Directing the Film

Film Directors on Their Art

The American Film Institute Series

Directing the Film

Film Directors on Their Art

by Eric Sherman

for The American Film Institute

Little, Brown and Company
Boston — Toronto

FIRST EDITION

T09/76

The author is grateful to Southern Illinois University Press for permission to quote from *Cinematics* by Paul Weiss. Copyright © 1975 by Southern Illinois University Press.

Library of Congress Cataloging in Publication Data

Sherman, Eric.
    Directing the film.

    (The American Film Institute series)
    Includes index.
    1.   Moving-picture producers and directors — Inter-
views.   I. American Film Institute.   II. Title.
III. Series: American Film Institute. The American
Film Institute series.
PN1998.A2S49   791.43'0233'0922   76-16494
ISBN 0-316-78541-5

Designed by D. Christine Benders

Published simultaneously in Canada
by Little, Brown & Company (Canada) Limited

PRINTED IN THE UNITED STATES OF AMERICA

For Paul Weiss: teacher and friend

Gentlemen, there are no rules. Cinema is an art. Anybody can learn it, providing he knows how.

— Jiri Weiss

Acknowledgments

Special thanks to James Powers, Rochelle Reed, and Jeanne Poling at The American Film Institute.

This book is made possible by the time and patience of all the filmmakers who have appeared in seminar at The American Film Institute.

The material with Samuel Fuller and Arthur Penn, and some of the material with Peter Bogdanovich, was taken from special interviews conducted by Eric Sherman.

Portions of the material on Allan Dwan may also be found in Peter Bogdanovich's book, *Allan Dwan, The Last Pioneer* (Praeger, 1971). Portions of the material on George Cukor may also be found in Gavin Lambert's book, *On Cukor* (Capricorn, 1973). Both of these books were based on the Oral Histories funded by the Louis B. Mayer Foundation and administered by The American Film Institute.

Additional thanks to friends and colleagues who have read and commented upon the manuscript or portions of it — most notably William C. Hocker.

Preface

The material in this book was gathered from the files at The American Film Institute Center for Advanced Film Studies. Once a week for the past several years, professionals and students have met in seminar and exchanged thoughts, ideas, and questions about the filmmaking process.

The first volume in the AFI / Little, Brown series, *Filmmaking: The Collaborative Art* (Donald Chase, 1975), details the work of the producer, screen writer, actor, director of photography, production designer, costume designer, script supervisor, editor, composer, and special effects people. While relating to us their areas of concern, they also usually describe the director as the ultimate shaper. For them, it is the director who creates the context in which their work is made evident. Certainly, all the participants are unique individuals with much to offer, and the ideal film is one in which everyone functions at his peak level of efficiency.

There are films in which the director obviously has had the strong hand. There also is abundant evidence of projects where no single controlling influence is so felt. This book explores all the situations as widely as possible. To achieve this broad view, some words are included from *all* of the seventy-five directors who have appeared at The American Film Institute. No selections of material have been made on the basis of critical vogue. The chief byword of this endeavor has been to describe what is the director's job — in its full extent.

To this end, the book is divided into four sections. In "A Director Is Born, A Film Begins," we learn of the backgrounds and training of those who became directors. The hard facts of economics also are discussed there. The script, that starting point for almost all films, is described, technically and theoretically. In "Film as a Battleground," there are such topics as casting, budget, rehearsal, and a thorough discussion of basic shooting methods and principles. The third section, "Under the Lights," describes the actual filming — the director's interplay with actors, cameramen, editors. Finally, in " 'Cinema,' " we have the reflections of directors on the aesthetics of their medium. Also, the subjects are brought up of the audience's role, "message" films, critics, and film education.

In addition to the quotations from the directors, there are several essays — on directing itself and on the subsumed processes of camerawork and editing. It is hoped that these essays will help to clarify any unresolved issues mentioned in the text. The chapters on script writing and acting are thorough, and comments have been added only to underscore the most significant ideas.

Thus, *Directing the Film* takes the reader through all phases of the filmmaking process. No book such as this can ever be complete. But, as unities necessarily issue forth from diversities, it is hoped that this volume will serve as something of a backbone for the film student, the film viewer, and the film enthusiast in general.

Finally, two points should be emphasized. First, the inclusion or exclusion of a director from those quoted here in no way constitutes a critical judgment as to his value as filmmaker. Rather, these are the directors who have given of their time to participate in American Film Institute activities. Many more already will have conducted seminars by the time this book appears, and it is hoped that many will come in the future. Second, no still photographs have been printed in this volume. The primary reason is that rarely would they have illustrated the specifics of what the directors discussed. Therefore, they would have added to the book an expense not necessarily warranted. Other film books and film magazines are replete with fine photographs, many concerning the works of directors quoted here.

CONTENTS

Three — Under the Lights

INTRODUCTION
THE FILM DIRECTOR

I must start with this cup of coffee. Is this coffee? It's probably very good. Allow me to try it. No, your coffee is not excellent. But from such a cup of coffee you can start a story, a wonderful story. This is, I believe, the way directors work. . . . I don't believe that a good filmmaker must abandon the direction of the picture during the writing of the script, during the cutting — all those things are one operation. It's like in literature: you start a line, a sentence, and you don't finish it because you don't find the right word. Perhaps the right word you have to find for a picture you would find in the cutting room. *A picture is a whole*. You cannot say this is the beginning, this is the end, and the middle. No. What is a picture? You know, I am looking for my answer now. Don't be surprised if I am hesitating. I believe that *a picture is a state of mind*. A picture, often when it is good, is the result of some inner belief which is so strong that you have to show what you want in spite of a stupid story or difficulty about the commercial side of the picture. Yes, it's a state of mind.

— Jean Renoir

In *Cinematics,* Paul Weiss's philosophical speculation on the nature of film art (Southern Illinois University Press, 1975), he offers:

A great film conceivably shows a director's impress more than it shows that of any other, but ideally others make their distinctive styles also evident, while instancing what the director has in mind. Film that is dominated by a director is only one possible form of film. Film without any director, or film which shows no influence of a director, is film which is less than it ought to be. A good director makes sure that all the parts are creatively produced and brought together in a single totality. That totality should reflect his fundamental idea. Together with the others he should provide determinate, limited, vivified versions of what initially is quite general. This the scriptist articulates, and the director envisages — both before anything is in fact filmed. . . .

A director interprets the script, coaches the performers, suggests to the cineman, works together with the montagist, and interrelates them all, incident after incident, thereby articulating what was initially considered. He begins with a vague idea of the entire film and uses this to help him determine what is to be done. Usually he expresses that idea in the form of a narrative line; marks a beginning, ending, and vital turning points; imagines an aesthetic whole with its major contrasts; and makes use of a space, time, and dynamism which encompass and are embodied in all the incidents. These factors are distinguished in being specialized; and they are specialized in the course of a film making. . . . A director learns from the film that is being made what his unity visually means, for it is initially only schematic, general; it is made determinate through the actual creation of the film. . . . There need be no destruction of the unity of a film when others are allowed to add their own creative elements to the creative work of a director. Unity is not necessarily lost by giving some freedom to others. Full control need not be exercised in the beginning, nor even throughout. It is sufficient that the director take hold and see that what would otherwise appear to be discrepant, or what does not help produce maximum excellence, be altered. If a director insists on having a point of view in advance, which he keeps to regardless of the contributions that others are making, he will end with something which bears the unmistakable mark of his peculiar kind of ability, but it will be less of a work than could have been made. He gains most when others are given their freedom to show what they know.

Throughout the course of this book, we will see that the position of the director in the traditional filmmaking process is highly varied and complex. His work often is compared to that of the conductor of an orchestra or the captain of a ship. The film director is seen usually as some sort of leader of others, as providing a kind of guiding force. According to this view, the final outcome is more or less predetermined by exigencies of script, camerawork, acting, and editing (as with the conductor's composed score and the captain's necessary destination and maps), with the director providing a certain organizational context.

Judging from the comments of most professional directors, there is very little agreement as to what exactly their function is. There are some directors who say that they must concentrate primarily on the structures of the script. If their films are to be works of art, it will be because of the inherent beauty in the narrative and dialogue patterns in the script. Other directors are occupied primarily with the performance of actors. To them, the beauty of film will be correlative with the quality of acting. These directors attend not only to the performance as a whole, but to endless minor nuances and gestures throughout. Some directors attend primarily to the camerawork, their chief concern being for a pictorial beauty and smoothness of execution. There are still other directors who say that the art of film resides in the editing process. For them, all the steps prior to editing yield crude material, which will be finally shaped and lent an artistic worth through their imaginative juxtaposition. Indeed, most formal film theoreticians posit the editing process as that which sets film apart from all the other arts. The point is that there have evolved nearly as many theories of film directing as there are directors.

The work of the film director is not easily discernible. It is evident in a film everywhere and nowhere. Were we even to observe the actual day-to-day functioning of the director, I do not think we would emerge with a much clearer view of his import to the art of film. The clearest course to follow is the evidence in film itself. We must look to the film and determine what is there that could only have come from someone in the position of a director. We must decide which of a film's dimensions of expression are the working domain of the director alone and of none of the other participants.

The conductor of an orchestra is essential to its production. Without him, there would most likely not be as tightly knit a unity to the whole performance. Although the musical composition from which the conductor and orchestra work represents a unity, in translating its arena of expression from primarily one of temporality to one of dynamism, the players and conductor must shift the dimension of expression and interpretation. The conductor of a group of musicians approaches the performance with a sense of the whole in mind. His sense of the whole is born primarily out of having lived with the piece of music to be performed. He has read the score; he may have heard other performances; he has experimented with different types of instrumentation to achieve the desired effect; he has an understanding of the other works of that particular composer. In some cases, his goal will be to vitalize those themes — that idea — that seem to be inherent in the written composition. In others, he will take it as his function, or even duty, to lend his own particular brand of musical vision to the performance of the written composition. In either case, the results of his work become apparent to spectators upon encountering the performance.

Musicians, too, come to a performance with a sense of the whole already in mind. They have studied their parts. They have gone through rehearsals. They, too, more likely than not, have heard other recordings or performances of the material. Their conductor, in describing how the parts should be played individually, and how they should blend together as a whole, will have presented an additional interpretation to them of the entire written composition that will definitively point the way toward each's performance. The final performance, then, will be colored by the sense of the whole that the conductor has expressed to the musicians as well as the sense of the whole that each performer brings to his part from recent rehearsal as well as past musical experience.

However, one can imagine a musical performance that seemed highly unified without the presence of a conductor. In chamber music, each musician has so finely tuned an understanding of the implications of the composition as a whole, that each performance may be said to be conductorless in person, or multiconducted, with each musician participating in fact. Also, there are often occasions when a professional orchestra is called upon to perform without the benefit of a conductor. In this case, each musician's experience comes into play to help create a unified whole. In such an instance, we may find that the leader of each section of musicians may be serving as some sort of mini-conductor, who explains how their particular ensemble sound must contribute to the whole. However, this is primarily a preperformance organizational function. No one individual takes the traditional place of the conductor. It would not be correct even to say that because of an amalgam of each musician's past experiences in performance we have a sort of conductor-in-absentia constituted out of all previous conductors of that piece. What we really have is simply a musical performance without a conductor. This is possible not only because we expect a high degree of technical competence on the part of each musician, but because the composition itself contains enough signals, enough information to point the way toward a unified performance.

Thus, if we were to compare a film director to the conductor of an orchestra, we would be forced to conclude that there could be a unified film without someone serving as a director. That is, we would have to imagine a script that was so explicit in its verbal description of visual ideas that the images could be committed to film in only one way. Similarly, the script would not only contain dialogue for the actors, it would have to describe precise gestures, movements, and so on. Too, every camera position and movement as well as lighting patterns would have to be delineated. Were there such a script, it would then be possible for each person involved in a production to read it and come through with a completely clear notion of the entire film. If each active participant had the entire film in mind before production, then a unified film might be constructed without a director. There are several problems here, though. As will be discussed in the section on screen writing, it would be impossible for a written script to contain all of this information. It could be as big as an encyclopedia and still not adequately describe all the work necessary to make a film out of it.

Were a film actor to have not only a completely clear idea of all the gestures and movements of his performance, but also how this performance should blend in with the other parameters of filmic expression, he still would not be able to affect the overall appearance of the film unless he were also somehow set apart from it. He would be responsible not only to himself and the other actors; he would somehow have to guide the camerawork and editing in order to preserve the unity of his performance that he had had in mind. Unity in a film performance does not yield unity in a film. Should an actor successfully dominate the other participants, he would not so much be showing how acting can unify a film as assuming the traditional role of a director. Thus, when Orson Welles, Buster Keaton, or Jerry Lewis directs a film in which he also appears as an actor, the unity to that film comes more from his directorial stance than from his work in acting. This is verified when we watch a film in which these men serve only as actors. Certainly we recognize all the familiar traits of gesture and movement. However, we do not find the connecting threads, the overall intensity — the unity of images with actors and actions — that seem to characterize their directed films. On the other hand, we notice that, say, *The Magnificent Ambersons,* which Welles directed but did not appear in, bears more resemblance to *Citizen Kane* (which he directed *and* acted in) than to one of the many pictures in which he acted but which he clearly did not direct.

It might be said that some screen actors, such as Marlon Brando, seem to dominate a film whether or not they have directed it. To dominate a film, though, is not to provide it with an artistic unity. In the theatre, perhaps, if a play is written around one character in particular, we can see how the character has the potential to dominate and unify the play's performance. However, in a film, even if there is only one actor written into the script, we still cannot conclude that that actor is in a position to unify the film. Unless he somehow extends his range of control over the camerawork and editing as well, there is no way for any one actor to provide that integral unity we expect from a work of art.

It might be easier to see that a cameraman could provide a certain overall visual unity to a film that the actors and script writer cannot. After all, his work is evident at every moment of the film. The question becomes, then, what determines the cameraman's placement of objects, arrangements of lighting, and positioning and movements of camera? If he lets the narrative constructs of the script determine his camerawork, then he might misjudge the import of the actor. If, on the other hand, he allows the actor's mode of dialogue and manner of gesture to guide his work, then he might miss some key story-line elements. The cameraman, being responsible first for a technical excellence of execution, directs his attention primarily to the pictorial qualities of his images. Unless he attends equally to the demands of the script and the emphases of the actors, his work cannot lend an overall depth of expression to the film. This is not to say that a cameraman is powerless to alter the dimensions of story and acting in a film. There are directors (for example, Josef von Sternberg) who have been driven to taking up the practice of cinematography in order to insure that the camerawork best represents their intentions. Similarly, there are cameramen (William Fraker, Haskell Wexler) who have turned to directing because they have felt that the desired extent of their work pushed them toward a fuller mode of expression. Indeed, there are many cameramen (for example, Gregg Toland, Arthur Miller, Stanley Cortez) whose work is readily identifiable whether or not they are working under strong directors, writers, or actors. The point is, then, that a cameraman's work may be extensive enough to lend a certain visual style to a film. However, visual style alone does not insure artistic unity. That style might be opposed to the essential dimensions of the story. Without a deep underlying relationship to the other aspects of filmic expression, camera style alone tends toward a superficial excellence. Indeed, it is one where we can say about a film, "What beautiful shots! What excellent camerawork!" and nothing more.

The editing of a film's images may also dominate its overall appearance. Yet editing, as a practiceable craft, will tend toward a sort of movement (juxtapositional and extensional) which may or may not correlate with the larger movements of the film as a whole. Moreover, the editor's raw materials possess a finality which virtually precludes his being able to provide a unity if there is not one already hinted at in the images themselves. A consistent imaginative juxtaposition of images may be an excellent quality for a film to have. There is no denying that the work of editing wields a sort of power over the final appearance of a film. Indeed, the very fact that so many directors have protested formally that the editing has ruined their intentions demonstrates the extent of the editor's control. However, a director's protestations do not mean that a film has been robbed of its essential unity, nor that an alien unity has been added. It means rather that the ideal totality for that film has not been reached. In fact, we might even conclude that the editing of a film becomes more significant the weaker the images are. In this case, the editing work is in a position to provide a certain professional gloss, but, by analogy, a sentence with uninteresting words does not become excellent by being punctuated properly, or even imaginatively.

Thus, we arrive at the point where a film may possess an excellent and unified script, acting, performances, camerawork, and editing and yet still not reach an overall unity, that sense of integral wholeness that is necessary in a work of art. The majority of professionally made films probably displays some excellence of craft or even stylistic uniqueness in one of several of these dimensions. If we concentrate on detecting some sort of style in the various modes of filmwork, we usually will be misled into a search for innovative techniques. Innovative stylistic techniques are the easiest thing to spot in a film. New types of shots or special effects are striking to the eye. However, their production often requires so much energy that the overall intensity in the film necessarily suffers. For this reason, films that are voted "the best of the year" often appear, in retrospect or upon multiple viewings, to lack that consistency and depth of expression so necessary to enduring works of art. Usually, in a filmmaker's career, his early works will be marked by a restless grappling with the tools at his disposal. Startling techniques may be sought after with an eye toward stimulating the audience and critics. However, the films made by older, mature artists evidence a certain calmness, or rather, a certain consistently sustained level of excellence, of beauty that places them in the realm of art. A search for works of film art guided by the appearance of innovative techniques is not a fruitful one. While it may help construct a valid history of cinematic development, it will not point toward any deeper appreciation of the film art.

The emotional power of a film is determined not so much by any one element, line of dialogue, shot, cut, or acting performance. Rather, we look for the film as a whole to possess an overall unity of expression, intensity of purpose, and beauty and completeness of vision. The performance of a musical composition might be excellent, beautiful, and unified without a conductor because the written score will successfully contain enough information for all the players both to perform their individual parts and play off one another. In film, though, there is no tool analogous to the written musical composition. Rather than being related to the conductor of an orchestra, then, the film director is more properly seen as lending that guidance that the composition in music provides. The director in film is the only participant in a position to grasp the whole of the film.* (It is important

*See comments by King Vidor in *King Vidor on Filmmaking* (McKay, 1972), especially section 2, "On the Set."

to note that by "director" I do not necessarily mean the person so entitled. Instead, I refer to whoever it is in the course of a film production that is able so to extend his moment of self-expression that his particular vision comes to signify the film as a whole.) He provides a unity where there could not have been one, even though all the other participants may have been working at their very best. The fundamental meaning of unity is that whatever is distinct from it is accepted by it as a special instance of itself. Unity faces nothing other than a plurality of fragments of itself. This would mean, then, that for the director, acting, script, camerawork, and editing merely instantiate in a limited area that very unity which he has in mind. The director's function would be to insure that all these particularized unities are exemplifications of the one fundamental unity that will be the film as a whole.

Two erroneous implications may be derived, though, from this idea. First, there may be too much emphasis on the necessity for excellence in each of the areas of filmwork. That is, a film could possess all the qualities of art without individual excellence in acting, camerawork, and so on, if the unitary vision brought to it by the director were strong enough. I suppose the effect of this statement, though, would be to alter the definition of excellence in filmwork. That is, excellence is not so much a quality extracted from the realm of each dimension of filmwork. Instead, excellence becomes a matter of correlation with the overall designs of the film. Thus, a complete and controlled acting performance will not insure an excellent sense of filmic appearance. Likewise, an amateurish acting performance does not necessarily diminish a film's artistic potential. A pictorially beautiful image may distract from the thematic and visual consistency of a film. An excellently constructed narrative situation may interfere with the linearity of a film's development. An imaginatively edited sequence may not contribute to the particular vision of the world that a film seems to be about. Thus, when we are watching a scene in a film, we might think to ourselves how much better it would have played had the actor scratched his nose differently, had the camera angle been slightly different, had an insert been cut in, and so on. However, we might also come to recognize an overall contextual dimension to the whole film that would render any such specific comment rather insignificant.

A film is to be accepted on its own terms. "Its own terms" are not constructed from the contributing parts but are seen to emerge out of the totality. Once we recognize a dimension of unity in purpose, then we can go back and see how particular shots, acting gestures, and so forth contributed to or detracted from that overall sense. However, we cannot, while watching a film unfold for the first time, point to this shot and that line of dialogue and fully appreciate their ultimate relationship to the whole. Similarly, the actor attending to his gesture, the writer concerned with logical narrative and engrossing dialogue, the cameraman dealing with an excellence in isolated image, and the editor concerned with the rhythmic flow and juxtaposition of images are not in the position that the director is to grasp the film as a whole. Only the director stands apart from any one particular contributory element but lends to all of them a sense of the totality.

The second erroneous implication derived from this suggestion of the director's role in filmmaking would be to think that he must actively organize, control, and dominate the participation of all the other contributors. Many of the strongest directors have disavowed virtually any function other than that of a vague overseer. Alfred Hitchcock, Frank Borzage, and John Ford, among many others, claim never to look through the camera. Their cameramen have stated that they felt as though they were working with a great sense of freedom. Also, we have learned that Ford's control of actors seems to have been limited to placing them a certain way in a scene, then nodding if their performance were acceptable and turning away if he felt they needed another take. Ford also claims never to have participated in the editing of his films. Indeed, he claims never to have participated in audience reaction "previews," or even to have seen a completed version of any of his films. What I think this means is that the context of a Ford picture was so strong, his vision was so powerful and unified, that he was able to exert a subterranean control over all the contributors to his films, that the force of his artistic overview was strong enough virtually to necessitate certain camera positionings, acting styles, editing rhythms, and so on. One need only compare the way of filming various types of situation among Ford films and then look to other films produced by the same cast and crew when working under different directors. It becomes clear that Ford might just as well have given exact instructions to all the participants. I do not think that this is so much a matter of the film director suppressing anyone else's self-expression. The director, whether he explicitly controls all the subordinate work in a film (for example, Robert Bresson) or merely creates a certain context through his very presence (for example, Ford), is the only participant in a film's creation whose moment of self-expression is wide enough and, thus, whose artistic vision may come to characterize the film as a whole.

In this sense, the film director, rather than serving a function similar to the conductor of an orchestra performing from a written score, might possibly be better compared to the leader of a group of musicians who are improvising upon various themes. In a jazz group, for example, there are many elements that may serve to unify a performance. There might be a single theme whose basic chord changes will provide the structure for all the musicians' solos. There should be a level of technical competence that gives an audience the sense that the group will be able to go with the music wherever its energy at that moment seems to be pushing them. There may even be a shared level of spiritual consciousness and artistic sensibility among the members of the group that underscores the unity of all the music at any particular moment of expression. However, it seems that jazz music best reaches the level of artistic import when it is conditioned by the overall context established by a strong leader. We note that in the music of John Coltrane, for example, what always seems to come across most vividly, what always seems to push his music into the realm of art, is the power and totality of his vision, his way of making music. This is not to say that the quality of any one performance was not affected by the contributions of the other members in his group. Indeed, one might say that it was the sympathetic relationship among the members of his quartet that helped to add that high degree of unity that so characterized his music. However, without any active suppression of the individual freedom of the members in the group, their performance always evidenced the musical vision of Coltrane. Although any of the other members may have been artists in their own right, while performing with Coltrane they were not functioning as unrestrained artists. Their range of control over the music was implicitly limited by the strength and breadth of Coltrane's vision.

In positing that in film it is the director who best has the potential of being an artist, we do not deny the full expression of any of the other contributors. The whole that the film director envisages does not overshadow some unity that the other participants might see. It is just that the director's envisagement is the only one allowed for, the only one that can come across in all the extended dimensions that constitute a whole film. The director's very role in the filmmaking process forces him to attend — explicitly or implicitly — to the entire film as a whole. Were all the other participants in the filmmaking process to possess as complete and strong a sense of the whole as the director does, then either their work would serve simply to intensify the director's vision (if their sense of the whole is in line with his) or dissipate and make diffuse any unity, any singularity of artistic force that the film as a whole might have displayed (if their view of the whole is in opposition to his).

Ultimately, the screen writer's concern is with the situational flow and the vocal sound of a film. The cameraman must attend to the particularities of each shot. The actors must concentrate on specific gestures and movements. The editor will be confronted with piecing together raw materials that either make implicit an already finished artistic vision, or evidence so little unity that his work becomes one of *re*construction, of attempting to produce some coherence, although his contribution in such a case will have been obstructed at the level of professionalism rather than art. It is for these very reasons that it does not really matter whether or not the film director actively dominates all the other contributors, or assumes those roles for himself (for example, Josef von Sternberg in *The Saga of Anatahan*), or merely allows his extended presence to shape the final appearance of a film.

The director approaches a film with a more or less well defined sense of the meaning of the totality. For him, this limits and determines what the basic thrust should be of all the other contributing elements. The director provides the unity for the totality, a one for a many. While that one is made immanent by the many, is pluralized by it, we nevertheless recognize that the director's concern always is conditioned by a sense of the whole. He selects and guides all the other work and shapes it along the necessary route to achieve that finality he has in mind.

This is not to say that in a director-dominated film we find a monotony of units. Indeed, as noted earlier, many of the strongest directors do not attend concentratedly to any one of the other functions. Neither does the presence of a strong director necessarily inhibit the individual interpretations of the other participants. But the director is in a position to sense when those pluralities that are being issued during every moment of a film's creation do not possess the intensity of direction that will allow him to construct a unity. When we say that the director approaches a film with a sense of the whole in mind, we obviously do not mean that he has a complete foreknowledge of the totality in all its parts. In fact, a director learns, as the production of the film progresses, exactly what it was that he had envisaged. However, those films that are works of art evince an intensity, a unity that characterizes one vision. Unless we allow for the highly unlikely probability of joining five or more individuals with an identical artistic vision, the only way to account for the singular sense of existence that we perceive in a great film is to look for the presence of one artistic sensibility. A film constituted out of complete and beautiful contributions from the realms of camerawork, script writing, acting, and editing need not be a work of art. The localized beauties expressed in these instances do not provide the depth and reach of expression we require in order to label some labor as an art. The appearances produced in any of these endeavors are not of a great enough moment, do not extend any one of the dimensions of existence to a great enough degree, to take on the responsibilities of artistic creation. Certainly the beauty resident in great films is due in a sense to the work produced in these areas — but not due to the extracted qualities of this work in its plurality. Indeed, there is no "beautiful shot" or "great cut" that has not been conditioned by the overriding vision of the whole that only the director provides.

Now it might be argued that film, by its very nature, because it requires contributions from a number of diverse modes of creation, is some sort of compound art; that each type of work that contributes to a film has a wide enough moment of control to constitute its own being as an art form. Then we would only need look for excellence in these various areas in order to determine what sorts of artistic sensibility are being expressed. In the case where there seemed to be a strong directorial vision that lent a certain unity, we would recognize this as being only one of many different kinds of film. We could similarly find a film that seemed to be dominated by camerawork per se, and conclude that this was another type of film. And so on. Finally, if we were to find a film that was marked by excellence in all of these different endeavors, then we would be attending to five different sorts of artistic vision. However, taking this approach seems to deny any potential unity among all of the film's dimensions, except, of course, in the rare (if not impossible) case of five or more identically matched individual visions. It would seem that in viewing a film, we would have to attend at all times to five mutually exclusive dimensions of filmic expression; that is, if we were concerned about scaling the overall film as a work of art.

If we say that film is some sort of repository for various types of artistic activity, then we would not really be interested in its overall standing as a work of art. It would be in these five areas of work, as separated from the film as a whole, where we would determine whether or not a film evinced artistic creation. We would be interested only in whether the camerawork were excellent or not. And so on. If, by some chance, all the different work seemed to be aligned along some common thematic thread, then we might be inclined to term the whole film a work of art. In such a case, though, the unity itself would possess none of the personal intensity that we traditionally expect from works of art. Instead, the overall film would be a sort of anonymous conglomeration of excellently produced materials.

But can that power, that far-reaching emotional experience that we expect from the traditional arts, and that we do find in all great films, come from an anonymous source? Can it be born out of a plurality of group excellences? Does the film experience necessitate that our attention be at all times divided into a number of areas of interest?

Ultimately, the film-viewing experience, like all encounters with art, is a self-contained phenomenon. Any external measures that we bring to it in order to classify or concretize it are doomed unless they throw some light upon that emotional arena that is explored and energized by the film. Certainly, film is one of the newer art forms. Certainly it is unique in the number of different sorts of work that go into it. Unlike opera, where one might comment quite lucidly upon the music, the dramatic flow, the performances, and so on, film does not lend itself as well to fragmentation in analysis. The distance of the film screen, the frozen finality of the images, the potentially cosmic overtones of acting gesture and nuance born out of often mythic presences, the temporally and dynamically charged fluidity marked by camera and editing: all are combined inextricably. While it may often seem that films arise out of more technical and commercial conditions and restrictions than the older art forms, the experience that great films give us is in no way of a lesser order than that which we derive from encounters with, say, music, painting, and theatre.

As art transcends the everyday world by extending the dimensions of existence, so film's appearances inform our knowledge of those appearances we encounter in everyday life. The responsibility of the film director as artist is great. His attention must be pervasive and insightful. However, with a strong enough vision, he can wield control over the plastic realities presented to the film camera by script, actors, and scenery, later to be shaped and polished in editing. This is no easy task for one person; indeed, we might say it is no "task" at all. The artist creates not because he wants or desires to, but because he has to. Perhaps it is this drive, this consuming need to reshape those resistant and recalcitrant materials of everyday reality, that places the film director in a most likely position as the potential artist during a film's production. While writers, cameramen, actors, and editors all may have as cosmic a view of things as the director, their moment of self-expression, in terms of a film as a whole, is limited. Though the beauties produced in their activities are real, there is no indicator to which we may turn to reflect upon their status apart from the whole.

The "film shot" is an ambiguous unit, since it may last from a fraction of a second to the entire length of a film. A script seems more related to the art of story and speech (unless it has set for itself the impossible task of being a surrogate film: that is, describing with visual and temporal emphasis something which cannot be described in words). An acting performance, while illuminating what individuals are, the many guises they may assume en route in their careers, is robbed of any completely independent appearance when considered apart from the imagery that has captured it on film. Film editing is a constructive process, although impossible to consider on its own, since its moments of evidence are virtually instantaneous. The resistant material with which it is concerned presents too great a conditioning context to allow for the emergence of editing alone as the causal process that produces that emotional cosmos that we can and do encounter in films.

Film direction, though, when present at all, is ever-present. In an excellent film, a singular vision may be extracted. That vision, which we sometimes find in seemingly all the aspects of a film, is evidence that the film director has used the medium as artists in the traditional arts long have used theirs. This is not to suggest that all films are marked by a strong directorial vision. Nor is it to suggest that films that are not so marked are to be excluded from any consideration as having potential artistic worth. However, no film offers so cosmic a sense, no film enables the viewer to live through such a whole new world, no film suggests as decisively all the potentialities of the dimensions of existence, no film so illuminates the nature of entities — material and nonmaterial alike — as the one created through the complete directorial vision.

ONE

A DIRECTOR IS BORN, A FILM BEGINS

1

Who Is a Director?

WILLIAM FRIEDKIN: Directing is a nice job. It's the best job for me. If I had
to pay money to do it, I would do it. If they changed all the rules and they
said, "You've got to stand in line to pay money to do this work," I would
be the first guy in line. It's problematical. It's disappointing often. It's
very challenging. It's frustrating as hell. It's extremely demanding and
totally satisfying work. And if I wasn't doing this, I would have to do
legitimate work for a living. There are guys out there really working for a
living, cleaning streets or coal mining, teaching. Directing is playing.
Acting.

RICHARD ATTENBOROUGH: If somebody said to me, "Well, look, movies are what you want to do. We understand that. Now then, you make your decision. You can either photograph them or act in them or whatever," I would unhesitatingly say, "I want to direct." Because obviously, I don't have to tell you, cinema is the director's medium beyond all others. I operate as an actor in terms of intuition and instinct but I have an enormous desire to communicate. The exciting thing in the theatre is my talking to you, to have a direct contact with somebody. I find it exciting, rewarding, and thrilling. I adore it. In movies, this is not the same at all. Movies — you act for the director if you act for anybody. But if you're directing, you have the opportunity to put your signature on the bottom of the frame. You have the opportunity to say, "This is what I believe. That is my credo. That is what I wish to state."

ED EMSHWILLER: For years I was a painter and I was stuck away in a room, in a very internalized kind of world where I regurgitated back strictly internalized things that were all controlled, fed through my own head in this exchange that my artwork was. But when I'm a filmmaker, I find that it's an encounter art. In other words, the world is very intractable and I am engaged in a form of conflict in order to achieve the making of the film. I have to deal with other people and they have their own momentums which I either have to work with or to oppose, to find some way in which their momentums will coincide with my needs. You have all the logistics and all the physical, production, aesthetic . . . you have all kinds of problems.

KEEP THIS IN MIND — OR, SOME BASIC PRINCIPLES

GEORGE CUKOR: I can't tell you what are the basics. I wish to Christ that I could. You could turn me inside out. That is the knowledge of a lifetime. Don't think that you can learn it that way. Life is not that way. You learn out of bitter experience, trial and error. Life teaches you that. As sincere as you all are, you can't learn it all in school.

ABRAHAM POLONSKY: First of all, directing is an idea that you have of a total flow of images that are going on, which are incidentally actors, words, and objects in space. It's an idea you have of yourself, like the idea you have of your own personality which finds its best representation in the world in terms of specific flows of imaginary images. That's what directing is. Now, I know particular things to say like the "mise-en-scène," how to keep pace going, how to set up shots, what angles to use, what kinds of lenses to use. But these are all part of the profession that you learn. And you don't have to know a single one of those things, and you're a director. And you can direct your first film without knowing a single thing about that. Nevertheless, if you know all that, it'll be a better film. You can be sure of that. But I think you have the gift in some kind of way. And all the work you do adds to it.

ROBERT ALDRICH: I don't think that this is a gift or a talent. I think that it has to do with patience. Of all the necessary ingredients in making a viable director, the key element is patience. Sometimes the work is dead, dead, dead dull. If you don't have sufficient patience to get excited when somebody presses the button, then you are going to lose it. You are out there night after night. And often it's not a lot of laughs. You don't want to associate with the actors, and how many stuntmen can you talk to?

ABRAHAM POLONSKY: Directors are like generals, political dictators, aggressive people. You don't have to be aggressive in a malevolent way, in a hostile, disagreeable way. Actually, you have to be the opposite way. You have to be a real leader. That's to say that you have to let those who are doing their work do their work. You are a guide, and you're a "tell-it-to," and you're a prophet, and you're a boss, and you're a slave, and, in the end, it's your fault. And everyone in the film is always grateful if you can tell them what to do.

BARBARA LODEN: That was the big problem for me. It was hard for me to ask people or to tell people what to do because I was never in that position before. Another hard thing for me was to make decisions because it has always been difficult for me to make decisions. But when you make a movie, you have to make quick irrevocable decisions sometimes and that's really nerve-racking. . . . I think it's a personality problem. I don't think it has anything to do with whether you're a man or a woman. It has to do with your kind of personality — whether you're authoritative or whether you can get people to trust you and to believe in what you're doing.

JIRI WEISS: Some directors shout, some of them are gentle, some of them are I-don't-know-what. But they must communicate. The director must know what actors want to do and also he himself must know how people behave. He must know life.

ABRAHAM POLONSKY: If I had my first choice in the world, I'd prefer to be a political dictator. But barring that, I'd as soon be a director because it's the same job. You have to take the responsibility.

ROBERT ALTMAN: Your own ego is the only trap that I think you can fall into.

PERRY MILLER ADATO: If you are the director, you have to take credit or blame for everything that is good or bad. Nothing goes in that you haven't approved. You have to react. If the editor does something, you have to say, "No, that's not good. That doesn't go in." Or you may say, "Oh, that's wonderful. Let's keep it in." But all of the decisions and all of the responsibilities are yours.

OSCAR WILLIAMS: You have an idea of what it's going to look like, what you want to do. And because you have an idea of what you want to see, you shoot it that way. . . . Things happen while you're shooting and sometimes you capture those things; sometimes you go back to what you originally had. Sometimes you just let it happen. Sometimes there's a magic that takes over the cast, the crew, the director, and everything starts to work.

ROUBEN MAMOULIAN: All the equations in the film world are absolutely personal. There are really no rules. This is not the army, where you have a general and a colonel and a lieutenant and a private, nor is it a factory with a foreman at the head of it. The field of competence and authority varies according to who's the producer, who's the executive, who's the director, and who's the star. Sometimes the star is so outstanding she outweighs the whole caboodle of them, and she's got it her way. If the producer is important and the director is not so important, then he has the last word.

JACQUES DEMY: I don't think it is good to tell everyone, "You must do this. You must do that." Many times what you think may be wrong. You don't want to force something when it is completely wrong. Usually the crew and the actors want to please the director. They are usually very nice, and it is not right to make them do something that is completely wrong for them and for the film. It is best to combine your views and see what is best. But, if you feel that it is wrong you must tell them how you feel.

RICHARD ATTENBOROUGH: Obviously the most important talent, it seems to me if one uses that word, that a director acquires is his ability during the shooting of the picture to be able to contain and maintain in his mind, in his eye, the entity, the whole, the shape, the tempo, the graph, the thrust forward, etc. This applies to tempo; this applies to emotion; this applies to character development and everything else.

FEDERICO FELLINI: You know, technical things are involved; one has to know technique. But one is born with technique. I never think during the night what I am shooting the day after. I mean, I never think consciously. Certainly I live always the picture. I am not a director who is looking to find the shot, looking in the camera. I have no problem in this sense. The camera is just my eye. The thing has to work anyway. Certain kinds of movement have to be decided, certainly. . . . It is very difficult for me to talk when I am outside a picture because it is a particular atmosphere that when you are out, it is difficult to remember well what are you doing exactly. . . . The picture is in your head, in your imagination, everything.

JACQUES DEMY: Something struck me when I was eighteen or nineteen. I had an interview with Jean Renoir. He said that movies were not reality. If you want to see reality, you can find a better seat from a terrace or in a café on the Champs Elysées. You can find reality when you watch people and hear them speaking. But, when you are doing a movie, you have to do something else.

VINCENT SHERMAN: I would say that the director is a storyteller. Whether he is telling a story in terms of farce or in terms of drama or tragedy or comedy or melodrama, he's got a story to tell. How he tells it and the way he tells it are what distinguish his work. He is searching for the most effective way to tell it.

HOWARD HAWKS: I'm just telling a story. I don't take a job unless I think I can tell a story. And if I get talked into doing a picture I don't want to do, I'm always sorry for it.

ROBERTO ROSSELLINI: . . . You always have to approach the thing in a very simple way. The main thing is to be very simple, very straight, very direct, and never to think of yourself because if you look at yourself, you want to illustrate yourself and to show your intelligence.

JIRI WEISS: A director is like a man who catches butterflies. There are people who set in advance what kind of butterflies they catch. There are people who say, "I've got yellow butterflies, blue butterflies, I've got this and that." And they might employ other people to get them, if the catching is easier. And they all know they can catch them in a room. There are other people who, with a net, run around before us and catch them where they are. And the disadvantage is they don't know what they get because they might, you know, get nothing.

BREAKING AND ENTERING

> To be honest, you must hit the nail on the head right from the start. In order to make a motion picture, you must have money. And in order to have money you've got to woo people. And in order to woo people, you've got to bullshit 'em. . . . The last thing in the world to be worried about is how to make the picture. After the money, the most important thing to worry about is the erection you get of wanting to make a film, a certain film, and nothing would stop you. A man in prison who wants to draw finds a way to draw. A millionaire who wants to paint, paints. This can't be taught. You've got to have an emotional reaction inside.
>
> — Samuel Fuller

There have been as many paths to entering the business of filmmaking as there are filmmakers. Intention and accident both play a role en route.

ALFRED HITCHCOCK: I first started in 1920, in an American studio in London. It was called Famous Players–Lasky, and all the technicians were imported from Hollywood. There were no producers in those days. There was a scenario department, so you had a scenario editor and his assistant. My job at the time was designing the titles, because titles were very important since whole stories could be changed, characters could be changed, merely by the wording in the title. Then I was given odd jobs of going out to shoot odd little entrances and exits on exteriors. So gradually I practiced my hand at script writing myself. I took any story and after the script was written it was handed to the director.

Eventually the studio closed down, and it became a rental studio. So then we waited around for jobs, and eventually a group came in and I was going to be the assistant director. They said to me, "Do you know anyone who can give us the name of a good script writer?" So they said, "What do you know about it?" So I said, "Well, here's one I've written." I gave them the example and they accepted it. So they said, "Well, what about the art director?"* and I said, "I'll do that as well." So for three years after that, I wrote the script on each picture and then became the art director. In that way, I learned the whole technical end — the process of every facet of that part or that department. But it all started with my being in the scenario department.

PAUL MAZURSKY: I started out as an actor. In fact, I was in Stanley Kubrick's first picture. It was called *Fear and Desire* and was made in 1951. After that, I got into writing out of frustration. Unless you get terrific parts, acting is a very frustrating thing. I was a theatre actor in New York mostly; I was a nightclub comic for about three years; then I came out here and I was still acting and doing comedy and fooling around, writing my act, and I started doing Second City.† The acting thing was getting worse and worse. I was either playing juvenile delinquents or bizarre, crappy parts. Then one day I got a job writing for Danny Kaye. I did that for four years. I didn't really enjoy it, but it was interesting and I learned something. The frustration of doing that started me into realizing — at that time I was about thirty-two, I guess; I'm forty-three now — that either I was going to direct films or get out of show business and open gas stations. And then with Larry Tucker, I wrote *I Love You, Alice B. Toklas*. I was supposed to direct it, but there were complications which would take too long to tell you about. Then we wrote *Bob and Carol and Ted and Alice,* and at this point I was determined that if I couldn't direct it, we wouldn't sell it. This would be hopeful, I guess, to you. We brought the script in to a man named Mike Frankovich, who read it and liked it, and he said to me, "Why should you direct it?" I said to him, "I just won't give it up. Either I direct it or . . ." He said, "But why?" I said, "Because that's the only reason." The next day he said, "You can do it." And that's how I became a director.

ROGER CORMAN: I started as a writer and I sold a screenplay for Writers Guild minimum, which I think was three thousand dollars at the time,

*"Art director" is a term used almost synonomously with such current expressions as "production designer" or "set designer." Basically, this refers to the person whose function it is to design the overall "look" of a film's sets and locations. Usually, this person works intimately with the director, cameraman, producer, and, sometimes, the writer.

†A Famous Chicago satiric improvisational group whose alumni include Mike Nichols, Elaine May, and Shelley Berman.

and . . . since I tried to get more from the producer, we compromised and he agreed to give me associate producer credit and three thousand dollars. I accepted that. On the basis that I had three thousand dollars in my hand and I was an official associate producer, I raised five thousand dollars more. With eight thousand dollars, I felt that if I could get ten thousand dollars, I'd make a film. A fellow came in to direct it because I wasn't directing at that time. . . . He asked me how much I would pay him, and I said, "If you can raise two thousand dollars more, you can direct this picture." He did, and we made the picture for ten thousand dollars in cash and a series of deferments. . . . The picture made money, and it was simply a matter of taking profits from that and going back into another picture and each time filing it back.

IRVIN KERSHNER: I come from documentaries. I did three years on television, in which I was shooting and directing and acting, writing, putting the music on, and editing a series that was one of the first documentary series on the air.

BUZZ KULIK: I'm a television cat. I was in New York and I was a messenger boy at an advertising agency. Television had just begun. The network at that time was New York and Washington and Philadelphia. The established directors of the theatre . . . were interested in coming into television. . . . So there were a bunch of us who were down at the bottom of the barrel. We were fortunate enough to be there. They picked us up and said, "Hey, you're a director," and we kind of did an on-the-job training because nobody knew any more than anybody else, and we learned from our own mistakes. One summer they said, "Would you like to do some *Gunsmoke?*" which was a CBS television half-hour film in those days. I said, "Oh, boy, would I like to. . . ." I did and I made an ass of myself because I discovered that the motion picture is a medium that's unique unto itself, and again, I was able to kind of do an on-the-job training program, so that when live television and tape television kind of went by the boards, I was able to make the transition into films for television. I don't think there's any one way to do it or any one way not to do it. I think we can come from wherever.

WILLIAM FRIEDKIN: I started in the mailroom of a television station . . . then became a floor manager, which is like an assistant director in films. I was directing by the time I was seventeen. I did about two thousand live TV shows in about eight years, and I would probably still be working in live TV if I hadn't been fired from every station for which I worked. . . . Once I really wanted to make an hour-long documentary. I went and did a big selling job on it and they said, "Can you make it for five hundred dollars?" I said, "Absolutely." You know, there's no way you could make this for five hundred dollars. It cost about seven thousand dollars. They went crazy and I got fired from there. But that won the San Francisco Film Festival award and David Wolper saw it and he hired me, and that's how I came out here.

HAL ASHBY: As far as an academic background in drama, I have none. . . . When I started out I went into running a Multilith machine. I got my first job through the state employment department. Like a jerk I went down there and told them I wanted to get into motion pictures, and that woman looked at me like "What the hell is that?" and started going through the little index file and said, "Well, here's something."

So I said, "All right, I'm willing to start at the bottom."

"Well," she said, "here's something at Universal with a Multilith machine. Do you know what that is?"

And I said, "No."

So she said, "Do you know what a mimeograph machine is? Well, it's like a Multilith machine. They don't particularly want experience." So that was my first thing as far as getting into a studio. Then I started looking around and I said, "I'd really like to direct films one day." So I started to ask questions about what to get into to become an assistant director. I was that naïve. Well, as soon as I went to two or three people and asked them if they could help me get into assistant directing, they all said, "No, no." I was that naïve at that point. And they all said, "Go toward the editorial thing because that, in the end, would be a better school," although none of them really explained to me, which I found out later, that the editorial thing is so good it does get you in because you have everything that goes before coming out of that piece of thirty-five-millimeter film right there. You can run it back and forth and inspect it and see why you like it and why you don't. That can go for everything — from the lighting to the costumes to the casting, to the way it's played.

My boss, Norman Jewison, said, "Where do you want to go? Do you want to stay in editing?"

I said, "No, I want to direct films. It seems like a lot of fun to me."

So he said, "Why don't we see if we can find something for you?" He was constantly getting scripts in. We were looking at things all the time.

It wasn't much longer than that when he said, "Why don't you go ahead and do *The Landlord?*"

I said, "Great."

JACQUES DEMY: I went to Paris to a cinema school. . . . It was a good school. At that time I was twenty-two. After graduating from the cinema school, I wasted five years running around, calling people, and so on. Meanwhile I was writing screenplays. One day I sold one.

JAMES BRIDGES: I came out here to be an actor and that didn't work out, and then I became a writer. I wrote eighteen of the Hitchcock television shows. I worked on twelve features as a writer and then I decided to become a director. I started in the theatre, because nobody would believe that I could direct. So . . . I went to New York and directed a play. I came back with the reviews and said, "Look, I'm a director, it says so in *The New York Times*," and everybody now said, "He's a director." So they let me direct the first picture, and then I did another.

ROUBEN MAMOULIAN: I was lucky to have done a series of very successful shows on Broadway. So Paramount came to me — sound had just come in. They wanted me to sign a seven-year contract. First, I was to help a silent screen director by directing the dialogue for him for a couple of years. Then, if the studio felt that I had learned the business, they would let me direct a film. Well, you see, I was in a lucky position. I didn't need films. I was going strong on Broadway. I laughed at the whole thing. I said, "Look, I'll tell you exactly what I would like to do. I'd like to do only one film. No seven years. No options."

They said, "You're dead for films because we never sign a contract without options."

It's one of my few original achievements — I have never signed an option in my life. I said, "No options. And there's only one way we can do it. Let me go into the studio. Allow me to be on the set, to watch the shooting, the projection of the rushes, the cutting, and so on. And when I come to you and tell you I am ready to direct, that's when I do a film."

I guess they wanted me enough to say finally, "Well, we're dealing with a crazy man, but let's do it." So we signed this contract and I went to Astoria Studio.

There is no great mystery to the mechanics of motion picture making, I think you can familiarize yourself with all of it in five weeks. I was asking George Folsey, the great cameraman, about lenses, to tell me what a "thirty-five" does, or a "forty," or a "four-inch," silly questions in the cutting room and so on. After five weeks I felt that I knew enough about it. So I went into Mr. Lasky and Mr. Zukor and I said, "I'm ready."

They said, "Ready for what?"

I said, "I'm ready to direct a film." They laughed at me.

I said, "Look at the contract. What does it say? When I tell you I'm ready, I'm ready."

ALLAN DWAN: I planned to be an electrical engineer. I'd studied for it, graduated from the university, and was busy at it long before I thought of moving pictures. . . . At school I was in the dramatic society and acted — in fact, played King Lear and Richelieu and other little roles. Mostly Shakespeare. I was quite a ham on the campus between football seasons. . . .

After working his way to the burgeoning film "business" on the West Coast, Dwan, as a troubleshooter for the home office,

. . . found our company at San Juan Capistrano, way down in a little hotel. They'd had about eight actors in stock and a lot of cowboys, some horses, and they were sitting there doing nothing. I said, "Why aren't you working?"

They said, "Well, our director has been away on a binge for two weeks in Los Angeles, and we don't see him very often. So we haven't made any pictures."

Well, it looked like a pretty sad situation, so I wired back to the office and said, "I suggest you disband the company. You have no director." And they wired back, "You direct." So I got the actors together and I said, "Now, either I'm a director or you're out of work."

And they said, "You're the best damn director we ever saw. You're great."

And I said, "What do I do? What does a director do?" They said they'd show me, and they took me out and showed me. And it worked. Except, of course, I had to write the story.

MICHAEL WINNER: I was, I think like most people, fascinated by film from a very early age . . . in my case, my earliest living memory. At the age of five, I was giving shadow plays on walls and telling stories to go with them. I was fascinated by film, and seeing film, and reviewing film on the school notice boards, and I was the critic of the Cambridge University paper. I was writing about films. I was a film critic in London. . . . And it was just a determined ambition from my earliest consciousness. Now, of course, getting in was a disappointing, difficult thing because you have to accept that it's a fairly small mat, and there are many more people trying to get onto it than there's room for. Well, you don't accept that when you're young. You have an absolute belief that you intend to be a film director, and you will be a film director. Of course, a great sadness occurs in most people's lives who have that desire because they do not become film directors or, if they do, perhaps they don't gain the freedom they believed in their youth they would achieve.

I remember my first interview for a feature film. A cockney producer had taken his life in his hands and was offering me my first feature film. I went to see him, and he handed me one sheet of paper — the film was starting two weeks later in Switzerland — and he said, "Here is the script." This was one sheet of paper . . . with not many words on it.

I said, "It's a little short. What's it about?"

He said, "Well, I'll tell you. It's about this man. He goes into this restaurant, and this woman is there, and then he goes into this church and this same woman is there and then he goes into this Arab tent — I happen to have some Arab tent material — and this same woman is there."

"That's fascinating," I said. "Who is she?"

He said, "Well, you'll have to work it out."

So, a couple of weeks later I wrote a script that was even worse than that, and we were making this film in Switzerland, the idea being that he had a documentary to make in Switzerland. He kind of stayed on in the hotels and made this B picture film, a thriller.

We were doing a scene where the leading man jumped over a wall and was chased . . . very big action scene, one man and a wall . . . and he hurt his leg, this man, and he was then sent back to England, and my first feature film was in terrible jeopardy. This fellow recovered very quickly . . . he hadn't hurt his leg very badly. So I said, "Let's do the film in London. No one will know. It's meant to be Geneva. We'll film in London and say it's Geneva."

Now, we didn't have an art department then to transform London into Geneva. All we had was three thousand cardboard Swiss registration plates for cars. We used to go into the street and Cellotape these registration plates onto the cars, and that automatically transformed London into Switzerland. We didn't own the cars but we owned the Cellotape. Then, of course, people came and drove these cars away. London was full of people driving Swiss cars. One thought at the time that "this is a lunacy that will ultimately end" . . . that the real film business is terribly sane and proper and this sort of thing doesn't happen . . . and you learn fifteen or sixteen years later that it happens all the time . . . that it gets no saner.

Eventually, in the early 1960's, chances got better because of the combination of the pop world, which had a lot of young people making records and producing records, and the French "new wave," which gave films to people in their early twenties. In the American cinema the people were all very old — and in England, too. There was a kind of mystique that you had to be forty before you could be a director. Some magic thing happened to you at forty . . . knowledge and skill were automatically instilled into you, you qualified. There were being made in England at that time — as a result, I think, of the Beatles and other pop influences — a whole lot of very seedy pop musical films, one of which starred our imitation of Elvis Presley . . . a man called Billy Fury . . . and they tended to give these to young people to direct as a kind of brave sop. Sidney Furie got his first film that way . . . Dick Lester too, and I got this one with Billy Fury, which was Britain's first twist film. Except nobody was twisting there yet, so they didn't quite know what it was.

That was my inglorious entrance, which was indeed very welcome at the time. I think I was twenty-four. Working on a feature film of whatever caliber was obviously preferable to sitting at home waiting for the phone to ring. All over the world where I go and meet young filmmakers there is this terrible problem of "How do you get in?" . . . and I'm rather unsympathetic to it . . . I must say . . . because if you haven't got the stamina and the ability to get in, it's too bad. We know that we are choosing a precarious business. You know that. You know going in it's difficult, and of course there will be injustice, but I'm a great believer in welcoming anyone who makes their own opportunity. I can remember years on end when I was totally unemployed . . . afraid . . . convinced that I would never get anywhere, and somehow or other one kept going and eventually you came out of it.

After his early years writing film criticism and personality articles, Peter Bogdanovich says,

I always considered myself a director who was sort of making a living writing about pictures, not the other way around. In other words, I always wanted to direct films, even when I didn't know it.

KING VIDOR: The way I got to direct the shorts was that I knew how to run a camera. I had a job with a fellow making a travelogue as a cameraman. I showed a lot of initiative, and he finally wrote some shorts and promoted them and gave me the job of director. Then I tried to get from the short category to the feature film category, and they said, "He's not a feature film director." So I glued three of these shorts together and tried to make them look like one film and didn't fool anybody. They always said, "It looks like three shorts glued together." For some reason, I couldn't make the change. So I figured that the only thing to do was to write a script and show it to people and if they were interested I'd say, "There's one catch; I've got to direct it." And that's what I did.

JOHN SCHLESINGER: It's no loss of face to confess that you've made a mistake, which we all do and will till the grave making films. People are very uptight, particularly in this country. We make commercials in England. No American director would ever do it because they think it's loss of face or position, something like that. I find it quite useful. First of all, it's just interesting to do a quick job in the middle of cutting something when you're bored with a film. You suddenly go and get out and do a one-day shoot on something. Jolly useful. And also can work with new technicians, see if you like them or not.

LOUIS MALLE: I made documentaries. I spent three or four years with Jacques Cousteau. That's how I started in film, as an underwater cameraman. I filmed fishes for three years, but the good thing about it was that technically it was fantastic. I was in charge of everything — camerawork and editing. So after those four years, I really knew enough about all that. I don't mean that it's necessary, but it helps; it helps control the people you work with.

ROBERT ALTMAN: I was in Kansas City. I was working for an industrial film company back there, and I quit. Independently, I did an industrial documentary film. I got this guy who owned some theatres and he put some money together and I wrote a script and did it for nothing. I produced it and directed it and drove the generator truck, got it through, and they sold it. I made a documentary feature called *The James Dean Story* after that. Then Hitchcock saw both of those pictures and at that time talked about putting me under contract. I wasn't interested in that . . . anyway, I did a couple of his television shows. Once you do one of those things, there's no way you can't keep doing them. They're dying for directors who can work and come in on time. The only thing they don't want to do is give anybody a first chance. Once they know you can do it, which is remarkable to me, they say, "That's fine."

To put it most simply, to make a film, one must make a film.

PAUL WILLIAMS: If you are talking about the reality of getting people to trust you with money to do films, then you have got to do films. That means either shooting very, very, very low budget films with sixteen-millimeter equipment and somehow being so brilliant that people want to trust you with a bigger production. Or you have to do the kinds of productions that can go both ways. One other alternative is to find somebody with a lot of bread who is willing to believe in you to do your very personal project. . . . Most people do genre things and then hope that they can do their movies someday. Stanley Kubrick did a couple of genre films first. You do learn a lot the first few times out. . . . There is definitely something to be said for getting to work.

PRODUCERS AND OTHER STRANGERS

One is a director either when one decides that he is, or when his experience and achievement show that he is. But one's state of mind and background are only indications of a future. Film, by economic necessity the most public-oriented of the popular arts, is dependent largely on money and the people who raise it, handle it, and deal it out. A film is derived from an idea — an impression, a story, a script — but that idea will never be realized without the support of fuel. For a filmmaker, fuel comes in two forms apart from his own inspiration: producers and money.

The Producer
ALLAN DWAN: They used to say, "You're as good as your last picture." My idea is you're as good as your last producer.

JAN KADAR: A producer for me is a man who is a creative person. His creativity is such that he develops and gives birth to a child. I don't think that a director should do everything. There should be this kind of perfect marriage between the people with different talents. But the producer has to love what he is doing. I don't think that the producer is somebody who is putting together the deal or who is finding the money. That is a secondary thing for me. If he is doing his job well, then he is being a creative person.

CARL REINER: "How do you produce?" I didn't realize, even though I had been in the business for so long, that anybody who has taste is a producer. That is all you have to have, with a little bit of ability. If you can be a producer without taste, you have to have money. You have to have one or the other. Also, it is nice to have some kind of heft. You can also have a piece of property. That will give you heft. You can say, "I just bought all of Joseph Conrad's manuscripts, all of the unpublished ones." That will give you heft until they say, "Who is Joseph Conrad?" That's when you've got no heft. But many things can give you heft. One successful production will give you heft. An attitude will give you heft. Also, you can have heft if you are a very smart guy who knows what you are doing.

PANDRO S. BERMAN: At a certain time in the history of the film business, things began to change a bit. I think that Louis B. Mayer was responsible more than anyone else for what was loosely called the "producer system." He had Irving Thalberg. With Thalberg, he was able to set up a method of making pictures whereby he felt he could save a lot of money. He hoped to hold the directors more or less in check financially by giving the producers authority. He made them responsible for finding the properties, and watching over the development of the screenplay with the writer. It may seem ridiculous to you today, but very often under Mayer's system the stable of M.G.M. directors, which was rather extensive, would be called in to make a picture two weeks before the production started. Very often the director would be finished within six days or so after the picture finished. That was one way that Mayer saved a lot of money. He would get a lot of pictures every year out of his directors that way. Today, I would imagine that a director starts from the beginning with the idea, and by the time he is through editing the film, maybe a year or a year and a half has gone by.

In those days, the producers had authority. If they were intelligent enough, they would delegate a lot of that authority to a bright man who was the director. In many cases I hope that I was smart enough to let the George Stevens and the John Fords and the top directors who knew what they were doing carry the ball. I hope I let them carry it to their ultimate conclusion. I always believed that a picture should be the result of one man's feeling and thinking, whether he be a writer or a director or a producer. I never believed that it should be messed up by too many people having too much to say. If you had a director who really had a concept, then I believed in letting him carry that concept out.

ROGER CORMAN: When I back a young filmmaker, I generally keep not a great deal of control during the shooting on the basis that I don't think anybody can have a great deal of control in the shooting unless they just come in and take over. Most of my controls are before the shooting and afterward. For instance, I'll check out the script very carefully, the production staff, the casting, and so forth, and then I'll probably have some sort of control over the cutting. During the actual shooting itself, on most of the films that I've backed, I never even go to the set. I really feel it's best on the basis that I say, "O.K., I'll back this man as a director. He should have the opportunity to simply go and direct his film." The only time I'll generally step in is when I'm looking at the rushes; when I see something that really causes me to jump out of my chair looking at the rushes, I may have words with him about that. Or if he falls a great deal behind schedule. But if the work looks even somewhere near what I would consider to be commercial, acceptable standards and he's near his schedule and his budget, I prefer, frankly, not even to talk to him. Just let him make the film. . . .

STEVE KRANTZ: I think a picture producer has a responsibility to let a director do his thing within confines. I think the director has the right and responsibility to have first crack at everything. I think the producer has a responsibility to hold a checkrein with respect to the director if only from the standpoint of another body viewing the material.

RALPH NELSON: You can't divide the producer and director that easily because there are overlapping functions. The only parallel I can make is that it's like a father-mother relationship. I liken the mother to the producer because he originally buys the property or negotiates for it. He selects the writer to do it, he selects the director, and he nurses it all the way through, even after it has been screened and is in release. There are two distinct parts of making a film: making the best film you can, and then seeing that it gets the best distribution possible. There have been good films made that got terrible distribution and then got lost. And the father of the film is the director who comes in, has a few weeks of fun, and then is off to something else. But they overlap so, and I find it's good when you have different points of view because if you are the producer and you see a scene or casting problem differently than I do, then you state your position, I state mine. I've worked with good producers; I've worked with terrible producers.

FRANKLIN SCHAFFNER: You will find that there are, as in life, all sorts of people, and there are all sorts of producers. There are producers who are terribly good in terms of contribution to the script, and can turn out to be terribly bad in contribution to casting the picture. There are producers who are terribly good in finding the property and raising the money for it, and absolutely no help at all in the rest of the productive process. There are producers — and these are the worst kind — who have twenty-twenty hindsight. That is, they can look at dailies and tell you where you are precisely wrong, although they have had the same material to deal with that you have had all along. The only difference is you've had to commit and they haven't. One shouldn't judge them too harshly unless they are inhibitive.

Film is no more of a charitable enterprise when controlled explicitly by a government.

SERGEI BONDARCHUK: In the Soviet Union, as you know, cinematography studios belong to the State. They're supported by the State. We have no private studios. In the Soviet Union there are fifteen republics, and almost every republic has its own studio. I work at Mosfilm Studios. At the studios there exist these creative unions, sort of . . . branches; we have seven of them. And every union has its own administration, and has a script branch division to it, and an editing branch. As usual, what generally happens is that a director will submit an application for the writing of a script. And the application itself can be very brief, or it can be more involved. The creative committee actually is the one that discusses and investigates this application. They are the ones that decide whether to accept us to make a film. They contact the script writer and the director, etc.

Ideally, a producer provides not only fuel, but serves as the intermediary from committee to filmmaker.

VINCENTE MINNELLI: I remember *Meet Me in St. Louis*. No one wanted to do that because they had read the script and they said, "There's nothing there." And on the face of it, there isn't if you read it. And even Judy Garland didn't want to do it. She thought it would ruin her career. She was told that she was trying to get away from that sort of thing. But my producer, Arthur Freed, and I saw certain things in it, great nostalgia value and so forth, and so I completely ignored all those people. But Freed — his record with the company was so good that L. B. Mayer, who was very, very close with him, said, "Well, let Freed make his folly." But I must say that all said afterward that they loved it.

And this establishment of source material is not only a starting point; it conditions the entire filmmaking experience.

WILLIAM FRIEDKIN: The most important thing that I think the director does is choose his material. That's the single most important thing you do. In other words, how are you going to spend your time for the next whatever it is? In my case, on *The Exorcist*, it was two years, which is excessive. But generally, on a feature film these days, it's anywhere from six months to a year. So number one, it's what are you going to do? What do you want to do? That's the most important decision.

VINCENTE MINNELLI: Once you find the right idea, then go ahead and embellish it.

The Money

With material chosen and money committed, the director's task only has begun.

JOHN SCHLESINGER: I think one of the jobs of being a director is practicality. You hang around for months or years trying to get something financed. Then, it's go, go. A lot of the energy goes into the creative thing, but a great deal more goes into seeing that they don't piss it all away down the drain.

CURTIS HARRINGTON: There is only one reason, at least in America, that people put money in film. That is to make a profit. There is no other reason. You have to think in those terms, because nobody else thinks in any other terms. You can't go in and say, "This is going to be a beautiful picture." That doesn't mean anything. You have to say, "This is going to be a beautiful picture that everybody will want to see. It will make a lot of money." When you set up a picture deal, you not only need the money to make the picture, but you have got to have a completion bond or completion money. That means that if you go over budget, the people who have given you the money to make the picture, they are assured that from some other source there will be money forthcoming to complete the picture, no matter what. They have got to know that the picture will be finished, or all the money that they put in at first position is of no value. A non-completed picture is of no value whatsoever. Investors insist upon completion money.

Again, the Iron Curtain provides little protection for the film artist.

TAMÁS RÉNYI: In Hungary, since the expectation is the commercial success, those directors who cannot achieve this financial success are not fired, but nor are they encouraged afterward to make another commercial venture.

It seems that, the world over,

STEVE KRANTZ: The three qualities in respect to your relationship on the pecking order are: number one, are you working? Number two, is your last picture successful? And number three, can you give me a job?

PAUL WILLIAMS: I am really convinced that nobody cares about the effect of the film on the audience other than whether they will come to the film or not. I mean, if they are convinced that this film is going to make money . . . You get the picture made.

VINCENT SHERMAN: If you are making hits and if your pictures are successful, then you get a little stronger with each picture and your position improves. They listen to you a little bit more. They say, "Well, the last one was a hit. The one before was a hit. The guy must know what he is talking about."

ROBERT ALTMAN: . . . I would caution you not to think that this economic aspect of filmmaking is not related in an important way. Most of these pictures are cross-collateralized, one against the other. If you have two or three flops, you will quickly discover that your independence and your freedom to do what you want to do disappears. It is very much related to how well the picture does.

MICHAEL WINNER: I don't like that at all, having to be conscious of "commercialism." I'm very aware that when I go into some of the films that I make, including something such as *The Mechanic* or the picture I'm making now, that in one respect I really shouldn't be doing them. They do not give me enormous artistic pleasure to make. They give limited pleasure only. I think that you then say: "What are the alternatives?" One of the alternatives which I see a lot of my English colleagues adopting is to make very few films indeed. They say: "I'm not going to go into that film until I'm totally satisfied with everything." And they wait two, three, and four years between pictures. During that time they make commercials. They choose to go and direct a box of chocolates or some washing powder. I don't see that as a way out of anything at all. You can wait three or four years for what you think is the masterpiece, and it quite frequently can be as big a dud as something you picked after six or seven months.

And, remember,

ABRAHAM POLONSKY: . . . The fundamental part of this business is some form of pornography. It's either the pornography of violence, the pornography of sex, pornography of politics, or it's something. And they're selling it. So you're not dealing with people who have high principles.

2
THE SCRIPT— A DIRECTOR'S CURRENCY

The first basic element in creating a film is the script. The script is basically the guideline. Even if it is very precise, it is a guideline. Later, the period of the shooting will bring you a lot of surprises. Then, the editing still is a completely new experience.

— Jan Kadar

The script is the director's currency, the beginnings of the raw material from which is derived the resultant images that, strung together, constitute a film. As suggested earlier, scripts may come from ideas, impressions, stories, plays, paintings, music, poetry, dances — in short, any perceptible realities.

What must a script do? What must it contain? What is the interplay between form and substance? What is the extent of a script's value and import? How are directors matched with projects?

When Thomas Mann authorized Abraham Polonsky to adapt his story "Mario and the Magician" for the screen, he told Polonsky that he was looking forward to its translation into the "sphere of the visible."

Economic considerations aside, all films begin with a concept suitable for this visualization. This concept represents an attitude towards character(s), event(s), environment(s), object(s), and so on. Without such an attitude or stance, there is no unified film script and, hence, no complete film. Rightfully, even the most abstract film follows some sort of narrative line.

STAN BRAKHAGE: Very often my contemporaries and I are attacked or scorned because it is said we are not involved in narrative, and narrative is the only true art. This is not so. I think narrative is intrinsic to any continuity art. There is always a story, but it may be a different sense of a story than the normal Hollywood film.

As a continuity art, film is constructed out of an eventful flow. This ongoing thrust characterizes the most successful films — it provides an entrance for audiences into the film.

ALLAN DWAN: I can't recall any particular thing that drew me. Any human thing did. Any good story. If somebody came along and told me an interesting story, I was interested, terribly interested. . . . Like adventure and romance. I deplored tragedy. I didn't like violence. I used it occasionally to gain a point. But I would say adventure, movement, and romance were the basic things. And, of course, always hope. I hated an unhappy ending. Now they're arty, but I don't like them even now. I wouldn't care to handle one.

VINCENT SHERMAN: I went to Warner and told him that I didn't like a story he had sent me, and I didn't know what we could do with it. I said that I liked the two writers very much. They seemed to be very bright and intelligent. But I thought it was an impossible story. I thought we wouldn't come out well on it. Warner then said to me, "Look. This is my situation. I've got eight actors on salary here and they are doing nothing. Now fix this script up and put them to work. For God's sake, I can't pay people to sit around here week after week and do nothing." He then named Gordon MacRae, Eddie O'Brien, Viveca Lindfors, Dane Clark, Virginia Mayo. Anyway, Virginia and Viveca were the two women. And Eddie O'Brien and Gordon MacRae and Dane Clark were the three principal men. We also had two or three others that were under contract to the studio. There were a total of about eight people on that one. They were under contract to the studio and were being paid a salary.

Warner said to me, "Now you can't expect to make an Academy Award every time. Sometimes you have to do something for the studio. Just make me ten or twelve reels of passable film here and I'll be satisfied."

I said, "But they don't fit these parts."

He said, "Make them fit."

I said, "There is no part for Viveca. She is a very fine actress and a wonderful gal. She is a personal friend. There is no part for her. I would have to change the whole concept."

He said, "Change it."

I said, "She's foreign. She can't play just a straight American girl. Because she is a foreigner, we have to give her a different character, and tell who she is and why she is."

He said, "Fix it and change it."

I told Warner that I would make a deal with him. I said, "I understand that the studio has *The Hasty Heart*. You are going to do that in London."

He said, "That's right. No rush on that, though."

I said, "I'll make this if you let me do *The Hasty Heart*."

He said, "O.K., it's a deal."

I said, "This is going to put me so far in the hole that I'm going to need something to pull me out." And that's how I made *Backfire*.

MICHAEL WINNER: What normally happens in this town is that somebody gets a script and says, "Let's give it to somebody else," which I really can't understand at all, and ten writers later and six arbitrations later . . .

Sometimes very good films are made that way. Some of the finest films ever made have been through many writers in the most extraordinary manner. Quite frequently what happens on the way is the script gets so expensive through all these writers working on it that it's then abandoned in quite a good state and no one can afford to take it over, which is even sadder, really. But, you know, we enter a business of power . . . very much a business of misuse of power. Sometimes intentionally and sometimes accidentally. That is part of the imperfection of any society of which, in a way, the film industry is a microcosm. One can only attempt to move through the microcosm honestly and truthfully, and that's all you can try to do. You will fail frequently. There's no doubt of that. I don't think there's anybody who doesn't fail frequently.

GENRES AND MECHANICS

HOWARD HAWKS: I don't think any action picture is thoroughly worked out. You can't sit in a room and write an action picture. You have to get out and get ready to make it. But the form of the picture and the sequence of the picture and everything is worked out. If the writer puts in the fact that somebody says something coming into a room on a run, you can't do it. I mean you've got to get your action first and then use your dialogue, put your dialogue in afterward. At least, that's the way I work. . . . In working on *Rio Bravo* . . . , we found ourselves with a choice of two things, either of which we thought was pretty good. So, the one we didn't use we made a note of. . . . Very often in a story you run up against sometimes two, three, four situations. You don't know what one to use. Sometimes you even want to flip a coin to see which one you use. Sometimes there is no real reason why you pick one instead of the other.

RONALD NEAME: I don't believe that an adventure story is good enough by itself. I think that there should be within that story characters that you can relate to. I see a lot of action films in which I couldn't care less about the people. I don't know who they are, where they came from, where they're going to, what makes them tick, and therefore I'm not with them or for them. And so when I agreed to make *The Poseidon Adventure*, the first thing I insisted upon was that up front, before we started our cliff-hanging stuff, we did at least get to know just a little bit in depth, but not too much because you cannot afford the time, but just a little bit into what kind of people we were dealing with.

VINCENTE MINNELLI: To me, musicals are no different than dramas or comedies or farces or anything else, or tragedies, because they have to be real and right. You know it takes just as much concentration and use of intuition and imagination to make a musical as it does to make any other kind of good picture. I see musical numbers as scenes, you know. They're like scenes. They're dialogue. They have to put forward the story, have meaning to the story, and have a reasonable place. You can't just have a scene and stop and have a number. . . . I always feel that you have to do that so that it isn't noticeable, isn't an abrupt and comical breaking into song. That can be very bad. It has to be done subtly, and it has to be started in such a way that you accept it as though it were dialogue.

RAOUL WALSH: In a gangster movie, in the first place, you had to keep it moving. You had to have lots of bullets. At times, you had to have a bit of sympathy for the party who was going to get killed or wasn't going to get killed. And a fairly slight love story going through it to hold that part of it together. But, there's no set rule; they're all different.

ROBERT ALDRICH: There is a thin line between how much exposition you can put into a film and still not lose the continuity of the action and the concentration of the audience.

ROUBEN MAMOULIAN: Another word the majority seems to hate like poison is *symbol*. They hate "symbols," yet they'll live by symbols. Symbols are stronger influences throughout mankind's history than any reality ever was. We still live by symbols. Symbolic imagery.

ROBERT ALDRICH: I thought *The Dirty Dozen* would make a fascinating movie. Kenny Hyman had bought the script when he was with M.G.M. I always loved the book, but I hated the screenplay. I really loved the book. At that time I didn't realize that I could get Lukas Heller to come over on the screenplay. We agreed we would have to rewrite the screenplay. M.G.M. and Hyman agreed that the screenplay wasn't as good as it should be. It looked like a 1940 Warner Brothers war movie. There was one Italian and one black and one comic and so on. It appeared to be very old-fashioned. The book on the other hand was not old-fashioned at all. We thought it could be much more fun, more entertaining, and certainly more exciting than the script showed. . . . It was a patrol picture. We had to get here and then we had to get there and back again. We were careful in laying the foundation and we hoped that the action would take care of itself.

ALFRED HITCHCOCK: It's really a matter of utilizing your material to the fullest dramatic extent. For example, in the picture *Rear Window,* James Stewart is a photographer, so naturally he fends off his attacker with the use of photographic material, such as a flash gun. That's only because it is indigenous to him.

JOHN HUSTON: My own trending . . . is that there must be a plot. I see plot as a very noble thing. It's making a formula, a geometric formula, if you will, to become abstract about it. Reducing a theme down to a formula. And so when you draw that last line from the hypotenuse, the thing is demonstrated. The plot is the demonstration of the theme and, I think, completely valid considered in those terms. I think the moment plot becomes obvious to the point where it is melodrama, when you begin to see the stitches, then it is twisted and bent and not a true reflection, demonstration of the theme.

MERIAN C. COOPER: My theory is the three D's: danger, distance, difficulty. Or better still, difficulty, distance, danger. And if you go through those three D's, you get a picture at the end of it.

HOWARD HAWKS: I don't think plot as a plot means much today. I'd say that everybody has seen every plot twenty times. What they haven't seen is characters and their relation to one another. I don't worry much about plot anymore. Quite a while ago I made a picture called *The Big Sleep*. Somebody said, "Who killed such and such a man?" I said, "I don't know." Somebody spoke up and said, "I think so-and-so killed him." And we said, "No, he couldn't have done it." So we sent Raymond Chandler a wire and said, "Who killed Pete?" And he sent a wire back, "Joe did it." And I sent him a wire saying, "Joe is out in the ocean; he couldn't possibly have done that." And after people liked the picture and everything, I thought, "Why worry about plot and everything? Just worry about making good scenes." . . . So that's all we try to do is to hook it together with something that keeps your interest.

If you can get a new plot, well, I'll be glad to hear it. If you're any good as a director, you are good as a storyteller. Bob Hope wouldn't tell certain stories, and I just tell stories that appeal to me. People that I know, things that I've done, flying, racing automobiles. I like stories of the West merely because they are so, oh, really fundamental, basic and honest. It's a question of life and death. It's fun to do it. And the people like them.

LASLO BENEDEK: You know, three or four good effective scenes is enough to make a picture interesting. That's all you want.

The form finally chosen may dictate to a certain extent the content.

ALLAN DWAN: Everything was triangles with me, everything I did in a story. If I constructed a story and I had four characters in it, I put them down as dots. If they didn't hook up into triangles on lines, if any one of them were left dangling out there without relationship to any of the rest — or sufficient relationship — I knew I had to discard him because he'd be a distraction.

HOWARD HAWKS: I'd say that the whole thing in making something success-ful is to have somebody you're interested in. If you get a picture going where you've got a character that the audience is interested in, then

they're with you. . . . Wayne, when we made *Rio Bravo*, was beginning
to age. You don't want a romantic scene, so you had to make the girl the
aggressor. It was a theory I used in a picture called *Hatari*. The more
somebody likes somebody, the more he is liable to get angry at them and
mistreat them because he doesn't like himself falling. It made a good
relationship in that picture.

VINCENT SHERMAN: The big, big thing always was: does the story have
suspense? What is keeping the audience in its seat? I think that is
something that is still valid in anything, whether it is a comedy or a
serious story or a drama. There must always be a problem that is in the
process of solution. There must always be a problem that an audience is
interested in through the human beings involved in the problem. The
quicker the problem is set up and the stronger the problem is — putting
people in danger or creating an emotional problem between them — the
better for the audience. I learned along the way, too, that each scene in
the story or in the film has to be related to solving that problem. It has to
be on whatever the theme is of the picture. If you go off the story and off
the problem, then it shows up as a weakness immediately.

I have tried in any script that is handed to me to humanize the villains
of the piece. There is another thing that I have discovered. Your hero
becomes greater as his opponent is greater. If you have a formidable
opponent you raise your hero. You can't have a puny and petty opponent
and make your hero a big man. There is no contest. I think that Iago
makes Othello more interesting as a human being.

ABRAHAM POLONSKY: A good script is very complex and developed and full
of all kinds of relationships that are not expressed in the words, but are
implicit. So if you've got someone else's screenplay, you've got to do that
job now. You've got to find out what it's about, you've got to agree that
that's what it's about, you've got to believe it, and then you've got to start
to assemble it, whereas if you've written it, you've already done the
assembly. What you haven't done is the expression. But with someone
else's screenplay, you've got to do the assembly before you do the expression. And many a director who hasn't done that has come on the set and had
a lot of trouble, trying to find out what he's doing. And the picture's bad
for that. Directors have to work very hard, but, of course, if you're working in the convention of a studio where they give you a detective story to
do and there are a hundred more like that, and you've done forty of them
yourself, what you do is to use old-fashioned assemblies.

KING VIDOR: I always thought my job was about half done if I worked on the script, particularly the story, and if I'd worked with the set design and the picking of the locations and the casting. That's at least half of it, before you ever start to shoot on the stage. You can't help but visualize as you go along, if you're working on the script and the continuity.

The first year that I made silent films we didn't have any budget to buy stories. You just had to write your own. I made four pictures the first year, and they were all right out of my past. But you can't keep doing that. The picture *Hallelujah!* was a bunch of things that I had seen happening in my boyhood in Texas and Arkansas. I made a list of all the stuff that I'd seen and that was the film. We connected it up with some sort of story thread. Fellini's still doing it. He's psychoanalyzing himself all over with practically every picture he does.

ARTHUR PENN: I think one just does the film that he feels he has to do. Once you launch on something like *Night Moves*, which breaks with some of the traditions of a genre, the film that comes out is the film that comes out. It tends to reflect your inner state. It's not visible to me during the making of that film what those inner states are, or how that might resonate against the tenor of the times.

There's no accounting for how an idea strikes you. There's something absolutely impure about it. Maybe that's the way cinema is born. I would suspect that much of Hitchcock's cinema is born that way. "There's a terrific stunt. Now, how do I make that stunt work backward for me?" One tends to censor those moments as being somehow not appropriate to art, or some kind of high-minded crap like that. In point of fact, I think that it's the very essence of cinema.

For some, the choices of raw material are basic and classic.

GEORGE SEATON: To me there are only three stories: man against man, man against society, man against himself.

For others, common life on the streets may trigger the whole development of a theme and tale.

MILOS FORMAN: The source for *Taking Off* was this very tragic event in the East Village in New York about three years ago. This girl, Linda Fitzpatrick, and a guy called Groovy were murdered. When I read the interview with her father, that was the first moment I realized that this could be our work, to dig for a story because already in that interview was everything: the tragedy, the comedy, the puzzlement, everything was in this interview. Then I started to do research, hanging around the East Village, talking to the kids with a friend of mine, a French writer, Jean-Claude Carrière. When Jean-Claude left for Paris, we continued with John Klein, doing research and talking to the kids and their parents, and slowly we started to structure the story. At the beginning the story was more focused on the kids, but the more I learned about the whole scene, we shifted the interest slightly more to the parents. . . . I met a man who was commuting every weekend during a four-month period from Miami, Florida, to New York looking for his runaway son and hanging around the East Village hoping that one day he will bump into his son. And one day his son bumped into him and said, "Hi, Dad, what are you doing here?"

"I'm looking for you, my son."

"I'm all right."

"Why don't you call or write us, let us know that you are all right? We are dying not knowing if you are O.K."

"O.K., I will."

And tell me, is this tragedy or comedy? I don't know.

ADAPTATIONS

What constitutes the "right material" for any particular director would, of course, depend on his orientation, the sense of his own function.

ALFRED HITCHCOCK: It is very difficult. It would depend upon which direction you were going. You may be making a psychological murder story or a chase story. I make many, many different kinds of pictures. I have no particular preference, to be quite honest. Content — I am not interested in that at all. I don't give a damn what the film is about. I am more interested in how to handle the material so as to create an emotion in the audience. I find too many people are interested in the content. If you were painting a still life of some apples on a plate, it's like you'd be worrying whether the apples were sweet or sour. Who cares? I don't care myself. But a lot of films, of course, live on content.

JOHN HUSTON: I never look for film material. I don't read things, unless they're manuscripts that are sent to me. But I don't read books with the idea of making pictures out of them. Very often it's something I read in my youth even and keep harking back to and one day say, "My word, that could be a film." It comes out of my interest in the material itself.

Because of the many superficial resemblances between theatre and film, plays often have inspired movie versions, not without hazard.

MARTIN RITT: A good play is created in the heat of time and place. When you start to "open it up," which is a movie phrase, you can wreck it. You lose the power. If you make a play, in most cases, I would say that you shoot it. You get the best performances that you can. You shoot it as honestly as you can, and then you let the play sit.

ROUBEN MAMOULIAN: A good play sometimes is not going to make a good film. Because there's a reason why it's a good play. A good play is a succession of words. It's dialogue. It's usually one set, two sets. If you're going to distort it or widen it to make it fit the film medium, you're going to lose certain advantages and virtues the play had on the stage. If you bring in something that belongs exclusively to the screen that makes up for that loss, then you can make a fine film. I think usually the best films are made from originals, or from just the idea of a novel. Then you can start out by structuring the whole edifice of your script in graphic terms. I do believe that even though we have talking pictures, the main force of the cinema is in imagery, not in words. Obviously, words are necessary to get the main ideas, so you also have a dramatic progression in words. But that progression on the screen is really not comparable to a progression on the stage. On the stage you can have a scene that lasts for thirty minutes and it may be the best scene in the play. On the screen it would bore you to death.

You just cannot have an equivalent of that. On the screen you should achieve the same thing in six minutes. So right there you see how the architecture of the words has to fit the screen.

Novels, for love and money, have been the source of many film projects.

HOWARD HAWKS: Hemingway and I were shooting down in Cuba, and I wanted him to go into pictures. He was afraid. He said, "I'm number one in my own field; I don't want to get mixed up in Hollywood."

"Well," I said, "you're always broke and you could make some money." I said, "We can take your worst story and make a picture out of it."

He said, "What's my worst story?" He didn't like that at all.

And I said, "Well, that horrible thing called *To Have and Have Not*."

"Oh," he said, "you can't make a picture out of that."

And I said, "Sure." So we started talking about it and he threw aside his story and we started talking about how maybe the girl met Harry Morgan. Then he didn't want to have anything to do with it, so I came back and bought the story from somebody who owned it who hadn't been able to do anything with it. We made it into a picture and it was very successful, a very successful picture.

I saw Hemingway and said, "You got ten thousand dollars for the story. I bought it for eighty thousand dollars and I made close to a million." He was so mad he wouldn't talk to me for six months, because I had told him he could have half of anything I made on it.

COSTA-GAVRAS: In adapting *Z*, we had to first simplify it but without taking out truth. The book was based completely on a file submitted by the investigator. It had movie-like details. Second, it was essential to discard folkloric details. Third, not to talk too much about psychological explanations. Make out of it a tragedy with entertainment rhythm. We did not want to give all the keys and solutions.

In adapting a classic for the screen, some directors do not hesitate at freely interpreting all those underlying elements that may not have been made explicit in the original work.

JOHN HUSTON: I must have read *Moby-Dick* eight or ten times without ever thinking of making a film. Then I did think of making a film of it and wrote a script and put it away and gave up the idea. It was several years after that that I returned to it. The material fascinated me, and it was a preoccupation — how to get it on the screen, and, indeed, how to define it. In many respects it is a random book. It has many faces; I finally perceived at least to my own satisfaction, what the point of the book was — a blasphemy — and there, by the way, was the most difficult problem in writing the screenplay: the realization on the part of the mate, the second mate, and the crew of the *Pequod* that they were engaged in an unholy undertaking. The whole script was right except for a scene that would point this up. I had even started the picture before it suddenly dawned on me what the material of that scene should be. It should not consist simply of the reaction to the pursuit of the white whale, but — which is what we tried to do — when Starbuck realized that Ahab was out to kill a whale, this in itself didn't seem to have a particularly diabolic meaning or significance. What turned the trick was my realization one day — a ray of light hit me — that they were not doing what they were supposed to do: to furnish oil for the lamps of the world, light. In this they were committing, according to the Quaker mentality, a sin; and it was then the realization hit that they were engaged in something devilish. . . . The scene was in Ahab's cabin when Starbuck confronts him. That was really the heart of the picture and not in *Moby-Dick,* not in the book. I think that Melville would have approved.

Perhaps mere changes or additions to the narrative need not constitute an unfaithful position with respect to the original source.

GEORGE SEATON: . . . I think you should remember, if you're adapting somebody else's play which has been successful or a novel which has been popular, that a screen writer has to be sort of a literary impersonator. He has to pick up the same quality of the original writing.

SWITCHES

When films are the inspiration for future films, the "community" or "collaborative" nature of filmwork becomes more evident.

ALLAN DWAN: . . . If I saw a Griffith picture I liked, I'd give it a few little twists and put my cast in it, which made it different. Different actors made it a different story. But it was his story or wherever he got it. I don't know where *he* got it. He got it from someplace, maybe an old stock play or something. But we'd buy them.

VINCENT SHERMAN: I became oriented toward the idea of "switching" stories, which I discovered was a very common thing in Hollywood. The more adept a man was, the more skillful he was at switching stories. In fact, years and years later, I met Dudley Nichols, who was a marvelous man and screen writer. We were having some trouble at Columbia getting a picture ready for Rita Hayworth, and he said to me, "Why don't you do a switch?" He told me that, in reality, *Stagecoach,* which he had worked on, was a switch on a de Maupassant story. So, there's nothing to be ashamed of in switches. You'd be surprised how many there have been in this town that have gone unrecognized. I made a film later on called *The*

Unfaithful, which got quite good reviews. It was a switch on a story called *The Letter*.

Directors even have "switched" their own works.

RAOUL WALSH: I remade *High Sierra* as *Colorado Territory* because Warners was stuck for a release. Everybody had turned down scripts and nothing came up. I had a talk with Warner and said to him, "Make this a western." He said, "All right. Start tomorrow."

However, it always should be kept in mind that free choice of material has not been the standard case in Hollywood.

RAOUL WALSH: The director could turn down a script, if it didn't fit him or something. But then, they'd generally plead with you. You see, most of these pictures were already sold and had to be released on January 15 and here you were in December. "How are you coming? Do you think you'll finish tomorrow?"

THE CRAFT

What must be in a script to make it suitable for filming? Usually, we associate with the idea of "script" two functions: narrative flow and dialogue. With the rule of thumb of "one minute of screen time per page," scripts may contain anywhere from sixty to several hundred pages. However, although many scripts employ a similar form, there is a wide latitude regarding the inclusion of detail — environmental description, suggestions for visual style, and so on. This latitude, of course, is vital to the interpretations to come of directors, actors, cameramen, and editors.

SAMUEL FULLER: It's a question of what kind of script you write. If you write a very detailed script, generally you write that when you're at a big studio so that every department will know in advance what they're going to do, what you're going to demand of them — props, special effects, etc. Or, you have a very loose script, where you answer all the questions later, at meetings. But whether it's detailed or loose, to me, it's very flexible because what I say or think at the typewriter certainly takes on new forms, aspects, and size when on the set.

JOHN HUSTON: I think of a script as an organization, you know, like an engine. Ideally, why, all the parts, everything contributes and nothing is in excess and everything works. . . . It isn't an internal combustion engine until a scene makes it spark and the wheels begin to turn on each other. When this happens, why, the rest is comparatively easy. Everything has its function and, I hope, more or less, varying degrees of success.

GEORGE STEVENS: I think there's nothing more unfortunate than to know something about a story idea, and then to read the script and see this continual introduction of "long shot" and then nomenclature and definitions like "P.O.V." You'd think a Russian spy is going to read it. All of these things interrupt the course of whatever visualization an individual might be making of it. It's so often good, if one is doing a film script, to put what is superfluous in another document, some supplementary document, so the visual concept of it can be somehow apprehended as you go through the reading of the pages.

FRANK CAPRA: I work together with a writer, and you spark each other. When you get somebody that you're really in cahoots with, why, that works just wonderfully because you're your own audience and your own entertainer. I work a long time on the script, in preparation, a long, long time — maybe five months, six months. I may throw it away, throw all the scenes away, but the body of it is there, and the idea is there, the structure is there. I don't fool with the structure. I only fool with details. So a great deal of preparation goes into it. What I look for is entertainment, interesting characters, interesting people.

JOHN SCHLESINGER: One sets out to make a film because one likes the subject matter. I believe the script is never finished. I constantly work on the script, either with the writer, or, if the writer's not there, with another writer, or with the people that are working with me. I think the script is a blueprint and then it has to have a life of its own. The night before you shoot, you have to do what we call in England "prep," and I draw constantly little drawings. Nobody else can read my drawings except me, and I can't always read them. But it's at least a plan of campaign for the next day's work.

GEORGE SEATON: Everybody works differently. A lot of people just go boom, right into the screenplay because they feel that the original impetus . . . they'll lose it if they start to think about it. What I like to do is a treatment. I do a biography of every character — ten or twelve pages. . . . I turn these over to the actors. . . . I hate to have things on white paper with black typewriter ink because there's a finality to it which I don't like. I write longhand and I'll do it first on yellow paper, then green and blue. I don't mind for some reason changing those colors, but when you see that final black on white, then you're loath — at least, *I* am loath — to change something. I like to keep myself fluid as long as possible, but I do a treatment. Sometimes I just do maybe a sketchy outline first of nine or ten pages, you know, saying A so-and-so, B so-and-so, and then start to fill in, and then you say to yourself is C necessary? Why don't you go right from this to this? Because if you start writing a whole scene in screenplay and then say to yourself, "Oh my God, I don't need these forty pages," then you've done an awful lot of work and expended an awful lot of creative energy.

CRANE WILBUR: I don't write anything for myself at all. It's all in the head. I don't write the story as a story. I write it as a script, as a thing that is ready to shoot.

PAUL MAZURSKY: When you finish a first draft of some kind, it's like when you finish the first rough cut of a film. For the first time, you realize, "My God, it's so long. It's so boring. I don't need that scene. That's ridiculous. Why did I go to the Grand Canyon? What do I need this for? That's all nonsense — they know this already." And you thought it was great. It's the same with a script. It's a hundred and fifty pages and suddenly it's . . . You realize this and then you start cutting it away. I think you have to write more, put it all down, and then edit it yourself or find somebody to help you. Or, if you are not going to direct it, the director will then assume that function with you. It is probably better to over-write the first time. Don't edit it yourself. It's easier to take it out than to put it in. The same holds true for the film. . . . I knew where I was headed with *Blume in Love* in one sense. I knew about the end of the picture, but I didn't know what would happen all around it. . . . I try to figure out who the people are, but I don't know the whole thing, necessarily. No, I let a character take me to the next place.

To what degree is writing for the screen a craft to be learned, or an art that is felt?

ABRAHAM POLONSKY: I think that writing is something you learn at the same time that you have an ability to do it. Writing is not one kind of thing. I think it's a lot of talents. They're all different. Some writers have them all. But narrative ability doesn't mean you can write good sentences.

Writing good sentences is a gift. And writing good dialogue is a special gift. And having a sense of philosophy and history and meaning is another kind of gift, and the sense of significance. But some writers have it all, and they're very great writers. Some have some of it, and they're significant writers. Some only have one.

MICHAEL WINNER: I think any script by nature has a leading role, or, as you say, two leading roles. In fact, one is conscious of this when the script is in preparation, and the writer is conscious of it because he wants his money too, and a lot of it comes on the first day of shooting. Who are you going to be able to get? And if the leading role is for a seven-foot-tall Pakistani, you're in big trouble. The age group is very important. There are far fewer younger stars, for example, than middle-aged or older stars. You look at the list, and it's a very short list, and there's no doubt the acceptability of the picture depends on that. I think that's very sad, actually.

BERNARDO BERTOLUCCI: In Italy, we write on two columns, not as in America, where they write the dialogue right across the page. At the left side, you have the description of the location, action, also psychology, and the right side you have the dialogue. When you see that you have too much left side, you start to try for a balance.

Whatever the format, the words on the printed page are not necessarily the be-all and end-all for the future film. For Jean Renoir, the story evolves slowly from an idea. "In any domain, the problems are the same: slow digestion." Unlike Marcel Pagnol, who had once told him that "ideas come on like lightbulbs," Renoir's ideas were more likely to be in a state of constant evolution.

JEAN RENOIR: You know, I don't believe that a man is steadier than a tree. We change, and our ideas change. There are many lightbulbs in filmmaking. . . .

Even the famous character, Octave, which Renoir himself plays in *Rules of the Game,* was derived from a story necessity that arose only after much of the script had been written.

JEAN RENOIR: I thought certain situations needed a comment and that I should add to my story a kind of master of ceremonies, like in a review of the stage. And I found out that this master of ceremonies would have to say everything that I myself, the author, had in mind. And I say, "Well, why not say it myself?" . . . He was not originally in mind when I began the picture, but I found him before finishing the script. . . . Let's say I had about half the script.

CARL REINER: All writers are improvisational actors. They act on paper when they write.

Though a script establishes its own guidelines, slight variations that may arise later often affect the entire quality of a sequence. This may be true especially in comedy, where the tone of the humor is as important as the substance.

GEORGE SEATON: For instance, I guess two of the biggest laughs — line laughs — in *A Day at the Races* — one is, "Either he's dead or my watch has stopped." You know, that's when Groucho is taking Harpo's pulse. Well, the first time it was written, it was "Has my watch stopped, or is he dead?" Now, we had a conference about it because basically there was a funny idea there and Groucho was the one who said, "Let me try it as a statement instead of a question." And suddenly it all became clear, because when you ask a question in a funny way, you expect a funny answer. It's the old story of "Why does the chicken cross the road?" or "Who was that lady I saw you with last night?" You expect a topper. So that if you can, on a one-liner like that, make it a statement instead of a question. Your chances are a hundred to one that you'll get a better laugh. The moment that Groucho did it as a statement, "Either he's dead or my watch has stopped," boom, the roof went off.

The other line that I'll never understand why it gets the biggest laugh . . . is when he's got Kokey Flo and she says, "Hold me closer, hold me closer," and he says, "If I held you any closer, I'd be in back of you." What's funny about that? What's funny about it? I threw that in a matinee in Minneapolis and again the roof went off.

PETER BOGDANOVICH: You set up something. You get a laugh with it. And then you top it. The trouble with most comedies today is that nobody understands the principle of topping a joke. This means that you get a laugh and then if you get a laugh on top of that one, it's always the big laugh. Most times you see a comedy you feel kind of like you laughed but you wish that you'd been able to have a big release and the reason you don't have it is because they haven't topped the gag. That's all it is, as simple as that.

My favorite example of that in *What's Up, Doc?* was the sort of classic gag which was the one where the cars are all making a U-turn and they smash into this Volkswagen bus which is parked along the curb. There are three cars and each one smashes it and each time it gets a bigger laugh. It never fails. The third car that hits it is a bigger laugh. Now I could have left it there because I did three — one, two, three — and each one was bigger. Well, the topper is when the guy runs out who obviously owns the car, opens the door, and the whole thing falls over. That's the topper and that's the big laugh. The audience actually falls apart because you have led them up to that. It isn't that they're happy. It's a release. Because it's laugh, laugh, laugh, and you want one more and there it is. It finishes the situation — no way you can get another laugh with it.

CARL REINER: The best scripts that I have ever read were scripts with no laughs in them. . . . My executive producers will say, "There are no jokes. There are no laughs in it." I remember saying once, "That is the single funniest thing that I have ever written." They will say, "Yes, but there are no laughs in it." I always am suspicious of a script when I read it and there are word laughs and word plays. I call that curvy writing. Everybody is talking so cute that you can't stand them. Nobody will say hello without finding a cute way to say it. What I am saying is tell a straight story and tell it with straight feelings. If you have a comedy bone in you, then every so often you will lighten the moment.

The classic story demonstrating the potential gap between written word and seen image is Mamoulian's tale of the last shot of Greta Garbo in *Queen Christina*.

ROUBEN MAMOULIAN: The power of the screen. The director has so many tools in his hands which you don't have on the stage. On the stage the actor is on his own. No help you can give him in the middle of the stage — five people around him — it's up to him to hold the tension. But on the screen you help the actor with the angle, the movement of the camera, the framing, the foreground piece, the background piece, with props, with lighting, all that. Now, when you've prepared something and you're reaching the climax, the climax here being a tough one — a queen resigns, abdicates her throne for love, she gets on the boat and her lover is dead — what are you going to do? What words are you going to use? Anything you say is going to sound phony, silly. So I thought, "The only way to do it is with silent imagery."

Just before I was to shoot this, Mr. Mayer called me in. He said, "Look, we forgot something. All the producers read this script. You must change this ending."

"What do you mean, change it?"

He said, "Make it a happy ending. You can't have John Gilbert dead."

I said, "Let's not be ridiculous. The whole film is written for that."

"But," he says, "it's depressing. It's very unhappy."

I said, "Mr. Mayer, I don't believe in depressing people any more than you do. If an audience leaves a film of mine, or a play, then I have failed miserably. Because the purpose of the theatre and its function is to excite, to stir, to stimulate, to uplift a person. The greatest uplift comes from a tragedy. A tragedy is not cheerful, but when you leave a tragedy you feel marvelous, because the final effect of an artistic thing is uplift. If this ending turns out to be depressing, then let's get together and I'll be willing to discuss it. But right now, that's what I'm going to shoot. We'll have a preview and if we find it depresses the audience, they walk out grumbling, then we'll do something about it."

So I shot it purely visually and rhythmically. If you'll notice the movement of the sailors, all is preparatory for Garbo coming up to the front. Now, she comes to me and says, "What do I do?" Indeed, what? What do you play? Do you cry? Do you have little glycerine tears running down? Or do you smile for no reason or do you laugh? What do you do? Everything is wrong. Because for me, I'd say, "My God, this woman is inhuman, she's smiling." For you, you'd say, "She's a weak sister, she's crying." For the others, they insist on a queen going hysterical. "Can you imagine them being so insensitive?" Nothing you do is right. Therefore, I said to myself, and this works — if you do it right it always works — "I'm going to have every member of the audience write his own ending. I'm going to give him a blank piece of paper — as John Locke said, *tabula rasa* — nothing on it. Let them write sadness, inspiration, courage, whatever they choose, whatever they prefer. We have prepared the scene. They'll fill it in."

So I said to Garbo, "Nothing. You don't act. Nothing. You don't have a thought. In fact, try not to blink your eyes. Just hold them open. Just wear a mask."

And she did just that, for ninety feet. You'd be amazed. Some people say, "Ah, the courage of this woman." Others say, "Oh, the sadness that is beyond tears." "You know, the serenity . . ." Everybody thought she felt the way they wanted her to feel. So everybody's satisfied. But actually, what they're looking at is zero, a very beautiful one, but zero.

COLLABORATION

Because the script is an implied "is-to-be," it is difficult to approach it with the finality we do other arts. The script is a means to an end, an end firmly grounded in the area of popular and commercial appeal. With an eye to this future, the craft of script writing often lends itself to becoming a collaboration between screen writers, or between screen writers and the intended director of the project. In fact, in the practical arena, a good deal of attention is paid by the writer not only to directors' possible necessities, but as well to many other potential exigencies.

ALFRED HITCHCOCK: For *Frenzy,* I went to Covent Garden first. You must choose every place you're going to put in the film. You know your rough story line. Then you go around to your locations and so forth. Then you come and sit down and go through that three-month process of making that film on paper — discussion after discussion. You may only get two sentences down in a day. . . . Very often scripts are written, and then the location manager is called in, and they try and find some location that fits the script. I don't believe in that. I think you should go to the location first, and then put it in the script. Now, years ago, I did a film with Thornton Wilder, *Shadow of a Doubt,* and it was laid in a small northern California town. We went up there and stayed a week before a line was written. I usually work with the writer on the treatment. Now when you say treatment, it is really a description of the film, and it describes exactly what is coming on that screen. There are indications of shots in it, and so forth. Then you give that to the writer and let him go off.

GEORGE PAL: I think a writer should be cast to a project. Usually a producer has an idea of what he is going to do. Sometimes it is an idea and sometimes he found the idea either in a book or in a play. Very often a creative producer has an idea and then he follows it through. Then he looks for a writer. . . .

MILOS FORMAN: I don't like to work alone. I don't know if it's because I'm so lazy, but I like to work with somebody because it's a dialogue. The film is a dialogue. You are telling a story. As a filmmaker, what you are doing is just using film images to tell some story. So writing a script you have a partner to talk with to provoke you. I always work three people together, which is very good because if two are in the argument, the third one can make the judgment. If one falls asleep, two still can work.

MARTIN RITT: There is one problem about getting too involved with a piece of material. You lose your objective relations with the material. Once your own creative impulse is in, then you tend to like the writing more than you might ordinarily and fall in love with your own ideas. If I were a producer or if I were a studio, I would prefer to have a different man directing and a different man writing, if I had genuine respect for both. I would want to have the value of both individuals.

GEORGE CUKOR: . . . I respect the writer a great deal. I am very dependent upon him. If they give you a good scene, there is an old theatrical expression, "The scene plays itself." A good scene is the one with support. It will move you. If I respect the writer, I encourage him and I influence him when I can. But, I don't intrude myself on him too much.

CURTIS HARRINGTON: I consider myself not a very good writer of dialogue. I am pretty good on construction. Therefore, now that I can do it, I much prefer to work with a writer rather than write it all myself.

ROMAN POLANSKI: When I work with Gerard Brach, it is very loose. We often live together when we work together, and after breakfast we start playing a little chess, you know, and then we start talking and we say, "Maybe we should start working," or something, and then we walk around and talk about themes and exchange ideas and Gerard goes to write it and he goes to the room and writes and I go and do something else. Sometimes I write some dialogue or make a couple of telephone calls and then I come back and I say, "Read it to me." If it reads well, we go to the next scene. If not, we will try to rewrite it . . . or we play some chess. . . . It depends on the script.

HOWARD HAWKS: When I hired Leigh Brackett, I thought she was a man. I had read a book of hers. She came in, and Bill Faulkner was out here, and we did *The Big Sleep*, which was a very well written thing. This fellow was one of the finest of that type of writers. It took them eight days to write the script. Then Leigh worked on others, and she got more and more used to my way of working. We'd talk about a thing. She writes a thing and then I go over it with her. Then, after we cast the picture, I go through the script and change it to suit whoever is the personality. . . . Well, I can change the dialogue for a character . . . in two or three days, so that's my participation.

WILLIAM FRIEDKIN: For *The Exorcist,* Blatty had written a screenplay that I read and didn't like. He departed from the book considerably and I wanted to stay close to the book. I went back, and I have a copy of the book at home. I went through the book and I literally marked up the book and I gave it to Bill and I said, "This is the script," and then he took it and he reworked — he rewrote the script from that, and then day to day, he would get new ideas, bring new stuff in. I went out and saw an actual arteriogram and a pneumoencephalogram being performed. I wrote down what they did, gave it to Bill, and he put it into script form. We talked out the dialogue. We talked out what we would keep of the book, what we would cut. He went away and put it into a screenplay.

STANLEY KRAMER: With every writer, some more than others, deadline is the most vicious enemy in the history of man. So therefore you have to be flexible on that and allow the time. I think every writer is different, and as for myself, I have to participate the full way with the writer without intruding either through credit or obstinacy. I have to be close with him, because I can't go on the stage unless we put it through the wringer that way. For better or for worse, mistakes or not, at least we worked on it and I sweated it out and I knew everything he knew. If I don't know as much about the script as he knows, the motivations and the whys, any dis-agreements are only on the basis of not being able to get together as people working together, and I think it's essential and it has to be. I don't think you can make a film unless you're working on the basic product and you know the initial stages.

FOLLOWING THE PLAN

Collaboration or not, of what final use is the film script? Confronted with the demands of the actual shooting experience, to what extent should and does the director rely upon it?

GEORGE SEATON: Mel Brooks said that he's learned one thing in two pictures and that is if it's not in the script, it's not going to be on the screen. Being a follower of that philosophy, I completely agree with him.

MICHAEL WINNER: The script is the basis of everything. I think that is really *the* creative work. The director and the actor are interpretive. However many scenes you may add to the script, or write anew, you are doing it from a basic creation, and I don't think you'll ever get that much better than the script.

RONALD NEAME: I think that a fine director with a fine crew and fine artists can plus that script by about twenty-five percent. I think a lousy director with a lousy bunch around him can minus it by about twenty-five percent. I think that basically the picture is the script. That is why I think you get the anomaly of somebody who you know is not a very good director who will turn out a pretty good film. Equally, you have seen some fine directors work and you say, "How could that man who is so marvelous make that awful picture?"

GEORGE SEATON: Years ago I did a script called *This Thing Called Love* . . . one of those comedies popular in the thirties. In the very opening you see Rosalind Russell and Melvyn Douglas arguing in a bedroom and they talk about other arguments. They've been arguing for six months, and so forth and so on. . . . It went on and on and on. Well, this is exposition that is just deadly. No matter how fast you tried to go, it slowed down. So I figured I had to get some visual trick . . . not trick, but an effect, that would tell all of this. So you see them in an argument, and she picks up a shoe. He runs and he closes the door just in time and the shoe hits the door. We went up to the door and we saw fifty scars. In one shot it told they had fifty arguments before. Well, when the picture was reviewed . . . they said it was one of the best directorial touches they had seen in years, but this was in the script. That reminds me of when Lubitsch instructed his writers to "give me a lot of Lubitsch touches."

Alfred Hitchcock often has said that for him, when the script is finished, all the creative work is done. However, his sense of script is somewhat different from the traditional.

ALFRED HITCHCOCK: I have had problems with writers because I find that I am teaching them cinematics all the time. You have got to remember that with a lot of writers you have to go by the page, what is written on the page. I have no interest in that. I have that square, white rectangle to fill with a succession of images, one following the other. That's what makes a film. I have no interest in pictures that I call "photographs of people talking." These have nothing to do with cinema whatsoever. When you stick up a camera and photograph a group of people, and pick up the close-ups and two-shots, well, I think that is a bore.

What, then, can and should a film script contain?

SAMUEL FULLER: Let's say I've been given a contract to make a picture, the money is there, they say go ahead, write your script, and shoot it. Fine. Now if I wrote that script the way I visualize it on the screen, it would be about eight hundred to nine hundred pages. It's impossible, of course.

VINCENT SHERMAN: In *The Adventures of Don Juan*, there were the scenes down in the dungeon. Now, all of that stuff I had to develop myself. There were things that were not written in the script. For all of the action scenes, the script said, "A fight takes place." Mike Curtiz shot for four weeks on *The Charge of the Light Brigade* when the script just said, "The brigade charges." I had things that said, "The café breaks into chaos." That took four days to shoot.

RONALD NEAME: I think that anyone writing a script should not put, "Medium shot. Close shot. The camera zooms in. The camera pans out. The camera does this, that, or the other." You cannot know what that camera should do until you have rehearsed with your actors. That is, unless you have worked it out so carefully in your mind that you are going to tell the actor to move over to the door or to the window or to sit down.

SAMUEL FULLER: I have a scene of us sitting here talking. That's the opening shot. We're about to shoot it, and I get an idea because looking out the window I see a bird following, chasing, another bird. I say, "Wouldn't it be great if I could catch them while they're chasing each other? No cut. Then pull back, and here is this man chasing this other man. There's no advance in civilization. Or a cat chasing a cat. Or a dog chasing a dog." Now, from a writer's viewpoint, if you put that in, then automatically, the studio says, "Oh you've gotta get dogs, trained animals." Now you multiply all this, and the writer says, "The hell with it" — unless it's that essential — "I'll just have the man chasing the other man in the office. If they can get an artistic approach, fine." This is just an example of what can happen. You don't have to create everything on paper, but the reason for making it is on paper. A director has to do with the eye what the writer has given to the heart when anyone reads the script. It's an emotional experience.

ABRAHAM POLONSKY: If you have a marvelous script in which every detail of direction is done, and you have a director who is just obedient, you will not get a film as interesting to look at. That's just a fact. Because unless the director does his work, you're not going to get anything. Film is an expression, by a director, in this medium. That's what a film is, no matter what kind of a film it is, whatever it is, whatever category it falls in or whatever genre it falls in. Now the genres or the categories themselves have aesthetic factors, so you can discuss those too. A powerful writer who's an artist, when he writes a screenplay, has got to have a powerful effect on a real director. There's no doubt about it. He may have an overpowering effect on a nondirector. But he will have a more interesting effect on a real director. That's just a fact, but he didn't direct the film. There's no way to direct the film except to direct it.

VILGOT SJÖMAN: I felt very strongly that I somehow had to get away from the well-written screenplay. . . . I was trained by Ingmar Bergman. I learned how to write screenplays by him. And so the whole idea behind *My Sister, My Love* was to do a very well-written screenplay, the way scenes followed each other almost choreographed. And that was a dead end somehow. I had to get out of that, and start to work with the camera as a pencil.

BERNARDO BERTOLUCCI: It's two different experiences — writing and filming — because to write a script for me is a literary experience. I think a movie must be independent, must have a sort of life of its own. It must be autonomous.

SAMUEL FULLER: How do you direct a scene in a way to make the man who wrote it happy? It's almost impossible. If I wrote a script and someone else directed it — the picture didn't do well and I was disappointed in the way he handled it. And the box office was bad. I would generally and normally say, "He ruined my script." However, if a director took my script and not only topped it, but what he did to it, or added to it, or how he changed it . . . made it a smash, then it's difficult for me to go around and tell anyone, "He ruined it." So, the whole thing is a tremendous big fraud. All of it depends on money. All of it depends on how successful it is. All of the rest is horseshit.

IRVIN KERSHNER: I think that everyone that I have known who has written a film has felt the same way. "If it had only been shot the way I wrote it, then it would have been a masterpiece. It would have been perfect." In their mind, they are right, because you write perfection. You can say, "And fifty thousand come through the canyon and immediately twenty-five thousand fall off of their horses dead, because the cannon was so accurate." You can see it in your mind. It is so perfect. But, when you go out to shoot it and you realize that you can't get fifty thousand horsemen through there . . . When you lower the figure to two hundred you realize that it won't look like anything. Everything is a compromise with the writer's "perfect" conception.

THE EVOLVING SCRIPT

As Kershner points out, once on the set with ever-changing conditions, all sorts of liberties may have to be taken with the written word.

ALLAN DWAN: A script is a lead sheet. It's something you can work from but you've got to ad-lib a great deal. With the best of scripts, you have to introduce things and sometimes things that are right on the spur of the moment are the best. . . . Otherwise you'd be idle. You have to improvise constantly. You have to take advantage of accidents and, well, many things.

BERNARDO BERTOLUCCI: I must be completely free when I'm shooting. I can't follow the script. My dream would be to dream the night before the shooting what I will shoot the day after. It happens sometimes. Not always, but I need to be on the set to decide what kind of style, of language, to use.

BARBARA LODEN: Once I started shooting *Wanda,* I would never look at the script much because . . . everything was different when I got out to Pennsylvania. I couldn't get locations that were indicated in the script, I couldn't get people to say the lines, I couldn't get people to do the parts as they were written, and so I had to use the people just as they were. I just quit looking at the script. It didn't serve any purpose. I knew the general story of it, what I would do. It was good to have something to deviate from, but I would never write down all that stuff that I had. It's written for somebody to read. What I would do — I would just write for myself what I needed as a filmmaker to make the film.

SAMUEL FULLER: I have one bad habit. And it's my fault, nobody else's. I break my ass on a script, many times till four or five in the morning. Now, I can mention several pictures I shot when I never even looked at the script. That's terrible. Days later I say, "Oh my God, I forgot a little touch there that I had thought of as a writer." But I had put in stuff while I was shooting from a directorial viewpoint that I never thought of as a writer. So, one balances the other.

RAOUL WALSH: Well, when we get the script and go over it and over it, then you make notes and stuff where you can boost it up and then, also, when you get on the set, sometimes the words don't sound too good.

HOWARD HAWKS: Don't ever think that a scenario is sacred. I used to get into quite a bit of trouble in the beginning when you had producers who would tell you what to do. I'd written the story and the script and I'd start to change things in the script. They'd tell me, "Hey, you can't change that." I said, "Why can't I? I wrote it." But they seem to think that once it is printed down and on a piece of paper that it becomes gospel, and that isn't so. Not in my way of thinking . . . Very often we have a story point and the collaborating writer says, "I think it would work here." I'll say, "Well, write it there, but also write it in another place." Then the writer comes back and says, "I can think of another place," and they write the same story point. We don't shoot them all. Sometimes we shoot two of them, sometimes only one, because as you get to telling your story you begin to realize where the story point ought to come. . . . The first thing we want is the action. There's a whole problem about making a scene if the people haven't any attitude. I can give you a pretty good example. We were doing *I Was a Male War Bride* with Cary Grant. We had a scene where Cary as a French captain had to answer the questions from an American sergeant that would usually be asked of a little French girl who is marrying a GI. Such questions as, "You ever had female trouble?" And, "Have you ever been pregnant?" and all kinds of ridiculous questions, and we looked forward to making the scene. We got up to making it and it wasn't funny at all. We didn't know what was the matter. And Cary said, "It's falling flat, isn't it?"

And I said, "It certainly is." Well, I said, "I don't know where from, but the suggestion came that a man like Cary Grant would be amused at the sergeant having to ask him these silly questions."

"Oh sergeant, female troubles, I've had them all," you know. All of a sudden, "We can do that, we can do that," and he got over in the corner with the sergeant who was asking. In two or three minutes the scene became very, very funny because the sergeant was embarrassed and Cary was having fun with him. And we had started an entirely different scene.

ROBERT ALTMAN: You can always manufacture something that'll work. If it really doesn't work, it means that something is wrong with your concept; the scene doesn't work. Every time I come to a scene and we start staging it and it doesn't work and it continues not to work, you start seeing what the problem is. The problem is in the material somewhere and the scene shouldn't be there. Something's wrong. You run into a lot of those things where there's slow spots and we'll do a lot of things where we think, "Oh, that doesn't work." Well, we can lose that.

We shot two days on a location in Nashville and all during the shooting I thought, "This is really terrible, and anyway, I know the film's long enough. We'll just drop it." But we saw it cut together and it's wonderful. Sometimes those things will work out of a plan. In other words, the design makes them work. Other times, they work out of the energy and even go beyond the design of it. Every film I've made, I'd say the average film took me forty-five days. What actually ends up on the screen uses up twenty-five days of shooting. They'll say, "Why don't you cut out that stuff that you cut out ahead of time? You don't have to waste time shooting it." You can't do that. You have to do the whole thing and then pick from it.

Other directors, though, acknowledge that while a certain amount of spontaneous creativity takes place on set, the script still is the thing.

HAL ASHBY: Basically, I feel that once you start out with a screenplay, that format, that you lived with and worked with long enough, there is an obligation to each scene within it; and when you start changing the obligation of the scene you can be in trouble. You can change what's going on within the scene, or the dialogue within a scene, as you go along, but basically stick to the obligation of what that scene is. Because I've always had a feeling that if I didn't I could end up all over the place.

For the abstract filmmaker, a written script may actually come *after* the film. Here, it serves as something of a repository for accumulated thematic notions.

STAN BRAKHAGE: After several weeks of photography I began to make a kind of script, about the only type of script — after three films — that I have made at all. This is still about the only type of script which I'll make — thematic, writing down certain themes that occur to me. The title very often comes first in my work. *Anticipation of the Night* — this whole life I was living, the childhood memories of it, were simply anticipation of the night or the death that was to come. Then from there the rose, and I would write all of the things that would occur to me about the rose. My writing is just to get rid of the superficial levels. Once I have written so I'm rid of all of the clichés, then I toss the writing aside and start filming. I try in the filming not to follow what I wrote, rather to go on from there.

Finally, whether preceding or following the film, whether a sketch or a detailed blueprint, whether abided by or revised on the set, it must be remembered that the script may serve one additional function.

MICHAEL WINNER: . . . This is the basic thing, to write screenplays. I think that you have got to start with the written material. If you are a young director, or wish to be, the number one thing you've got to have is a screenplay. You can't win your millions on the roulette table unless you've got a chip to put on the numbers — and your chip in the film business is a script. If you've got a script, you can go to any studio and say, "Here is my script. I'd like you to make it." If you look at most young people who get into films, that's what they've got. Scripts don't have to cost you any money. You can write it yourself or con or persuade some other struggler to write it for you. Then that's your currency. The people who are waiting for someone to anoint them with work are unlikely to get it.

Two

Film as a Battleground

3

Forming an Army

THE COMBAT FIELD

IRVIN KERSHNER: Making a film is a war. There are many battles every day. But, then there are battles that constitute entire sequences. Even in the beginning, there are battles fought over the script. There are battles for casting, and there are battles to get the amount of time that you want for specific scenes. You battle against the technicians, who all feel secure and safe thinking that they can do things the way they have done them before. This is a constant battle. There is the battle with the cameraman, who has his ideas, and who really is usually a frustrated director. . . . He

55

would like to direct, and therefore he gets himself involved in the entire production. He tries to visualize the scenes as he would do them. This, of course, I encourage. I choose him very carefully and I want to make him a participant. But, the price that you pay for that is that he is a strong-willed person who has been given his head, and he is going to fight for what he believes. This is constantly going on.

ROGER CORMAN: I'd like to have unlimited time, unlimited budget, but it has not worked out that way. So there's no point in fighting the fact that you've got three weeks to make a picture, and there's no point in spending half of three weeks bemoaning the fact that you've only got three weeks. You simply go out and do your best shot in three weeks.

LASLO BENEDEK: This is a situation one has to face. You can say, "Well, I'm sorry. If I don't have six month's preparation, I won't do the film." Or you go in and do the best you can. I once couldn't do anything because in the four weeks, I had to work on the cast, find the locations, work with the art director, prepare all the technical problems of photography. You see the film day or night practically all the way through. Then, naturally, during the shooting, I had a chance, because fortunately for me, I got the actors on my side to make some changes. I did a great many changes during the editing.

IRVIN KERSHNER: There are two ways of looking at it. I think that it has to do with your own personality and life-style. You can take the position that you will do anything to get a break and to make a film. You can try to do this and try to make it as much your film as possible. You may try to do their piece of junk, so that the next time you can do it your way. That is my attitude. Most people take that position. "This is for them. The next one is for me." You have got to be very careful, because this "one" for them becomes the first one, the second one, the third one, and the fourth one. Suddenly you don't know who you are. But it works for most people.

The second position is "The hell with them. They are all idiots. Everybody out there is an idiot. The companies are idiots. The money men are idiots. The writers are idiots. Everybody is an idiot. I am an idiot because I know the film I want to make and I don't care if it costs fifty million, I am going to make that film. O.K., I'll compromise. I'll make it for half a million. But, I am the one who is going to do it my way, and if I can't do it my way, then the hell with you." Many men make that work for them.

And you have to decide where you fit in and where you can best function. . . . I have operated in both categories and that is why I am so upsetting to so many of the businessmen. I start out sounding like I'll compromise, and then I go crazy. They think I am a maniac and they can't deal with me.

FRANKLIN SCHAFFNER: This is the area of the responsibility of the director to a production. And one is occasionally asked what the duty is. The duty is only one, and your duty is only to the film. It isn't to yourself; it isn't to the actor; it isn't to the writer; it is not to the producer; it is not to the distribution company. It is to the film, which is my way of saying it is to yourself, I suppose. But I think that a producer and a writer, unless there are extraordinary circumstances, work together so closely that the moment you make the commitment to do a film you had better be fairly sure not only that you want to make that film, with all its faults and with all the problems, but that you're going to be able to live with this guy. He's got a certain point of view, too. He does not, he will not, make the film, but he has a certain point of view about it.

I've been luckier more times than I have been unlucky in this respect. There are various ways in the same way that you will deal with the writer, in the same way you will deal with an actor, in the same way you will deal with the cameraman. There are ways that you will, on a one-to-one basis, learn how to deal with the producer. I am always fascinated when a producer or a production manager comes to me and says, "O.K., we've got a ballpark figure." It's always a marvelous moment.

"What's the ballpark figure?"

They say, "Ten million."

You say, "That's fascinating. Now what's it above-the-line and what's it below?"

And they say, "Well, we figure three and a half above, and we figure six and a half below." Which means to say that "You, buddy, the director, are responsible for six and a half and I'm only responsible for three and a half. . . ." Right. What you do, therefore, is learn to protect yourself.

If a man says, "Can you live with six and a half million below the line?" you call your department heads and tell them as specifically as you can what you are going to need, what you think the script is finally going to be, how long you really think it's going to take to shoot, and the details within all of that.

As an example, the assistant director may have ten days where he has

extras that will amount to a thousand dollars per day, and on the last day
will amount to twenty-five hundred dollars. A costumer, a designer who
has got to be responsible at that moment for twenty-five hundred costumes, and for the next day has got to be responsible for something
designed by Jean Louis, those people are responsible for coming back to
you and saying, "This is what it's going to cost."

And when you have their figures, the assistant director's, the special
effects, the designer, the designer's costumes and sets, etc., etc., etc.,
you are fairly well in the area where you can say, "Yes, I think it's going
to cost about six and a half, although you really know it's going to cost
about six and a quarter."

And it's a matter really of your experience, and leaning upon the
experience of those people who have been used to doing this far more
often than you have, to give you the honest figures that will pull it all
together. Now mind you, once you commit to that, then it is your total
responsibility. When that production manager brings in the board, and
you have gone through that board, and you have gone through the script
with the assistant director, and you say, "Ninety days, I can do it in
ninety days," there is no reason why you shouldn't be responsible for
doing it in ninety days, even if you have weather problems, because
nobody forgives weather problems. Nobody forgives actors being sick.
Nobody forgives the fact that there have to be retakes for technical
reasons. You said ninety days, and you're supposed to be experienced,
and those things happen. So somehow or another you bring it in in ninety
days. And don't worry too much about it. It's really possible to do.

JOHN CASSAVETES: When we were putting together *Shadows*, we said,
"Sure, we'll make a movie." We had this loft, and they started to build
sets and everything, and I went on a radio show, and I said, "Wouldn't it
be terrific if just people could make movies instead of all these Hollywood bigwigs who are only interested in business and how much the
picture was going to gross and everything?" The next day, two thousand
dollars in dollar bills came in.

Not only that. Shirley Clarke, who was working in those days as one of
the few independent filmmakers, had the only equipment in town, so she
brought it down and said, "Go ahead, take it, I'm not doing anything for
six months. Take the equipment." So we had the equipment, and one girl
came in with a moustache, and she really looked like an ogre. She was
enormous, maybe four hundred fifty pounds. Stringy hair and a print
dress. As soon as she saw me she said, "I listened to your program last

night," and she got down on her knees, and I said, "What are you doing? This is shocking; stop this."

She said, "What can I do? I'll do anything."

I said, "Don't do that, whatever you do." I said, "Grab a broom, sweep up this joint."

So over a period of three years we worked on this film, *Shadows*. And none of us knew what to do; I mean we didn't know anything about filmmaking at all. I had made movies, but I was only interested in myself. I didn't care where the camera was. All I heard was, "Roll them, action, print that," so I would say, "Print that." There was no one to write that down.

So when we got through with this film, I had about five or seven thousand dollars in it. I said, "That's enough. . . ." It cost forty thousand by the time we were through. Tremendously hard work, but it was thoroughly enjoyable, and we made every mistake that you think is possible to make until the second picture. But, you know, "Print it."

So when it was finished, we didn't have enough money to print the sound, and it was improvised; the whole picture was improvised, there was no dialogue, so every take was different. So we looked at it and said, "What the hell are we going to print here? I don't know what they're saying. It looks terrific, everything's in focus, the exposure's all right, it's beautiful — we'll lay in the lines." Anyway, I thought, live sound is everything, we have to print that sound.

So we had a couple of secretaries who used to come up all the time and do transcripts for us, but they volunteered their services. They had nothing to do; we had all silent film. So we went to the deaf-mute place and we got lip-readers. They read everything and it took us about a year. We had a wonderful time, though. We knew a liquor store down the street. We were drunk all the time, happy. It was a happy experience. It took us three years to put the film together.

IRVIN KERSHNER: The biggest battle, well, there were studio battles. And then there were script battles, and there were producer battles. With the studio, the big problem was to get sufficient time to make the picture. It began with the studio sort of liking the script for *Loving*, but not really being enthusiastic. The story department at Columbia did not care for the script. They used what I call "the old fashioned way of looking at script-ing." They will say, "Does the character change? . . . With whom do we empathize? We don't like anybody." They were using the old idea of Hitchcock's that the stronger the villain, or the stronger the evil, the stronger the picture. Columbia would ask, "Who is the evil in this? . . . What is the resistance? . . . Who is the bad guy?"

Also, the film didn't seem to fit into three acts. It appeared to be one long act. It had only one climax, and that seemed to be right at the end. They knew nothing about the wife and her life. They knew nothing about anyone. They sort of saw everything from the outside in, because we cut out, on my insistence, any description of the character from the inside out. In other words, anything that you couldn't describe with the camera I refused to let it in the script. So, therefore, we weren't presenting a selling script, and that is what all scripts are in Hollywood. Rather, we were presenting a script the way I wanted to see it, because I had been working on the script for many, many months.

So the first fight was one of us trying to get the picture made. And the story department said, "No." And they sort of wanted to have me make a film there. It seemed to be a good buy to them, and we finally got the O.K.

The next battle was how long it would take to shoot. They wanted to make it for as little money as possible, because of the nature of the project. They wanted me to do it in about thirty-five days. They were making it very possible by saying, "Let's shoot it in Pasadena, then we'll go to New York with just the cast and doubles and shoot there for two or three days, and then come back and shoot the rest of it in Los Angeles, using some exteriors and some sets."

I said, "No, I refuse to do the picture if I can't shoot the entire thing on location." I didn't want to do it in a studio. I told them what I needed for this film, which I call a tonal picture, I needed reality. Therefore, I wanted the cold of winter to present the picture the way I saw it. We fought about that and finally at one meeting, I said, "I can't shoot the film on sets, because I want to constantly look out windows. And the way I have seen, in my mind's eye, the staging of the film, we are constantly going to be looking out of windows and doors."

And so someone in the studio said that it would cost a great deal to put "process" behind all of the windows. And that seemed to sell them on the idea that we should go to New York. Of course, we blocked out all of the windows with light. Finally, we kept upping the time, until we got forty-five days. This is pretty tough on location in New York, especially on an improvisational picture. But, we raised it to forty-six, and we shot a little over fifty, because we lost many days with a big storm. The scenes that you see with the snow in the end, we had to actually come in with a dozen men with snow shovels and all kinds of vehicles and move some of the snow away to make it possible to shoot. But that was the second battle.

Then, when they said, "O.K.," we came to the battle of who was going to do the main role. Who was going to play Brooks? They had a good deal with George Segal. I thought perhaps he was too young. They suggested Rod Steiger. I have great respect for Rod Steiger. I think he is a fabulous actor. I felt that possibly he would be too heavy, too overpowering, too theatrical. I wanted to control the actor, so even if he didn't know what he was doing, I wanted to control him so he would appear to be out of control. I didn't want him to always be precisely in control of every situation. Steiger can seem this way.

So I got Segal. Then, I got a woman star. I had to get a star because, again, they said that they are going to invest a lot of money, and if they got George Segal, they'd have to care also about the woman. . . . So, in order to cover themselves, they wanted a star for both roles. They wanted Lee Remick. That fell away, and I thought of my old friend, Eva Marie Saint. I didn't think that she could do it, but I made a real attempt to get her. I was finally quite satisfied that she would be marvelous in it because of the very things that I knew about her. She finally said, "Yes," after much soul-searching. She had a chance to do another film, a big film. But the problem was which was she going to choose. She finally decided to do this. That was the next battle. . . .

The studios want a name to put on the marquee. They want a name for the distributor. When they show the film to distributors, the cigar-smoking old men all sit around and say, "Who's in it?" That is the first question that they ask. You say some name. If they have heard the name, then that is something. It may be that when they were fifteen years old, they went to westerns and they remember the name. Well, Eva Marie Saint, she is a respectable actress. And people know her name, and you can get television time and you can get space in magazines with her. So that is all we needed to constitute a name.

Then I went to New York, and the understanding was, with the writer, who was also the producer, that we would continue to write the film right through to the last day of shooting. It would never stop, because the film was never that type that was set. It couldn't be set. I wanted the film to keep speaking to me. Now, it had stopped speaking to the writer, and I could understand that. It was fixed in his mind and it was a perfect thing. It was not a perfect film, but he had gone through the experience of writing it, and therefore, in the process of struggling to find the words and images, he had concretized every moment. Naturally, you don't write something unless you feel that it is right. So he had written the script, and he felt that with a slight manipulation, it was all there.

I found that it wasn't. I found that there were moments that were false to me, or moments that were simply jokes. It was full of jokes, gag lines, slapstick, and social comment. It was full of all of these things that you do because you are trying so hard. We went out to West Hampton and locked ourselves away for a couple of weeks, and that couple of weeks actually changed about sixty percent of the script. We threw out sequences, brought in whole new sequences, and at that point conceived of the television sequence at the end. That didn't exist before that time. When this project was sold and we went to New York, there was no such thing as the dollhouse or the television sequence.

What happened at the end was that there was a party. It was a much different party, in which there were confrontations between the wife and the girlfriend and everybody. It was very dramatic, because it was a series of confrontations. At the end, he takes Nellie out to a car and they make love and some people are leaving the party and they look in, and they see what is going on. They call the other people out, and they turn on all of the lights on all of the cars. He comes out of the car with the girl, and the husband attacks him and the wife is there. It's a debacle right there at the car.

I was quite dissatisfied with this, because I felt that fate wasn't taking over. What the film began to say to me was that if a man doesn't make a decision, then life will insist on making the decision for him. Life has its own pulse. It continues its relentless movement, not a movement toward anywhere, but just a movement. You have to move with it in some way, or you will be shunted into some area where there will be a reaction to what has happened. So I didn't want the nasty rich boys, the boys that had the argument on the stairs, I didn't want them to look in and say, "Aha, now we've got him." That was the reason why he was caught. I told them that I didn't like that, so we threw that out. That was quite a big battle by the way, and we began to play with ideas, and, finally, the television idea materialized. Also, the dollhouse came off and it grew after that. That was the next battle.

Then the next major battle was on the set. That was where all of the scenes worked, but all of the dialogue stunk. It didn't work, and I made it clear that I wanted to start changing it. I was accused of not knowing what I wanted to do, of not having a mind of my own. I was accused of everything.

JEAN RENOIR: I will tell you how I made *La Grande Illusion*. I was shooting *Toni* in the south of France. *Toni* I made almost entirely on location. Nearby was a big airfield, military airfield, and the planes, the pilots, could see that I was shooting a picture, that somebody was shooting a picture — the reflectors, the cameras, the trucks. They were above my head the whole day long. I couldn't record any sound. I decided to pay a visit to the commanding officer of this base. I found a man just the copy of a general — as I am not — and more medals than you can wear. I was confronted by a man who was a very good friend of mine. As a matter of fact, during the first war, he saved my life. Several times. He was in a squadron, he was a fighter in a squadron of fighting planes. I was a photographer.

That's the way I became interested in movies, by taking photographs from above. You know, planes carrying cameras, etc., were not very fast, and we considered each time we were confronted by a German fighter that was the end. Several times my general — who was no general, he was just a noncom at the time — arrived with his little squad and tak-tak-tak, the Germans were too happy to run away. It's why I consider this man saved my life several times. His name was Pensal. He's dead now. General Pensal. Pensal had been shot down by the Germans seven times. He escaped seven times and went back to his squadron seven times.

We were happy to find each other, to meet again. We took the habit in the evening to have dinner together in a little joint. During these dinners he told me the story of how he escaped from the German jails. I thought that could be a good suspense story, an escape story. I asked his permission to use a few of the stories he had told me, and I wrote a screenplay. I wrote a screenplay convinced I had written a very banal escape story. I thought it was very commercial, very popular, and that I could find the financing very easily.

That's what I thought. During three years, my dear friends, I visited every office in the Champs Elysées or in Rome or anywhere, and everywhere I had the same answer: "No girls in your picture and we are not interested." Good. Finally, I met a man who was, well, I don't like to insult people, but I don't find any other word but the word "crook." He was a brilliant, successful crook — that was his profession — and he told me he just had made several millions with an operation — I don't know which one, I don't understand anything about such things. He told me, "Jean, I believe in your picture."

I said, "Because you are not in the film business, because people in the film business don't believe in it."

"That doesn't matter. How much do you want?"

I needed two million old francs, real francs. He said, "O.K., you will have them. Let's have an agreement." And I shot the picture and the picture was successful. . . .

Now, the screenplay I wrote, of course, didn't follow the adventure of Pensal. That's what I want to tell you: I discovered that *La Grande Illusion* had another meaning. I discovered that *La Grande Illusion* was perhaps a little approach to a big problem, which is the problem of surrender, and the problem of nations, which is the racist problem, the problem of how people from different religions meet, how they can understand each other, how they cannot understand each other for some reasons. *La Grande Illusion* became this question — I am crazy about such questions — to me, the only thing which is important in the world is how to meet. And *La Grande Illusion* was, for me, a possibility to tell everything I had on my heart about this question. But when I wrote the screenplay, I didn't know. It was just an escape story. In certain scenes between Fresnay and Stroheim, we talk only of questions of surrender, questions of adaptation, questions of how to get along together, but I don't ever forget that it was an escape story. And the escape story was insignificant.

For instance, I have a scene between Dalio and Gabin. They are preparing a rope to escape, and they talk, frankly, about racists. And it seems apparently that it doesn't belong to the picture, but it does. It works.

I had entire scenes which were done only to express this expression of origin, nation, races. For example, I have a scene where half a dozen French prisoners are preparing a show, costumes they are sewing, and so on. I have a very serious conversation having nothing to do with the scenery, with the costumes, with the show. It is a question of "Where are you going, where do you come from?" I could put fifty situations like that in my pictures, where the shell is just a shell but where what I was fitting is inside the shell. You have to break the shell to find it. . . . The head of a studio, a very nice boy who wouldn't kill an elephant, gave me the money to shoot this picture *La Chienne* with the idea it was going to be an hilarious farce. Of course, I didn't contradict him, being sure that if he knew the truth I would have to stop shooting. And he realized that I was shooting a somber drama when everything was shot. He told me, "At least I want to try to save the situation, and you won't do the cutting."

I said, "O.K., I won't do the cutting." We started a fight. With our fists. I was stronger than he was. But the next day when I went to the studio I found a policeman, who very politely said, "Monsieur Renoir, non non non. It is forbidden."

I was saved by a wonderful man, the man who was making the money for the studio. He was Mr. Monteaux and was president of the most important shoe company in France. And this man who understood so very much about shoes, it seemed to me he also understood about pictures. He was indignant. He even asked the head of the studio to stop any money. And I was restored to my cutting with only a few shots missing.

BUDGET

PAUL MAZURSKY: I think once the director gets to work on the picture, he is always aware of the budget somewhere in his head. But once you start the actual work, I don't think you begin the morning by saying, "I'm making an eleven-million-dollar picture. What am I going to do?" You say, "What am I going to do about this scene between this guy and that guy?" and "How am I going to photograph it?"

RAOUL WALSH: They gave the schedule to you in those days by the day. For a short picture you got thirty-two days, and for an extra-long picture they gave you forty-two, maybe forty-three. They would tell you you had five days on location; you'd go on location and it would rain for five days — they'd put the five days back again and we'd struggle through it.

PETER BOGDANOVICH: I think that why so many of the older directors were good was because they had a discipline that was imposed from outside. I think there's nothing better than being told, "Look, you've got to do it in three days; you've only got this much money, and do it, kid, or you're not going to get it done." As soon as you start saying, "Look, we've got all the time in the world, all the money in the world . . ." You should have that kind of pressure making movies or anything else, that sense of economy. In the old days, somebody like John Ford, he had just so much film, let's say a thousand feet of film. It wasn't that they wanted to be economical — they just couldn't have any more film. The guys said, "That's it. Shoot the picture in that much film. That's all you've got."

And, you know, at Columbia, for years, they wouldn't let you print more than one take. Now, sometimes that's good.

PANDRO S. BERMAN: Right now, obviously, the director is running the show. That has been true before. It was true in the early days of filmmaking. There were no producers. The D. W. Griffiths and the early directors were producer-directors, and they made the pictures.

HOWARD HAWKS: I think I probably started a vicious thing when I had too many pictures to look at so I hired an associate producer. So people found that people with less talent could function as associate producers if they surrounded themselves with the right kind of talent. Usually it was an associate producer who prepared the story. Then they'd get a director and start all over again. Now there were some producers that were really fine, good people. Sam Goldwyn was. Irving Thalberg was a name. Zanuck. You know they had qualities that you haven't got today. To some directors, they'd turn it over completely. To others, they'd say, "Don't change anything in that script, just do it this way." There are different kinds of directors. But there are no conflicts when you are the producer and the director. There's only conflict when you are one or the other and there is a disagreement, and that happens quite often. Hasn't happened to me too much.

ROGER CORMAN: I feel that any script can be made for any budget, but the result will be somewhat different. You can make *Doctor Zhivago* in six days for fifty thousand dollars, but it's going to look somewhat different. At the beginning, I tried very much to hold down the number of actors, the number of locations, the number of moves . . . in other words, to bring it down to a small tight unit. . . . I feel that you're better not to try to make a spectacle on a low budget. You're better to try to work in depth on a subject that lends itself. If necessary, if you fall in love with some huge project, you can do it, but I think you dissipate a great deal of your efforts in that your work as a director and your production manager's work and everybody's work is then . . . your concentration is given to making something small look big rather than taking something small and making it look good.

HOWARD HAWKS: You need a certain type of a crew. A good cameraman gets paid a lot of money. A crew gets paid an awful lot. I started to work during a college vacation. We got sixteen dollars a week. Nowadays, they make four or five hundred a week. An awful lot of expenses. Today, the studio isn't the most expense. You go all around town and the studios are losing money. You rent space, make a picture without paying any overhead. The studios used to charge you twenty-five percent overhead. That's a big amount. I would say that a first-class picture today is bound to cost you two million dollars.

VINCENT SHERMAN: . . . Jerry Wald once told me, "Vincent, you have to spend a lot on a picture. If you spend a lot, then you can be assured that they are going to push it. If you don't spend a lot, then they have no obligation to try to sell it."

ROGER CORMAN: Cast and crew comforts are very nice for morale, but when you're really strapped for money, you have to con a little bit and jolly people along as much as you can. Again, if you're trying to make a good picture for a hundred thousand dollars or less, it's very, very difficult — you want to put your money where it shows — on the screen. . . . If you're young and starting, you get a tremendous amount of help. I was still claiming to be a student filmmaker ten years after I was making films and going on location trying to make films. Don't bypass that; don't go into the trap of trying to say, "If I pretend I'm from Metro, I'll be accepted better." Go the other way and say, "I've got a little amount of money and I'm trying to get started." In general, people will try and be glad to help you.

ROBERT ALDRICH: You have a moral responsibility. Are you going to tell a guy to come and work for you, and he will get some of the profits? That may be fine if you control the profits. But, if you don't control the profits, you cannot insulate that person so that he is protected and will get what he is due to receive.

HAL ASHBY: On *Harold and Maude* we had the normal insurance — which is very, very expensive, terribly expensive. It covers all kinds of things: it covers illness, somebody dying, something happening to the negative — which is usually the biggest thing. Sometimes something will happen to the negative; if it happens in the lab — forget it.

PAUL MORRISSEY: I don't prefer the low-budget way or the million-dollar way, whatever that is. I don't think I have a preference. When you hire fifty or sixty people to run around on a film, they all do something. They set the lights or they put an extra light somewhere and the camera is moved very smoothly. I think it's great. I have nothing against it, I just never did it before. I don't think it really matters whether a film is photographed to look fantastic or whether it looks really awful. If you come away from the film and you have had a somewhat amusing time, then you've seen something that approaches a good film. . . .

All this goes back to Andy Warhol. He always wanted to get rid of his money before income tax took it and he didn't know any other way to do it so he just kept saying, "Let's start filming again." I thought it was terrific. To tell you the truth, *Trash* was going along and the cans were coming back. We used the big reels, twenty-five minutes on the Auricon, which was the only reason we were able to do this improvisation, because changing reels wouldn't interfere with the camera set-ups. We could let the scenes run on. I'd been filming for a few weekends on *Trash* and Andy said, "How much film do you have now?"

I said, "Oh, seven hours, eight hours."

He said, "That looks like enough film. You must have enough there."

I said, "Yes, I guess so. Maybe we do." When he thought the stacks of film were high enough, it was the end of the film. We didn't do any more scenes.

I said, "Well, we could throw in a few more scenes."

He said, "Oh no, you'll spoil it if you do too many scenes." I think he was right. We didn't scrutinize any of the material. Andy financed *Trash* like he had financed all the films he had done himself.

PAUL WILLIAMS: I went two days ahead of schedule after the first day. I knew that it was possible for the money to run out at any moment. I just wanted to get the film done. So after Ed Pressman raised the extra money, I could slow down a bit. Then we decided that we had deferments from the lab and we had deferments from the sound studio. It took over a year and a half to two years to get done, so we were getting money all along. The final picture cost us one hundred seventy-five thousand dollars, not including the deferments to the lab and the sound studios. That is an important figure, because we were ready to go bankrupt and not pay them.

CASTING

Perhaps nowhere are directors' differing methodologies more apparent than in their interactions with actors. Of these, the first is casting.

ARTHUR PENN: One of the blessings is to cast well, to cast carefully. I have a terrific associate in this. We tend to cast for good actors. People who have emotional availability, who have technique and skills. I'm under the assumption that once we cast the person, they *are* that character. After all, a character on a page is really only a dozen lines of dialogue. Once you assign those to a whole person, he or she becomes that person.

LOUIS MALLE: Casting, I think, is half of it. It's terribly important because even directors who think they're geniuses are really in trouble if they cast wrongly. You could be clever enough to make it look all right but you're in big trouble.

MILOS FORMAN: . . . In directing the actors, the most important thing is to choose the right people. The work, the most important work, is done before the shooting starts, because once you tune the actors with what you want, the direction is no mystery at all — it just works somehow.

PAUL MAZURSKY: Casting is ninety percent of what happens with acting. If you cast wrong, you are in a lot of trouble.

STEVEN SPIELBERG: I like to do my own casting. I think eighty percent of what you contribute to the film is in the selection of the actors.

SAMUEL FULLER: I have a tremendous respect for actors. . . . An actor can make or break a scene completely. You might have a beautifully written scene and a beautifully directed scene. Beautiful. And what goes wrong is . . . bad or wrong casting. So now you have the question, why did the actor accept it? Why did the director accept it? It's either name quality or money. One of them wanted the money. One of them wanted the name connected with it. So the character was diminished immediately. Sometimes, you can take a weakly written character, even a weakly conceived character before it was written, and moderately staged . . . and the right actor just makes it a superb thing; the whole thing explodes and you're in business. That's a thrill. So, you see, every case is different. A lot of it is personal like and dislike.

STARS — "CREATURES OF THE CAMERA"

ALLAN DWAN: What makes a star? When you see a star, you don't see an actor, you see that person, always the same in anything you put him in — costumes or out of costumes — he's the same. You like him for some reason, and you yourself must analyze the reason. . . .

A fellow like John Wayne is the same in every picture, but you like him because he's Wayne. And you like to see that walk of his, that strange walk. And you're satisfied. Here he is. What he does is a matter of how'd you write the story, because there's no change. He can play certain scenes very well, his way, and you accept them his way. And if there are scenes that he can't play well, he just won't do them. You don't get him caught that way. He doesn't go into bad scenes. Some of the actors unfortunately bit off things they shouldn't have attempted and they got hurt. But the majority of them . . . well, take Fonda, for instance . . . he's always Fonda. And Jimmy Stewart is always Jimmy Stewart, no matter what he's playing. And you like it. You like him. And personalities are very important.

GEORGE CUKOR: They carry their own excitement, their own fascination. There are some extremely good actors. But, often you don't really care. They don't involve you. They don't fascinate you. You see certain people who carry the center of the stage with them, even when they are doing nothing. Sometimes it is a physical thing. Sometimes it really is an intensity inside. Often it is the way the light hits the eyes. They are born to be creatures of the camera.

RICHARD ATTENBOROUGH: I think your breed of actors like McQueen are very exciting to act with and bring a marvelous immediacy. They are stars, and I know it's a sort of a dirty word in a way, but stars are actors or creatures that look as if they are going to blow up any minute. They have an in-built violence within them. If you think over the majority of great movie stars in the past, that's what they have.

PAUL MORRISSEY: The hard thing is to appear in front of the camera and be interesting. I think you're either interesting or you're not. I don't think anybody can learn to be interesting in front of a camera. That's the part of filmmaking that is a mystery. It doesn't make sense. Why is somebody funny? Why is somebody sexy? Why is somebody unusual? It's the most interesting thing about filmmaking, from my point of view. . . .

The public likes the security of knowing the actor before he goes in. They like when Clint Eastwood is Clint Eastwood. If he tries to be someone other than Clint Eastwood, they resent it. In effect, Clint Eastwood has created that artist man, Clint Eastwood, on the screen. As an artist, he has to be Clint Eastwood. If he was a commercial illustrator, he could do any type of illustration. But if he was a serious painter, he would always do the same painting in some way.

JACQUES DEMY: A star has no meaning to me. I really don't care. They are just human beings, and what I consider is what they are as human beings. That means if I hear too many stories about the biggest star in the world and if she is making trouble, then forget it. I am not going to work with a person like that. If I find someone who is unknown who has great qualities, then I would welcome the opportunity to work with that individual. Catherine Deneuve, who can be considered as a star, is a lovely person. It is because of that that I am working with her.

It is important to try to establish a true relationship. Doing movies you get very much involved. It's fascinating. I don't know why. In making movies I find that there is a passion associated with it. You have to deal with people who are very passionate.

OUTSIDE THE ORBIT

The star, the lifeblood of the film industry, is a persona to which audiences are readily and pleasingly attuned. The essential identification processes between viewer and screen presences necessitate that expectations should be fulfilled to maintain the viewer's equilibrium — and, perhaps, the star's as well.

RAOUL WALSH: We gave Cagney a big death scene in *The Roaring Twenties*. . . . In those days, Cagney and Bogart were the only two stars you could kill in a picture. You couldn't kill Flynn; you couldn't kill Gable; you couldn't kill Cooper or any of those fellows. The exhibitor wouldn't even play the picture. But, with Cagney they accepted it and with Bogart. So, I thought, as long as they accepted it, we'd give them a good load of it.

ALFRED HITCHCOCK: How do we derive character values in a story like *North by Northwest?* First of all, you have available to you a film star by the name of Cary Grant. The value of having Cary Grant, the film star, is that the audience gets a little more emotion out of Cary Grant than they would from an unknown, because there is identification. There are many members of the audience who like Cary Grant, whether they know about his character in the scenes or not. For example, we couldn't have him as the murderer in *Suspicion*. But I wasn't in charge at that time. I had to be more or less compromising.

I was loaned out to RKO by Selznick and they had the whole thing set up. The whole subject of the film is the woman's mind: is my husband a murderer? The ending, an ending which I had to compromise, was that he was not. But the real ending that I had for the film was that he brings his wife a fatal glass of milk. She knows that she is going to be killed, so she writes a letter to her mother: "I'm in love with him, I don't want to live anymore, he's going to kill me, but society should be protected." Folds the letter up, leaves it by the bed. She says, "Would you mind mailing that for me?" She drinks the milk, he watches her die. Last shot of the picture is Cary Grant, whistling very cheerfully, going to the mailbox and popping in the letter. But that was heresy, to do that to Cary Grant in those days.

JOHN HUSTON: Bogart had never played anything like *The African Queen* before. There was a part of Bogart that I knew . . . that sneering face . . . quite the opposite of the man in control of his own and everyone else's destiny. A little pie-faced runt of a creature. Well, that was in Bogart.

ROBERT ALDRICH: You have got to be an idiot if a guy like Don Sutherland comes along and you don't realize that the guy is a natural. I didn't know Don Sutherland and he didn't know me. Don came in and he was going to play Vernon Pinkley in *The Dirty Dozen*.

One of John Cassavetes' big disappointments in the original script was that John went up and down and pretended he was the General. But, if you have got a guy like Don Sutherland there, you say, "Christ, this guy is a natural." You don't have a preconception, because you have never met the fellow. But when he walks in you see an actor who is so unique that you say, "Give him the business. Let him do it. He can do it much better."

It wasn't going to destroy the character of John Cassavetes for being the company cutup. If you are rigid you lose those kind of advantages. Would you take the basic character from Lee Marvin and give it to Jim Brown? No, I don't think you would.

WILLIAM FRIEDKIN: The most important decision after choosing material is who's in it? Who are you going to put in it? The casting becomes the next single most important decision you make. Not simply who's a star or something, because I never think in those terms. At all. I never cast that way. But who do you know or think you could achieve, be *simpático* with, in order to be able to communicate through this person to an audience. Because what a director's doing is communicating and he's doing it largely through actors — through other things as well, but largely through actors. So I try to envision the kind of person I want or don't want in any given role.

More importantly, the first quality I look for in any actor is intelligence, what I consider to be intelligence, because I think that's what makes a good performance. And in *The Exorcist,* in the case of Father Karras, I was not going to hire any actor who had not had a Catholic education. I went on a search for someone and came up with Jason Miller. I had never seen him act; he had never done a film before. He had never done a play on Broadway. He had acted in a few off-Broadway shows, a few regional theatre things, but he had never done anything, what they call, major.

But I met Jason and he fulfilled all the requirements. He was trained to be a Jesuit at a Catholic university for three years. He was extremely intelligent, and I thought he had an inherent sensitivity that I could photograph. I felt I could work with him. In the case of Linda Blair, I auditioned five hundred girls and went with her because I felt she was the most intelligent, most pulled-together youngster I had ever met.

BOB TAYLOR: You cast an animator just like you cast an actor. There are wacky animators — guys who can do crazy things with personalities and stuff, and there are subtle guys. There are guys who can do stuff that's very subtle, and doesn't move me a hell of a lot, but there's a certain personality that comes through.

PAUL MORRISSEY: I only look for combinations of people who would be interesting. When you think back on Hollywood films, the incredible casts they came up with. I was recently thinking of Myrna Loy and William Powell in *The Thin Man*. How could they have gotten such a great combination of people? Over and over again, they found great combinations. Spencer Tracy and Katharine Hepburn. Cary Grant and Katharine Hepburn. Cary Grant and Jean Arthur. All those people were fabulous people to combine with one another. *American Graffiti* was a good film and the whole cast was great — those combinations of kids went together, it was really exceptional. *Paper Chase* had a great group of kids playing students. You came away from those films knowing a few things about people you had never met before.

MICHAEL WINNER: The casting of secondary players is terribly important. I think that again and again one falls into this. You read through the script, and there's somebody with three lines, and you kind of don't bother. . . . I'm talking about the very small parts. You'll say, "We'll get a local man in Washington," or "He only says one line," and suddenly you're on the set and everyone's in a certain rhythm and pacing, and in comes this awful man and says one line. You cringe and you think, "My God. This is too awful." It's so important. Anyone who speaks can make or mar a scene. Sure, you can always get round it . . . you can always disguise it. You can always loop it, or put someone else's voice on it, or not show them with so much prominence. But you suddenly realize that you are losing what could be a plus. So I frequently get very good actors — if they'll do it — for tiny parts.

ROBERT ALDRICH: Different people work in different ways. If I bought a book or a play, I would hire a screen writer who will say, "This part is for somebody like . . ." You may discuss a combination of two or three different people. In terms of intellectual casting, you must ask yourself, "Who is it like?" That is when you really start casting. You and I might think that you are not going to get Gregory Peck to play *To Kill a Mockingbird*. But, you will say, "I want a man like Peck was in *To Kill a Mockingbird*." You talk about that kind of a character. In casting you begin by communicating with the writer.

CURTIS HARRINGTON: Sometimes in the conceptual stages I have an idea of someone that I would like. I may have an absolute first choice very early on. I wanted to have Marlene Dietrich for *Games*. I wrote that for her, but we weren't allowed to even approach her. Often I will have an idea like that. All things being equal you try to get your first choice.

MILOS FORMAN: Before the final draft is written, I like to know approximately who will be the people in the film because it helps you develop the characters.

JAN KADAR: A bad casting is a built-in failure. I think the most important function of a director is the casting, and the right instinct will help you a lot. Try to do it in advance when you are just writing the script. Try then to see whom you feel would be good in a part. I don't believe that it can be any one of "this, that, or a third." It has to be one and only one. You have to feel this right from the beginning, because if you don't then you will be in trouble.

JOHN HUSTON: We go right back to the material. It depends entirely on the role. I'm not star-minded. And I never start off with an actor. The only reason Bogart was in so many films of mine was not because of our association, not because I liked Bogart, but because that face and voice and figure fitted in with the kinds of stories that I like to write and make.

KING VIDOR: In *The Crowd*, I had a vision of a fellow, an ordinary man, the average man, and I saw a bunch of extras walking out of the studio. One guy stopped and walked between me and the man I was talking to. It was James Murray. I saw the face and I saw the figure of the guy, and I chased after him.

FEDERICO FELLINI: I don't have a particular system for choosing actors. It depends, picture by picture. Certainly the part of choosing the faces is very, very important for me. I think that it is the real moment when I start to see the face in the picture, because I think when one is writing the picture, when one is thinking about the picture, it is always a very easy time. Living with a very vague imagination . . . that's that, but when I start to choose the cast for the picture, that is the real moment . . . the area of imagination. That for me is the hardest moment of the picture because I have to choose. Sometimes I choose someone for the character I have in mind not only because he is a good actor, but because I see that his eyes, or his voice, this particular human being, is in *connection* with the character I have in mind. It is very difficult to explain the system.

ROBERT ALTMAN: I have always had control of the casting of my films. . . . We just cast a film the way we think. The thing of using a lot of the same people — I don't feel I have a repertory company, but take an actor like Ned Beatty, for instance. Say I've never seen Ned Beatty, and I see him the way he will ultimately appear on the screen in *Nashville*. And say I didn't make *Nashville*. I'm going to sit and say, "Oh, that guy's very good for this kind of thing." I may eliminate him from six or seven other possibilities, but working with him and seeing how he works with other people, you start to see the range of the actor. I just have more knowledge of the range of these actors than a director who hasn't worked with them. It's comfortable to know that you've got somebody that you can communicate with and who understands what you're doing or at least responds to it. It's fun to see people in three or four different pictures really do different things and do them well.

JIRI WEISS: When you cast the picture you should never go out with a conception of how a personality should look. . . . The most important thing is to fill the slot in your drama. Find out by which means, physical means, the actor will fill that slot. It's arbitrary. Entirely arbitrary. Because if you say you want to have a fat man, you find that the fat man may not fill the dramatic part. And he will be only fat. Big or fat or long or small or whatever, as long as he's got this wonderful charisma, this wonderful thing which distinguishes a personality from a nobody . . . Presence. Screen presence, that's what I'm speaking about.

JAN KADAR: I never used a casting director. My assistant director made the casting with me. The most exciting thing was how to use an actor or a person who was already very obvious . . . and not to make typecasting.

JEAN RENOIR: Casting is where I like to have my friends, technicians and other people, help me. Because I am very bad at casting. I am very bad and sometimes to be bad helps me . . . in the way that I am attracted by a certain innocence.

VINCENTE MINNELLI: I think that the best results come from finding a character that sticks together. The actor and the director — you have to allow for their personality. In some rare cases, though, it can be most rewarding if they work against their personality. One of those was Kirk Douglas in *The Bad and the Beautiful*. He was very strong and had to be full of charm; he had to play against that strength, because you can't imagine why all these people would have worked with him and he could con them into anything unless he could charm the birds off the trees. So, he played it all for charm but the strength was always there. . . . No matter what he did, how charming he was, he was always strong and ready to strike like a cobra.

HOWARD HAWKS: When we made a picture called *Scarface*, everyone was under contract in Hollywood, every good actor was under contract to a studio. They weren't about to loan us any actors at the time because we were working independently and they didn't like that. Howard Hughes decided to make this picture and we couldn't get anybody, and I told

Howard I'd go to New York to see if I could find anyone back there. I found Paul Muni in the Jewish theatre on Thirty-ninth Street playing an old man. I asked him to come out and make tests and he said, "No, I'm a sedentary man; I couldn't play a violent man."

"Well," I said, "come on over." We put him on boards about this tall, and we got little people to work with him, had a sweater underneath to make him look big. He became a star. Georgie Raft I saw at a prize fight. He had never worked before, and Ann Dvorak, the girl who did so well, was a chorus girl at Metro.

RAOUL WALSH: I liked the script of *High Sierra* when I first read it. Warner put George Raft in it. They sent the script to Raft and he read it and he turned it down. So Warner said to me, "Raoul, you're a good friend of George's. See what the hell he turned it down for. It's a good script." So I went over to see him. He didn't want to die at the end. He refused.

I said, "Well, look George, the censors will demand, after you kill a couple of people, that you pay the penalty."

He said, "I don't give a damn about the censors. I don't want to do it."

So I went back to Warner and told him, "I can't talk him into it, Jack."

He said, "We gotta get started. Who the hell can we use?"

I said, "Well, you got a guy here under contract called Bogart. I'll take a chance with him."

So he said, "All right. Go ahead." and Bogart got the part.

BUDD BOETTICHER: . . . The first thing that you do when you cast a picture, and you are satisfied with your casting, is to spend as much time with the actors as you can and find out what they do. The skeet sequence in *The Bullfighter and the Lady* originated when we went by a skeet shooting place and Bob Stack said to me, "Gee, it's been a long time since I've shot."

I said, "Do you do that, because I don't."

And he said, "Yes."

And I asked him if he was any good, and he told me that he was the world champion for three years. Well, wham, all of a sudden that is in the picture.

PAUL MORRISSEY: I don't go looking. It's by accident. You can find anybody if you keep your mind open. You find them. You meet them at a party or they're a friend of a friend.

ALLAN DWAN: Our actors came from anywhere. We picked them up and made them; we trained them; or we just said, "You're an actor."

"What do I do?" You'd show him what to do and he'd do it. Girls were a natural. Children are great actors because they're always acting. They're always making believe.

ROGER CORMAN: What I normally do is interview a great number of people for each role, generally people who have been recommended to me or ones whose agents, or friends of mine, say, "I know So-and-so, and he or she is good," or an agent whose opinion I think is reasonable will say, "I know somebody." Then, I will put these long lists together, talk to a number of people, really one every ten minutes, and ask them to read. And the way it works is they come in, I talk with them, give them a few pages, tell them to go out and look at it, and somebody else comes in, and it's just sort of a leapfrog arrangement like that. Based upon that, which is a very rough look at a large number of people, I work it down to, say, my top six or seven — it could be anything from five to ten choices for each role, then I will have them come back, read again, read different scenes and do improvisations, and based upon that, I'll either make my final decision or maybe have the top two, if I'm uncertain, come back a third time, and the third time is generally just improvisations. I'll make the decision from that.

HAL ASHBY: Sometimes, especially when dealing with the younger people, you're not quite sure what kind of thing they'll have when they do really get in front of a camera. It's not so much the freezing up of it; it's just a way of carrying themselves. . . .

When I do test, it starts out with meetings, I guess what you call an interview. For instance, on *Harold and Maude*, I'd say for the part of Harold I probably met fifty young actors. It seems like fifty — maybe it wasn't, maybe it was just twenty-five or thirty. That went over a period of time, a period of four to six weeks, while meeting other people also for other parts. And then settling down to try and pick out five or six that you think are really good, heavy potentials; and then setting up the test from there. . . .

On *Harold and Maude* I used videotape, so I could shoot it up at the house, and so forth. In New York, with a girl, I just used my camera crew to give us a chance to work out a couple of things — but it's just to put it on film so you can really see it on film and take a look at it and study it that way, and see where those people are, because they'll all do different things.

PAUL MAZURSKY: I don't read too much. I go mostly by what I think a person is like. In every case, it's a different problem. I'll talk about the part of Elmo in *Blume in Love*. That was the hardest part for me to cast, the part Kris Kristofferson played, because I was not able to find an actor who I felt would be real in the part. There may have been some, I saw about a hundred people, but most of them were playing at being free and easy, playing at being hipsters or whatever. Then I started seeing musicians, and I saw some who were interesting, but they had no acting experience and I felt they couldn't handle the *other* side of it. I just kept looking for a feeling. Then one day Kristofferson walked in and said, "How's it going?"

I just said, "You've got the part." That was it. I mean, that's all there was to it, but it happened after I had seen about ninety-nine people.

ROMAN POLANSKI: I started about four or five years ago taking pictures of actors. I understand it is now current fashion to take Polaroid pictures of people that you audition. I started doing it for the simple reason that even if they leave their photograph with you, when you see forty people, you are not able to remember them anymore, even if you look at the photograph that they provide you. "How about the man called So-and-so?" says the casting director or whoever helps you with the auditions, and you say, "Which one is that? I don't remember the name." He grabs the photograph and you can't even associate it with the person who showed up because they look so different; so I came to the conclusion that snapping a Polaroid or even a regular photograph — Polaroid is better because you have it ready right away — even if it is a bad photograph, you can immediately remember the man because you took it and you immediately associate it with the person you saw. You remember a few things that he said, you remember the subject of conversation. It's just visual association. Actors resent it tremendously, because they know they don't look well on those photographs, but they are too dumb to understand that that's not the purpose.

JACK NICHOLSON: In *Drive, He Said,* I wanted the lead to be a certain height so that I would be getting the tops of people's heads in shots. I wanted him to be able to play basketball because I like sports myself and I wanted it to be the first American movie which was shot pretty authentically, so the action of the game looks real and yet has the central character in it. So I decided if he couldn't act, he'd have to be able to at least play basketball. It never became a problem. Bill Tepper was really the only guy who came in who was ever right for it from every point of view. There was no rigorous mental problem with the casting. He just came in and that was it. He had played basketball in college and then had dropped out just a year before, so that he was still that age and still pretty much into his game.

JAMES BRIDGES: In *The Paper Chase*, I would never make a final decision until Timmy Bottoms, the star, was there. I read every single person with Bottoms before I cast them. I cast around him.

MARTIN RITT: I have had two experiences where I offered an actor a part and he said to me, "You son-of-a-bitch." He knew why I had offered him the part. That is the key to casting. You cast what you feel about that person.

MICHAEL WINNER: I think very few films are made with unknown actors by choice. Most of the great stars were discovered because an existing star walked out, wouldn't do it or wasn't available and, in desperation, the company turned to a newcomer . . . not because they wanted one. Then he or she became the hottest thing around.

PROFESSIONALS AND NON-ACTORS

Evidently formal theatrical training is not a prerequisite for a successful screen appearance. Perhaps the professional film actor is not so much trained in playing roles as in being himself in front of a camera. Of course, that self must be magnetic in some dimension or another to be attractive to an audience. Nevertheless, it would seem that someone with no prior experience might well embody and become suddenly an engrossing film persona.

ARTHUR PENN: I have a preference for professionally trained actors. On certain occasions, I don't mind working with amateurs. On *Bonnie and Clyde*, for example, during the family reunion scene, when Faye and Warren have gone home to see Faye's mother, that woman was a woman we found watching us one day down there. We felt that she bore an extraordinary resemblance to Faye, and we employed her as the mother.

In point of fact, I think that the effectiveness of her scene, despite her certain dryness and some of the little compliments and accolades that she's received, is not so much in what she did, but in the way that the two professional actors responded to it and dealt with it. *They* converted a relatively primitive piece of acting into a complicated and sophisticated piece of acting by the way they responded to it. Now, had they been three people without technique, I think it would have been deadly.

JOHN CASSAVETES: I have that confidence that I can take anybody and have them give a good performance, because I don't think there's anything to acting except expressing, being able to converse. The mistakes that you make in your own life, in your own personality, are assets on the film. So if I can just convince somebody not to clean themselves up, and not to be someone that they're not, and just be what they are in given circumstances, that's all that acting is to me, and I don't think it's very difficult. Only when the lines go against you, it's impossible for you to say them. Or that the character's inconsistent. Or that it's an impossible circumstance where everyone's so hostile that you don't feel like acting.

ROUBEN MAMOULIAN: I always get the best actor I can possibly get for every part. But in certain cases it is almost advisable to get somebody who is not an actor. I think anybody — and I'm not exaggerating — anybody is capable of giving one hell of a good performance. You can take somebody off the street and put him in a short scene and he can be great on the film. All you have to do is get it once. You hypnotize him or you browbeat him or you convince him or you trick him, but he winds up by doing it once in a very excellent way.

MILOS FORMAN: In *Taking Off*, these three guys are the real Hell's Angels, and so they are nonprofessionals. They were very nice to work with. It's true that with nonprofessional people, sometimes it's easier to improvise, because professional actors somehow become used to memorized text. It's part of their profession, and they feel very insecure when suddenly you want them to improvise.

MICHAEL WINNER: If you pick someone off the street, you've got to give them the time, of course, and you've got to frighten them or cajole them or charm them into standing in the right spot . . . and all the technical things that go on in a film. When you say to someone, "You not only say the line, but you end up exactly on that spot, because if you don't, Mr. Burt Lancaster is going to have to turn his back to the cameras to look into your face," or something, there's a whole lot of things that you're suddenly throwing at them . . . and some people can do that and some people cannot.

Some people get so flustered that they come in with their eyes down looking for their camera mark, and then they look up and say the line of dialogue, and then they look at the camera rather nervously to see if they've done all right . . . and by that time you're kind of under the table. Yet someone else will stroll on and do it with enormous naturalness. And some quite well known actors will be quite incapable of hitting the same mark twice, you know, or saying the same thing twice.

MILOS FORMAN: In *Fireman's Ball*, for example, I used non-actors; you have to get just the best reactions of the non-actors. Where you have professional actors, you can stage the scene and develop it. It's a little bit quicker to work with professionals, but not very much. But it's a little bit easier to work with nonprofessionals because they ask less questions. They really think that things are as they are told they are, but professional people, they already have certain experiences — bad, good — back in their minds, and they are always asking why is this and what will follow that and why so-and-so and not so-and-so. . . .

Psychologically, you must from the very beginning convince the nonprofessionals and make them understand that this is just fun; it's nothing which is important. When they start to feel the importance, something strange is happening. Something is stiffening inside them. This is the first thing, to get them rid of this feeling of importance and make them feel like doing it for fun. It's not at all the way to become a star.

ROBERTO ROSSELLINI: When you work with nonprofessional actors, each one has his own technique, so I don't want to say that my technique is the only one, but I can tell what mine is. When I make the choice and want someone to play a role, I have the patience to be with him for lunch or dinner so I can discover what kind of work he is suited for. I discover what kind of gestures he does mainly, and when I do the scene, I do the scene thinking of it. So when we rehearse, I give him the suggestion to do himself. Normally, we don't see ourselves, you know. . . . So you suggest to them to just be themselves. They don't know that. . . . Never, even to the actors, do I give the script. Otherwise, you have to do twice the work. Can you imagine those people there memorizing the script so they do only their interpretation of the character of the scene? So you have to break down that kind of thing and start again. I give them the dialogue and scene at the last moment. I reduce the time. . . .

ABRAHAM POLONSKY: An actor works the way a writer works, by remembering and inventing. That's what an actor does: the exact thing a writer does. So what you've got to do is to get the actor to start remembering. He knows all the technique if he's a professional actor. If he isn't, if you're working with nonprofessional actors, then you've got to supply that which they don't have. But it doesn't make any difference. You've got to make them work. And you can make every actor work. When you can't make the actor work, you just don't use him. If he won't work, don't use him. Except if you just want his name.

JACK NICHOLSON: Bill Tepper, the lead performer in *Drive, He Said*, had started to major in theatre arts in college. I don't think he'd ever acted outside of the school background at all. He was writing; he had an agent as a writer. In fact, it was my agency who sent him to me.

One of the reasons why I cast him is because he had a very similar aura to the aura I felt the character in the book had. Bill had it when he came in.

One of the things with Bill was to get him to be himself more often. In other words, very often he would come in with an intellectual interpretation of the role. I constantly said to him: "You are the character. Don't make that separation; nobody's going to come along and recreate *Drive, He Said*. It's not going to become a classic vehicle. Forget about what I wrote or anything like that. You are it; you will be it for all time — that's it. You're it." That's the way I approached his problems. I read him a little bit of the script and I thought he would be able to do it fairly easily, outside of technical problems, which I told him to completely disregard. I said "Don't listen to anything that any professional tells you about what to do in terms of acting. If you want to walk out of the scene or say something else, or spit on the floor, or stop — I prefer if you don't stop, let me do the stopping — but anything that you want to actually do, go ahead." It creates problems later on but I thought I'd give him that. It wasn't like going into Louisiana and getting the gas station attendant. I mean Tepper had written screenplays and stuff like that, so the dialogue with him was much the same as you would have with a professional actor. The jargon and the talk is almost the same.

CURTIS HARRINGTON: My development as a filmmaker began very early. I started right out being a filmmaker. I didn't do anything else prior to entering this field. I made my first film when I was about fourteen. When I made *Night Tide*, which was my first feature, I knew very little about working with actors. All of my experimental films had been made with non-actors.

I have consciously preferred to work with non-actors. Not knowing very much about acting and the meaning of it, I found that working with non-actors in those short experimental films gave me a feeling for their humility. They would simply do anything that I told them to do. Actors don't do that. They don't do just what you tell them to do. They give you problems. But I learned when it became apparent how I should deal with actors that that was fine. They will make problems and then you deal with those problems.

ABRAHAM POLONSKY: You don't need actors if you have all the time in the world. But remember one thing. Actors are special people, and they're different from non-actors who play roles. Actors are very different people, just as gifted as writers, dancers, physicists, all the rest. They have their gift, and they're going to give you something that you can't get from people who are not real actors. So you're not just using actors because it's the cheapest way to do it. You're doing it because that's the best way to do it. You see? Yet there are some pictures where you don't want actors because you want a different feel.

4

Drilling the Soldiers—
Rehearsal

The second director-actor interaction is the rehearsal. Again, we find as many rehearsal styles as there are directors.

JOHN SCHLESINGER: Maddening though they are, actors can make considerable contributions to the work. I also think that more and more people demand a period of rehearsal with actors before starting a film. It's not so much that you are actually getting specifics — you know, saying, "Right, we move here." It's not like a television rehearsal. You're not actually plotting camera moves necessarily. It's that you have the opportunity for throwing around the script, for throwing around the characters so that actors are going to get used to a way of making relationships before those relationships are totally upset by shooting the film out of continuity, as you inevitably have to do.

I always have a tape recorder around me when we're improvising, and I have the screen writers there, because so often they can see really interesting developments taking place, rather than you going to the screen writer and saying, "Look, this scene can be better if blah, blah, blah," and they're in the bathroom and not part of the process.

I think it's terrific if they're there, witnessing something that's growing and happening and changing relationships. Of course, actors improvise reams and reams, much too long, but out of it can come wonderful ideas which you can then give back to the screen writer, and if you have the tapes transcribed, you will find ideas out of that improvisation which you can then put into a more formalized way into the script.

PAUL WILLIAMS: I am very actor-oriented, and I am very concerned with performance. I don't know how to do it without rehearsals.

BERNARDO BERTOLUCCI: I don't rehearse too much. I try, if I can. I only do a mechanical, automatic rehearsal. For example, only the movement from there to here, and in general, it's a rehearsal more important for camera than for actors. Idealistically, I would like to keep the first take.

ROBERT ALTMAN: I don't have any real rehearsal period. I'm embarrassed in a rehearsal because I don't know what to do. I keep thinking that you should really do something. . . . Finally, I'll rehearse any way that the actor wants. I mean, everything changes really a little bit, but the improvisational part of it usually is the rehearsal.

GEORGE CUKOR: I don't really believe in too much rehearsal. I think you can do a certain physical rehearsal and set things up. But, I believe that the actual thing happens when the camera goes. . . . I will tell you why. The camera must catch that immediacy, that freshness. The camera must do that. I find that if you overrehearse that whole thing, or if you talk about it too damn much, then the magic goes out of it. It depends upon what kind of thing you are doing. This is something very interesting. . . .

When you do a costume picture, the pitfall there is to sort of act and posture and all of that. You have to walk in a certain way. You have to talk in a certain way. For example, in *My Fair Lady*, we rehearsed some.

But, it really never springs to life until the camera goes. That is not to say that you don't prepare.

MICHAEL WINNER: I don't believe in rehearsal for a film. I think to get into a set plan in the very beginning can deny you all the experience you have day by day as you get closer to the characters. I think you discuss with the principal actors at least the line of the film as you see it . . . the emotional changes, what it means to you . . . and they can then add what it means to them. But I'm personally, I hope, a very intuitive director. I'm very happy to change day by day, or hour by hour, and to be ready to soak in, as it were, any thought that comes as a result of what we're doing.

I think if an actor is playing a part alien to his nationality, he should research that very carefully, and you should have helped him research it. In *The Nightcomers*, Brando was an American playing a man from Ireland, and by the time he had made these researches with our help, he was able to detect the part of Ireland from which an Irishman came . . . and accurately . . . his ear was so good . . . better than I could. There I think great preparation was necessary.

ROGER CORMAN: I have a small amount of rehearsals. I don't have a great deal and the reason is you have problems with the various guilds on rehearsal time. So, again, it's a matter of knowing that a little bit of rehearsal helps you and a great deal of rehearsal — you end up paying your actors so much money, you might as well be shooting with them. On a bigger budget, I would go for rehearsal.

RONALD NEAME: In the case of *The Prime of Miss Jean Brodie*, I had ten days' rehearsal before the film. The producer tried to arrange the contracts with the artists so that we didn't have to pay them a fortune during that rehearsal period. Most directors would like to rehearse, but the management and agents are inclined to say, "Oh no. We can't let Joe Doe rehearse with you for ten days." One just can't afford that. I think a rehearsal is tremendously important, though.

RALPH NELSON: One of the exciting things about live television, in the days of the *Playhouse 90*, for example, was that you had a three-week rehearsal period that gave you a great opportunity to work on the script, improve it, alter it, and work on the performances as well. You don't have that opportunity very often with a screenplay.

JACQUES DEMY: I always dream about rehearsing the actors before shooting. I have been in the business for ten years, and it was only for my last movie, *Peau d'Âne*, that I could get a rehearsal for one afternoon. I asked for a week and I could get the cast together only for three hours on one afternoon. That was all we rehearsed. And even while we were all together, we weren't as efficient as we should have been. Every two minutes one of them had to get up to answer a phone call or do something. It was insane.

JIRI WEISS: . . . It is sometimes very important to rehearse actors a long time before you shoot. A long time before you shoot. There might be people who need to rehearse two to three weeks before shooting. Because, you see, there are people who are picking up the elements of the personality. Especially people who do a lot of theatre. They are used to a process. I believe if you permit something to ripen it will be so much better.

MARTIN RITT: When I rehearse I realize that most of the scenes are not going to be shot for three months. I try to get the actors to a point where they really know what the scene is about, but they haven't nailed it. I don't want it to sit there for three months nailed and rehearsed and cold as ice by the time it gets out on the screen.

FRANKLIN SCHAFFNER: There is one thing that influences rehearsal method beyond any other single factor. Generally speaking, you don't have a chance to go into a rehearsal period on a picture before you start shooting. A number of factors mitigate against it. One is that the production is moving so frequently. The production may be taking place in Spain: to carry on an actor may be prohibitively expensive. And, quite frankly, there are some actors who don't like a rehearsal period. Generally, therefore, it is totally unlike the theatre. It is totally unlike live television, because there you do have rehearsal periods.

You shoot out-of-sequence in motion pictures. Therefore, both you and the actor have to know on the second day of shooting that you are shooting the last day in a man's life. You have got to be able to bridge that entire hour and three-quarters; he in his performance, you in your concept, and so forth. It settles down to a day or two of readings before you start principal photography, so that you can explain your point of view, so that all the actors can be exposed to one another, and to you.

And then you go on a day-by-day rehearsal period. You get the cast on the set without makeup or wardrobe, block the scene, technically, so that now the production department has a chance to take over. Then you take the actors and work with them in that time on that particular scene. Now mind you, this is not the most satisfactory way, but it is the way that is dictated by the mechanics of the medium.

ROBERT ALDRICH: If you are aware enough, porous enough, to absorb all the kinetic energy that is in the rehearsal period, then you can be very creative. The kind of work that you do on a script is studious and thoughtful and can be very creative because you are determining what they are going to do. If you work with a great writer on a good story, then the script will become better daily. But in terms of how much imagination and creativity that you, the director, bring to the movie in x number of minutes and x number of days, I find that I do more in those fourteen days in terms of putting something on top of the story and putting something on top of the writer and something on top of the actor, than I do in the fourteen weeks before or the fourteen weeks that I'm shooting or in the fourteen weeks that I cut. That doesn't mean that you don't have other contributions. You do hope that they are important. But that is the imagination time. Everybody isn't sitting on the payroll while you say, "That isn't the right way to do it. Let's try it this way. . . ." Usually, you discover the broad strokes, the big things, when you are rehearsing.

JEAN RENOIR: Usually when you work in a picture the schedule is too slow, the money is too rare, and you have to hurry. But if I had the time, I would work first in a rehearsing room with no props. That is a very old idea. The name of this kind of work is *à l'italienne*, to rehearse the Italian way. It was very much in favor in the time of *la commedia dell'arte* in Italy, and they brought this method to Paris, to London. I tell you what it is: you sit down around a table, the most important characters and the director, and you read your texts without any expression. You must read the lines as you would read the telephone directory — blah, blah, blah . . . monotonous, flat. If the actors in the beginning of the rehearsal give you an expression . . . Let's say, for instance, we have a little scene which represents a mother confronted suddenly with the death of her son. Well, you are working on this scene and you ask the actress who will do the mother to help you find expression. The actress pulls a little drawer, a symbolic drawer, and she finds four, five expressions she's used already a hundred times and other actors in the world used millions of times.

It's very dangerous if you forbid her to give an expression in the beginning. The situation, the text, grows inside herself, and perhaps sometimes, not often, all of a sudden among the actors who were reciting this flat text you see a little sparkle. Oh, you cannot miss it. You see a little sparkle; it is the baby. The midwife did her job. And when you have one proof that the sparkle does exist, well, you start, you go to the stage, you rehearse, etc. This method is never used because it takes too much time and time is money in the picture business.

RICHARD ATTENBOROUGH: To a degree, you've got to be a psychologist. You've got to explain in the sort of language an actor understands and in values that an actor appreciates and thinks is important. The moment you deny those importances and those priorities for the actor, the actor loses confidence in you. You're the only person he can play to, and if your judgment is something that he is not able to accept, he's floundering. He's absolutely at a loss, and the poor devil doesn't know what to do. I think it varies a great deal, actor to actor, right from the word *go*, how much he wishes to know of the technique, when he's going to come to rushes, if he wants to know whether he's in this shot or whether he's in that shot. I think there's a great deal to be learned by that.

HAL ASHBY: I try and let the actor go. You block him and give him his marks, but still in rehearsal I like to keep it as free as I can in the movement of it and work accordingly with my camera. I have them go through it once or twice to see how it feels, and if it feels right, then the next rehearsal is to keep them going, and then we mark there and do whatever we have to do technically.

RICHARD ATTENBOROUGH: I start on the set, if possible, with a scene of any sort of consequence. I start off by virtually emptying the set and working with the actors. So, to block out a scene with the actors, without the actors having the opportunity of feeling uncomfortable, I believe that a director should arrive on the floor with a blueprint which he is prepared to abandon. He must have a form and shape and a tempo in his mind, in order that that particular moment in that particular scene in that particular sequence can be properly adjusted and placed in the entity.

You must never leave them floundering. You must never let an actor feel a fool. You mustn't leave him so he has to turn to you in embarrassment and say, "Well, where do I move now? What do you want me to do now?" You must never place him in that position. But, at the same time, you must grant him the freedom to be able to move other than the manner in which you've discovered.

Personally, I would rehearse. I would then fetch in the prop boy and say, "Mark out the marks." I would bring in the cameraman and the sound mixer and say, "Is this possible? Does this work? Can we take him from here to there?" You may have to modify again and let the actors go away.

Then you've got your set lit. Because there's nothing worse than bringing the poor devils on the set, getting them to a point of rehearsal where you're about to take and suddenly, you know, the cameraman says, "Well, what the hell are you doing, Jack? You've moved him here now and I can't cope with that position." So the actors have got to go off and come back. Actors need cosseting, they need loving, and they need helping.

ALFRED HITCHCOCK: I talk with the actors privately in the dressing room. Not demonstrably so. I don't rehearse the scene. Oh, with dialogue scenes, you can, a duo can be rehearsed, but if you've got very competent actors you can get them to go off on their own.

HOWARD HAWKS: I don't rehearse a lot. I go over a scene. John Wayne, before he learns a scene, comes around and says, "What am I supposed to do here?"

"Well, you're supposed to get mad at this fellow first and then he pops you." I tell him the theory of the scene, then he goes and learns it. I know what I'm looking for and I know what I want to tell them. I'm not that interested in what the actors want to tell. I want them to do what I tell them to do.

ROGER CORMAN: Pictures like *The Wild Angels* and *The Trip* were shot in three weeks. So, knowing that we work quite rapidly, what I do is this. I talk extensively with the actors, before the picture is ever shot, about the characters, about what I think of them, the unit relationships, and so forth. If time, then I do improvisations, which I have great faith in, all with the final cast. I bring them all in for a day or two days and I'll make up scenes in and around the picture and will improvise that, which I think helps to set relationships between the people.

CARL REINER: In *Where's Poppa?* we rehearsed for two and a half weeks. You can only rehearse the interior things. We couldn't go to a park to do it. There is a big logistics problem. If you bring your actors in too early to rehearse, you have to put them on salary and carry them, and all of that stuff. But we did rehearse with our principal actors, the ones that we knew we had to pay for the whole time. We rehearsed with the principals for about two and a half weeks. Then, at least we knew the material enough so when we got on the stage, we could invent even more there. Things change when you have props on your hands and you have all of the sets up. We rehearsed without sets for a couple of weeks.

PAUL WILLIAMS: Before I even walk in on a project anymore, I just say that I am not interested in doing it unless I have four weeks' rehearsal time and ten weeks to shoot. I will say that without even looking at the material. I have learned a certain amount now, and I know how to make certain things work. It just takes time to do it. . . . The actors want the rehearsal. If you cast good people or people who want to be good, they will give you a rehearsal. . . . You use rehearsals to make mistakes. If you are on the set, you cannot make a character choice in reel one that is not going to work in reel eight. But if you are rehearsing, you say, "Let's play the guy like James Bond today. . . ."

In a way, we rewrote the whole script for *The Revolutionary* in the rehearsal. We rewrote all the dialogue and did improvisations and all that kind of stuff until we got the material working. I learned a lot about the processes that one should go through when making a film. In fact, I think that we worked too hard at the rehearsals. Two weeks, ten hours a day, and I was literally exhausted by the time we were ready to begin shooting.

RICHARD ATTENBOROUGH: It can be quite, quite frightening if you've got two actors in a scene — one who needs rehearsal and the other who is poisoned by rehearsal. There's a scene in *Young Winston* where Bob Shaw has a row with his son in the breakfast room and he sends his son up to his bedroom. If you remember the scene, you will see that there is scarcely a two-shot which is not on the boy's back. The reason for that was I rehearsed with the little boy for an hour and a half. I knew that if I rehearsed with Bob for an hour and a half, Bob's performance would be out of the window, gone, finished. So it is shot, in single shots, and over the boy's back, and the boy's performance is totally unimportant and we can lay in the track afterwards, which would grant the best performance. And I think Bob's marvelous in it, but it's take two.

PAUL MAZURSKY: The important thing is to try to break the barriers between people. But again, I don't want it to sound like that's my rule, because in certain instances you might want people not to know each other. You might want a barrier, because it is right for that scene. For example, Dyan Cannon never met the psychiatrist. I didn't want her to meet him for that scene in *Bob & Carol*. She never met him. She kept asking who was playing the part and I told her it was an actor that I had found in New York. The couple of takes she did with him in that case, not rehearsing, paid off. I didn't rehearse at all. She just started to talk and he made her very nervous, which is what I wanted. Of course, as an actress, she was doing certain skilled things that she knows about. What I'm saying is that it is different in different instances. . . .

Almost every actor goes into almost every picture very frightened. He is positive he really can't do it. The bigger the star, the more frightened he is. . . . What I generally do is rehearse with the actors; I get to a certain point, which is not nearly finished, and then I leave on some pretext. I have to go to the bathroom or something. I go into another room or somewhere and they usually continue to do the thing with me not there. I kind of look in, so they get to know each other as people.

The worst thing that can happen is for two total strangers to walk out on a sound stage with everybody nervous and crazy and meet for the first time, and then begin to work on something important. It's very hard to do. It's very easy for good actors to get results, to indicate and do very good glib things. But it is very hard for them and for the director to trust or delve so deeply and take the time, especially when you are shooting and time becomes money, it's very hard then to get past that surface place. I think that most of the pictures are surface.

HAL ASHBY: Talk about actors and how actors work. We were rehearsing one scene for *Harold and Maude* where Cyril Cusack was standing by the ice and he was using one of those five-pronged ice picks. We were just rehearsing while he was talking to Ruth Gordon and Bud Cort — the dialogue — and he was chipping away on this thing, and he had these kind of wool mittens on, and while he was rehearsing I saw it go into the glove but he kept right on going. I thought, "Wow, that's wild. Thank God it just went into the glove." Because there was just a moment's pause. But still it was only a rehearsal.

And we finished the rehearsal and he said, "I believe I've stabbed myself." I said he should take off his glove and he was right. He'd gone right into the bone. And I said, "Why didn't you stop right away? That was only a rehearsal."

And he said, "Oh? Was that only a rehearsal?" That's his power of concentration and where he gets to.

WILLIAM FRIEDKIN: Now, the way I generally work with an actor is first of all I plan every shot. I plan the entire sequence on paper because if you do that, you can be flexible enough to throw it out, but if you don't have a plan, then you don't have enough flexibility. I'll plan everything very carefully. And then in a rehearsal with the actors . . . I rehearsed *The Exorcist* for two weeks. I rehearsed the first forty-five pages of it and then did a lot of talking about the rest of it. In those two weeks, what I largely tried to do is communicate with the actors, set up a situation whereby they could talk to me and I could talk to them about anything on our minds. And if it happens to be about the staging or the meaning or the part or something, great, but if it's about something else — like Jason Miller and I never talked about anything but the New York Knicks and I used to talk to the little girl about far-out stuff, but almost never what she was doing.

In rehearsal, I'd then suggest a staging. I wouldn't insist on it, but I'd suggest it. And the actors know I'm only suggesting it. So they're free to then find something that works better for them. If they find something that works better for them and I like it, then I'll keep it. If it looks like they're just groping around and getting nowhere, then I'll go back to my staging. Whereas, usually, if you cast the part right, it comes down to a problem of pacing or the emotional intensity that the director wants to accelerate or decrease. Usually these are, I find, the most common acting problems. The facing of a scene or the emotional intensity that the director feels is needed there.

What I usually try to do, because I like a thing to be as spontaneous as possible, I'll tell one actor one thing and the other actor something else. I'll never tell the two of them at the same time, anyway, because sometimes I want you to be a little *allegro* and you to be a little *andante,* and I don't want you both to know what I'm asking you to do. I don't want you to know what his barometer is, because in life he doesn't want to know what yours is going to be. So I try to balance those barometers, the emotional barometer of the character, and also control the pacing musically.

GEORGE CUKOR: I don't believe in rehearsing the emotion of a scene; you can rehearse the mechanics of a scene. In fact, I used to urge Rex Harrison, "Don't play it, don't play it; let it come out." Wise movie people don't do it; they go through all the mechanics and they just let it happen when the camera's turning.

IRVIN KERSHNER: For *Loving,* I brought Eva Marie Saint to New York. We locked ourselves away and we began to work on the script, on every scene that she and George Segal were in, that we were going to shoot. Now, what happened at those rehearsals was quite exciting, because we questioned everything in the script. It was as if we were coming to it fresh, as if someone had just handed us the script. We were remaining flexible, that is what I am talking about.

You should know what your concept is and you should know what you are working toward, but you should not fall in love with the pieces that you are working with. So, we questioned everything, and some things we ended up liking and sticking with. And many things we ended up doing complete improvisations in the rehearsal. We would do improvisations from different points of view, and I took notes.

I entered into the improvisations. I would often take the part of Eva. I would take the part of George. I would take the part of the husband. George would take the part of the husband. Eva would take the part of George. Do you see? We kept manipulating each other, and tried to find the truth of the situation. This was always done after I had explained what it was that I was after in that sequence in relation to the whole.

Now, there are many things that I never told them. There were many secrets that I kept from them. I never told George that to me he was a man who had never grown up. He was a case of arrested development, emotionally. Had I told him that, he would have been playing that. He would have been real boyish and sort of charming, weak, and so on. You don't tell actors many things. . . . I told George that he was trying very hard to find a solution to his problem and that his problem alternated. At one moment his total problem was a goddamn job. Between the two problems he would get thrown. I would tell him that as soon as one problem gets tough, then you think it is the other problem really that is bothering you. In other words, if he is having trouble with a girlfriend, then he thinks it's his job, and vice versa. He was constantly jumping across the tracks, and it makes for a complexity which you don't have when you work on one level.

FRANK CAPRA: There are no rules on rehearsing that will apply to everybody. It's all instinct, anyhow. The way I used to do it — suppose I had a scene with five people in it — well, I would spend the morning with the people around a table and they just read their parts. I didn't want them to learn whose parts before they came in. If I thought they'd come in with their parts glib, and they knew them, I'd change them. I'd take lines out of the middle of the speech and put them at the end, just to break them up, because if they came in with an idea of how the scene should be played — well, they don't know what the scene before was, or what the scene following is going to be. Pictures aren't shot in a sequential order as they are rehearsed on the stage. On the stage an actor gets a chance to see how a part develops from beginning to end. How the hell does an actor know if you start with scene twenty-five, or maybe scene four hundred? Only the director can keep that in mind, and that's why it's a director's medium. He's the only guy who can tell that actor where he is in time and space, and in relation to the other actors — in degradation or in uplift, or in whatever the thing is.

RALPH NELSON: Working with Mickey Rooney on *Requiem for a Heavyweight,* and also Jackie Gleason, we had a rehearsal period. On the first day with Jackie Gleason, we were rehearsing the first scene, which was in the dressing room where Tony Quinn had been told that's his last fight or he'd suffer permanent eye damage. Jackie Gleason was railing against the fates, storming around the table, shouting. I said, "Jackie, if you do it like that, it's going to be just like Ralph Kramden in *The Honeymooners,*" which was his popular television series at the time.

He stopped for a second and said, "You're right, pal." And he changed.

Now, shortly after that — I heard this later — we took a five-minute break and it was our first day of getting together. Rooney sat down next to Gleason and said, "Who the hell is that guy? The next thing he'll be telling me I'm doing Andy Hardy." Five minutes later, I walked in.

But Mickey had a remarkable facility. First of all, he can read a three-page scene as fast as the eye can travel down and he knows it, just cold. But when I said I didn't like what he was doing, he gave me eight different readings on it and they were totally different.

VINCENTE MINNELLI: The penny arcade scene in *The Bandwagon* was very carefully rehearsed. Every movement. Astaire has to have everything exactly in his mind. He has to know every minute. He's very inventive himself, but he has to have worked out every single bar of music and every step that he's going to do as to how it looks and so forth. That was in rehearsal for several weeks. He worked before the picture was started and during the picture when he wasn't working with someone else and so on. And then finally the musicians take it down and orchestrate it and then record it.

PAUL MAZURSKY: I think it's a question of when is the best moment to start shooting. That's a tricky thing. It's that moment when you have to decide not to rehearse any more; when you just do it and you set up a series of circumstances.

5

First Principles— Shooting Methods

While it is impossible to present a lexicon of technique, we can indicate the range of areas over which directors focus their attentions. Several of the filmmaking phases discussed here appear also in other chapters. However, the actual techniques, the hard facts of daily preparation and shooting, are here brought together to suggest the flavor and scope of this aspect of the director's task.

PREPLANNING

"Storyboarding" is one of the ways by which filmmakers prepare for a production. This technique consists of making a series of sketches or diagrams where every basic scene, and every camera setup within the scene, is illustrated. Thus, in storyboarding one has something of a visual record of the film's appearance before shooting begins. As with most stylistic techniques, the application of this method varies from director to director.

Storyboards — Pro and Con

PAUL MAZURSKY: I've storyboarded every picture. I throw out some of it, but I use a lot of it.

STEVEN SPIELBERG: For *Duel,* the entire movie was storyboarded. I had the art director sketch the picture on a mural that arced around the motel room. It was an aerial view that showed all the scenes and the dead ends and the chases and all the exciting moments. I think when you make an action film, especially a road picture, it's the best way to work, because it's very hard to pick up a script and sift through five hundred words of prose and then commit them to memory. The movie was more of a concept than a page-by-page description of what had to be shot, so I felt that breaking the picture up and mapping it out would be easier for me.

ED EMSHWILLER: I've been involved in a lot of different kinds of films and every film is somewhat different. I always have some preconceptions. I have themes. I have to have techniques to approach a film. I define certain kinds of ideas I want to explore within a certain framework. Very often I'll make little sketches or a brief storyboard, thoughts or notes on three-by-five cards. I use these things, but unlike the novelist, who then creates it all out of his head, I go out then and struggle with people and places to form the film.

BOB TAYLOR: It starts with me from boards, and I work out the angles, I work out the perspectives, I work out the scene cuts from the dialogue and the action. I draw it all out — storyboard it — as I go. . . .

GEORGE PAL: Good preplanning is probably the most important thing, if you want to make a picture within a reasonable budget. If you don't want to waste money, it is very, very important to plan it out. That's why every script that I have, I go through it and I practically rewrite it. I don't use it, but if I rewrite it with my handwriting in the script, I can visualize it. I make little thumbnail sketches all along, and it works. This came from the animation technique. That is what taught me to make storyboards. . . . My background in this area was very, very helpful. Preplanning is very important. Of course, first you have to have a brilliant idea, and then comes the brilliant screenplay and so on, but then comes the technical part of it, and that needs to be very carefully digested before you get on the stage. And that is why it is so easy when you get on the stage. When you shoot, it is very simple because everybody knows what is going on. The cameraman has a Xerox copy. Everyone has a copy of every page of the written script. So, they all know what the next step will be. And what we do, we only try to improve what we have already on the paper. The paper isn't necessarily the Bible. You can improve it. At least, hopefully, you are not going to make it worse, because you already predesigned the whole thing.

ALFRED HITCHCOCK: I sometimes storyboard, not always. It can be done. You can storyboard key scenes. The less important shots, they're nothing. You storyboard in *Psycho* where the man [is] coming up the stairs, to make sure that you get the contrast in the size of the image. In *Vertigo*, there were moments when you needed that, but you don't necessarily storyboard all of those, because it's very hard to do camera movements. Your artist usually draws a big arrow, which doesn't really convey where the camera is going. I think you more or less have to leave that till you go on the set. But you have it in mind.

RICHARD ATTENBOROUGH: I don't actually storyboard. I do a sort of rough shorthand in my script, but I don't actually storyboard. I do some storyboard in conjunction with the art director in very, very early days, but they're not strictly storyboard. They're mainly with a view to discussing with him which is to be our fourth wall, which we take out or what I might wish to move or where I might basically wish to shoot from, in terms of a piece of setting or what might create for us an exciting setup, etc. In terms of the actual scene, it's in my head. I don't storyboard precisely.

HOWARD HAWKS: You don't storyboard all the angles. You tell the art director what you want. You know which way the men are going to come in, and then you experiment and see where you're going to have Wayne sitting at a table, and then you see where the girl sits, and then in a few minutes you've got it all worked out, and it's perfectly simple, as far as I am concerned.

OSCAR WILLIAMS: I don't storyboard. I do that myself on my script when I'm working at nights before I come in. I draw a diagram of what I am going to do.

BERNARDO BERTOLUCCI: I never make any storyboards, designs. In fact, I write out my own scenes and then, at the moment of shooting, I really do the opposite of what I have written, generally speaking.

FRANKLIN SCHAFFNER: Just floor plans. I'm very ambivalent about models, set designs. There are many set designers who will spend a great deal of money and go to a great length of time, not only to build models for you, but to sketch sets, indeed to sketch storyboards. I've never really found those particularly helpful. It seems to me that a set designer obviously designs with a certain amount of artistic eye for a scene. He's got to function beyond that, well beyond that, and that's to design for the drama of the scene. And this is where you as a director fit in.

BUZZ KULIK: I don't storyboard. What I do is an extraordinary amount of homework. I think that a great deal of the success or failure of the film can be in the amount of preparation that one does. Again, that's my way of thinking, through knowledge of not only your script, but of the subject as thoroughly as you can.

I spend at least two to three hours every night before tomorrow's work, going over and making sure that I understand what I'm supposed to be doing tomorrow. I don't nail it down. I try to lay out specifically tomorrow's work from the standpoint of what it is that I want to achieve from the scene and how do I want to achieve it.

Diagrams — Pro and Con

WILLIAM FRIEDKIN: What I do is first make sketches, and from those sketches I write out in longhand a complete verbal description of every single shot in every sequence. I have those mimeographed, those notes mimeographed, and duplicated by the assistant director to everybody concerned with the scene. And they all, either two or three days in advance, have a copy of my notes so they all know what I want. They all have an idea from reading this thing what the cutting sequence is.

I see an entire picture in my head before I do it. And then, like a novelist, I set out and write a visualization, instead of prose — narration and dialogue. I write out a visual novel of the movie. . . . I plan these things so damned carefully. Every shot is laid out. I get to the set and I work it out.

I always use a viewfinder off a camera. I don't like those director finders. I take the viewfinder off the camera and I hold it up and I move around and generally I see something through there that's beyond my wildest imaginations. So, generally before I shoot a scene, I'll take the finder and walk around and just, you know, move around and just stand there until something feels right.

TAMÁS RÉNYI: I make my films by almost always precisely knowing the camera setups in advance.

JAN KADAR: There are some things that you have to put in the script. But, when I started to do pictures, I always had a thick book with me of all angles. Everything was drawn. It was mostly because of my own exactitude. I was insecure, so to feel self-confident, I would write everything down. I would draw everything out. I think that is necessary to do sometimes. But I finally realized that doing that places certain limitations on you. I don't want to tell you not to do it. Please do it in the beginning. Later you won't need it.

ROGER CORMAN: I sketch a large portion of the picture. I always hope that I'll sketch the whole damn picture, but there's never time and what it amounts to is certain key scenes, key shots, I have worked out in my own mind. I'll block the scenes very loosely with the actors, giving them the opportunity to change the blocking on the basis that there's a certain way of working where you don't plan anything in advance and you work it all out. On a low budget, I consider that to be disastrous because it slows you down. I'll have a kind of plan with certain symbols that I've invented for myself — arrows and dots and moving things — so it's looking down that way, and I'll see actors moving this way and the camera moving over here, and so forth.

STEVEN SPIELBERG: I had the entire picture *Duel* planned on IBM cards, the first time I've done that. Every sequence was plotted on the cards and I had them mounted on a bulletin board in the motel room in Lancaster, so rather than taking the script and opening it to a page, I would select, let's say, ten cards. That would be the day's work, and when the cards were finished, I'd tear them up. I saved the pieces, but that's the way the picture was shot. On the cards was the gist of the scene, how it was going to be shot and how many setups I needed for the sequence.

ROBERTO ROSSELLINI: I don't diagram. Not at all. I have a camera and I look through the camera. That's all.

HOWARD HAWKS: You don't have drawings. You visualize the thing, and you get so that you know what you're going to do.

PETER BOGDANOVICH: I never sketch. I know what I'm going to do but we never sketch it out. Sometimes I know a shot or two, but usually I do it the night before. I plan how we're going to shoot it, and then I don't tell anybody till we get on the set in the morning unless it's a very complicated shot — then we explain it the night before and set it up.

JIRI WEISS: There are moments when a director must know in advance what he's going to shoot because it costs so much money. I must know in advance how the shot will look. Possibly I ask the art director when he starts building to make for me a mock set. So I have a model now, and I take a viewer and I look at it. On the other hand, if I do a love scene, I know nothing. It depends on how two people will be; how will they do it? When they do it, I will be able to see where to place the camera. In the cinema, there is no method. There *is no method*.

Preconceptions and Chance

RONALD NEAME: Most new directors, young directors — and I was exactly the same myself — they set in their mind what they are going to do with a particular sequence before they go on the stage and shoot it. I think the problem with new directors is that they are so anxious to appear to be the director and to show that they know what they are doing that they have too strong a preconceived idea of the way the sequence should go. If you've got the opportunity to rehearse, you can do all kinds of things. You can extemporize all over the place. You can change things. You haven't got a crew of electricians and carpenters and painters and cameramen and so on, all waiting for you to shoot. There is an enormous cost that is involved.

JOHN CASSAVETES: You do think out certain things, but after a while, you begin to shorthand, like breaking down a board. You do know what you want to shoot, and you do break it down greatly. But I've never seen a scene that looks the same once you get there. No matter what location you scout, it just seems so hopeless.

ROBERT ALTMAN: We work with a blueprint script. We get locations, cast, and I very rarely do any preplanning on what I'm going to shoot, how I'm going to shoot it, until I actually see it happen in front of me. We'll do certain things. If we go into a location with a member of the crew, I'll say, "Well, I think I can shoot this room. We'll need that door. We'll take this corner." I'll say, "I'll never shoot you back into this corner," so that they can generally go ahead and sketch it in.

ED EMSHWILLER: My films are preconceived to the extent that I don't just go out and wave a camera and shoot everything and then wonder what I'm going to do with it. But they're not preconceived in the sense that I know what the movie is going to be when I start it. I have certain themes, certain visions, images that fascinate me, that interest me, and that I want to explore. Then I start, through the mechanics of filmmaking, to try to engage those themes directly by seeking out the images or by creating them. When I've got a certain number of these, they start to inform me. The accidents of the process — learning, exposure, looking into things — teach me, so that the film becomes an organic growth. A life experience is really what it is.

Research and Preparation

ROBERTO ROSSELLINI: Surely this work is a very careful work of research. But in a certain moment when you have made that analysis, that analysis gives you a result. The main thing is not to start with a preconceived idea.

WILLIAM FRIEDKIN: What I try to do before each film is immerse myself totally in many peripheral or tangential phases of that subject before I make it, so I'm literally swimming in it before I expose a frame of film.

MERIAN C. COOPER: I always write the history of each character from birth to death, so when you get anyone playing the character, you know all about it.

FRANKLIN SCHAFFNER: I have found one of the hardest lessons to learn, particularly in preproduction, is how to budget your time. Now this might sound entirely insensitive. It isn't. Because most of the solutions you arrive at in preproduction are going to solve an enormous number of production problems. You are paid to make this machine run so that you are using all of these devices, shortcuts, etc., so that when the moment comes when you have to really spend the time for the magic moment, you've got that time, and can still cope with your schedule.

STEVEN SPIELBERG: Before a picture, the best thing to do is go to the gym and spend two months just working out before you get on the stages. That's what George Roy Hill does, and he's done this for every picture, because making a picture is an endurance contest with yourself. There comes a time, I swear to you, a time comes when your legs don't work — they're jelly. Your mind is very sharp, but you can't get your body to respond. But you've got to pour it on six days a week, twelve hours a day.

STAGING FOR THE CAMERA

Masters

The "master" is usually a complete run-through of the scene, taken from one camera position. The position chosen is such that all the actors and action are visible. This shot then becomes a kind of "reference" shot for the scene.

FRANKLIN SCHAFFNER: There is, in any set, a basic master shot you are going to make — unless you work in a totally different technique. But I think the most satisfactory one, at least for me, is to set up the master shot first. Now, dramatically the set has to accommodate that shot. There may be specific instances for inserts, quarters, this kind of thing, that are going to have to apply to cutaways, but on a stage, as in a one-proscenium, (which is literally what a master shot is), that design has got to accommodate all the drama of that moment.

A master shot does provide a number of services. One, it creates enormous order on the set. If you stage a master, then everybody knows literally what really the day's work is going to be because they can then see how you're going to cover on a reverse angle, how you might cover on a reverse master. They at least know all of the action in the scene so that the assistant, therefore, can set up his timing problems. The camera-man knows where he's going to have to light next, the actors have used the master scene as a basic rehearsal period — if not the final one, a very basic one.

It's astounding how often you may think to yourself, "I'm wasting time. I'm staging a master. I may not use the master except for eight seconds in a sequence that might run for three pages." The fact of the matter is, more often than not, when you get into the editing room, you're going to fall back on that master for a number of reasons. One, in a moment of complete privacy, what you thought might have been useful, a close shot, it turns out it isn't useful at all, that the moment of privacy is much more eloquently played in a huge, wide shot. For example, there may be a magic moment with a single line of dialogue that you got in the master that you got no other place. You can take that line of dialogue and you can lift it and you can use it for your visual purposes when you want to.

ROBERT ALDRICH: In any scene, you have to draw in the center line. You don't necessarily have to do the master with that in mind, because the center line doesn't have to be centered. But, you have to do one establishing shot so that you know that Ernest Borgnine is looking left to Lee Marvin and will always be looking right to Robert Webber. The cutter will usually say that the master is the longest shot that he has, even though you may only use it for one walk-in. That is not necessarily true. What is important is: if you have more than one master, you must never cross the line. You must never go over three hundred sixty. You must never flat over so that somebody is working the other way. If you do, then you have the old joke — if you cut to the dog with the ring around its eye, you cut to the insert, and cut back and flop over; you really can't get out of the room sometimes. Lewis Milestone is the great master of this. You will see this all the time in his pictures. A whole sequence will be lined up one way, and in the end it will be completely different. You realize that he has cut to a telephone or he has cut to a flower, or maybe somebody has come in, and you will see an insert, for some unknown reason, of the door handle.

Blocking

ROBERT ALDRICH: I know that when I block I don't consciously say, "Now, he is going to be on the left side of the film." You just know that he is going to be there. You are always the most surprised guy in the set when the script girl comes up and says, "He is looking the wrong way." It's something that you don't think about. You try to make the action fit. If you know what a fifty-millimeter lens will accomplish, and if you know what will happen if you have to drop back to a forty to get everyone in at once, I don't say that you are always on the sideline, but you know pretty well what is happening. I hope that you discover that an actor is in the wrong spot before you shoot. Very rarely are there physical restrictions.

ALLAN DWAN: We'd plan where to put the actors — the position and composition we wanted. I'd never let them get on a line, a straight line. I broke them into little groups. If there were too many actors to make an artistic setup for a group, then I'd break it into sections of that group and photograph various sections and relate them with cutting. But all those things were sort of automatic and instinctive. And once in a while we would undertake the imitation or reproduction of something artistic — a famous painting, let's say — and then we'd work on that. We'd say, "I want that reproduced," so everybody connected with the enterprise would do his best to make it look like that painting.

GEORGE CUKOR: I don't do blocking, but I rehearse the scene. If I were supposed to go over here and pick up this coffee cup, then I would do it. I would let the thing flow and would do it naturally. That is one element: whether or not it was natural. Also, you have to have a sense of how that will photograph. It is possible to get that in a camera?

I have a rough idea of how the scene should go, but not absolutely definite. I have a rough idea that they have to go here and come there, and this and this happen. I don't start with nothing in my head. Then, you rehearse it and you see, "Yes, this is the way to play it." You know, there is something very curious when they say, "Setup." When you place the camera in the right place, then it all falls into place. It's like a jigsaw puzzle. This is after the blocking and you have the camera over there. It just doesn't do it. But, once you have the happy thing of saying, "Yes, this is the point of view," that doesn't mean that you can't vary it. You have to have a sense of that. The movement of the thing is what people will do and what you think is effective.

Camera Placement

FRANKLIN SCHAFFNER: A lot of guys like to hide behind a viewfinder and a megaphone, or a bullhorn. First of all, I have never found a viewfinder that was accurate. I can put it on a thirty millimeter, and I say, "Put it here," and they put it there and it's not the same shot. There is no viewfinder that is accurate. The only good a viewfinder does you is when you go on location, where you can get at least a sense of what the scope of the limitations of the shot is on an exterior. It doesn't do any good on a set. You can get a floor plan and lay a protractor down, and see what you are going to get.

Quite specifically, I take the cast on the floor, and only because of years of training, my eye is good enough; I outline the choreography with its specifics involved. Then, by that time, the cameraman, who is no dumbbell, obviously, sees where the camera is going to have to be, at which time you talk it over, generally with the operator beside you. You then refine that. You decide you'll put a little move here, a truck here, a little depression, a little height, what have you. Operating techniques are different in this country than in England. It's always terribly fascinating to make that adjustment to an English operator, because the director shouldn't look through the viewfinder at all. But it takes about two days to get to be friends on that issue.

ALFRED HITCHCOCK: You see, it is very, very essential that you know ahead of time something of the orchestration: in other words, image size. What I mean by orchestration is, take the close-up, well, that's like in music: the brass sounding brassy, loud sound before you need it. Sometimes you see films cut such that the close-up comes in early, and by the time you really need it, it has lost its effect because you've used it already.

Now, I'll give you an example where a juxtaposition of the image size is also very important. For example, one of the biggest effects in *Psycho* was where the detective went up the stairs. The picture was designed to create fear in an audience and then gradually transfer from the screen into their minds. Hence, the very violent murder to start with, another one less violent — and more frightening — and they've got the thing in their mind. Then, as the film goes on there is no more violence. But in the mind of the audience, and in the anticipation of it, it is all there. Here is the shot of the detective, simple shot going up the stairs, he reaches the top stairs, the next cut is the camera as high as it can go, it was on the ceiling, you see the figure run out, raised knife, it comes down, bang, the biggest head you can put on the screen. But that big head has no impact unless the previous shot had been so far away.

So that is just where your orchestration comes in, where you design the setup. That's why you can't just guess these things on the set.

Long Takes

ROBERTO ROSSELLINI: I prefer the long takes because you can put a lot inside of the take. You build through a lot of things, the atmosphere around, certain kind of detail, certain kind of mood, certain kind of passage in the thought, and attitude, physical attitude, too.

In "montage," you have to split things up. When you have a short take, it's more difficult to put in a lot. So you have to divide, and the whole thing becomes a demonstration instead of something which is contextual to the thing. But it's a personal taste.

VINCENT SHERMAN: The truth is that with each picture you do, you learn a little bit more about your craft: how to cut, how to stage the scenes, etc. Sol Polito made me conscious of one thing. He said, "Why take scenes that are too long and make the actors sweat it out when you know that they are going to be cut?" So, I really only made cuts when I felt that it would be necessary. I didn't want the actors to go through those long four-minute scenes when you knew damn good and well that you were going to have to cut them anyway.

Movement

ALLAN DWAN: To get the real effect of a dolly at any time, you have to pass something. If you're not going past anything, you don't get the effect. You pass buildings or you pass a tree or you pass something, and it's very interesting. We used to notice, years and years ago before any of these effects were tried, or anything like stereoscopic photography was thought about, that if we passed a tree, then the trees became solid and round. If you dolly past a tree, it seems to revolve. It turns around. It isn't flat anymore. But stand still and photograph a tree and it's just a flat tree. But move past it and it rounds right away. Just becomes solid. And we used to get that effect. We'd take certain buildings — buildings with pillars — and get a wonderful effect going past those pillars if we dollied. The pillars seemed to revolve but they got solid because as you went around them you had the feeling that they were of substance and not just flat.

JOHN HUSTON: If it is right, it is usually very easy to find the camera angles. The best scenes I've ever shot, so far as the camera is concerned, are never commented on. I move the camera a great deal, and my people move, and I try to get sometimes three scenes instead of one, so that one scene goes into another scene visually and a whole new atmosphere and visual circumstance is created. This will happen with the camera moving, with the people moving, with a change of environment so that you are inside and then outside. It will go from a medium shot to a close-up, back to a two-shot of people walking or something else, and they get into a car and the car drives away. Now these shots are almost ballet. The camera is having a dance with the actors and the scene. These are never seen if they are good. The audience never sees them, never realizes what's happening.

I remember there were a number of scenes of this kind in *Treasure of the Sierra Madre*. In fact, they were in *The Maltese Falcon*, too. I remember one scene that was marked on by the cameraman. There were twenty-six marks, where the camera moved, dollied, and crabbed, and so on. There can be as many as that.

SHOOTING IN SEQUENCE

HOWARD HAWKS: We try to start at the beginning of a picture and go right through. You can't do that when you start on location because you can't do your interiors. But you run over the interior that comes in between, so that the actors know what the attitude is going to be. Then you keep on going.

I try to shoot as much so-called "continuity" as possible, because you can get into horrible mistakes if you don't. It's very hard sometimes to get out of continuity. I think almost all the people that I would say are good directors use that. I don't know.

They're telling a story and how the deuce are they going to tell it when they start in with the finish and then jump around and everything? Then they're not storytellers. They're reading a script and say, "It says here that they come in here and so you come in there and you come in here." They play a scene and there is no growth of any feeling. I think that's what makes good scenes, that's what makes a picture get more interesting.

I've done a play a couple of times; then, it wasn't hard at all because I knew what the play was like and I knew the attitudes and the pitfalls that were coming and we were able to shoot in any kind of order. But it is a very, very difficult thing to jump way ahead and commit yourself to the attitude of somebody who has finished a really good scene, and all of a sudden you realize that you made a scene that follows and you can't make the scene that you want beforehand because you can't follow it.

JOHN HUSTON: Usually it's quite possible to shoot in sequence. There are occasions, of course, when you have to jump out, but each time I work on what you call a "board," there's almost always a way of doing a thing in sequence and not losing the time. You know what the board is? It's the schedule, the days and the places that are all put down on the scripts — the dates and scene numbers. Things will occur spontaneously if you're working in sequence. For instance, if a man gets hit in the nose, it depends on which side his head is struck. Well, if you show him in the hospital after he's been hit, and it's on the left side, then you have to shoot the scene according to the requirements of the hospital.

ROMAN POLANSKI: I always prefer to shoot in sequence, but often it is impossible for production reasons. Often it would cost twice as much money to shoot in sequence.

FEDERICO FELLINI: The first trick of shooting is to start with a sequence in the middle of the picture. One is obliged to give an explanation of the sequence that makes it richer. I think for myself it's psychologically a good thing not to follow chronologically the production schedule.

COVERAGE — LOW AND HIGH SHOOTING RATIOS

LEO MCCAREY: I never shot a lot of coverage.

PAUL MORRISSEY: I don't cover much. "Let's do the next shot. Come on. Let's get over there." They tell me that directors here in Hollywood cover everything. They have one scene all typed up and they photograph it here, then they photograph it there. And they photograph it here again. They put it together in the editing room and it's so fast and it moves along so great. They spend a couple of million dollars in the processing, and it seems like a waste of money.

ROBERT ALTMAN: I shoot a lot of film, but I don't do a lot of coverage shooting. I don't do a lot of takes and I don't do a lot of coverage. The only reason you use coverage is to get you out of a situation. You get a situation and you have to get out of it. You need something to go to. I can shoot a scene that would play beautifully if it were a perfect scene between two people. There's no reason to have to go to a close-up of him and a close-up of her necessarily, so you just shoot the scene. If it becomes too long or if it's immaterial, you say, "Jeez, I've got to get out at this point. I want this out of there," so you go to the close-ups. That's really the main advantage of it. In *Nashville,* I have twenty-four people going, and if I get bored with what one person is saying, I'll just cut over to somebody else and come back and pick him up later. I didn't have to do any coverage.

ALFRED HITCHCOCK: By shooting with a lot of coverage, you're bound to the objective, you see, whereas I'm a believer in the subjective, that is, playing a scene from the point of view of an individual. But if you do your master, and then you go in close-up, that's like the theatre to me. That's like sitting in the orchestra looking at a play — purely objectively. Whereas we have the power in film to get right into the mind of a character. And I'll give you an example: I made *Rear Window.* It's strictly pure cinema. It cannot be done in any other way, except perhaps by a novelist. But of James Stewart, you do a close-up. He looks. Then you go back to him and he reacts. So you set up a mental process. You can't do that by doing a master and these various individual shots.

ROUBEN MAMOULIAN: I visualize a whole film in my head before I come to the set and then I try to match it. And I usually have the cutting in my mind.

PAUL WILLIAMS: From a production point of view, I generally try to make virtues out of liabilities. In a film like *The Revolutionary,* you have to shoot very, very fast. I wanted to get a certain level of performance from the cast. I spent a lot of time and effort on performance. Whenever there was a choice to be made, I would always go for performance rather than for coverage. That may seem like an artificial dilemma, except that it wasn't in this case. I knew we had Jon Voight, who had just finished *Midnight Cowboy,* and also *Catch 22.* They had six months to shoot. We had six weeks. Professionally, we wanted it to look O.K. We wanted to get some interesting things. So, very often it is a matter of deciding how to do a scene in an interesting way, visually, but extremely simply and with very long takes. It was just a matter of a time and a day, so that we could get the kind of performance that we wanted and still not hurt the film visually. You find that half of the scenes in *The Revolutionary* are one shot. Sometimes they are fairly carefully worked out, but still just one shot. When we got a scene and we knew it was working, that was it. It was not as if we had to go past a scene which was not working. When we had it, we knew it. Then we could go on the next thing.

ALLAN DWAN: We would never use over two thousand feet. I was very
sparing with film. All of us were. But very often, too, we'd repeat things.
For instance, if I had gone out and hired twenty extra horses and men and
I needed a chase for the film I was making, I'd make two or three extra
chases, more than I needed, because I was paying these men for a certain
period of time. . . . I had a library, so I'd sometimes reach in the library
for stuff. And having a stock company with the same actors, and being
careful not to let their costumes change too much, I would use any scenes
I wanted to in any picture I wanted to — like a ride-through or an
entrance or certain obvious things, coming into a street riding in, a
stagecoach arriving, any of those things, the same one over and over
again. And so that was economical. That saved us from doing it over and
over.

HOWARD HAWKS: I know pretty well what I am going to shoot. If I don't like
a scene, I protect myself so I can cut it down. If I like the scene, I make
it so nobody can cut it. You know, just by shooting it and that's it. You
can't lay down any rules. Frank Capra and I were working at the same
studio, and, as a matter of fact, our pictures made more money than the
rest of the studio lost. And so we were going pretty well, but they'd
always get worried because Capra would finish an ordinary seven-reel
picture in twenty-two reels. The head of the studio would worry that I
didn't have enough film because "When you get through cutting it, we
don't have a full-length picture." I said, "You're going to have a hell of a
time cutting it because I happen to shoot that way." Capra, who was more
successful than I was at that particular time, would shoot thousands of
feet, different angles, then he'd have to guess what to put together. If
you're going to direct you have to be a storyteller and you have to do it
your own way.

VINCENT SHERMAN: Having seen many of John Ford's pictures, I can imagine that he does a lot of cutting with the camera. We couldn't do that at
Warner Brothers. If we started doing that at Warners, we would have
been in trouble right away. We knew that we had to cover a scene from
many angles so that there would be a choice, so Wallis and Warner could
have a choice of what they wanted. Now, sometimes we wanted to have a
choice ourselves on things. I think it is very difficult to say, "This line I
want in the long shot. This line I want in a medium, and this line I want
in a close-up."

It's a strange thing. When you go to put a film together, many of the things that you thought in the beginning have changed. Sometimes, in the cutting of a film, a scene that you think is vital and important to the film turns out not to be important. It ends up being one that you can leave out. A scene that sometimes appears to be slow, if something is taken out ahead of it, the tempo of the scene seems fine. There are all kinds of things that you discover at the end of a film. I don't think that anybody is that good that they can anticipate everything that they can do with a film. While I say that some of the shooting that we did was conditioned by the fact that we knew that Warner and Wallis wanted certain things, there were other reasons. We ourselves felt that we wanted a choice or the possibility of a choice. That is the reason we covered things.

HOWARD HAWKS: The only cover shots that you make is if, watching the action, you see something that's a good bit, you go in and get that. And then you use it if you wish to. If you see something else, it's silly not to do it while you're there. You may want to be a little closer to somebody when they shoot a gun, or you may want to be further away. We put up a couple of cameras and shoot it, and we use whichever angle we want to do it. But you plan the cutting of a scene before you shoot it.

HAL ASHBY: I would rather not limit myself except for rare instances which I visually lock into a thing and say, "That would be a sensational transition." I'll still probably cover myself so I'll have two or three different openings and ways to get in and out of the film or out of the scene and make those transitions work. For *Harold and Maude* we wound up with just about three hundred thousand feet in the cutting room and ended up with eighty-one hundred feet. I print a lot of what I shoot — I would say up to eighty or ninety percent.

ROBERT ALTMAN: For *Nashville*, we shot three hundred fifty thousand feet of film and we printed that much. The picture in a good first cut would be six and a half hours. We hope to get it down around three. The studio hopes to get it around an hour and forty-five minutes.*

RALPH NELSON: It's a mistake, I think any experienced director will tell you, to camera-cut. There's a temptation when you think "Well, the studio's going to take over, I'll fix them, I'll fix it so they can't change it,"

*Ultimately, *Nashville*'s running time was 159 minutes.

and you start camera-cutting. And you usually cut your own throat. Get the coverage.

ARTHUR PENN: I shoot at a very high ratio — almost indecently high. You shoot according to the economics of the situation. When you're in a given geographic location, you tend to conclude all the material that's in that location. Equally well with a given actor who is available to you for a certain period of time. You tend to shoot all of his or her scenes. Consequently, you're shooting extraordinarily out of sequence.

Then, one has to account for the magic of movies. What you feel on the set that given day in August is not at all what you're going to feel when you deposit that scene in the continuum of the narrative of the film on some day in September in a cutting room three thousand miles away. To assume that the rhythm you maintain on the set will carry over suggests either that you have a superb musicianship, or, as is in my case, a recognition that you have a tin ear and had better get a lot of material. This is not to say that you get a lot of options, but you get material with which you can either increase or decrease the rhythm, the dramatic rhythm of a scene. A scene which happens at the beginning of a film clearly has a different rhythm from a scene at the end of a film. I like to be able to develop the internal rhythms of a picture in the cutting room. That's where I think it truly happens. In fact, the shooting is the cheapest part.

Look, if you get Marlon Brando and Jack Nicholson together on a given set and you have only a few days to do some stuff with them, then clearly the amount of film you expose is minor compared to ever getting those two guys together again on that same set.

JAN KADAR: I cover, yes. But, I never shot a quarter of a million feet. We have a ratio, and I always use the highest. The ratio is one to ten. One time I went to one to eleven. I used mostly, well, if a picture was three thousand meters that means five thousand feet. So, I used about ninety thousand feet in American terms. You have to cover it, but if a director is effective, that is one of the ABC's of the routine. First of all, you have to know exactly how you are starting your chess game. When you are going to shoot a scene, you have to know how you are going to build it. I have never done a so-called "master shot." I know that exactly half of it will go to hell.

Sometimes when I am doing a long scene, I do three sequences from the same point of view, maybe in a long shot. You have to cover the scene in such a way that I take into consideration that if anything goes wrong, I could change the written and work with the script. The worst thing is when you don't have the coverage, and you have to run certain sequences, and you don't know what to do, and you have no more material. The directors in our country talk of it in terms of a "reasonable covering" or a "desperate covering."

ROGER CORMAN: I used to shoot on a very low ratio. If I'd have a finished film of, let us say, six, seven, eight thousand feet, I would shoot maybe thirty thousand feet. But now I'm shooting maybe a hundred to a hundred fifty thousand feet to get just the same thing. It's one of the luxuries as you move up a little bit. Once you get beyond your immediate coverage of your cast, I believe that you should shoot a lot of film on the basis that everything is there — you're paying for dressing rooms, you're paying for lunches, you're paying for all this nonsense. It's not really nonsense, but you're paying for all these things that don't show on the film, and when it's done, all you have is the film itself. So I now believe in shooting a great deal more film.

BARBARA LODEN: The cameraman and I never did have to do many takes. The people that were not actors you couldn't rehearse because they just got more inhibited the more they had to think about what they had to do. I found I had to start the camera and just have them all try and see what happens. If it didn't work, we'd do it over. We just had to keep the film running because you just didn't know when you could get something that you could use later in the editing. A lot of the scenes were really made in the editing room — I guess as most movies are — because a lot of times we would get somebody saying a line that was O.K., but then we wouldn't have the picture to go with it. So we would have to compose a scene like that.

STEVE KRANTZ: Animation is like playing a game of cards, whatever game it is, with fifty-one cards in the deck. However you shoot, if you're good and decent and kind to your producer, you'll only shoot six, eight, ten to one. If you don't care, if you're profligate in terms of your film, you're up to fifteen, eighteen, twenty to one. Cover shots up the wall, every kind of way you're covered, and so on. In animation, it's virtually one to one, or one and a fraction to one, anyway. What you see is what you get. What you see in your head is what you get. Period. You have no room to maneuver. Now, we took the same approach, unfortunately, in the live action shooting that we did. We had absolutely no coverage, none what-soever, and all that we had were the techniques of juxtaposition of sequences, use of opticals, and going back to animation, if we were going to create some new animation. So we had those elements. We had fifty-one cards to play with, and we needed a full deck, and so it was a question of juggling all those things in the air, and hoping that no one would ever count the cards.

BOB TAYLOR: As you know, you can always overshoot, and overshoot, and overshoot, right? And then you can pick your takes, and you got coverage and everything else. In animation, it's got to come out right now. It's got to be there, because from the beginning, from the time I board something with the shots, and the perspectives, and the angles, and the acting that goes on with the characters, from that point till the time it's on film is four or five or six months. At that point, it's sometimes too late to change, and there is no covering shot. There's nothing we can cut away to unless we do an insert shot. There're no two or three camera angles to choose from. So it becomes a little difficult from that point of view. It's also challenging.

BUZZ KULIK: If there's one piece of wisdom I can give you, it's shoot as much film as you can within the framework of your schedule. There are people like Mr. Ford, but God, there was only one John Ford; you knew he was cutting on the stage. Well, that's brilliant. I don't think there are many people that can do that. He actually put his hand over the lens and then he took it away and he never went to see his rough cut because he knew there was no other way to cut that film; all in the way he did it, you see. I think that's special.

For the rest of us . . . I did *Brian's Song* for TV in fourteen days, and I shot like eighty-five thousand feet of film, but I want to have as much film in the cutting room as I can because it's there that I don't want to get stuck. I don't want to get hung up and say, "Jesus, if I had only had that." I print two and three takes because there's always a variation in time and tempo. There are certain companies in this town that will not allow you more than one take, one print. They tell you you can only print one.

MULTIPLE CAMERAS

MICHAEL WINNER: I never know how many setups other people use. I use what I think the script dictates. For example, the film *The Nightcomers* is a period piece, a slow mood; it had something like eight hundred setups. *I'll Never Forget What's 'Is Name* and *The Mechanic* had something like sixteen hundred. In an action film, such as *The Mechanic*, you have these chases and things where you have three- or four-foot shots of cars or guns or whatever. You tend to have an enormous number of setups to keep it moving. You are not able to linger on two people having a conversation which you can obviously shoot at some length in one shot. You've got cars going from here to there, and people shooting and blowing up. That sort of thing requires, to show it in all the different settings it takes place, an enormous number of angles and, therefore, setups. So it's the material that dictates the number of shots that you do — and they do vary, as I say, between six or eight hundred and fifteen or sixteen hundred. But a lot of those, of course, are two, three, four, five cameras on one shot . . . although that's counted as one setup.

So you can end up with really more then than the fifteen hundred shots in the film. Right now we're shooting an action picture in Hollywood, and today we were shooting in the Century City car park. Cars crashing into each other and blowing up. Well, you cannot afford to blow up a car too often, so you tend to shoot it with five cameras, and then you're covered. You don't have to take five separate shots and blow up five cars to get all the angles.

ROBERT ALDRICH: I would say that I save twenty-five percent of the time by using two cameras. I never make an over-the-shoulder without making a close-up. Film and labor are the cheapest elements in making a picture, so if you are doing one shot, if you put an eight-inch lens on the other camera, then you can use the close-up there, there, and there. When you work in this way you eliminate the necessity of going back to get that shot later.

RALPH NELSON: I've used multiple cameras many times. . . . Particularly in action sequences but sometimes in a scene where you want the actors to overlap and one may be off-camera. Then I'll shoot two cameras at the same time and they can overlap and you could cut the sound track.

PAUL MAZURSKY: For a scene in *Blume in Love* where the three actors George Segal, Susan Anspach, and Kris Kristofferson were on the couch and she's playing the guitar and then he takes the guitar, that scene was very tricky because I wanted it to really feel like it was being made up. Yet, because of the music problem, I had to rehearse the song so that it would appear to be a certain way. I put two cameras on it three times. In other words, I had six setups, and each time I put the camera on it, they would start doing the scene. But I wouldn't roll until a certain point, so they didn't know when I was rolling every time. It's just intuition.

You see, what I do with the second camera is prearranged with the operators that when I tap him, he'll move to another character. I would tap him once for one person, twice to go to the next person, and the other camera was set holding a three-shot. The second camera was moving and then a couple of times I even whispered to him that I didn't want any hands. There are things that you do at the moment. You see something happening that you didn't know would happen. You need a little luck, too.

CONSIDERING THE ACTOR — STAYING LOOSE

ROMAN POLANSKI: I always set up with actors, without thinking of the camera. I observe them while they rehearse, and then later I try to film it.

BERNARDO BERTOLUCCI: I'm really ready to change a lot of things during the shooting. What I can't change is the presence of the camera. That's very important for me. It's my point of view, my physiological presence, near to the actors.

VINCENT SHERMAN: In *The Unfaithful*, when I had long tracks rather than lots of brief cuts, it wasn't by design the night before. It was working on the scene as you see it and as you see the values in the scene. You say, "Here I would rather track in than make a cut because the suspense is sustained better that way." Each shot becomes more effective that way.

I think that happens generally with every director. He goes in with a general idea of how he is going to do a scene, but things develop as you rehearse the scene. You have to be prepared to take advantage of these things. Some of the best things happen spontaneously and unexpectedly. You, therefore, take advantage and you shoot it. You are always trying to make the scene as effective as possible. You want to make the story point as effective as possible.

RAOUL WALSH: Setting up shots is easy once you're there with the script. You know it, and you know how it should be set up. Of course, the difficult thing about making pictures as compared with the stage — in those old days, we used to work until three or four o'clock in the morning. When I'd get home, at daybreak, there'd be a script on my lawn, like the newspaper; somebody threw it there. We went back and started work at nine o'clock.

Knowing setups comes from experience. I'd always directed crowds mostly: big movement, you know. I guess it was instinctive. A lot of directors fight away from crowds. They sort of get a bit panicky, particularly young directors coming in, but they never panicked me at all. The more the merrier.

You picked it out how they'd enter, then you'd get rid of them, and how you'd get rid of them. I made a picture in Italy one time, and I had four thousand extras. Well, we generally use four thousand people, say, for four or five days. Then you finally get down to more close-up shots and you only use two thousand. Well, the two thousand we laid off were waiting at the gate for me. With swords. Wanted to know why they were laid off.

ENHANCING THE ACTOR

ROUBEN MAMOULIAN: Notice in *Applause* when Helen Morgan is dying after she's taken her poison — today it's difficult to recognize what it is, but there are sounds coming through the window that are supposed to be the New York traffic. In those days we couldn't go out and photograph in traffic and then dub it in. I had to get the traffic on the stage to help the actor. You can help him by the counterpoint.

I don't know whether you noticed it, but while Helen Morgan is on that chair, you hear the elevator in the hotel corridor open, and two young people, very happy young people, saying irrelevant things to each other. And they laugh. Did you notice that? There's no relationship to the scene at all. So you say, "Why have it, then?" Because that happiness of somebody else makes her misery ten times worse.

There, I wanted the traffic noises to gradually build up so at the end I could bring in a siren, fire truck or ambulance, going by. There is no more desperate agonizing sound than the sound of a siren. It comes in naturally in the traffic. Well, it comes in towards the climax of her scene. And then you follow with a dissolve of a stick hitting the brass cymbals, doubly exposed over her head. Well, now, these three things make that whole thing immensely more powerful. I don't know how powerful you find it; but whatever you find it, it wouldn't be one tenth if you just had Helen Morgan alone there. Those things help.

VINCENT SHERMAN: The first shot of Bette Davis in *Mr. Skeffington* is one of those little things I tried to do when you are presenting the star and want to find an interesting way for them to come in. It's just a little attempt to dramatize the presentation. It was like the first time that you saw Miriam Hopkins in *Old Acquaintance* and her back was to you. She was talking on the phone. You heard her voice. Then as the camera moved up, she turned up. It was the first time that you saw her. I feel that wherever you can sort of dress up an entrance you do. I guess that comes from my training in the theatre. You always tried to give an actor an entrance. You tried to build it up for him.

ALFRED HITCHCOCK: In *Psycho*, you introduce Martin Balsam with a close-up. You bring him in like that because you are bringing in a new possible menace.

CUTTING TO A CLOSE-UP

VINCENT SHERMAN: We knew that it was important to have close-ups in a scene, not only because you might want to be in a close-up to see the actor's expression or his reaction to something, but also, if you want to eliminate a line of dialogue, you have to have someplace to go to eliminate the line of dialogue. There were many, many reasons why you did a thing the way that you did it. You didn't want to have to go back and do retakes. That's always painful. In fact, I don't think in all of the films that I ever did, I don't think that I ever went back more than once or twice in forty films to do a retake. When I had some doubts in my mind about a scene, then I would always make an alternate take. I would say, "That line doesn't sound right to me." Or, "That direction doesn't seem right. We may cut that." I may also say, "I think it would be better if we did the scene this way," and then we would do an alternate take.

ALLAN DWAN: My slate numbers are never over three or four if they're that high. And mostly one — the first take. Because if I'm going to break it up, it isn't important that I think one scene is perfection, as they call it. If it's nearly good, it's good enough. If you're going to put close-ups into it, you're going to break it up anyway, so don't worry. The close-ups will correct it. Cross-shooting.

Or you cut away to something. No, I tell you, if you know what you're doing, and your actors are good, things pop along. Actors will sometimes say, "Gee, I could have done that better," and I always say, "We'll fix it in the close-ups; we'll save it." And that makes them happy, you know. We don't intend to use a close-up, but we very often shoot them 'cause they get happy.

NUMBER OF TAKES

VINCENT SHERMAN: No formula. Sometimes I would print the first take. Usually I would see something in the first take, something of value that had not been exploited. I would say that my average was around four on a picture. But sometimes you would get a good first take, and you could never get anything better than that. Most of the time it would be two or three or four.

JIRI WEISS: There is absolutely no rule. I would say it depends on who the people are. If I could, I would shoot the entire picture, and then do it over again. After you see it on the screen, you cannot do it. By the way, never reshoot anything, if possible. Cut it. You cannot do it better. Everything which is reshot is always bad. It is impossible.

JEAN RENOIR: I believe it's a good thing to be committed, to play the game. You have the scene. You believe it's good. Shoot it. You know, I shoot my scenes usually one time. In the studios, our people proceed — they want at least five takes. If you have not five takes, you have not a great picture. When I can, I have one take. I like to be committed, to be the slave of my decision. If I know that I won't have those shots to cut, my main shot will be better. If I know that I will have those shots, I say, "Oh, that's not very good — but we'll have the close shots." I don't like this attitude.

ROGER CORMAN: I don't limit takes, takes per setup or number of setups. You just do the best you can. I try to hold to my schedules, and I do hold quite closely to the schedules, but you can't predict exactly. I'm shooting more takes now than I used to. I'd say I'm probably averaging four or five takes per shot, whereas formerly I would average two or three per shot.

NUMBER OF SETUPS PER DAY

ROGER CORMAN: It varies according to whether you're shooting interior or exterior on location. On location, exterior, you should be able to get thirty to forty setups a day. You can get much more. Location, interior, you'll slow down heavily because of lighting. Lighting anywhere is slower than shooting with the sun, and lighting on natural locations is slower than lighting in a studio. So if you're getting, say, forty setups a day, exterior, that might drop to twenty-five a day, interior. It can vary tremendously.

GEORGE PAL: I do on the average of about four pages per day, and this was at a time when the lighting was much more complicated than it is today. We made as many as thirty setups a day, and as few as three or four, depending upon what it was. But, we averaged around about seventeen setups a day. In page count, that is around three or four. For instance, with *The Time Machine*, I shot that in twenty-nine days, and the script, I believe, was one hundred twenty pages.

But in terms of lighting, there is a very big difference. Today it is wonderful that you need little light and you don't need the bulky equipment. It's really a joy. That's why I don't wear a watch, because it takes all the time setting up with the lights. I just tap my fingers and think about the time. So many times I've said, "Don't anybody look at your watch." I don't wear a watch. You have clocks on the desk and in the car and everywhere, even in the radio. You get trained to respect time.

SIMPLE STORYTELLING

HOWARD HAWKS: I don't think there is any effort in using a camera if you're just telling a story. People get mixed up if they try to do fancy things with it. If they tell it from a viewpoint as though you're looking at a thing, and then you're telling a story and you say, "And then she drew a gun," well, you want to be able to see that she draws a gun, so you go up and make a shot of drawing a gun. Usually a good cutter comes out on the set and you tell him how you shot it. Occasionally he'll say, "I got an idea for doing it a little different way." Well, that's fine, because you can always put it back the way that you did it. Very often you're very pleasantly surprised. He has got a much better way.

MICHAEL WINNER: I do like my films to move. I must say unless you're making a very deliberately slow film, which sometimes I think you should, I personally like the thing to get along, and that perhaps takes more setups than Satyajit Ray, who shows fifty-two steps being walked up by one man in one setup. Most people would skip forty-eight of them and get him into the room a bit quicker. But that's personal styles of filmmaking. I am not in any way criticizing the slow style, but, in the Western world, in the English-speaking cinema, you have to face the somewhat regrettable fact that you are making a film for mass audience. This mass audience is, on the whole, going to the cinema to be entertained. They are not going for anything else at all. You are employed in the hope that you will make a film entertaining enough to recoup at least the cost of its production and hopefully show a profit.

ROUBEN MAMOULIAN: Some people like to be shackled, spiritually shackled. To some people a prison gives great security. The army is great security, I'm sure, because everything is done for you. Why shackle yourself? That's just plain silly. You have this marvelous gift of a camera that you can do anything with, and you want to confine it to eye level — because of what? Because you see life at eye level? This is not life. This is art. Of course, if you go up on a ceiling for no reason at all it's kind of silly. Camera placement depends on the scene.

In *Jekyll and Hyde,* the first reel establishes the camera, a subjective camera in the first person. This is the first time it was ever done on the screen. I had the camera play Dr. Jekyll. It starts out by his playing the organ. Then the butler comes in and reports to him, and he goes through the rooms and looks into the mirror. He walks out, gets into a carriage, rides through the square, another street, then he comes to the university, and that's where this thing started.

Experimentation is a very stupid occupation, unless it has a purpose. You say, "Let's experiment . . . ditch this, break this . . . then we'll see what happens." That's silly. You experiment when you say, "The conventional way isn't strong enough, isn't beautiful enough, isn't elegant enough. How can I do it better? What if I do this? Ah, let's experiment."

A scene tells you how it should be shot. You can't have just one way of shooting it. For instance, the traditional way of shooting a scene is: start with a long shot, go to a medium shot, wind up with a close-up. Most scenes are shot that way. But in *Mark of Zorro* I reverse the whole procedure. I start up close and go to a long shot. It fits the scene better. You must never establish — I say "must" — I have my favorite things.

After you've exhausted all the conventional things, and all of your own things, if you're lucky enough, something pops into your head. It doesn't come *out* of my head. It falls *in*. Maybe there are ideas floating in the air. Every good idea I ever had I never "thought" of it. It dropped. And I said, "Oh, yes, by God, that's it." Suddenly you'll discover there's a way of doing it and it's the very best way. Whether you've done it before or not done it before is irrelevant. I'd certainly never recommend to evolve any rigid method of shooting, or process of shooting, or forms of shooting.

Each scene should dictate its own method. In *The Mark of Zorro*, it was, as I remember it now, the scene of the corrupt Spanish governor. He was squeezing the poor peasants out of their taxes, insisting that they pay him even if they had no money. There was a scene of this evil captain, Basil Rathbone, and a sergeant collecting taxes. The sergeant sat at a table and the peons stood in front of him. Each came up with his poor pesos. Some didn't have it, so they had to be whipped.

I said, "What's the point of showing a long shot of this? I'd like to show it the way the son of a bitch — excuse me — looks to the poor peon. He's a beast." So I showed this poor peon trembling — as they were — and then I cut to a large close-up of the monster. Then a long shot, once I had established this. In this case, start with a close-up. It carries into the long shot. If you start that scene with a long shot, then you don't get this feeling. If it comes in at the end, it's too late. It's a short scene. You want to hit it in the beginning, the relationship of master to people.

CHASES / GAGS

RAOUL WALSH: Chase scenes are very easy to shoot. Just keep going, keep going, keep going. Get up on top of the mountain, turn around, bring 'em down again. Just hope there's nobody on the road.

LEO MCCAREY: In the early days, comics had a tendency to do too much. With Laurel and Hardy, we introduced nearly the opposite. We tried to direct them so that they showed nothing, expressed nothing, and the audience, waiting for the opposite, laughed because we remained serious. For example, one day, Babe — that's a nickname I gave Hardy — was playing the part of a maître d' coming in to serve a cake in *From Soup to Nuts*. He steps through a doorway, falls and finds himself on the floor, his head buried in the cake. I shouted, "Don't move. Just don't move. Stay like that." Hardy stayed still, stretched out, furious, his head in the cake. You could only see his back. And for a minute and a half, the audience couldn't stop laughing. It's amazing how much thought went into what on the surface looked like lowdown stupidity. . . .

This is literally what happened. I came in one morning and I said, "We're all working too fast. We've got to get away from these jerky movements and work at a normal speed." I said, "I'll give you an example of what I mean. There's a royal dinner. All the royalty is seated around the table and somebody lets out a fart. Now everybody exchanges a *glance*. That's all." Everybody died laughing, but I got my point over.

In *The Awful Truth*, the car broke down and Cary Grant and Irene Dunne were stuck to stay overnight in their house but their divorce was up at midnight. So it got down to only an hour — whether he believed her that she had been with another man or not. It's the first time I remember that anybody resorted to double-talk in a picture. He was asleep or trying to sleep in the room across the hall and he'd get an idea — he was trying to go to bed with his wife but he couldn't forget his pride, and one of them had to weaken. So she said, "What brings you back?"

And then he went into "Oh, I got to thinking, we used to be so happy up here and now here we are again but everything seems so different. It's too bad things are the way they are because if things were different, well, they'd be different. Do you follow?"

She says, "Yeah. I follow."

"Well, that's all I came in here to say. So I guess I'll go back to my . . . well, good night." And it went on like that.

There was a cuckoo clock on the wall. I started at eleven o'clock and at midnight the divorce was up and they would be separated, so that made fifteen-minute intervals. Every fifteen minutes, I'd have the cuckoo clock. That was perfect timing — to do a gag three times and the fourth time you pay off. Most gags were based on "the rule of three." It became almost an unwritten rule. As a gag, I used to have different sized megaphones for long shots, medium shots, and then I had a little tiny megaphone for inserts.

LOCATIONS VERSUS SETS

ABRAHAM POLONSKY: There's no difference between a set and a real place, except that a set has fewer things on it than a real place does. Therefore, a set's harder to work on because there's less help from a set. When you plan a set, you've only got what you've planned, but if you go into life, it's got things you never thought of.

MICHAEL WINNER: I make all my pictures on location. I never go in studios — I hate them — and I always try to go to the real places. Of course, you do have difficulties and sometimes they're in places you wouldn't expect. I think the funniest one of those was on *Scorpio*, which is a CIA picture, and obviously the CIA figures very strongly. The production manager in Washington said to me, "What sort of building shall we get for the CIA?"

I said, "Well, you get the CIA."

So he said, "Ha, ha, ha. How can you get the CIA?" I didn't think he'd get it in a minute, you see, and about a week later he said, "Well, I phoned the CIA. They said we could come and shoot there."

Now, this is a picture that shows the CIA assassinating people left, right, and center. They're killing themselves, they're killing everybody, and sure enough, that film is shot in the CIA.

But getting into places, especially since location filming has become so popular — and has always been to me — you know you end up having to get into sixty, seventy, or eighty places, and they are your film. They are your sets. They are your dressing. They are your image on the screen, and they're terribly important. A great deal of tenacity is required in the selection and in the gaining of admission and in the legalizing of the position once you are in.

I always say that you have to have that done, not only way ahead, but you have to say to the staff, "I must have physical sight of the signed release, a legal document, three weeks ahead of the shooting, or four weeks ahead," because people often say, "Yes," but when you finally come to them with a piece of paper which they have to sign, they realize they are now doing something quite irrevocable and rather formal, and they change their minds. So it's a vital piece of mechanics which is of great artistic importance, and it's not enough to say, "My God, we went to the mayor's office and he said we could shoot there on Wednesday." That's meaningless. You've got to have it in a written manner which the mayor would be too embarrassed to renege on, and until you have that, you're not there . . . and you can't wait, you know.

They'll say, "We'll sign it tomorrow. We'll send it in the post." I don't ever go by the post. I say to a production man, "You go down and get that document, and if you don't get it in your hand, you'd better start thinking of something else."

HASKELL WEXLER: There is a certain assurance when you are in a real place. You do know that you have at least what will make it real. And so all you have to do is to light it real. Whereas if you are on a set, if it's a bad set or not quite a good set, or if you are not sure that the real doors really have things like that, then you sort of have double worries. If you are in a real place, which is supposed to be what it is, then all you have to do is photograph it. On a set, however, you have to cover up for some things and not show some things.

BERNARDO BERTOLUCCI: In general, I try to shoot in a true location, not in the studios. I need to be there because the life outside, the weather, inspires me and so I try to be completely neutral when I go on the set. Then I try to imagine and I feel that the great emotion, the best emotion, is to invent the shot. This is the best moment for me in shooting, and then to shoot is sort of verification of my idea.

JACQUES DEMY: I must have the place in my mind when writing the script. I have always worked this way. I will see a location in town, and then people will come in. I start to think about the people after I have the location firmly set in my mind. It was the same for *Umbrellas of Cherbourg*. I had to escape from Paris, and I took a drive along the coast. One evening I was in Cherbourg at sunset. It was beautiful, and I went to a restaurant to eat and then went to find a hotel room, and everything came to me. I was wandering in Cherbourg and everything came to me.

CURTIS HARRINGTON: I have nothing against shooting on location. But, I haven't had occasion to. In the case of *Helen* and *Games*, if someone had said, "I want you to go to New York and shoot in a real townhouse," or if they said, "Let's go down and rent a real building for *Helen*," I would say no.

The reason is because in those kinds of stories, the layout of the sets needs to be controlled. I like that control that you get on the sound stage. The layout of those sets is such that everything is designed for the action of the picture. I would never find a location that would enable me to stage the continuity as smoothly as those sets. They are all worked out specifically for the film.

FEDERICO FELLINI: *Satyricon* is completely shot in the studio, except for the ocean scenes. I don't think my producers would put the ocean in the studios. I wanted to make everything in the studio just because I think that an inventor must invent an atmosphere, something very realistic. And so, to go on location, naturally, is something to disturb you if the picture has this rigor of recreation. For that reason, I wanted to do all of the sets in the studio.

WIDE-SCREEN

"Wide-screen" is a general term used to describe a film whose "aspect ratio" (the relative size of a frame's width to its height) is greater than the "normal" — 1.33 to 1. Panavision, CinemaScope, VistaVision, Cinerama are all "trademarked" names of particular lens processes that provide ratios such as 1.85 to 1, 2.55 to 1, 2.35 to 1, and so on. As with most other technical innovations, directors differ widely in their response.

NICHOLAS RAY: My affection for CinemaScope initially was my affection for the horizontal line as I learned it from having been apprenticed to an architect who was someone named Frank Lloyd Wright.

FEDERICO FELLINI: Technical things sometimes have to be accepted. I'm not agreed to remain faithful to the old size. I like to change.

VINCENTE MINNELLI: In *Brigadoon*, that was the first time I had used it. At that time, we hadn't developed close-ups very well. They were always distorted, but actually I was appalled by this. It makes no sense to me even now. But I've used it since because you have to, because it's there. It's the shape of a mural instead of what you would ordinarily use. I think what you call 1.85 to 1 wide-screen is much better than CinemaScope, though the theatres prefer CinemaScope, and that, ultimately, dictates what the studio will make. . . . The long horizontal gives a sense of calm, because you're not getting more on the sides, you're getting less on the top and bottom. . . .

I always used close-ups and things like that very sparingly, only when they were necessary because my feeling was always that if you use them all the time, then you have nothing left for big emotion in moments. Lots of times I would just pull a scene through one camera and that was it.

When you want to show a full-length figure, you are showing an enormous amount on both sides, rather than height. I think that the wide-screen is very good.

HOWARD HAWKS: I thought wide-screen was awful. I made one called *Land of the Pharaohs* with it. That's all. For years and years you were used to a certain type of thing, and then, all of a sudden, the studio wants you to do it wide. It becomes very unnatural, very hard to work in. I think it's very undramatic. In only a few pictures is it workable. Just to get a little more room, look a little different from TV. I don't like this real wide stuff. It's too hard to compose a picture. You spend years trying to focus, and all of a sudden you get people with a whole lot of stuff going on around them. It's unnatural. Abnormal filled-up background — everything's so busy. Film is so good and it carries so much focus nowadays, you really are in trouble. The good still man today will work so the background is really out of focus. When everything comes out of your background, you can't tell what it is going to do to your portrait.

LEO MCCAREY: I hated CinemaScope. It was much too wide for its height. My cameraman told me to ignore it. It seemed silly to me if I'm taking a big head close-up of you that the television set way over here is in. I'm shooting a close-up of you and the property man says, "What are you getting in on the sidelines?"

"From here to here." Everything. Whole side of the room. So you couldn't compose the picture.

LENSES

ROUBEN MAMOULIAN: Each lens serves its purpose. If I have to pick a lens that I prefer, it's purely for a nostalgic and sentimental reason. It would be the forty-eight millimeter. You know why? Because in the last shot of *Queen Christina* — you know, you won't get a face like Garbo's every Monday — I wanted that close-up at the end, and the buildup to it. I wanted to do a shot, a dolly shot that would start with a long shot and come into a two-thirds close-up of her face, and then hold it. Bill Daniels, one of the great cameramen, said, "It can't be done."

I said, "We've got to invent something. Do it somehow."

He says, "What you'll have to do is cut or dissolve. You'll get the long shot with a thirty-five, then get into a two-inch, then a three-inch, then for the last close-up we'll use a six-inch. We'll be about an inch from her nose."

I said, "That's no good. You're chopping it up when what I want is a rhythmic flow, ooze into the close-up and hold it."

"It can't be done."

"Well, if we do — let's take a middle lens, say a two-inch, and start a little further up."

"Well," he says, "you'll have to bring it in so it touches her face and then every pore on her face will look like craters of the moon because you don't have the diffusion." As you know, the closer you are, the thicker diffusion you have to use for a close-up. The whole thing comes down to graduated diffusion, and there's no way of graduating it.

I came on the set that morning. I didn't know how to do it and I hated to give it up. And suddenly something popped into my head, after all the sleepless nights of coming up with nothing. Suddenly, like a gift, I walked on the set and I remembered when I was seven years old and my parents gave me a magic lantern. A little red lantern. It had a kerosene lamp in it and it had an opening here, and you used to hang a sheet. I had all my little cousins sitting there. I was giving them a show. It had a glass slide about this long. It had four color pictures on it. You put the first one in and they all loved it and applauded it. You pushed it in and showed them the second, and the third and the fourth. Suddenly that pops into my head and I said to Bill, "Eureka, I've got it."

"What?"

"The diffusion."

"To what?"

"Magic lantern."

He said, "You are going hysterical?"

I said, "No. Bring in the magic lantern."

He said, "What?"

I said, "Why don't we take a piece of glass, instead of four pictures, start it without diffusion, then increase it, get it thicker, thicker, thicker, till you've got enough here that the forty-eight lens would take a face?"

"Well," he says, "we've got no contraption to handle it. It has to be fitted to the . . ."

I said, "Let's make it." We had a whole laboratory over and I told them, "Magic lantern this; do it." It took a whole day. They put a new contraption in front of the lens. Garbo usually quits at five-thirty. The thing came up at six. I said, "You must stay. This is the last shot in the picture." We made two takes because it had to be very smooth. I saw it the next morning. The first take was bad, impossible. The second take is in the picture. So if I had to pick a lens, it's that forty-eight with a lot of diffusion.

PETER HYAMS: There's a really wretched invention called a zoom lens, which is the most abused, single abused, thing in filmmaking. It's more abused by young filmmakers than anybody. It's just a vile piece of equipment. As for tricky scene transitions, I know directors who sit down and literally look for those things as ways to get from scene to scene. I mean, what is the point of starting on a blade of grass with a blur behind you and racking focus then to the lady? I mean, what is so critical about that? I mean, why are you doing that?

And then, the zoom lens thing does something that I don't think people understand. When you zoom in to something, you are not bringing the audience to the subject. You are bringing the subject to the audience. Major emotional difference. People do not realize that. You zoom back, you are not moving away from that subject. You are pushing the subject away from the audience. It's a tremendous difference.

COLOR

ROUBEN MAMOULIAN: I consider that color on the screen must be used as an emotion. If you use it directly as the emotional expression of what you're trying to do in the scene, it takes care of its own aesthetics. It will always be beautiful, emotionally correct. If it is emotionally or dramatically wrong, it will ruin the scene. It will spoil the actor's performance. It will spoil your film.

Now, you're dealing with color, and color has a definite impact on any human being, whether they're conscious of it or unconscious. Some of them are soothing and others excited. Certainly, the most exciting color is red. A progression of color should lead to a climax, which can only be red. Not blue, not yellow, red. In order to lead to it, start with black and white, go to dark blue, dark green, then yellow, then light green, then orange, then red.

Now, how do I do that in *Blood and Sand?* That would mean that the officers leave last. It doesn't make any sense. You have a dilemma. You have to choose. Now, every time you have a dilemma like this, naturalism — physical naturalism I'm talking about, not truth of emotion — on one side and utter stylization on the other side, pick the latter. That's what the audience will take. So I told my stage manager, my assistant, to divide all the guests into groups of thirty — the first being black and white, the second dark blue, yellow, green, orange, and then the last people to run out would be the officers in red.

He really thought I'd lost my mind. He said, "How could they do it that way? The officers should go out first."

I said, "Well . . ." — I didn't go on from there.

"Then how do all the blue dresses get together?"

I said, "I don't know how. But they do. We've got to do it this way." It looked crazy, and that's the way I shot it. Each cut was more intense color. Not a single person ever said, "This is not right." Color impact is stronger than the naturalism. It doesn't even occur to you.

LIGHTING

ALLAN DWAN: I liked the backlighting which Griffith used extensively — reflected it back at the people rather than blaze the sun at them directly. And, he and Bitzer [D. W. Griffith's almost constant cameraman] were superb at composition in general. Backlighting, I would say, and sidelighting were the two principal things we caught. There's not enough of it used even now. Very little of it.

HOWARD HAWKS: I like cloudy days. You get the best stuff in the world on this kind of a day. Bright sunlight is the toughest thing to shoot. We generally work against the south, where the sun is coming from. I often use a sort of a net above the people when we get into close-ups, and then just a little fill light in front. So we get away from the harshness of the sun. A diffusion net — it's like a fishnet, very fine. It cuts down on the hard sunlight and enables you to work on faces.

ROBERT ALDRICH: Low-keyed lighting has nothing to do with the classic painters. It's a terribly simple question. For example, I am looking at this lady in the second row. I would like to know what she is thinking. If there is more light on the wall behind her than there is on her face, then I am not going to concentrate on her. This has nothing to do with Rembrandt. It's not that complicated. If you pour light onto a wall behind people, your focus of concentration is not so intense.

In Metro, in the old days, if a cameraman would come in and he didn't light the room, then they fired him. If they were going to spend *x* thousands of dollars on a set, then they wanted to be able to see it. My feeling is that I don't want to see the set. I know that it is there. But, I would rather see what the lady looks like.

SPLIT-SCREEN

HAL ASHBY: I just have a feeling it can still be used, but it should be planned in advance. Then you can work it out, every shot, and make up your board and say, "O.K., we'll put this shot in here and this shot in there." But basically you should have that going for you as to why you're using the technique. I would love to use it anytime there's a film you're really going to get into.

For instance, if there were one or two main characters, and you really wanted to get to know them better by visual means, then I think it could be very effective if used early in the film — anytime you could take them and in two minutes' time put up ten minutes of film in visuals — maybe to show you someone's background, how they arrived to this particular point in the story, or how they grew from here to here, and you could do that in two minutes where it would normally take you ten minutes and you might eliminate it because it would take too long that way. That could be very, very effective; and it would give you the chance to set up the pattern early in your film. Then, you might start seeing other areas where it could be used. There's something that fascinates me about the use of it; I think it's just dynamite because I think people are into absorbing the images of it.

LOOPING

"Looping" or "dubbing" refers to the process by which sound is added to a motion picture after the images already have been shot. Sometimes this is necessitated by production circumstance, and sometimes by the filmmakers' choice.

HAL ASHBY: I guess it's from my early schooling in looping that I got around to thinking the only time I wanted to loop was if I thought I could improve the performance, because there's something very dead about looping. It can be a very deadly thing. You're into a sound stage and you try to get perspectives, and the clarity is so sharp that it sounds unreal to me.

MICHAEL WINNER: I don't see any way out on a location film. You can minimize it, but I don't think you can tell if it's well backed up with soundtracks. Actors always think they lose quality. I was always told Marlon Brando would never loop, and he had to loop. And he turned up quite happily to loop, and as he was looping — he didn't loop everything, of course — he said, "You know, I'm improving a lot of this." And I think you often do.

FILM AND TELEVISION

BUZZ KULIK: I don't understand the big screen. I really don't. I'm an anachronism. I love television, forgive me. I love working for television. I understand it. I've done seven theatrical films. I still don't understand that. I don't understand how to serve that big frigging screen. Basically in our business there are two divergent points of view. There's the point of view that says you make a setup; you set the camera here and you play your actors to it, you know? I guess Eric Rohmer is the epitome of that, but that's been going on since the first years of making motion pictures.

You can't even pan too much because you'll spin the set, they say. Then there's the other point of view which says, "Move it, baby." Now, I was raised in the Orson Welles scheme of things. Orson Welles was our guy when I got to understand what I was doing in television, and his films, I thought, were the most incredible kind of things from the standpoint of storytelling, and of movement, and of variance of setup because, Christ, he put the camera down on the ground which was unheard-of. I think so many of those techniques come right from Orson Welles.

But there's this other divergent point of view which says, "Hold it here and let the actors and action come to you and go away from you, and pan slightly." Well, if you're Orson Welles, you're spinning the set all the time. Not only that, but you've got *The Magnificent Ambersons* with, for me, technically and mechanically, camera-wise, the best stuff I've ever seen. It has a boom shot that starts on the third floor of a staircase and goes down into this little dining room and all the rest of it.

I don't know what to do — I'm telling you now — I don't know what to do when it comes to the big screen. I've tried holding it here and letting the movement come to it. I've tried movement. I love the zoom lens. I can use it intelligently because you can't see the focal length change on the television as much. They say you can't use it on the big screen because that focal length in the background changes. Baloney. I can use that tool, and I can use it well. I can do all kinds of things with the zoom lens. When I get to do one theatrically, I worry. I don't use them. I start taking it off and putting flat lenses on, and it's a whole other thing to me.

INSTANT PLAYBACK

RALPH NELSON: For the last few films, I've used a device which has been of enormous help to me. I come from a dozen years in live television, where I worked in an electronic medium and saw all four, six monitors and whatever they were projecting. When I first walked out onto a sound stage, I was astonished at how old-fashioned they were. First of all, all this heavy iron and scaffolding, the slowness of the film itself, the parallax conditions where even the operator was not seeing what he was filming . . . He'd look over here, then he'd rack-over the camera and be looking through the viewfinder, giving him a parallax situation. Then he would describe to me what he saw and I wouldn't see it till the next day, or, if we were on location, not till four days later.

A lot of changes have come in since then, and now, the last few films, I've used, shooting through the lens, a black and white television and I have instant replay on tape. I first used it on a picture with Jim Brown for M.G.M., and they were hesitant about the cost of it. I convinced them that Jim Brown had recently become an actor and was basically a football player; that I could get a much better performance from him if he could see with me these replays, and it turned out to be true and they felt the investment was worth it. Since then, I've always used it because I see things immediately. There are no surprises when I see the dailies because I've seen what the operator has seen.

SPECIAL EFFECTS

HOWARD HAWKS: For the train sequence in *Rio Lobo,* you go down to see where the train is going to start. A good shot at the station would be to take it out left to right. So we took everything left to right until we got to the top, and then we turned it around and went right to left. If we had switched that you would have gotten all confused. . . . So you send out a note and say, "Just remember that the train going to the destination goes left to right; coming back it goes right to left." Of course, if we do run into a good shot that works the other way, we flip the film over. And even if you can't read the lettering on the side of the train, it works fine. People's coats are buttoned on the wrong side; they have left-handed guns; but nobody seems to notice.

GEORGE PAL: With crowds you will very often use special effects. Do you know why? Because the extras are so expensive. For instance, I will tell you what happened once in *Houdini*. There was a frozen river where Houdini is supposed to go into a hole. There is a bridge, and people are supposed to be standing on the bridge by the thousands. We had the camera low so that you couldn't see more than a row and a half of people at the most. And fortunately there were eight lampposts on the bridge where we shot it downtown. We shot thirty-two people at each lamppost, and we split the screen eight times, and we had a crowd. And actually, there were noises of thousands of people. So, if you do it really, that costs eight times as much because you have to have eight times as many extras to shoot. Sure, it costs you a little money to put it together, but that is a one-man job in the lab. It's fun. There is a certain amount of satisfaction to fool people.

RONALD NEAME: As you must know, the ship itself in *The Poseidon Adventure* is a miniature. I think it's not a bad miniature. It is a hell of a good miniature. But may I say right out in front that I loathe miniatures just on principle. This one was about twenty-six feet long. She really is absolutely beautiful. In the mill they took something like four to five months to build her. She is built from the plans of the *Queen Mary*. The *Queen Mary* used to travel her own length in fifty seconds when she was cruising across the Atlantic. Our model traveled her own length in five seconds. So, by turning the camera ten times normal speed, she took fifty seconds to travel her own length. That brought her up to the right sort of proportion, as it were.

Three

Under the Lights

6

On the Set

THE DIRECTOR'S ROLE

LEO MCCAREY: You drive to work and you don't know what you're going to do and as you get near the studio, the pressure begins to catch up with you and by the time you get to the gates, you can't wait to start dictating.

FRITZ LANG: I made a rule to be the first on the set in the morning. The rule is that you should start your first shot at nine o'clock. I consider the crew very close to me because we are working together. I mean, if someone pushes the cart on which the camera stands and he knows he has to stop exactly on one point for a certain reason, if he doesn't understand why, he may go too far, he may not go far enough. So I was always the first one at the studio at seven o'clock.

139

And do you know why? For a very simple reason. Look, sometimes you have to go into overtime. If necessary — and you usually should — you send your main actor home because if a woman gets up at five o'clock or six o'clock and is made up and starts to shoot at nine o'clock, the close-ups which are made at five or six o'clock that evening can't be very good anymore; that's natural. So you send her home and then you work maybe one hour later. I don't want to hear from the crew, "Naturally, Mr. Lang, you come at nine o'clock in the morning. It's very easy for you to work one hour or two longer." But when I come at seven o'clock and work with my crew and sit with my crew and have a cup of coffee with my crew, then they could never say this. I never had trouble with anyone.

ALLAN DWAN: On my first picture as director, the cast told me what to do. The first thing they did was give me a chair and say, "You sit here." And they gave me a megaphone and said, "You yell through this."

And I said, "What do I yell?"

"You yell 'Come on' or yell 'Action.' Just tell the cameraman when to start the camera and then tell him when to stop the camera. Just say 'Cut' and he'll quit; he'll stop turning. Say 'Action' and he'll turn the camera. And then you wave a flag or something and we'll ride over the hill, or we'll walk in and do our scene."

STEVEN SPIELBERG: One of the things Henry Hathaway told me is that you just have to know what you're doing every single minute of the day. His advice was: even if you don't know what the hell you're doing, pretend you do.

JACK NICHOLSON: I tried to utilize whatever professionalism I found myself surrounded by and tried to get people who weren't going to be frightened. On *Drive, He Said*, I had an organized crew and the organized crews that I've worked with are really trying to imitate the other crews that I used to work with — the so-called disorganized crews. That really means that they just had less people working. Every movie crew is disorganized to a certain degree.

Every movie has a totally different set of circumstances and problems, you know: how do you get the doughnuts from the Grand Canyon Motel down into the gorge and keep the generator running at the same time? It was very much a learning experience. My theory on it was that I didn't know anything about it to start. I related to somebody who was a professional in their job. I would say, "I don't really know anything about this, so if I go overboard or if I start bullshitting you in some way, just let me know. I won't be nervous about it. Just tell me, you know, and I would like to learn because it's not the only movie I'm going to do." They were always helpful.

In other words, if you did nothing, the movie would get shot. If you want to sleep all day, the technicians would go on. They have their own style. It's really how much you affect their style as opposed to vice versa.

PAUL MAZURSKY: When nothing is happening and it's not working, it's great to have feedback. But usually you can find somebody. You can go down to the coffee shop and ask for a Danish and a cup of coffee and while you are chatting about Nixon and all that stuff, you say, "Do you think that if a guy actually climbed over a fence . . . ?" You can get it somewhere in the streets.

RALPH NELSON: I think that the atmosphere you create, the understanding of the people involved and the nature of their lives is terribly important. It's the foundation for me.

JAN KADAR: If you direct pictures, please try to have an excellent assistant director. Try to surround yourself with thinking people. Avoid the yes-men. They are the worst.

LEO MCCAREY: In the old days, *supervisor* meant being responsible for practically everything on the film: story, gags, screening the rushes, working on the editing, sending out the prints, cutting again when the previews weren't good enough. Also, sometimes it meant shooting sequences over again. But in those days, your name often wasn't mentioned in the credits. The industry knew who'd done what. Irving Thalberg, for instance, never put his name on anything. In my modest way, I tried to follow the same path. Though I made at least a hundred Laurel and Hardy films, I very rarely took credit.

STANLEY KRAMER: The power of the creative project is centered on our being able to create an atmosphere in which the writer and the actor and the director and the musician can come together, all of those people, and give of their talent. Now sometimes it ends up cottage cheese, but sometimes you get a glow because you worked together and did it.

HAL ASHBY: On *Harold and Maude* we tried to get people who were really interested in film. When we were cleaning up at night after working somewhere, someone might be lugging cable, which I would do too. What the hell, we had to help everybody move out so everybody could get some rest. So everybody would kind of chip in and help everybody that way. We didn't get into one of those things where everyone said, "This is my job and this is his job," which is what usually happens.

ROBERT ALDRICH: I don't want to belabor the "Keep them smiling" syndrome, because it is more important than that. Don't joke about the idea that the prop man comes up with. He may come up with the best idea in the picture. You will be surprised with the total contribution that is made to a film by people who are encouraged to contribute. I was at Paramount as an assistant when Cecil B. DeMille was there. At that time, nobody ever made a suggestion to DeMille. It just wasn't done. But that was unfortunate, because often ideas may have been suggested that would have had great merit.

VILGOT SJÖMAN: The trouble in directing is that it's such a superstructure. You are really sort of an authoritarian system. You have the creative people, the cameraman, the editor, the actors, primarily. You really must, as a director, be arranged so that they have a certain range of creativity because they are so — in general terms — so dependent upon you. So it's important for their wellbeing that you give them as much liberty as you can. It's horrible for a cameraman to have a director watching over every angle, every shot, every composition.

GEORGE STEVENS: One comes to the point where there's always the difficulty of one imposing a particular point of view on various people who have their own ideas of how things should be done. For real definition in the film, a singular point of view seems to be very necessary. That's why it's comfortable to know the other man's craft very well, so that imposition doesn't necessarily have to be made by seduction, just reasonable harmony and definition.

COSTA-GAVRAS: The director must know what one can ask. Each actor has certain susceptibilities, sensitivities. Often people say, "This can't be done" of certain things. It really can be done. The director must know this, and it is important that the cameraman knows he knows this.

FRANKLIN SCHAFFNER: Now there are many striking moments in this wonderworld where you are responsible for being prepared for everything that can possibly happen. And suddenly, you discover you have staged a master because, goddamn it, that's the way it really has to be. And an actor will come up with a moment which changes the texture, the intent of everything you have planned. He's right. And now suddenly you have to scurry to accommodate that. It's a marvelous moment in filmmaking when you discover that you were totally wrong. That somebody's concept was really great. It's marvelous.

ALFRED HITCHCOCK: . . . One of the biggest problems that we have is in terms of atmosphere, as I call it. We have a very strange system in this industry, and that is that the man that is called the art director leaves the set the moment it is painted and finished but not dressed, not even the carpet. And the new man walks on, called the set dresser, and he is the man who reads the script and then proceeds to dress the set: goes out and picks furniture, carpet, goes into the prop room, gets ornaments, paintings, and this man is in charge of what is the most vital element of the decor, the atmosphere. Instead of being a set dresser he should almost be a writer, because he ought to know the character of the person who lives in that room. But he doesn't, and that is why you see so many films that have an artificial look. It is because they are very badly dressed.

And the only way I have ever gotten around it is to send a photographer with a color still camera. In *Vertigo*, James Stewart was playing a retired detective who went to law school and who lived in San Francisco. So I said to the photographer, "Go to San Francisco, find out where a retired detective lives, make sure he went to law school, and go in and photograph his house. Get all the detail and bring it back and dress the set that way."

This is a very big problem. You can't always go on location. That's a decision that you have to make quite a bit. It depends. If you are shooting a long dialogue scene and you go outside and you shoot it in an open car in the street, you've got to dub the whole scene because of the external sounds. Now you've got to do that, or you can do the best back projection you can get. And it can be well done, and it can be badly done.

At least then you can let the players have the comfort of being able to play the scene naturally and spontaneously. On location, I think they'd be distracted. They'd be distracted by traffic, the guy driving the car. There have been a lot of pictures made that way, with the camera strapped on the front and the windshield taken off, but you do run the risk of having to re-dub the whole thing. No, when you're dubbing a whole long dialogue scene, you're not going to get the necessary emotion into it. That's the risk you run.

ROUBEN MAMOULIAN: I remember two examples where nobody believed that it would come out and they were all creative people. One of them was in *City Streets,* where I thought, "Why not take advantage of what a sound recording can do and use the thoughts and the recollections of a person and put it in audial shape over a silent close-up?" In those days, we shot everything on the set. There was no such thing as dubbing.

I had Sylvia Sidney in prison, in her cell. I wanted a large close-up of her. All around the camera I had Gary Cooper and the other actors, and doorbells, prison bells, all sorts of sounds; and over her silent close-up occurred her thoughts, what Cooper said to her, the other things that had happened. People on the set said, "This is absolutely insane because it's going to confuse the audience. They'll say, 'Where is Gary Cooper? You hear his voice. How can she talk when her lips aren't moving?' "

"Look, I'm sure the audience will accept this. It's pretty clear." Nobody believed it would work.

But it did.

PETER BOGDANOVICH: There's something that comes when you get control over the picture. Since *Paper Moon* and including *Paper Moon,* I've had final cut, but the problem with getting a certain amount of power is that people are afraid to tell you what they think. People are afraid to say, "I don't like that," or "Excuse me, I don't think I like that," or any form of that. Or they're afraid to say, "Why?" Now, that's healthy. There's nothing wrong with that.

I've always been very open on a set or with the crew or even with studio heads. If you don't like it, tell me you don't like it. Tell me what's the matter with it. People get more scared to tell you and that's a problem because they start saying, "Yes." It's like the yes-men, you know. And they do that to you and everybody starts saying, "Yes, sir." And sometimes you want to say, "Why?" And it's healthy to have that kind of question.

If you're lucky enough to have the power, the clout to say, "I don't care what you think, we're going to do it my way," that's great. But it's also good to be able to have people say to you, "I don't think that's a good idea," and you say, "Why? Tell me why."

JEAN RENOIR: I like to have a control on every part of the picture: the art directors, the cameramen, the actors. I like to know intimately what they do, and to suggest, to help them to decide when there is a choice to be done. But I don't like — I don't believe in specialists. You know it can happen that an actor in confronting me will tell me, "I don't like this part of the set," and we have a discussion about it, and change it if necessary. In other words, I like to keep the right of the important decisions and also the details; but I don't like to do it alone. I like to feel that around my direction many of the problems are going on, and that I know them and I am participating as well as the other ones, the technicians or the actors, are participating to my worries.

STEVE KRANTZ: The director's job in an animated motion picture is perhaps more difficult than the director's job in any other kind of picture. There is nothing that the director gets from a third party. He starts with a blank sheet of paper, and that blank sheet of paper has to be cast by him, has to be designed by him, has to be given attitudes, personality, characteristics, the voices have to be matched, or vice versa, every aspect of the thing starts from an image in your head. It's very difficult to do this without some sort of collaborative effort from one person to another.

In animation, your biggest individual cost in a picture is the guy with a pencil and a sheet of paper. We have a lot of these guys, and the wage scales for these fellows is extraordinarily high for the ones with substantial talent who are able to pick up on what Bob Taylor gives them in terms of what's called "personality animation," which is making those characters live. And the element of this thing demands an understanding of ass-scratching, an understanding of what the mind is doing, and obviously, an ability to draw.

You might say Bob [Taylor] has been instrumental in finding guys who have been passed over somewhat, young guys who have been passed over or who have been relegated to relatively subordinate roles in connection with other animation studios. Not the kind of traditional things: I meet you in Schwab's; I tell you I'm going to make you a star. That doesn't work. But there are people with spark, and there are people who have a feeling for this kind of thing, and a concept. Then the problem is getting them the equipment, getting them a pencil, and whatever.

STAN BRAKHAGE: I have made my living for years in the commercial film industry. That is a form of collaboration, all of us dedicated to selling soap. My first film was a collaboration; it had a different cameraman than myself. This didn't work out, so I immediately had to learn the camera.

I have tried, of late, to collaborate with others. The closest I've ever come on a film that came out as a work of art was on *Blue Moses*, where I wrote a script and an actor whom I very much respect memorized it. Then he and I spent weeks walking around a locale that I had chosen with him attempting to state the script in a variety of ways and places that would be meaningful to both of us.

When I felt we were at a point that was sufficiently thrilling, I began filming. Out came *Blue Moses*. It was very, very difficult. I don't feel, generally speaking, that it is really possible to collaborate in an art. I can give you the best example from a beautiful book called *The Flower Brueghel* on Jan Brueghel, the son of the more famous Bruegel. He had devoted his life to painting flowers. He and Rubens, who was a close friend of his, agreed to attempt a collaboration. Jan did the border and Rubens did the center. When you look at the result you could either laugh or cry. There are two geniuses struggling with each other.

Even if you divide the labors very carefully, as I did with Bob Benson when I was making *Blue Moses*, you have this tremendous, weird phenomenon. That is my experience. This is one of the problems that an artist has when he works in a studio on a film. He is always accused of being a dictator, and everyone always hates him.

ABRAHAM POLONSKY: You can say, "I want something to happen," and the crew says, "How do you want to do it?" And you can say, "I don't know. Let's go over there and find out." They're very happy to do that. You don't lose authority that way. You lose authority by saying, "Do that," and it's wrong. You never lose authority by asking how things should be done.

ROBERT ALDRICH: Someone once said that a director on an action picture has to be a very tough quarterback. The physical erosion involved with this kind of picture does make people short-tempered. If there is a boss or a quarterback, he should be as fair as possible. He should have a direction. He should know what kind of film he wants to make. He should treat everyone with equal consideration and with equal respect.

MICHAEL WINNER: If I ever seemed tough, I'm sure there was somebody on the crew who had messed it up, and who had got told off very thoroughly. I must say that I think on a film, a director has to show some strength.

You know, the chain is as strong as its weakest link. The weak link is a terrible hazard to everybody, not just to the director.

RONALD NEAME: One of the first things that you learn as a director is not to direct too much. Having said that, equally, you mustn't let them run roughshod all over you. They will do that if they get the chance. This is particularly true if you have ten stars, like I had. Given the chance, one of them will make a suggestion, another one will say, "Well, we could do this." Before you know it, you have bedlam. Then you have to be strong. Then you have to say, "Will you all shut up and let me think for a moment before you talk anymore?" You have to crack the whip a little bit. It's a matter of playing it.

ROBERT ALTMAN: If you saw *California Split,* we went down to the Olympic Auditorium for the boxing scene. So we decided we'd actually put on five bouts. We got some fairly good boxers and we put on regular bouts and we said that everybody could come in there free. We had three cameras and we put our three principals over in an area. None of us figured we could get what we wanted, in there and out in a day, and we were trying to because we didn't want to go for two days. We knew we couldn't get the crowd back.

Joey Walsh, who was the co-producer with me and who wrote it, was coming down to have lunch with us and we were finished at eleven-thirty. Once we started that, those guys fighting, and we started shooting and the actors knew what their attitudes were — the only thing we rigged was that little fight at the end between the two — we were through in two hours. I don't think I said a word to any of the actors. I stood over back there and they said, "Should we start?" and I said, "Yes." I literally didn't do a thing. I didn't do one thing except that if I hadn't shown up, they wouldn't have started.

ALLAN DWAN: I'd go in and study the set if it was a stage set, and figure out the best way to move the actors in that particular area. If it was an exterior, we were always inspired by the background. The background told as much story as we did then and sometimes more. So we'd take advantage of the background. An interesting contour of the scenery or a road or something would in itself suggest a dramatic thing. A tree would be an excellent place to hang a man or to make love under — whichever happened to be best.

HAL ASHBY: I was so nervous when I went out there that very first day, I couldn't talk, I had bronchitis, and I was physically ill. I had had a week of rehearsals to see if the whole thing was really going to go, and I had that going for me, just to see if I could get through it first of all. Then for some wild reason, for whatever it is that happened, when you start looking at your dailies you start seeing a lot of yourself in that film — a lot of things that you feel — and it just carries itself through, I think, and your humor will come through. Just basic things you do feel.

GEORGE CUKOR: About the climate on the set — that includes relations with the actor and the actress, and with everybody, in fact — the hours are long and you've got to be perfectly natural about the whole thing. Not patronizing. One is spoiled when you're on the set because you're the master. You're physically spoiled. You say, "I want a Coca-Cola," when you're in the depths of the desert, and this wonderful property man brings you anything you could possibly want.

We should talk about that, and we should talk about the crew. I'm talking about Old World crews. There's a tradition of moviemaking here since 1910. Certain expressions that are maybe not quite used now, but they would say, "You'd be out on Pico." Whatever that means, I don't know, and I used to say it all the time. I used to threaten people in the most terrible way.

I find that the password, at least for me, is a kind of humor. The reason I say that is, you're on the set under great strain from eight in the morning until seven at night. There are moments when you're desperately serious, but you can't spend the whole day with a cathedral hush over the whole place. I like it to be lively; I don't mind noise and things like that. But then I get very testy. I've got very sharp ears and I'm very curious. If there's a whisper on the set, I'm especially curious to know what it is, but also, it throws me, my threshold of concentration.

What I like is everybody working perfectly relaxed and cheery. There is a relationship with everybody, usually lousy jokes, but I enjoy to just talk. Then there are moments when . . . people are surprised because it seems rather permissive. But there is great discipline — when it's supposed to be quiet, it is quiet, and that is the wonderful thing about a movie set. At one moment, it seems absolute pandemonium. Then suddenly, everybody does their job and does it very well and it all falls into place. They know exactly where they're supposed to be, what they're supposed to do, whether there's a new move or not. If they violate that, there are rules of behavior where they get slapped down.

JAMES BRIDGES: I don't think you should get too close to your cast. I don't think you should spend that time with them, because you're going to be asking them to do certain things. If you get to know them too well socially, personally, I think it's a mistake.

JOHN CASSAVETES: If you are interested in films in this country, you want to be a director. It's like in music. You really would like to write your own stuff if you could. I think film and music are very close, since what you are putting down is really more important than just interpreting somebody else's material. But I think now there just isn't enough regard or interest in the beauty of the technical work interrelated with an overall story. I think that everybody learns how to take a camera apart, how to reset it, how to load it, and how to put in your sound sync. But what is the relation, what is the technical responsibility of the cameraman, of the focus-puller, of the various members of the crew making a picture in the overall sense? . . .

Directors don't really get along with a crew, because usually a crew isn't involved, unless it's the way you work where you're working with people. I walk in as a director and meet my cameraman. He's got his crew and that is his army. The guy in the sound department has his army, and the painter has to check with the cameraman to see whether to put shiny walls over there. At what point can I have some kind of a rapport with the operator?

CARL REINER: One of the best directors that I ever worked with was a guy who could never explain what he wanted. But, he gave us such an excitement. He used to be very complimentary when you would start to do something. This was true even if he didn't know where he was going. He would get you so excited. You got so anxious to please him.

I think part of a director's ability is his ability to be a social director. He has to make that set conducive to creativity. Some directors do this by scaring the hell out of you. Some do it by friendliness. Whatever way you do it, it must be done. You must have a way to do it. I happen to make a happy set. I try to let everyone have fun. When you are doing comedy I think it is better to be happy. We laugh and we joke and we play like otters. After that will come a lot of stuff that will come out in the scene.

JOHN CASSAVETES: Now, I've often fired cameramen. Not for any reason, except that I couldn't work in an atmosphere that was less than friendly. I want my wife or anyone else to come on the set; I want people to come on.

I don't want some sucker saying, "Who's that? Get back. This is a long scene, now quiet." Because it's impossible to function if you're sitting in front of the camera. "Now, shush, all right . . ." Where are you? I mean, you got to be dead. So, it should be a thing where people can work. The crew has their time to work, the actors have their time to work. They can work independently and respect each other and that's all that really is required, that each person on the thing either respects each other, or get rid of them, get rid of the people that they don't respect, or tell them, "You're a jerk, you're a fool, get the hell out of here. Come on time. . . ." It has nothing to do with me, really. So, if people don't get to that state, I don't want them to work on a picture.

In *Faces*, I took Lynn Carlin once, I was going to kill her, had my hands around her throat. The crew had me like this. I said, "Where's the kitchen knife?"

I mean anything, there isn't anything that you shouldn't be able to do to get people to do the kind of work that they need to do. You know, if it comes from kindness or sweetness . . . Seymour Cassel jumps off a roof and down a thing, twice, on the dead fly, could break his leg twenty-four times, shots we didn't even use. He could be killed. We're on the freeway, lying on our backs, screaming at the traffic for the traffic to come through.

BOB TAYLOR: You have to eat, sleep, drink the picture. It's crazy, you know, it's nutty. I find myself in the middle of the night mumbling, and my wife says, "Shut up," and I'm talking about a sequence. It's ridiculous. It's nice to be that involved.

PAUL MORRISSEY: There are many ways of making a film. People think because I make films in a kind of crazy way, maybe I think that's the only way. I just find it's something that amuses me. I don't suggest it for everybody. It just shows that there are thousands of ways to make a film, that's all. I mean, it looks like film. I don't know whether it's so great or anything, but it's sort of amusing.

FEDERICO FELLINI: One never does what he wishes; he does what he can. So, I am obliged to do what I can, and I am conditioned to say that I am doing what I wish. If I go to see what I have done, I see what I only can do, so it distracts me. I prefer to go on like a blind man, following with the imagination of the picture to delude myself that I am going in this direction.

ROUBEN MAMOULIAN: I find that the actual shooting of a movie is a very painful agonizing process of constant minor disappointments. What you've imagined ideally frequently cannot be achieved with flesh and blood and with the circumstances, so you feel with each scene that you're losing something. And it's a heartbreaking process. Frequently, when I wind up with a thing I feel, "My God, it's no good at all, it's terrible. It's so far away from what I thought it would be." But, if you try hard enough, it comes out good enough, and exciting enough.

JACQUES DEMY: In filmmaking, you are dealing with human relationships. You are dealing with human beings, and you have to consider them as friends. You know the word, "Play." You are playing like children do. You are playing together. You should never forget that. To play is to have fun. You should be free to do whatever you like. You should be able to do whatever you have in mind. You must never forget that it is really fun.

I have never worked in a studio in France. We usually begin at about eight-thirty. In the evening it is very funny. It depends upon the movie as to how we work then. I remember that on *The Umbrellas of Cherbourg*, we couldn't sleep at all. We didn't want to leave and go away from each other. We wanted to stay together. We got along so well, all together. It was fantastic. We had many laughs and everybody was in love with everybody else. I remember that the set designer said that we should have a place to go in the evening. The designer said that we should choose a restaurant or something like that, so everybody didn't end up going to his or her hotel.

When we were making *Cherbourg*, we were working in an empty building. We had two sets in this building and the dressing rooms and so on. We said, "Why don't we make a bar, a set of a bar, and we can use it every night?" We decided that we could have red wine and sausages and we could screen movies and dance and so on. We did that. Every evening after the rushes, everyone went to the bar and nobody ever wanted to leave. We were often together there at two and three o'clock in the morning. We really did have a marvelous time. I always try to do the same thing on pictures that I make now.

HOWARD HAWKS: Sometimes you look at a scene and see a dour face. If the actors don't seem to be enjoying themselves, I don't see why the audience should. It's much better to do a scene with a certain spirit than to do it way down.

JAMES BRIDGES: I like it much better being a director than a writer. I love the whole social experience. I was tired of being totally private. I look forward to the experience on the set, emotionally and mentally, although while I'm on the set I hate it. It's one of the most painful and exhausting things I can imagine. I look forward, as everybody does, to the cutting room, which is one of the great pleasures. Then you dread all the stuff that comes after that. But I really believe the director is the writer of the picture and I never have any problems switching hats.

FEDERICO FELLINI: The history of four months', five months' shooting is not only the private story of the director making the picture, but it is also a story of a trip, of mutual relationships, of love, of enemies, of vanity. So everything has to do with the picture you are making because everything that is happening is happening under this kind of atmosphere. I think I am helped from everything. Everything gives some stimulation that has to do with this particular atmosphere of this particular picture. It is just to live together. So I think it is more a lesson of morality, first of all. Just to try to acknowledge what is around you and what you are.

ROBERT ALTMAN: There are really three highs in filmmaking. Four, really, in the whole process. Each is like second wind and each one protects you in a natural way. First is when you get the idea of the thing and you say, "Oh, we're going to do this." Well, by the time we really get it worked out and we get the deal made and they've taken everything but your blood, and ninety-eight percent of your energy is gone, you want to just forget it. Then you start shooting so it's a whole new thing. By the time I finish shooting, I mean, it's almost a joke with my crews. The last day is the last day because I couldn't go another day. I would feel, "We don't need that." With *Thieves Like Us*, we finished the last shot at noon in the railroad station in Jackson, Mississippi, and I was on the one o'clock plane for Los Angeles. I just really can't go any further.

Then we start editing and it's a whole new thing again. We start looking at the film. By the time you're through editing the goddamn thing, you know, you're sick of the frustrations. And then the picture opens and you can have a nice time with it. If it's very successful you love that and if it isn't, you say, "Nobody knows anything." You're finished with it and you can let the ocean come up and take the sand castle away. It's gone and you can go on and do the next one.

SHAPING CHANCE

In film, as in all the arts, chance often plays a role in shaping some of the outcomes. The film director, though certainly not controlling fate, may find himself in a position to influence the directions in which random occurrences and accidents tend. The following tales illustrate some aspects of that zone where chance and intention sometimes blend to constitute portions of films consistent with their overall designs.

BERNARDO BERTOLUCCI: In *The Conformist*, when the professor knocks over the wineglass, it was an accident. It's life coming in the movie. In film, I think accidents are very, very important. They're casual things that happen to allow the greatest liberty inside, the greatest freedom inside of this camera presence.

PETER BOGDANOVICH: Almost everything that I'm happiest with in the pictures I've done has been first takes. John Ford said that the best things in pictures happen by accident. And Orson Welles on another level said that a director is a man who presides over accidents. It's true. You can create your own accidents, and that's the thing that I think you have to be prepared for.

ABRAHAM POLONSKY: When you direct, keep your mind open and remember that everything is subject to change. There're changes going on all the time, and there's better stuff going to happen than you ever thought of. So pay attention. I remember a story of a painter who's painting a watercolor in the south of France. He was a very famous painter, Pierre Auguste Renoir [Jean Renoir's father]. He was so old that he was paralyzed practically. He had arthritis. He could hardly hold the paintbrush. And he used to sit in front of the windows and paint out the windows. Beautiful watercolors. And he was painting, and someone talked, and he turned, and three blue dots went right on. You know, when that happens in a watercolor, it's a disaster.

And the people went, "Oh, there goes twenty thousand dollars." That's what the painting was worth.

He said, "Don't worry. I'll make three flowers."

And that's what happens on the set all the time, and that's what happens to all directors. . . .

Romance of a Horsethief is different from any other picture I've made. Technically, all pictures I've made before have been made in the company of great technicians, and they did what they were supposed to do. They made contributions because they were masters. Cameramen were masters and their staffs were masters. I was in a strange situation in Yugoslavia, and this is not to put down the technical capacity of these people, but we were in a situation where I could not talk to most of them, remember that. Everything I would say to them would go through interpreters, in the main. Not that I didn't enjoy that. I did. But events often happened in ways that were different than your expectations. And control was loose. So that this picture was different from all others in the sense that every picture is full of adaptation to accident, but this picture is full of the *use* of accident as a technique in making the film, which is one of the things that was so shocking to David Opatoshu, because this was his first script.

HOWARD HAWKS: We were talking up at the house about dialogue, and I said without a doubt the finest contemporary dialogue was Hecht and MacArthur's. I had a couple of copies of the book of *The Front Page*. There was a girl there who was a pretty good actor and I said, "Read Hildy Johnson's part, and I'll take the other part." And while she was reading it I said, "My God, they are better lines coming from a girl than they are from a man." So I went off and bought the story, which had been made before and was called *The Front Page*. I put Rosalind Russell and Cary Grant in it, and it was a very successful picture, *His Girl Friday*. Ben Hecht says it was much better that way. So it really wasn't anybody thinking of it. It just happened in front of our eyes.

RICHARD LEACOCK: Let me tell you about shooting a press conference. You wait till the press conference starts and, at the end, you start shooting. I'm terribly aware of an experience that usually the most interesting things happen before and after the thing you're supposed to film. I found this in going over, for instance, the Eugene McCarthy headquarters in Albany, where I was shooting this student. He was constantly drifting off after the thing he thought we were shooting had stopped. And all of a sudden some nut would walk in front of the storefront where they were working and something marvelous would happen and he was off chatting with somebody. So that kind of shooting, you've just got to be totally on it when you're doing it. Earlier films I used to write treatments, knowing I was wrong. Sometimes it's a good idea.

LEO MCCAREY: I'll tell you one of the funniest things that could ever happen — it's the funniest thing that happened in my entire life — and I don't see how anything could happen any funnier in anybody else's life.

There must have been five thousand people gathered around to watch us shoot. Laurel and Hardy ran between these two apartment houses, away from the camera. Their wives followed a considerable distance back and fired guns at them. When they fired, men jumped out of the windows of these apartments, putting their trousers on and whatnot.

Now, before I shot the scene, I didn't want anybody to get hurt, and we had stuntmen jumping from the second floor. So, with a megaphone, I explained to everybody we had to get it right the first time. There would be only one take on account of the danger of injury. Everybody listened attentively, and I said, "When you jump out of the windows in various states of undress, you run away from the camera and disappear in the alley in back." Everybody said they understood.

So came the big moment. I started the camera and called Stan and Babe Hardy. They came running in, the wives followed fifteen or twenty paces back, and as they were going down between the buildings, the wives fired at them, the men all jumped out the windows. Everything's going great and one foul-up jumped out the window, pulling on his pants, came running *toward* the camera and he disappeared on the street side right next to the camera. And I bawled him out. I said, "What the hell do you mean by spoiling this scene? Didn't you hear what I said?"

The fellow said, "Hell, no. I'm not in this picture!"

FEDERICO FELLINI: I shot most of the ending of *8½* with a train sequence. It was just for the plan of the production schedule. . . . But before the picture was finished I wanted to shoot a trailer. So, I asked the producer if it was possible to call all actors and all the extras who worked on the picture in that little circus at the end, just to shoot an extravagant trailer. So, they came — two hundred people — and I asked for seven cameras — hand cameras — and I said to them to go on the staircase and when the music started, to come down, to walk and talk. I said to the second cameraman, "You do what you want. Take just the people, because it is a trailer in which I want to make my voice." When the band started to play and all the people came down, I was very moved by this scene and this atmosphere. I felt this was the right ending for my picture. So, I said to the producer, "I have changed my idea. I don't want to use the train. I have a new idea for the ending."

LEO MCCAREY: We were right in the middle of shooting *My Son John*. My daughter called me one night and told me of Robert Walker's death. The whole crew was as floored as I was. Salaries were stopped and everybody went to work on other pictures. We stopped shooting for three months.

In the original version, the character doesn't die. In the original ending, Walker gave the speech that's in the film as a recording, but he gave that speech himself, which was all the difference in the world. Since Walker really died, we had to have him die just so we could have an ending. I had to use all the tricks I'd learned trying to transform the few scenes we'd shot into a real film. It took three months.

Bob Walker was overly zealous. He was so in love with that big scene. He memorized it and memorized it. Finally, he drove down to my house and he sat on the edge of my swimming pool and paced up and down like it was a stage — this was on Saturday and I was going to shoot the scene the first thing Monday morning. And in the hope that I would have additional ideas, he came down on Saturday to work with me on it. Well, we both got very enthused about it, and I said, "Jeez, I wish we had a recording of it."

And he said, "Why don't you call the studio? Maybe they can get ahold of a sound man."

I said, "A great idea." So we got ahold of a sound man and he and I got in his car and drove to Paramount, and they set it up and we got a recording of Walker's voice making that big speech. And he died that weekend.

So I had to rewrite the story so that he called the FBI and said he was coming over with a confession that he had recorded in his office. And that became the excuse for the speech.

But it was necessary for Walker to die at the end and I hadn't shot a scene like that. So I went to Hitchcock, who had just made a film with Walker called *Strangers on a Train*. We were going to buy the footage from Warner Brothers. That was the deal. But it's amazing how people will cooperate with you when they are really dedicated to their work. Hitchcock became interested in my predicament then, and in his mind he went over all the footage of Walker. He called me up and he said, "I think I've got a piece of film where Walker and this fellow, Farley Granger, were under a merry-go-round." And he said, "Let's run it and see if there's any separation between the two of them where Walker dies."

And I went over to Warner Brothers and looked at the stuff, and I was in such a state that I started shouting at Granger, "Get out of there." Finally, there *was* a separation between the two of them. And fortunately it was right when he died. For a second, Walker was alone, saying a few words.

I had our trick man and our technical men and the cutter, and all I could get was a piece of film under thirty feet in length, and then I could only use the head because there was a big close-up of this other fellow, Granger, and I couldn't use that. So I evolved a setting of the wreckage of a taxi cab and matted in the head of Walker. I myself dubbed in his last few words.

VINCENT SHERMAN: In *Old Acquaintance*, a very strange thing happened with that scene, where Gig Young tells Bette Davis he has decided to marry the younger girl. When we shot the scene for the first time, Bette remained seated when Gig told her. We put that scene together, and we didn't think it was as good as it could or might be . . . due to the fact that Bette was facing Gig all the time. It is very difficult to see the pain and suffering when you are facing the person that you do not want to reveal that pain and suffering to. She was the last one to ask for any pity.

So I discussed it with Mr. Blanke, the producer, and we decided that at the end of the film, we would do one retake. That was the only retake of the entire picture. I don't remember whether it was my idea or Blanke's or whose, but we decided that after Gig told Bette that he was going to marry the young girl, that she had to get up and find some way to walk away from him so that, in other words, her back was to him. While he is explaining how it happened, we can see the suffering in her face which she didn't want to reveal to Gig.

We decided at the end of the picture we would retake that one scene. So what you see now is this. By the way, we finished shooting that film at two o'clock on a Sunday morning. In those days we worked all day Saturday. At any rate, we wanted to finish up the picture on Saturday evening. We worked until almost midnight to clean up the sets and everything. There was always a big desire in those days to wind up a picture if you could. Rather than have a scene or two left over for Monday, we decided that we would also do the retake. So it was after midnight when we did that retake.

Now, the first part was shot weeks and weeks before. The scene where she gets up and walks away from Gig as Gig explains how he fell in love and how they decided to get married is played with his voice in the background and Bette walks right up to the camera in a big close-up.

Well, she was very tired at two o'clock in the morning on a Sunday morning. This was the last shot in the picture. That was when we finally made the scene. When we finally took it to the projection room, we had a recording of what Gig was saying, but we sort of blotted that out and let the music take over. The important thing was to see how painful this was for her to hear.

An amusing sidelight was when we went to the preview of the picture, Jesse Lasky, a very nice man, came out and walked over to me. He said, "You know. That woman is just the most remarkable actress I have ever seen in my life. Why, I saw her age from one shot to the next shot. She aged ten years, for God's sake."

JOHN CASSAVETES: We had the worst sound track in the world on *Shadows* because we were in a dance studio, and people were above us, below us, the traffic and noise and I didn't know. "How's the sound?"

"Great."

So I really think that we innovated in that sense, we innovated through an absolute accident. We spent maybe two months on the dubbing, two months trying to get the sound right. We couldn't get the noises out, so that's the way the film came out, and thereafter the commercials picked that up, and thereafter other filmmakers started to make films that way. For us, it was a terrible trial, but when we were in England, they said, "What a great sound track; you could finally hear life, you could finally hear other things going on."

GEORGE PAL: In *War of the Worlds*, the sound of the Martians was actually the oscillator that you hear in the projection room when they tune up the sound. It makes that sound when it goes at a certain pitch. We stopped it and played with that, and used that kind of electronic sound.

There was something else that we had a lot of trouble with, and that was *The Naked Jungle*, where we had to have the noise of the ants. That was a very difficult undertaking. What do ants do? And especially what do billions of them do? We tried everything and we asked M.G.M. to give us the sound of the locusts from *The Good Earth*. We put that in there, and it didn't match. Just somehow it wasn't there.

I remember one Saturday afternoon spending time working with the sound department. We had tried everything from crumpling paper to rubbing this and rubbing that. Nothing matched really. And we were really tired and we thought we hadn't solved anything, so we went over to a little restaurant across from Paramount and we had a Coke with lots of crushed ice in it. I did like this, and said, "What do you think of this, skeeosh, skeeosh," and that became the sound of the ants. It was Coke with crushed ice, stirred with a straw.

WILLIAM FRIEDKIN: In *The French Connection*, Bill Hickman and I — he was the stunt driver — he and I got in the car. I operated the camera inside and I had a camera on the front bumper of the car. I said to him — I had been building Hickman up to this for weeks — I said, "Hickman, you have no guts. You're chicken-shit. You need a couple of drinks to drive good." I kept getting his goat.

And he said, "I'll tell you what. I'll show you some driving if you get in the car with me."

So I got in that car and he went for twenty-six blocks with just the siren on top of the car. We broke every stop light. We went through everything. We went in and out of lanes. There was no control. At all.

HOWARD HAWKS: I made a picture called *Scarface*. We had a new actor called Georgie Raft, who had never acted before. He was a pretty lousy actor. I didn't know what to do with him, so I said if he could only be doing something while he was reading his lines maybe people wouldn't realize how bad he was. So we gave him a half-dollar to flip and he dropped it a few times and then he flipped it and he said his lines and was pretty good. So we used the flipping of the coin all the way through the picture. It didn't change the story, nor did it change the scenario.

7

Directing Actors

QUESTION: With which character in your movies do you most identify?
NICHOLAS RAY: Myself.

People in the cinema, on the screen, are not heroes from a novel, nor actors on the stage. They are merely dreams — shadows.

— Jiri Weiss

Perhaps more has been written about the actor than about any other participant in the filmmaking process. Most of the material is from a purely devotional point of view — personality, life-style, opinion. This is only natural, since most of the attention paid to films is dependent upon their performers. What little information there is about film acting technique and style is derived basically from a theatrical orientation.

STAGE AND SCREEN

The differences between stage acting and film acting are as great as the differences between film and theatre as art forms. For the film actor, there is

160

little, if any, linearity of performance — performance time usually being limited, at a maximum, to the length of one roll of film, about ten minutes. The film actor must maintain the unity of his characterization over a period of weeks and months, during which he might express only a small portion of it each day. Except in rare cases, the film actor will be called upon to derive his role in a totally nonconsecutive manner. It is not at all uncommon that a film actor first will play his final scenes and weeks later will have to introduce his character as though it is the first on-screen appearance. The film actor, due to contractual exigencies, may even have to portray a conversation with another actor who is not actually physically present — the director, a camera, or a stand-in serving as a surrogate.

JACQUES DEMY: We have two types of actors. One is the stage actor. They are known as "stage actors." They sometimes do some films. Also, we have the movie actors. Most of the time they don't work on the stage. They are unable to learn the lines or memorize a big speech. So, there are two types of actors. In England the actors are very stagy. This seems to be always true.

MILOS FORMAN: You can't become a good actor in the theatre without professional training. But theatre and films today are so far from each other that what does it mean to be professional in films? What counts is the talent and certain gifts, and personality.

ROBERT ALTMAN: What I'm looking for instead of actors is behaviors, somebody who will bring me more. The original thing of acting is the person who has the voice and the facility and the command comes in and I have a play here and I say, "All right, you five guys read this part. These words are what I want put on the stage so the one of you who can be the best interpreter of this part . . ." Well, I'm not looking for that. I don't have that part. I'm looking for behavior that we as the authors say that we want in a person. You bring something to me that I've never seen before but that I know is right. If you try to do it all from one person's brain, it's going to look like it. It can be pretty good, it can be a nice stylized piece, but it can't be as broad.

MICHAEL WINNER: I think the thing about Marlon Brando is that he really lifted acting from the theatrical style of acting — which was "acting" where you actually give a performance. Where you had to be, from historical development, your own microphone, your own loudspeaker, your own magnifying glass, to people seeing you in an auditorium from a distance. Now Marlon took that acting and turned it into film acting, which is really behaving. It is behaving absolutely naturally and letting the camera image see you as it were in real life without giving a performance in the theatrical sense of the word.

JAMES BRIDGES: An actor on stage, of course, has a chance every night to keep on refining it; they have a chance through the experience with an audience to change it and keep finding where it is. I think acting is harder on film than in theatre. Much, much harder, because it freezes in reality so quickly, and then you have to keep building it as you go along.

BUZZ KULIK: Actors on the stage and actors in live television were really in control of their own performances when they performed. You could rehearse with them as much as you wanted. You could set the performance, but they could, if they wanted to be nasty about it, change the performance totally. They had total control. In film, of course, we have the total control because we can go into the cutting room and change a performance eight different ways.

PAUL MAZURSKY: In certain cases, some very good actors in the theatre play parts that don't reveal themselves, whereas in films, some actors who may not be as great have some quality that gets revealed, that is very strong and works in the right casting. For instance, Gary Cooper in some pictures. John Wayne, in some pictures, is very interesting to me. I don't think he could act in a theatre. I don't think he could play something else.

THE DIRECTOR AS MIDWIFE

JEAN RENOIR: I divide in my imagination the directors I know in two big categories. One category is the directors for whom the work starts from the camera. You put your camera in a certain spot which is carefully chosen. It gives you a beautiful background; it gives you with the props a certain idea which can symbolically help the telling of the story; and then you take actors and you put them in front of the lens, and you go on. That means the role of direction is based on the service of the camera. Wonderful directors work that way. For instance, René Clair.

But I am the opposite. I like to start with the actors. I like to put them in a certain mood. Finally, you know, I consider that my profession as a director is not exactly like a supervisor. No. We are, simply, midwives. The actor has something inside himself but very often he doesn't realize what he has in mind, in his own heart, and you have to tell him. You have to help him find himself. I always try to start the work from the actor. You rehearse, you rehearse, and when you are happy about the rehearsal, you decide that you can give the rein to the cameraman, and you ask the cameraman to come with you, the soundman to come with you, and you decide what will be the angle.

I always try not to cut the film during the shooting. It's why I use so often tracking shots, pans, etc. It is for no other reason than I hate to cut the acting of an actor during his inspiration.

A great director, perhaps the top director in our day, Godard, is exactly the opposite of me. He starts with the camera. His frames are really a direct expression of his personality without the in-between worries brought by actors. I need the actor who comes to me and says, "Oh, I am so unhappy; I believe my mistress is cheating me. I cannot stand it." Well, that's my job, to open the door to such confidences, and to turn them to the best use for my picture. Sometimes they gave me wonderful performances.

LOUIS MALLE: I've absolutely no principles and I'm absolutely prepared to change everything if it does help actors. Sometimes, which is really interesting and difficult, you happen to have in the same scene two actors who have to be directed or helped in a completely different way. For instance, like the boy in *Lacombe, Lucien*, Pierre Blaise, and the girl, Aurore Clement, the boy was at his best usually on the first take and then he got bored. And Aurore, to get the best out of her sometimes would take eight takes. The whole problem is to get to the right moment where both of them are at their best.

BUZZ KULIK: Each director works his own way. The example I use is William Wyler, who could never articulate what it was that he wanted from an actor, but his genius was that when he saw what it was like . . . he recognized it, which is an incredible thing, because there are so many times when we see something that's great and we're not aware that it's great or we're not sure that it's great.

He would say, "Do it again." I remember Walter Pidgeon telling me that when they did *Mrs. Miniver,* he had to walk with his back to the camera up the staircase forty-seven times and each time, he would say, "Willy, what is it?" And he'd do it again, just try to make it a little different. The genius of the man is that when he saw it, when it was the right one, he recognized it and that's a perfectly valid way to work with actors.

There're so many things in the quiet of your own bedroom, the night before when you're doing your homework, that seem right and valid, but then an actor will come in and give you another point of view that's thirty times better than what you thought of the night before.

MARTIN RITT: Let me tell you something about actors. This is very important. I say this to most actors that I work with. The only thing that you in your daily life don't know is what is going to happen to you. You know what you feel and who you believe is good. You know who your girlfriend is at the time. Whatever. But, you don't know how you are going to end up.

Every actor does, in a play or in a picture. He knows what his destiny is. That is the most important clue. If you knew what was going to happen to you at the end of five years, that would be a very important clue as to how you would live the next five years. An actor knows. Paul Newman knew at the end of *Hud,* according to Irving Ravetch and Harriet Frank, Jr., who wrote the screenplay, and myself, that he was a son of a bitch. When we started to cast that part, we were very worried. I can very easily say to Paul, as I can say to any other actor since, "You know that you are a son of a bitch, but the point is to make yourself attractive to the audience all the way through the film." We could actually go about halfway through the film. Nobody ever believed that Paul was going to do what he did at the end of the film.

This is what I mean by structure of performance. If you know the meaning of the picture and the character in terms of the overall movement, then you structure the performance. You work backwards, so that the whole thing is clear at the end. The actor, if he is well-trained — and if he isn't you have to do it for him — must detail his behavior. In that way you lead up to what the logical ending is. In structuring the performance I always start from the end. I start from the destiny. Then I detail the life.

I spend a lot of time with actors. I like actors.

GEORGE CUKOR: I read what people are supposed to tell actors and I don't understand it. You create your own language, your own image, or whatever you're doing. I remember working with Ingrid Bergman, and the first day or so when they reloaded the camera, I would go in and tell her the story again. I said, "So and so," to create a pitch.

Then she looked at me very politely and she said, "You know I'm not one of these cool Scandinavians. I'm not stupid, you told me that before."

I said, "Oh yes, I'm so sorry," and I walked back. Then I wanted to tell her other things, and I was afraid. After two or three days, somebody said, "These people are acting as though they were underwater."

I said, "You're right, they are." So I started acting just like I had before. "Let these people get used to me." They were rather pleased about it after a while. You have to just make an atmosphere where they can go and certain people you leave alone and certain people you should talk to. It's all a very individual thing. I don't do it deliberately, impulsively, emotionally; I do it freshly all the time.

VINCENT SHERMAN: I told Bette Davis the story that John Barrymore once told me: that I wanted to see her suffering at the end. Barrymore told me this when I was acting with him in a film called *Counsellor at Law*. We were talking about actors and parts, and he said, "You know, most actors, when it's a stage play, all they want to see is how many pages of dialogue they have, how many 'sides,' it's called. They want to know how many long speeches they've got. And they will go through a motion picture script and see how many scenes they are in. Hell, I don't give a damn about that. There's only one thing that I want to know. I want to know who does the suffering."

That has been like a guideline for me. I can go to a script and say, "Wait a minute. Who does the suffering here? Who is affected by this?" I've also very frequently been able to sell actors a part when they said, "Gee, it's not very long. It's not very good."

I said, "Yes, but, look. You do the suffering."

BUDD BOETTICHER: One thing that Duke Wayne has taught me, and he does it better than anybody in the world, when you don't have anything important to say, do something. Saddle a horse, light a pipe, spit, do anything.

MARTIN RITT: You don't have to tone anything down that is real. When you talk about toning a guy, you are talking about a guy that is acting to the second balcony. He fits real and full. You don't want to tone him down. You don't want to tone down Babe Ruth. When you have a great thing which is true, then it is pure gold. If it isn't true, then it isn't really great.

HOWARD HAWKS: When the girl in *Rio Lobo* stumbled over a few lines I was very pleased with that, because people talk that way, and I don't attempt to change that. As a matter of fact, I tried to tell them to start one way and finish up another way, because when you're trying to describe something, that's the way you do it in normal conversation.

FREEDOM AND DISCIPLINE — FINDING THE KEY

In every director-actor relationship, a methodology must emerge to elicit the best possible performance.

PAUL MAZURSKY: My experience as an actor, when I worked for other directors, was that very few directors knew anything about actors. Very few could tell an actor anything that would be really helpful. I never worked with the great ones, and I have no way of knowing about them, but I do know about acting and how to help an actor when he's in trouble; but I don't try to help an actor unless he is in trouble.

JOHN HUSTON: I start out by getting as much as I can from the actor himself. If he goes off the track, then I try to put him back on. If his performance needs to be intensified, why, I try to help him in that. I have as few searching conversations as possible. I can tell you a story in this regard on *African Queen*, with Katie Hepburn.

In the first two or three days, Katie is a suspicious woman at best, and the first couple of days, she was playing the role as a formidable woman, icy cold and supercilious — she had her own characterization that wasn't very good. It was, indeed, banal, and whatever I'd tell her, she didn't pay much attention to my advice and suggestions.

Finally, after a couple of days we were in the heart of the African jungle. Really, we were living under very romantic circumstances; beautiful place, the jungle. We only had a couple or three weeks at this particular place that we built out of the jungle, because presently the soldier ants would march in.

Anyway, this night I sent a note across to Katie and said I would like to talk to her. I was going to give the occasion all the formality that I could to make it impressive, and she answered back that she would receive me at her bungalow, and so I said to Katie, "Look, I don't think what you're doing is right, and I'm going to talk for a few minutes, and when I'm through, don't answer me; just think about it. I'm going to tell you these things." And I talked to her, and finally I said she should be a lady and

"I suggest you pattern your performance after what you've seen or what you know of Mrs. Eleanor Roosevelt. Act like Mrs. Roosevelt." From then on she was just ideal. That's all it took — the key. Yes, that's right, the key. And from then on she was wonderful — couldn't do anything wrong.

JIRI WEISS: You must accept the psychology of your actor. You must never try to direct it.

JOHN CASSAVETES: It just seems impractical to me to say, "You're a husband, this is what you are, and you're a simp, and you wear glasses, and you sit down in a certain way." All he really is doing is parodying what I want him to do, you know. But I'd rather take a good actor and say, "How do you feel about this? What do you feel?" Study his speech patterns and study the way he works and how he really feels about it, and then start to write off of that. Sometimes it works and sometimes it doesn't.

RONALD NEAME: I first learned this lesson from Alec Guinness of being completely fluid when I go on the set. . . . As a director the first film that I made with him was *The Promoter*. It was only the third film that I had directed. I had got it all beautifully worked out. I had done my homework. We came on the set one morning and I said, "Alec, I thought that maybe you should do this, that, and the other thing."

He said, "Well, Ronnie, I've been thinking. I'd rather like to play this scene lying on my back underneath the table."

I said, "Lying on your back, underneath the table?"

He said, "Yes."

I said, "Well, you're out of your mind, Alec. What's that got to do with the scene?"

He said, "Now, wait a minute. Don't get impatient. Just bear with me a minute." Of course, he suggested something in relation to the scene and it was absolutely marvelous played on his back underneath the table. That was the way that we shot it. That was the day that I stopped doing my homework, because I thought it was silly.

If an actor can bring you something and wants to do it his way, provided that he is following the character accurately and he's not being absolutely stupid, then he should be encouraged to do it this way.

MICHAEL WINNER: Actors, I have found, are not terribly keen to discuss their roles among themselves. The older professionals are more used to an individual chat with the director about the part and then coming on the set and getting on with it. It's a kind of myth, I think, that they're all dead keen to spend hours of their lives going into it. You have an awful lot of time on the set even with a quick lighting man, you know, to discuss the whole thing . . . or piece by piece. That's really enough.

I think that it's important that your lead or your star, who goes through the whole film and by whose behavior everyone else is influenced, as it were, is very clear about the lines you hope to take. But again, I think the director must be a chameleon and go by what the actor requires. I always ask the star, "Do you want to rehearse?" And if they say, "Yes," I'm very happy to do it. Thank God they haven't said it.

You have to really give service to the people who give the most to the film, which is the leading man, woman, eunuch, or whatever. You cannot, regrettably, with big-cast films give enough time, because it isn't there, to every single player. You're going to have to hope they come along and do a good job and take a five- or ten-minute guideline as to what they're about and adapt it as you see it.

We shoot from eight in the morning to six at night, which means you leave the house at seven, rushes from seven to eight, you're not back to the house till nine, and you've got to be up again at six-thirty. There's a limited amount of time there to get everyone together for these intellectual discussions, and I don't think it's really necessary.

VILGOT SJÖMAN: You have certain ideas. Then, you find the important thing is what the actors have. You adopt the camera to what the actors are doing. Every time you try to do it the other way of pressing the actor to fit in a preconceived idea of the frame, how it should look, then you don't get that much out of them.

ALLAN DWAN: I always found that it was a good idea to let the actors have a lot of free play. I learned that in the beginning and I never got over it. I don't believe in telling an actor every move to make. Sometimes you find them so dull or so frozen or so frightened that you have to pet them and help them, but *not* try to teach them to act. A director's job shouldn't be to teach acting. That's another kind of profession; that's something else.

IRVIN KERSHNER: In *Loving*, this flexible style demanded a certain amount of work on the part of the actors. It meant flexibility on their part. George Segal sensed this and went with it. Instead of getting frightened, he would say to me, "Do you know what is so great about working this way?" He told me that he could be as outlandish as he wanted. He knew that I would edit it out, that I would say, "That stinks."

He said that he could afford to not censor himself, which is the key to great acting. If you censor yourself, you are directing yourself. That way you cannot get the most out of a moment. But, if you just let yourself go and then you say, "What happened? How was it?" When an actor can really say that and not know, then you are reaching the stage where the actor is using his whole instrument. But, when the actor says at the end, "That was great. Print that. It was great." George would often say that. And usually it wasn't right. I told him that it bothered me, but I would never tell him specifically what it was that I didn't like. He was going to do it differently the next time, anyway. When the scene didn't work I would usually tell him something like "You got up too fast."

He would say, "What's the difference?"

I would say, "You see, I am going to cut when you get up, and we already shot where you were standing when you get into the next scene, and so it won't work." So we would do it again, and it would change. But, George had a feeling, just by little things like this, that there were limits, and that he would be held in line, that there was a guidepost, even though he himself couldn't see it. It was a matter of confidence in something outside of yourself.

That is what the director's function has to be. The actor is in a dreadful situation. In Europe it is different. When Fellini talks, then the actors literally don't know what they are doing. I talked to some of the actors who worked on *Satyricon*. They would walk in the door, and Fellini would yell, "You."

He would sit them down and there would be a hundred people in the background having an orgy. The actor would be sitting down. Fellini would move in for a close-up and the actor wouldn't know what to do. Fellini would say, "Stare at this light." Then, someone would hold up a little flashlight. I have done this, and you can do it with character actors, but don't you ever dare to do it with a star unless the star absolutely loves you. Actors really resent this type of treatment.

But, in this story that was told to me about Fellini, the actor sat there and the camera kept moving in tighter and tighter on his face and Fellini was walking around with a little flashlight and he told the actor, "Don't move your head, just move your eyes." And that was the scene.

I asked the fellow what he was supposed to be thinking, and he didn't tell me. He couldn't tell me. I asked him if he had read the script. And he said, "Fellini would never let me read the script." Well, that is another way of working. And that takes a lot of love and a lot of confidence to do that.

Marcello Mastroianni will work that way for Fellini. Fellini will say,

"Sit down and stare out of the window." He won't say, "What am I supposed to be thinking?" He will just say, "All right, Federico," and he will stare out of the window. But, you tell Richard Harris to do that, he will punch you right in the nose.

HOWARD HAWKS: . . . You are giving the actors an attitude. Once they have an attitude, then it is up to them to read the lines. I don't care what they do about that, except when they've got the wrong attitude. If they are mad in a scene when I think they ought to be smiling, then I say, well, I want to have them do it my way. It doesn't seem to hurt their egos or hurt them providing you talk it over and tell them how you feel about it. Then they have a chance to say how they feel. I don't mean that that's inflexible.

For example, I told the Mexican actor in *Rio Lobo,* "Don't get tough because Wayne will blow you right off the screen. Your only chance is to be quieter than he is. He doesn't do it purposely, but he can, he's too big. There's some quality that he's got. The only thing is to be the opposite, study him, watch him."

. . . Sometimes you find the character's attitude in a hurry. I was making a picture one time with Edward G. Robinson, and about four o'clock in the afternoon, I stopped the thing. I didn't know him very well, and I said, "Mr. Robinson, this is going to be one of the dullest pictures that's ever been made. You are sour and the scenes are flat and I really don't think it's going to be any good at all."

And he said, "What can we do?"

I said, "Well, can you play a very talkative man who laughs and jokes and is fun?"

"Yes," he said, "if you'll help me with what I say."

I said, "I'll help you, but you're going to have to do a lot of it yourself." We made the picture called *Tiger Shark,* and he played a good character, and every day we had fun changing this whole thing around. I hate to think of what the picture would have been if he'd stayed in that dour, sour character.

Bogart was a joy to work with. He is one of the fine actors we've ever had. He was capable of doing many things. He was really awfully good to work with. I had a lot of fun with him because we were working on a story and we got an idea. We were talking about Bogart's insolence, because no matter what you wrote he was insolent. So we said, "Well, let's make a girl insolent." So we started to work and we worked out the part for Bacall. And I said to Bogart, "As long as it doesn't come as a surprise to you, we're going to make the girl more insolent than you are."

"Well," he said, "you've got a fat chance of doing that."

I said, "I don't know. I think we've got a pretty good chance. I'll tell you one thing. Every scene that we make with her she is going to walk out and leave you with egg on your face." He just looked at me, and I said, "After all, I'm the director."

He said, "Yeah, and you have a pretty good chance of getting away with what you're going to try, too." And we did it. Actually, we had an awful lot of fun with the insolence of the two people in their relation to each other. That's another thing about attitude. Mitchum, for instance, I liked him when he smiled. So we made scenes that he could, you know, have a good sense of humor.

JEAN RENOIR: I hate to discourage people. The truth is, if you discourage an actor you may never find him again; but you'll hide his personality behind a kind of mask, a mask of fear. We must not lose something in mind. It is that an actor is an animal extremely fragile. Extremely fragile. You get a little expression. It's not exactly what you wanted, but it's alive. It's something human. Don't kill it. Don't kill it by rushing, by pushing your own ideas into his imagination. No. Try softly, slowly, to help him find what you believe is the truth.

PETER BOGDANOVICH: I tend to show actors what I want them to do. I'll get up and act it out or I'll give them a line reading or whatever — only because I don't know how else to tell them. I don't know how to intellectually say it to them. I can do it if I have to, but it's so much faster if I just get up and do it. Some actors don't like it, and if they don't like it, then I don't do it because they won't respond well.

GEORGE SEATON: What I usually do is just say, "Let's see how you see the scene. Let's rehearse it the way you see it." Now if it's not the way I see it, and we can discuss it sometimes, maybe the actor has a better point of view on it. Maybe he sees something in it that I don't see in it. My God, how many novels have been read by people who have written critiques and saw things in the book that the author never intended or never saw himself.

So that with an experienced actor, with a good actor, he might say, "Well, look, I see something in this line that's not . . . that you don't see obviously." Now, if it's something that I don't see and it's valuable, by all means. I'm not a shouting director. I don't say, "Do it my way, or else." But I find a way to get around it if I don't agree with what they're doing, if they're going off on a tangent, because an actor has a tendency to make every scene so important. The director has to guide them as one paces a horse.

This scene only is valuable because it leads to this scene, but if this scene is too high, this scene is going to fall on its nose over here. That's the job — to control the actor. I have a technique which seems to work, and that is, you do a take and it's lousy, and you say, "Well, let's do it again for so and so," and you do a third take and you say, "Gee, but you've lost something which you had in that first take."

He says, "What's that?"

And I'd say, "Well, it was so-and-so. . . ." He never had it, of course, but this is what I want. The moment it becomes his idea, something that he did, he jumps on it like a trout going after a fly and says, "Oh yeah, gee, I missed that, didn't I?" He never had it in the first place. But little by little you can build a performance and get the confidence of the actor because I found that if you take all respect, self-respect, away from an actor, you're finished in the scene. You've got to constantly build him up.

COSTA-GAVRAS: I don't like the word *direct* very much because you have much more a relationship of collaborators — of people working together, than a sort of head with someone underneath you. I think that now there is completely a new way of relationship between directors and actors.

It's not anymore that the director tells to the actor, "Now you can do this at this particular time," when you are going to shoot the movie. They work it out before they are going to shoot. What is really important is that when the actor is going to start the shooting he thinks that he is completely responsible for what he is doing, that he thinks it is himself that is doing it, that it comes all from him. In fact, it all comes from a conditioning that the director does beforehand. But once you shoot, he is completely free.

From time to time we have rehearsals. The actor, like the one who plays the part of the seller of figs in *Z*, who has the little birds, he was completely lost; he just couldn't follow the part of the character. And he is a stage actor, so he has a continuous vision of the part. So we had to spend several evenings together to rehearse a scene, go over certain details. You can't really take all the actors together and say, "You have to do it like this." Every actor is a special person and a special character in a particular case.

PAUL MORRISSEY: I don't think Joe Dallesandro ever asks me anything. Just where to go. I tell him to say it very short and sweet and don't think about it. I never like actors to think about what they're doing. At least, I tell them not to think about it. They always do, but it's better to let them think about it themselves than to tell them how to do it.

MARTIN RITT: Discipline is the greatest quality that an actor could have. The actor is so alive that anything that happens affects him. If a door opens off stage and a gust of wind comes through, he will still play the play. That kind of life which is immediate is extraordinary. Every director when he directs a picture hopes that that is going to happen.

There was a moment in *Hud* that wasn't rehearsed. Patricia Neal was talking in the bedroom and her hand bumped into a light bulb. Now being the type of actress that she was at the time, she still played the scene. It's like a great fighter. A great fighter doesn't have to think. He is disciplined so he can do almost anything he wants to do. He does almost anything that he wants to do when the occasion arises. Any great athlete does that. That moment of improvisation is what makes you gasp because that is what it is. With a highly geared, perfected, controlled instrument, suddenly a moment of brilliant improvisation will come because of something that has happened which was not expected.

Whereas,

ROBERTO ROSSELLINI: I give the actor very little room. So they are there trembling, trembling, full of fear, not remembering the dialogue, and I am there pushing, pushing, pushing, but more or less I build what I want to build. Not what they want to build. They basically contribute the reading of lines. It depends on the film, surely. I have another need, you see.

AS YOU LIKE IT . . . OR, LET ME GIVE YOU A FEW EXAMPLES

STANLEY KRAMER: Actors are different, all of them. So any basic rule is ridiculous, it's just ridiculous, unless you're a total czar in personality, not in actuality.

MARTIN RITT: Many directors keep using the same actors. It is easier that way. It is a shortcut. When the actor gets so he understands you, it is just easier to communicate. If you have to start fresh each time, then it is not easy.

PAUL MAZURSKY: Some actors tend to fall back on what they do the best and they tend to be very concerned. Their biggest concern is who's going to direct their next picture. Who's going to take care of me? Who's going to watch out for me? How do I know he won't ruin me? That sort of thing. That does have something to do with making movies. It shouldn't, really, because that's about the star system.

JEAN RENOIR: A picture is a little world. Something very important in life is balance. You must balance all the elements. What is very dangerous in pictures is the fact that when you work with a star, this star became a star because the repetition of the same voice, the same gestures — the public got used to it and the poor soul makes millions but doesn't make anything about talent. To me it's something quite tragic to see a human being repeating, repeating always the same gestures, and those gestures not being even true, not being real, not being the expression of reality.

ABRAHAM POLONSKY: One of the things that you have to work out with actors is to be careful that they don't give you old acting jobs that they've done. Because good actors have played almost everything. Right? But when you ask them to read the part, right away they get a little bit from that one and . . . They've got a filing cabinet, a subconscious filing cabinet, and you get it, and you've got to be very careful not to take that filing cabinet. Because they're very talented people, you've got to make them work. The idea of directing is to make everybody work very hard. Each actor is different, and they demand different techniques. Some are cuddled, some are fought with, some are just talked to, some are marvelous and know before you say. I mean actors are different as human beings.

GEORGE CUKOR: With any actor I would just tell them whatever was wrong with their performance. I will tell you a funny story. Jack Lemmon had done television, but *It Should Happen to You* was the first movie he ever did. It was a picture with Judy Holliday. We were doing a scene. It was a quarrel scene, a funny quarrel scene. When it was over, they did it very well, and I said, "It's all very well and good, but I don't believe a goddamn thing of it." I asked them what they do when they are angry.

Jack Lemmon said, "What do I do when I get angry? I get sick to my stomach."

I said, "Then do that." He did. All the time he was fighting with her he was getting awful cramps.

I don't think there is any set thing that you say to a stage actor who is going to do motion pictures. You say different things to different people. Certain people you have to touch very lightly. A director should know when to talk and when to shut up. You should also know when the scene is going to be as good as it is going to be. That is part of your job. You work one way with certain people and another way with others. Let's say with Rex Harrison and Audrey Hepburn; he was very good in *My Fair Lady*. As some actors are, he was scared on the first take. But, on the second, third, fourth, and fifth, he was great. Audrey Hepburn, on the other hand, was all the better as the takes went on. Usually, when you do a scene, as a matter of courtesy, you always photograph the lady's close-ups first. But, I found it best to do his first, while she was rehearsing, rehearsing all the time.

ROUBEN MAMOULIAN: Communication varies with each actor. What succeeds in one fails with another. You've got to invent custom-made methods of dealing with each actor. Fredric March happens to be a marvelous actor who also is a very intelligent one. With Freddie you can reason. With some of them you can't reason at all, because they don't get it. You have to say, "Do you know how a ripe pear plops down on the ground? That's the way we want you to do it."

"Oh, yes, yes," they say — and they do it, if you give them a figure of speech, or an emotion, or you hypnotize them in a feeling. With Freddie you can discuss it.

BUZZ KULIK: The problem of working with actors is that every actor is a special kind of creature and you have to find the key. There are certain actors — Dick Widmark is a classic example. If we have a scene, very simple, there's a guy here and a girl sitting over there and the requirements are that he's to go over there and try to pick her up, you have to say to Dick Widmark, "Look, Dick, you want to get laid," so that's it.

Now, there are other actors with whom you have to become a psychiatrist. If you were to say those words to them, they would look at you like they don't know what you are talking about, you see. For you to use motivational reasons with Dick Widmark, he'd kill you, because he doesn't know from that stuff either.

Some have to cry, some you have to rub down, some you have to pet, and I'm talking about men as well as women. Each relationship is a different one and if you can find the key, I guess maybe through experience you learn how to treat them. Some, you have to yell at. They will not respond unless you yell at them.

HOWARD HAWKS: John Wayne was a cowboy star getting paid very little; nobody knew him and we made a picture called *Red River*. He is exactly the same now as he was then. I don't handle him any differently. I know what he can do, he can do well, and he does. He's a lot better actor than you think he is. He is not a method actor. He's got his own way of grunting a line. People like it, and he's got a quality that is very good. If he gets upset and starts mumbling to himself, I say, "What the hell's the matter with you?"

And he says, "Well, something's wrong." He doesn't know what's wrong, but he senses that something's wrong, and we fix it up. He works on a very simple thing.

I told him a long time ago that if you make three successful scenes in a picture and don't annoy the audience you'll be a success. In other words, don't try to do something with a scene that isn't there; get it over with as soon as possible. Don't let them remember how bad you were, but when you have a good scene, then really go to it.

I would say he annoys an audience less than any actor I know because he doesn't make any attempt to do things.

Now, Cary Grant is one of the best actors that I know of, and a great personality. He does something and says, "How was that?"

You say, "Pretty dull. The way you get mad is just like anybody else. Can't you find a new way to get mad?" We try eight ways and all of a sudden he begins to whinny like a horse and I O.K. that.

But you make use of the personality of the people. That's why some of them have lasted such a long time. They have something that you can use.

MARTIN RITT: Behavior sometimes is not physical. That is very important to remember. Also what you physically do is terribly important. Some people feel that Dustin Hoffman's performance in *Midnight Cowboy* was external. He chose certain characterization things and he relied on those to illuminate his character.

Not every actor works from the inside out. Some work from the outside in. There is no one way to work. That aspect of behavior is terribly important. The physical aspect is important. What do you choose to do? How do you choose to make up? How do you choose to walk? All of those items are terribly important.

When the inner life of a character is portrayed along with the physical aspect, then you can have a great performance. . . .

When I work with an actor I may have an idea that he can't do. I have only worked with one or two actors in my life with whom I felt completely free in asking them to do anything because I felt they could do it. If the actor can't do it, I have to find another way. Whatever idea I have has to be related to the reality of who the actor or actress is. If I can't get what I really want, then I have to try to get it as close to what I want as the actor or the actress can do.

VINCENT SHERMAN: Bette Davis, after about the third or fourth day of shooting on *Old Acquaintance*, came to me. Henry Blanke, the producer, had told me, "Whatever you are doing with Davis, keep it that way. It's the most wonderful performance that she has ever given, because she's not acting, she's just being herself. Just keep her like that."

Davis, on the other hand, said to me at the end of a day's shooting after I told her how happy Blanke was, "I'm glad everybody likes it. But at the end of a day, I just feel like I've done nothing. I just haven't acted at all."

I realized that the truth was that she hadn't been creating a character outside of herself. She had just been playing herself very simply without being wrought up inside with some neurotic problem. It was a new experience for her.

VINCENTE MINNELLI: There are many ways to deal with actors. Sometimes you will insist, and sometimes you will cajole. Sometimes they need great reassurance, and you have to give them that. Fred Astaire, for instance, always needed enormous reassurance because he never thought he was any good. And he was marvelous. It was easy to reassure him.

I always pay great attention to extras. I take great care in selecting them very carefully and make them do things that they ordinarily wouldn't have to do. The assistant director would say, "Now, you stand there against the lamppost and pinch your nose or something and begin to be cold," and that was it. But I would make them work, and so they were always having to adjust and asking more money for doing it.

MICHAEL WINNER: Charlie Bronson, whom I adore, came in on *Chato's Land*, and he had to cut free a naked Indian; she was naked in the proper version. The version shown in America was cut to ribbons and emasculated. But his wife was staked out naked, tied to a rope, in order to entice him back to rescue her. He came on the set, and I said, "What you do here is you crawl on your stomach through this bush, and you cut the rope, you see."

He said, "I'm not going to do that."

I said, "I beg your pardon . . . page ninety-three . . . crawls on stomach . . . very clear."

He said, "I don't appear on the screen with a naked woman."

I said, "I beg your pardon . . . page ninety-three . . . wife is naked tied to rope, you know."

He said, "I don't appear on the screen with a naked woman."

I said, "Oh."

He said, "Have you just put this scene in?"

I said, "Oh, page ninety-three, it's been there for years . . . in on the first version, that was." So, I thought, *Well, I can't argue about this,* so I said, "All right, take the naked woman away." This poor girl, who was waiting for her big moment to be cut free, was promptly put in a towel and carried away.

I said, "Crawl through these bushes, sir, cut the rope." But we only saw the top of the stake, and when the film was cut together, you see the girl lying naked and she looks up and Bronson appears and cuts the rope. Looks like exactly the same thing, you see.

So there's normally a way around it. Something like that's a personal thing which you don't necessarily agree with, but there's no point in having a lot of arguments about page ninety-three, you know.

FEAR AND TREMBLING

JIRI WEISS: I have a friend, a producer of Alfred Hitchcock's *39 Steps*. He told me a story how Hitchcock could not get Madeleine Carroll to exclaim this horror after opening the door. And she was really a good actress. She was a star. So they were shooting it for the tenth time, eleventh, fourteenth, sixteenth, seventeenth time. Finally, she opens the door — wide. There is sitting Hitchcock with his legs apart, displaying those parts you show only to the most intimate. She screamed. I have not done such a thing but I believe in shooting the human being, to be very near the actor.

RONALD NEAME: I feel that the director's principal job is to make absolutely certain that the very best of what these difficult but God-given creatures can do with their performances shall be presented up there and not lost in the first place by the director wanting to be clever and wanting to star himself and, in the second place, by the film not being professionally shot so that it can be joined in a way that will allow for everything that the actor or actress has done to be used.

OSCAR WILLIAMS: You've got to know these things; you've got to feel these things. One actor said in rehearsals, "I can't do that, I'm going home, I'm going back to New York."

So I just said, "Don't move a nail, don't lift a hammer until he comes back." I put it on him. He came back.

It's just feeling for people and having a knowledge of them and feeling as if you were feeling yourself. But, you can't let it take you to a position where you are pushed out, aced out, or stepped on and you lose respect in front of crew and cast. The minute that you do that you are finished. They won't believe you; they won't listen to you. They won't do what you say. You often find when you talk about a film that everyone wants to do it from his perspective. But the director has to look at the whole view. He has got to know that a certain actor or action has got to move at a certain pace. The actors have been doing their numbers, and what you have to do is scale that down so that it fits. They're ready to give that big performance all the time. So the director has to keep that view of the film because he is hired for his overall view of the whole thing. They hire him to tell the story on film.

RICHARD ATTENBOROUGH: Every actor without exception that I know, of any sort of caliber whatsoever, is terrified. I don't care who they are or what caliber they are or where they come from or what their background is — deep inside they are apprehensive, they are nervous, they are lacking in confidence. They may cover it with the most extraordinary show of confidence and bravura and pomp and ridiculous behavior or tears or sweat or whatever there is. The truth is that they are immensely nervous because they are unprepared. When you work privately in the theatre, you don't mind making a fool of yourself, you don't mind experimenting, you're with just the players and so there is a freedom, there is a lack of having to present. But the moment you go on the floor with not only the crew but other people on the set too and somebody shouts, "Quiet," and you've got to present your wares.

RONALD NEAME: Actors are a special breed of people. Alec Guinness and I were making a film called *Tunes of Glory* several years ago. At the end of about the first week he was very sulky. He was very low and miserable and grumpy and irritable. I said, "Alec, what's the matter? We're all trying very hard and you seem so miserable and depressed and it's getting us all down. We feel as though we're not getting a good picture and that you don't like any of us. Is there anything I can do?"

He said, "You know, Ronnie, I have been working on this picture for nearly two weeks and not once has anybody ever said to me, 'Alec, you are really very, very good. We think you are marvelous.' "

I said, "Well, good gracious, Alec, we think that you are marvelous. What we are trying to do is live up to you. We have taken it for granted that you know we think you are marvelous."

He said, "Ronnie, I have to tell you something about actors."

I said that I would be delighted to listen because I found them quite difficult to understand.

He said, "All so-called normal people, so-called ordinary people, want to act between the age of about ten and fourteen. They want to put on wigs or fancy clothes, or in the case of girls put on lipstick and all this kind of thing. Then at about the age of fourteen they grow up through this period of wanting to act and they become clerks or lawyers or engine drivers or pilots or what have you. But," he said, "the actor in the part of his mind that can act, always remains permanently an adolescent in this area of his mind. You must believe this is so, because it is so. It is also very difficult. Take me, for example, I am a pretty intelligent fellow. I am a well-read fellow. I'm an intellectual and this, that, and the other. But nevertheless when it comes to the acting, I am still a child. So when dealing with actors you have to remember this. You always have to have it in this part of your mind so that you remember that: you remember that we need praising. We need to be encouraged and patted on the back when we have done well. But equally, we need discipline. We need to be smartly put down if we go too far. If you would regard us as you would regard an eleven- or twelve-year-old child, then you will find that you can manage and handle us."

GEORGE CUKOR: I've had experience when there's a wonderful scene being played that's terrifying, that the actor is either scared or forgets his lines. But not this young man, he went after her, and he had a long, very important scene in which he shamed her. And then she did something extraordinary. This was quite a long speech he had. She turned around and you saw that all the anger, all the madness, all the fear has disappeared. It showed this lovely, tender, sweet look in her face, very vulnerable, her eyes filled with tears. Then I said, "Quick, we'll do it once more."

So they got her ready, dried her off. I find one of the hazards of pictures is that you get a scene and get it very well, and the next morning they tell you it was scratched in the lab or the sound didn't get it. So I said, "Let's do it immediately."

She did it. She did it differently, but wonderfully. Scenes can never be repeated; you shouldn't try to reproduce them exactly. They must have that sense of freshness: "Let's see how it comes out."

When it was over, I said, "You scared the hell out of me." She was very pleased because she didn't know what effect she'd made.

Always funny, always funny, she said, "Oh, that's not much; come to my house any afternoon, I do it every afternoon. But I can only do it once at home."

ROMAN POLANSKI: Acting requires total concentration and total relaxation, and you have to combine those together and to appear relaxed, and yet to remember the various things that you have to do: to remember your lines, to remember the marks, to remember the shadows and a hundred other little things which require tremendous concentration. You also have to concentrate on believing more or less the character you are acting at that moment. Usually an actor does it just before the clapper-board strikes in front of him and he doesn't even realize that there is a clapper-board. He doesn't think, also, whether the other actors are exactly on their marks, or if their lines are in the wrong places.

JACK NICHOLSON: If a scene wasn't working, I walked over and got into a conversation about it. You see if there's anything that can be said. Most actors' problems, professional or amateur, deal with tension and there are a lot of devices and ways of eliminating it. First, you've got to point the tension out to them and get them to acknowledge that it's there. Most of the people in my film were cast because they were right for the roles, so problems of characterization didn't come up that often. In a very professional actor, someone like Bruce Dern or Karen Black, the tension is because they haven't made a choice that has taken enough of their mental interest. In other words, they haven't made a vital enough choice; it's not up to a level that will engage their imagination and get them into pretending unselfconsciously.

Very often tension is from holding something out rather than something that's coming in on you. In other words, you're creating more tension because you don't want to think about your next thing, how bad it's going to be when you get there. Just keep it moving, what is it, go with it, deal with it. A real problem is shading. Actors don't like to play unpopular emotions. I had a hard time in the scene in *Five Easy Pieces* that involved the fight with Spencer. At the end of it my character was kind of pitiful. I don't mind getting the shit kicked out of me in the scene, but then to have to be laying around after it. It's the kind of thing that you just feel weird about doing. You know when you're doing it right, you're still going to look like a dumper on the screen.

Karen Black's role in *Drive, He Said* involved a woman in a disintegrating relationship. She, being the older woman, has more vision about what's actually happening so she's more active in it. It seems to be she who was saying "no" all the time. That made Karen, not wanting to be a bitch, ask: "Give me something, you know what I mean, so I'm not so hostile all the time." Sometimes she would be too hostile in scenes and that's a problem in shading. If you can tell Karen what it is, she can play it. In other words, if you don't get a performance from her, that's your own fault because anything you can say, she can do, and she's phenomenal in this way. If you say, "Do these eighteen things," you get it right now. It doesn't matter how extreme, how unmotivated. If you can say it, you can get it. With her, very often, it was just a case of explaining what my point of view about the character was.

PAUL MAZURSKY: The toughest ones to work with are actors who are coming in for one day to do one scene. You're all worried about the schedule and don't want to go two days if you can help it. The actor, at the moment of truth, who was relaxed and fun and great in the office, gets unsettled and nervous. He doesn't know the lines or is uptight, or something is wrong. I try a lot of different things. I try to make them forget. I try sometimes to get people away from the set. I try, sometimes, to improvise a little. I use a lot of different things, and sometimes they don't work. Those are the hardest things to do.

RALPH NELSON: Many directors say that actors are like children, and I disagree with that. It's the actors who are in front of that camera and the good actors, the professional actors — usually those two are synonymous words — are the trained racehorses. They're nervous and skittish. They're high-strung. It's my job to make it as easy as possible for them and to try and get their complete confidence in me because I'm there as their sole audience until the film is in release.

IRVIN KERSHNER: It is very simple. You give them love, and you give them confidence. You give an actor that self-assurance by giving him confidence in himself and in yourself. You take away fears. That is what it amounts to.

MODES OF COMMUNICATION

JOHN CASSAVETES: First you form a relationship with the actors, an alliance, that you're working together. And then you can beat them or hit them or be nice or they can be nice to you. Because they respect you. And you respect them. I find it unnecessary to say, "You stunk, you were terrible in that take," and I don't find that very creative. You say, "Look, here's a guy and he's going to run away," and you bring them into the story. And then you write off of that.

GEORGE CUKOR: The director has an enormous advantage of seeing the performance. The actor is involved and the director sees it. I think that she is depending upon my reaction. I can say, "Yes, that's great. I believe that. I think that was beautifully played." I don't think she would kill herself if I said that it wasn't right. I think that with every actor and every actress, they should feel that there is somebody out there who sits and will tell the actor if he has done something good. Also, he should know that if he has done something wrong he will know about that too. But directing isn't just that. With inexperienced people, the director can do a little coaching and a little unsnarling of things. But I think that a director sees things and can influence and lead performances.

In *Bill of Divorcement*, I taught Katharine Hepburn a hell of a lot. She was an inexperienced actress, but very talented. She had no experience on the screen. She didn't know what that was. I must say that she was at home the first day that she got on the set. She was perfectly at ease. Although she goes back to the theatre and likes it a great deal, she is still a creature of the pictures. I think she had a rather tough time learning her job on the stage. I think she had three or four rather struggling years. But, the moment that she came on the screen, she seemed perfectly at home.

Of course, she had to be taught certain things. It was extraordinary. The first picture that I did with her, she was very clumsy. She played the part with a great deal of feeling, but it still wasn't quite right. After that she did another picture and by the time we got to *Little Women,* she knew what she was doing.

Judy Holliday had been very active on the stage. She really didn't know. The first day we shot we were downtown on a street in New York. She was scared and she couldn't do anything. She was supposed to hit a certain mark and she couldn't hit it. She was still playing in *Born Yesterday* on the stage, and she said, "I can get you tickets for the crew."

I asked her why.

She said, "I don't want them to think that I am such an idiot." But they were all clever girls and they learned quickly. The longer they are on, the more they know.

JACK NICHOLSON: My main problem was that *Drive, He Said* is a college film; it takes place on a college campus. Usually they cast people a good deal older than college in these films, but I wanted to do it with people that were that age. I had a lot of people in the film who had done no acting whatsoever and people who had done a lot of acting. The problem was really a question of keeping an even working balance for all of the people because their problems would be very different in any given scene; I was glad, being in that situation, that I was an actor.

I'm happy with the performances: I think they're even. Everyone looks like they're in the same reality. It's not one style of acting over here and one over there. Everyone seems like they're living in the same environment, which they were. It's the advantage of shooting on location: they're forced to live with one another.

JACQUES DEMY: I speak a lot to the actor about the character he or she is portraying. Generally, actors are great talkers. They love to speak. When you talk with them you get a lot of ideas on what you want to try. It is very important to get together with the actors over dinner or lunch and just talk about the parts. It's playing, but it's not kids playing.

LEO MCCAREY: I talk to them a lot. I spend a lot of time discussing things with actors. I spend a lot of time discussing the scene.

PAUL MORRISSEY: I try to avoid talk at all costs. If I thought somebody wanted to talk to me about their part, I'd probably never hire them in the first place. I just prefer not to deal with it. Let other people work with it. It creates a kind of introspection that's heavy-handed. You lose the spontaneity when you realize somebody's thinking the hell out of their part.

FRITZ LANG: I think you have to work with an actor as you would work with yourself. You have to explain to him how you see the character that he has to put on the screen. You cannot use him. Maybe he is right and you have to think it over. Maybe he is wrong. There's something which you should get out from an actor, something which is under his skin, something which he himself maybe doesn't know exactly. I hate — and I never did — to show an actor how to play a role. I don't want to have twenty-five little Fritz Langs running around. I have too much respect for an actor.

STEVEN SPIELBERG: Usually the actor entertains a totally different concept of the movie, and that's where many of the battles begin. And I think that the director's first accomplishment, if he ever accomplishes this, is to get the actor to understand the director's vision of the piece. If the actor can't understand it that way, then you shouldn't hire the actor. Unfortunately, the way the business is structured, all the idealism is taken out of it. And if somebody gives you a picture to do with Steve McQueen, well, you're going to direct the picture Steve McQueen's way or you're going to withdraw your services.

STANLEY KRAMER: I have the flexibility, and that's why I feel that I can make contact with the actor because I come to the set fully prepared, if he wants, to lead him by the hand. I also come fully prepared to say, "Let's see how you feel it." Sometimes he feels it better than I do and sometimes I have to give him range.

There are some people who can take advantage of that if you aren't strong. The young actor who comes from a certain school can say, "I haven't the proper motivation to come in that door and cross to the table." That can drive you right out of your mind.

One day we were rehearsing a scene, and I had a young actor, and we went on and I was being very patient and nice and letting him work out his motivations. Once we cleared the set so he could sit alone on the set and figure it out. All he had to do was come in and cross to a table and wait for the entrance of another actor. He said, "I don't dig it. Why the hell do I come in the room that way?"

Finally, Spencer Tracy said, "You come in the friggin' room because it's the only way to get into the room and you go to the friggin' table because that's the place in the middle of the room and that's where the director wants you to go, and you wait for the guy to come in, that's what you do. See?"

Well, Tracy really wasn't that crude and he really didn't mean it when they asked him in Berlin at the world premiere of *Nuremberg* what advice he had for young actors — it's now seemingly apocryphal but isn't — and he said the best thing for young actors is to learn their lines and try not to bump into the furniture. It isn't a bad definition. He maybe seemed overly practical or overly simplified but really what he meant was to play it *au naturel*.

HASKELL WEXLER: I don't think that there is any magic in it. I do think there is a lot to learn from someone like Elia Kazan or someone who is dramatically oriented about acting, but I don't think that there is much to learn about communicating. There is not a big mystical thing about communicating with actors. If you can communicate this idea to a person who happens to be an actor, then you are a director. The thing with being a director with acting-oriented experience is that it does give you a language that people who act for a long time have developed. It's sort of a shorthand. They say, "Use this." Or they have certain semi-Freudian terms which actors use to describe how they do things. And I suppose that it would be of value to know those things, especially if you have an experienced actor who comes up to you to discuss a certain thing.

JAN KADAR: To work with an actor you have to be like a doctor. You are a psychiatrist at one moment, a friend, a lover, everything. When an actress is doing something and is looking at you, you are the only audience. If she sees a poker face, the actress will be lost. She has to see in your eyes whether it works or not.

RICHARD ATTENBOROUGH: You must never humiliate an actor. I believe there should be an atmosphere of secret dedication on the floor. You are creating something. You are displaying human emotions, emotions which are not easy to talk about, and if the actor is true, they bear a relation to his own emotions and his own experiences. And you must have an affair with your actors. You really must. They must adore you and you must adore them and you must want to work with them, want to create with them, and those who will do that, I believe, will get the best perfor-mance, and I believe those laughers and the roarers get nothing. I really don't believe they come up with it. I never give any direction from behind the camera, ever. I always go through to the actor. I always try and talk to the actor. The actor does feel that there really is a communication be-tween you and him and that that communication is absolutely vital both to you and to him. He gets fired by, one hopes, your excitement and your enthusiasm, and so you end up to a great extent with those who believe that performances are created on the floor, and those who believe that anybody can create a performance from an actor with a Moviola. I happen to be very much the former.

PETER BOGDANOVICH: I'll tell you something. I think that actors and actresses always carry on affairs with their directors. Climbing into bed with each other has nothing to do with it. It's a *real* love affair. It's the only way to create an atmosphere where they're comfortable. They have to feel at home. They do what I want them to do, but they don't feel like puppets. Cloris Leachman said something like, "You are a puppet when you work with Peter, but he makes you feel as though you're handling your own strings."

JOHN CASSAVETES: I think if you are an actor, first of all, you are set aside from a director. You basically don't like directors, but the director shouldn't worry about that. That's number one. Any director who worries about whether or not an actor likes him is crazy, because it's never going to happen. It will happen as the result of being finished, seeing the work, and then if he has time, he'll say, "O.K." Half of the problem that a director has is he's not only trying to adjust to the actors, but to the technicians, to the front office, and to the financial problems that are existent. He doesn't address himself to the problem of what it is he's trying to say.

I don't think it really has anything to do with liking somebody. I've liked directors that I thought were terrible. You can go out and have drinks with them, and they are really nice guys. You feel sorry for them because they don't have more talent. You hope they can work more, because their livelihood depends on it. I think a guy like Roman Polanski is enormously talented as a director. Even if I didn't like him personally, I'd like to work with him. If there was some way to work with a guy and not like him personally, then I'd work with him anytime.

FEDERICO FELLINI: I just use him for what he can give to me physically. I try to help him, if you like, with certain shots. But working with actors, I like it if they participate in a very strong way in what we are doing. It is a different system. Or sometimes even when working with some people who are not actors, I pretend they are something deeper than a professional or a physical work. I pretend there is something that he feels inside; I pretend to talk to know him; I want him to become the character. In that case, the cooperation is much the stronger.

ROBERTO ROSSELLINI: I give them their dialogue at the last second. I am so scared of actors that I prefer to give them the dialogue at the last minute, so I do not have to make the tremendous effort to demolish what they have thought.

TALENT AT THE CORE — INSTINCT, INTELLIGENCE, IDEAS

NICHOLAS RAY: A director cannot breathe talent into an actor, no matter how large his [sic] ego.

RONALD NEAME: I should tell you that I worked with Alfred Hitchcock on the first talking picture that he ever made in England. I worked on silent films, and I worked with Hitch on the first talking picture. I was an assistant cameraman. I know him very well. Now, Hitchcock regards actors in this way. As he says, they are puppets.* He pulls them around on strings. Of course, it may be so in the case of the film that relies entirely on suspense and on its situation. That, very often, is what a Hitchcock picture is. But the moment that you go into any kind of depth of character, then the actor to me is the most important element and must be catered for entirely.

JAMES BRIDGES: The guy who plays Ford in *The Paper Chase*, the first day on the set, he was so terrified. He had done one little bit before at Harvard, but here he was walking into a close-up, and he was so scared. We started at about three o'clock in the afternoon, and I couldn't get a

---

*Author's note — it should be stated here that regardless of Hitchcock's "actors are puppets" alleged attitude, many of his films are marked by their consistently fine, deep, and feeling performances. One need only point to James Stewart and Kim Novak in *Vertigo*, Ingrid Bergman in *Under Capricorn* and *Notorious*, and numerous others.

thing out of him. It was just terrible, and it got worse and worse. Finally, I printed about the eighth or ninth take, and I said, "You're terrific. The baptism in the fire is over. Go home and have a wonderful time and get drunk."

So he left, and when he came back in the morning I told him we had had a sound problem and that I was going to have to reshoot his scene. He said, "Fine." I didn't even look at it. I know that if you can talk to them, you can direct them if they respond, pretty much. It's only if they're too intelligent that you get into trouble. I think actors shouldn't be too intelligent. Because films don't have anything to do with intelligence.

HOWARD HAWKS: The newcomers get a lot of help from the pros, and John Wayne has been that all the time. The first picture I made with him was *Red River*. We had a new boy, Montgomery Clift, and after the first scene Wayne said, "This kid is all right," and he took an interest in him. He didn't mind working with him. He didn't mind my changing Clift around and trying it a different way, and then trying it still another way. Wayne will do anything to make a better picture. He is one of the most helpful people that I know.

When I hired Clift, it was his first picture; he had never made a picture before. We took one look at him and Wayne said, "Couldn't you have gotten somebody who could stand up to me a little bit?"

I said, "I think he can stand up to you pretty well," and he said, "I don't know." We made the very first scene and Wayne came over to me and said, "That kid is going to be good." He said, "He looks like he is just figuring that he can take me apart at any time and isn't worried about it." He looked a little like a Remington sketch of the two gunmen — a little wisp of a man leaning against a post chewing a straw, looking as though he were very capable. Wayne said one thing: "We can't have a fight."

"Why?"

"It would be silly."

"Well," I said, "you're a lot bigger and it would be silly, but it wouldn't be silly if you tripped and he kicked you in the face first."

"O.K., let him kick me in the face." And we did it that way and it made a perfectly good fight. We had an awful time because Monty Clift couldn't throw a punch; it took us three days.

JEAN RENOIR: I tell you a little story. It was during the shooting of my picture, *La Grande Illusion*.

You remember at the end Gabin and Dalio are walking in the snow, and Dalio is wounded. He had had a little accident and was limping, and he couldn't go farther. It was impossible. Well, I had written two pages of beautiful literature to explain the situation. Gabin was, you know, like a poet, explaining about what's good, what's bad in nature, no nature. It was fantastic. I was so proud of myself. And I was a little worried because the two actors, Dalio and Gabin, they didn't want to start the scene. They were finding reasons to do something else. Finally Gabin told me, "Jean, we'd better tell you, your two pages of beautiful poetry are just trash and we cannot say it." Which was true.

I was embarrassed because the snow — it was the end of the snow season and I had to finish this sequence as fast as I could — finally I had an idea — oh, perhaps Dalio had the idea, perhaps Gabin. He was humming a tune I already used in the beginning of the picture, "The Little Sailor." I took those very innocent words and they became the center of the scene. And the scene is good, I think. But without the reluctance of Dalio, without my belief in the help the actors bring you, I would have nothing. Nothing. Oh, I would have a perfectly drawn and conceived scene, but dull.

Now, that explains my point of view with actors. In other words, you must not ask an actor what he cannot do. You know, there is an old slogan very successful in our occidental civilization. It is that you must look to an end higher than normal. That way you will do something. But your aim must be very very high. Myself, I am absolutely convinced that it is mere stupidity. The aim must be easy to reach. And by reaching it you do more. You do much more. The trouble with us human beings is that we are often very stupid. Things are in front of us, we don't see them. An actress rehearses with a beautiful face full of emotion — you don't see it. You think of your camera angle. I'm not for that.

CARL REINER: Hopefully, you will get a creative actor to work with you. It is good to work with actors who think. They are going to read a script and they are going to bring something to it. Now, you let them make their choice. I always let them make their choices first. If their choices don't bump into the choices of the other actors, who might be right or wrong, then you let them have them. If you don't like their choices, you say, "Hey, if you continue to do that, then this whole scene won't work. If you are going to play angry in this scene, then it won't work because we don't want the audience to know that you feel this way." When you don't like their choice, then you try to do a rearranging of attitudes.

GEORGE CUKOR: Very often I say to an actor, "You think you're thinking, but you're not really thinking." A lot of these people think they're being individual, but they're really aping rather blindly what is the key to success at that moment. For starters, it's awfully good to have talent. Then you've got to learn, and you've got to be intelligent and disciplined. Sometimes when people have talent and they don't nurture it, it's destroyed. Certain people start with enormous promise that is not just the bloom of youth and they just become goddamned dull. I can't help thinking a lot of people haven't got the theatre or movie intelligence probably to nurture their talent. I see people and I think, "Why isn't so-and-so a big success. They should be." On the other hand, other people keep on and change and develop. I think it's in intelligence.

LASLO BENEDEK: Complete control . . . You see the delight, the pleasure of a director is with an actor like Max von Sydow. You can rehearse and rehearse and you try things and you say, "Well, I have an idea, why don't you try so-and-so . . . ?" And then he does it. Finally you agree, he and I together, or he and the director, agree that perhaps this is the best way. Now, Max will do it exactly the same timing, the same movements, the same look, the same way.

He knows the lights. On a scene I was making before, when he pulled the curtain aside to fill light the first girl and he looked, the one eye I wanted on one light, and the other light. . . . I looked through the camera and told him, "A little more, little more . . . no, this is it . . . now, fix yourself a point . . . how far you are going to come out of the curtain, where you are going to look at . . . ?" He said O.K. He could do it a hundred times the same way. But the point is that he doesn't get mechanical, and that's just the technical part of it. But he is also emotionally under complete control. He can play a scene as high or as low as we want to and keep it.

JACK NICHOLSON: My point of view is that your job is to give the director what he wants ultimately, no matter what it is. That has cost me a couple of times, but I think it's the only way to do. And if you disagree you bring it to him. You're like a nerve ending or a feeler for the director. The director is not a mysterious figure; they don't really figure everything out. A really good actor brings a lot of information back in. Actors come up to me and say things that are fabulous. I would never think of them, and they just do them. I feel that the actor, if he's in conflict with the material, just simply brings that argument to the director, espouses it for as long as it's creative, and then after he's done that, he does what the director decides that they should do. That's the way I always work. Usually they're right, I have found.

MICHAEL WINNER: I've never known a star who didn't listen to some reason. I've never known a greedy star. I've found the main trouble with stars is that they try to take their lines out, that they don't want to say things which they feel might not be essential. I think a real star — and I think that the stars that I've had have been real stars, thank God — is very helpful.

IMPROVISATION

NICHOLAS RAY: Improvisation has to be worked out as carefully as a three-act play. It has to have all of the elements of conflict and surprise.

HOWARD HAWKS: It isn't really improvisation. It is just trying to get the actors to be natural.

JACQUES DEMY: I like improvisation when it is good. I do like to see a film that has been improvised. But, it is very difficult to get something good all the time that way. I have seen so many films where the improvisation is quite bad. For me it wouldn't work. Therefore, I like the dialogue. With dialogue I think you can act marvelously. You have to make the dialogue alive, and not dead. When you write you are improvising as well. You are always improvising. Even when you think of something and you are telling it to someone, you are improvising. So, I prefer to write it down and then if necessary I will change it.

JOHN CASSAVETES: There's a difference between ad-libbing and improvising. And there's a difference between not knowing what to do and just saying something. Or making choices as an actor. As a writer also, as a person who's making a film, as a cameraman, everything is a choice. And it seems to me I don't really have to direct anyone or write down that somebody's getting drunk; all I have to do is say that there's a bottle there and put a bottle there and then they're going to get drunk. I don't want to tell them how they're going to get drunk, or what they would do, and I don't want to restrict them in being able to carry out a beat, to fulfill an action. You can't say somebody's drunk, or in love.

It always struck me when I used to go see pictures as a kid at Times Square that when it came to the love scenes everybody used to boo. But once in a while, you see a picture like *Red Shoes,* and no matter how tough the audience was, they would root for the love story because the whole picture was a love story. And these people didn't pretend to be in love with each other. Somehow it insults the audience when you're supposed to be in love with each other, and you open your mouth and they swap spits; it doesn't make any sense because they're not doing anything; they're two strangers getting together feeling very nervous.

"Is that all right?" they say after the take. "Was my mouth open too far?" or "How do I look nude?" All you're doing is overcoming some kind of embarrassment or feeling free that way. But to dig deeply into the way things are through people is what I like, and what the people who work with me like also. To find out the delicate balance between living and dying. I mean, I think that's the only subject there is.

ROBERT ALTMAN: *California Split* was improvised in rehearsals but when we actually got to doing the thing, it became fairly set. The background characters, we used all of Synanon for extras. Alan Rudoph, who was one of the assistants with me, worked very closely with those people. He'd set up a whole kind of life with them, and I didn't even know what was going to happen necessarily. He would come and ask me if there was going to be anything that he knew was going to change something. He'd say, "Is that going to be all right?" I would deal mainly with the two or three people that I was dealing with and then we'd say, "Go," and all this stuff would start happening around and yet our people were still responding with what they do. It's improvised but it's much more controlled than it appears to be or than most people think it is. We always knew what the intention of the scene was.

In many cases, they were written very specifically. The deviations from that are just the things that grow within. You set a boundary, really, and you say, "O.K., as long as you stay within these boundaries, it's O.K. When you start getting out and carrying the thing somewhere else, then we have to stop it."

FEDERICO FELLINI: It's absolutely impossible to improvise. Making a movie is a mathematical operation. It is like sending a missile to the moon. It isn't improvised. It is too defined to be called improvisational, too mechanical. Art is a scientific operation, so I can say that what we usually call improvisation is in my case just having an ear and an eye for things that sometimes occur during the time we are making the picture. In that sense I think to be strictly faithful to what you have written four or five months before is a little bit silly sometimes. If you see that the picture is suggesting something new, I think that one has to be open to this kind of suggestion because sometimes it is the picture that directs you when you work in an open and honest way. That is not improvisation; that is just being faithful to what you are doing. Improvisation has nothing to do with that kind of work.

GEORGE CUKOR: In *Little Women* they don't improvise it. They don't make up the words as they go along. This was a very respectable script. They learned the words. They didn't do a lot of goddamned nonsense. I can hear it when I see pictures when the actors go, "Eh, eh, oh, yes, well . . ." They are improvising. It tends to be disorderly and undisciplined. I think that if the actors are good and if the director is good, when you see a scene like that and it seems unnatural, then you can say, "I don't believe it really." When they are in the saddle, they play it. That is the part of a talented actor. He makes it seem as though he hadn't spoken it before.

ROUBEN MAMOULIAN: I believe in overall design. It's quite fashionable, I hear it so frequently, the fellow says, "Oh, I go on the set and I improvise." That's ridiculous. Improvisation is for the birds and for the amateurs. You don't improvise a statue or a painting. If you do it isn't much good. Michelangelo put it best when he said that he does not conceive of anything. He looks at a block of marble and, he says, he looks at it long enough until he sees the shape. From then on, he says, "I just take everything superfluous off and disclose what's in that stone." That to me is a marvelous recipe. You see the whole design, a shape. I'm talking about what to me would be the full flowering of a screen work. It isn't that you can't do it other ways. But the other ways, they're just not the full flowering of the screen potential.

ALFRED HITCHCOCK: Each shot must make a point. You know, people often say to one, "Well, don't you ever improvise on the set?" I say, "Certainly not. I will improvise in the office. That's the place to improvise, long before you go onto a stage." Why, improvising in the set is like a composer composing with a full orchestra in front of him, and saying, "Flute, will you give me a note?" And he gives him an A, and he puts it down. That shows you how stupid that process is.

JOHN CASSAVETES: It doesn't matter if the words are written, because improvisation has been going on in films by everybody. There's nobody that doesn't improvise to some degree. So it just depends on what degree you need.

VILGOT SJÖMAN: Last time, I had a couple of actors who liked improvising. That meant that you wrote the script during a period of three months. That is, we started to hear discussion, figure out the main idea, and started working on the scenes and the sequences. For instance, this opening sequence, how are we going to have it? Let's go and start and do some bit of rehearsing and improvising and that gives you new ideas that you incorporate in the thing.

PAUL WILLIAMS: Originally, you start reading through the whole thing, picking different texts. And then once you start figuring out your plan, you can start breaking it into units and doing that. The other thing is using rehearsals not as rehearsals, but using it really as script-writing time. In other words, I would write all of the dialogue in the script, but I don't know if a single word of this stuff is going to come out on the screen. I take the people, put them into situations, improvise, get it on tape, and we will rewrite the scenes, and in that sense there is a tremendous carry-over. When you get on the set, you are now dealing with a scene that was a product of improvisation, and it's now in words. It's amazing how those things come out.

PAUL MORRISSEY: In *Trash*, I found myself having to improvise where normally the actors would improvise. I always made up the story each day anyway, but now I had to make up the dialogue, too, and have it typed up by a secretary. I think the secretary made up most of the dialogue. I can't remember exactly. I said, "She said this and he did that." She typed it up and she handed me a whole bunch of this stuff, which was really very good. When I made up the credits, she said, "I made up so much dialogue, you should have given me some credit."

I said, "I forgot all about it. I didn't mean to take all the credit." I sort of improvised the dialogue, made up a lot of lines, and the secretary added to them and the script was typed up during the early morning, between nine and ten-thirty or eleven, when they set up the lights for the first shot.

It always takes two hours for the first shot — I don't know why — even in Italy, where they're very quick. Of course, I made the films in four weeks, but there was plenty of time to type up a whole scene for the actors to memorize. So I kind of forced into these films the carelessness of the earlier films. In those, the actors were given the scenes and they had some key lines to say, then they rambled in and out of those lines and I just followed with the camera. It was like a documentary of acting, really, not these rehearsed situations which become improvised. I never like that. I always prefer the improvisation that happens.

I used to like how we did it with Andy Warhol, where we wouldn't cut any of it. Like on *Chelsea Girls*, we'd leave the entire half-hour shot. We wouldn't take anything out. I think those films are quite interesting but whenever I see improvisation in the recent films, I find I don't like it at all. I don't know why. There's a funny discipline involved in improvisation that's very difficult to achieve. If we had any success with it, it's because we did it so many times, over and over again.

JOHN CASSAVETES: As the director of *Husbands*, I went under the assumption that sooner or later Peter Falk would know what he was doing, and sooner or later Ben Gazzara would know what he was doing, and we'd wait it out until we did know what we were doing. Then, that would be close to what the characters would want to express, for whatever reasons.

I was shocked by Peter's choices. I mean, it really surprised me that he would go off in a certain direction.

What happens is, everything is strength. How much strength do you have? Before you get to improvise on any kind of level, we would have to know that no matter what we did, we would be O.K. We had to know the material that well. We could improvise the rehearsal and come out great. We all have the instinct that if we got in front of the camera that that kind of delicate improvisation without any theatricality would lose some of its ease. All of a sudden there would be cameras, cables, guys around, people saying, "We can't move this thing over there," and suddenly the actors would receive very little importance.

And you start to fight to preserve what you have and you start pushing, and all of a sudden, it's gone. What had been terribly concentrated in rehearsals would dissipate. So I found that by writing scenes that we might never use, and writing them again and again and again, that everything that we had written and improvised was, therefore, in our minds, used and usable. We had investigated, then studied it. We knew what we were capable of saying to each other and doing with each other, so we got to the point where we could just give any kind of improvisation.

MARTIN RITT: If I insist that they improvise, first of all there would be some actors who would totally reject the idea, and they will never get free enough to function. My problem is how to get him free enough to function, not to make him work in my way. I have to adapt what my training is to make him work. If improvisation was not practical, then I would never do it.

In early films with Paul Newman and Joanne Woodward, yes, I improvised a great deal. They knew what I was doing. They knew what I wanted. They knew what I was looking for. With Paul, if we were shooting a take at a certain point, and I say, "Cut," he would say, "I know what you want." I wouldn't even have to tell him any more. He would know where I was oriented.

Many actors are that way. It is fallacious to think for one moment that that is the only way to work. Not everybody can work that way. To impose that kind of work habit on a man who has been formed and is good — some people say that certain kids didn't realize that they are great actors until the Actors Studio came around. It's as though they just discovered sex.

PAUL MORRISSEY: In *Trash*, the scene where the welfare worker is interested in Holly Woodlawn's shoes, none of it was written. It's very simple, really. If you find good character actors and personalities and people who are worth photographing, a lot of what they do is interesting. Holly and the welfare worker came in and they sat down and she asked for welfare. He said, "You're not eligible."

I told them all these silly lines to say, "You're not eligible, blah, blah, blah." So he just said them, his version of them. I wanted them to argue and I had to find the basis of an argument. There was not much in the damn set, but Holly was wearing a pair of silly shoes. I said, "Why don't you ask her for the shoes?" She didn't want to give him the shoes. O.K.

All that filming we did then was always a funny situation where if I told the people to come around at three in the afternoon, by six or seven we'd be finished with an eight-week film, an hour a scene. We couldn't actually show the whole hour scene, but we would edit it down and try to save the better lines. The little electricity between the social worker and Holly, it just came right there in front of the camera. It was really good, the kind of scene you don't usually see.

Most of the films I've done have been narratives that I made up each day. *Dracula* was not improvised, though. I told the actors what to say in the morning. They memorized it during the lighting setups and I went on from there. Each day, I'd think of what further absurdity might logically follow from where I began.

LEO MCCAREY: A lot of times in *The Awful Truth,* we'd go into a scene with nothing. We knew where it fit into the plot but we had such a tight schedule, I'd say, "See everybody at nine o'clock tomorrow morning," and I'd go home not knowing where we were going to start. I'd say, "Well, I know that there's a knock at the door and Irene Dunne opens the door and admits Cary Grant, so let's put the camera here and I'll see what to do in the morning." So somewhere along the line, I got the idea that Irene opens the door and says, "Well, if it isn't my 'ex,' " or something like that. "What brings you here?" And he says, "Have you forgotten the judge? The judge says this is my day to see the dog." And the scene developed from there.

WILLIAM FRIEDKIN: In *The French Connection,* we ad-libbed a scene with Jimmy Breslin and Roy Scheider and a wonderful actor named Alan Weeks, who plays the guy in the front of the picture, who gets interrogated by these guys at the "pick your feet in Poughkeepsie" scene. Breslin ad-libbed a line in that scene that I was dying to use in the film and I tried to get it into the film and I'll tell you why it didn't get in. He ad-libbed a line when he said to this guy in interrogating him, "Now, either you're going to give me the name or you're going to be a memory in this town." Now that line, "You're going to be a memory in this town," I mean, it just wiped me out. I thought, "This line is the core of this fellow's character in his interrogation of people."

After we ad-libbed the interrogation scene and I had Breslin — I couldn't go with him, so then we got Gene Hackman — I wrote out the interrogation scene, which was based on actual interrogations that I had seen Eddie Egan and Sonny Grosso do, plus I put that line — that line was the capper of the whole scene. "You either give me that name or you're going to be a memory in this town." And that line was the end line of the scene as written. Now, the first day of shooting, it was the first time I had ever worked with Gene Hackman, that was the scene we came to shoot, the interrogation scene, Hackman, Scheider, and Alan Weeks.

I had staged the scene as it usually takes place, in a police car, not on the street, but inside the car, with the two detectives flanking the suspect. The scene was staged that way and the lines were beautiful. You got to read these lines; they're poetry. I tried to give the scene the

Pinteresque flavor of the interrogation in *The Birthday Party*, ending with, "You're going to be a memory in this town," which I thought, "My God, if I win a Pulitzer Prize for the way this is written, I'm out."

And thirty-two takes later, the scene was stiff, didn't work, couldn't get it to happen. Scheider would be pretty good, then Hackman would blow. Alan Weeks was getting slapped around. Real blood was coming out of his face because they were slapping him up. And he was saying, "No, man, it's O.K. Hit me. Go ahead. Hit me." Then, by take twenty-seven he was saying, "It's O.K., you can still hit me." Lumps in his face. The scene's no good. Hackman and I had given each other long looks. Boom. Thirty-two takes. We lost the light. We got no shot. The scene was pathetic. Went home. I thought, "Jesus, I'm through. I'm going to be fired off this picture. I can't direct scene one." Really. I had literally nothing in the can that day except the whole crew, and they're looking at each other, "What is going on?" I figured, "Holy Jesus." I didn't sleep that night and I'm thinking, "Oh, Christ, I go to — oh, yes."

And as usual, it's like a voice to me, some voice apart from me. I'm like a vessel through which these ideas pass, if I'm lucky, but you open yourself up to being a vessel and you say, "Hey, baby, tell me something. Lay something on me, please, because I'm stuck." You do one of these numbers: "Holy Christ. I know what's wrong with that scene. This is not Harold Pinter. This is a street show. And these guys know what they have to do. I've got to let them improvise the scene. In order to do that, I can't restrict them to that car and this tight shot."

So I called up the assistant director in the morning. I said, "Get two cameras down there. Get two cameras. We're going to do it against the wall. I'm going to give them a whole little courtyard there. A whole little area there and let Hackman and Scheider and this guy just wail on the scene. Just give them the notion of the scene, now take it and swing with it and just use your own words."

That's the way you see it in the picture. One take, two cameras. I chose the best moments of it and got that wonderful tag line from Hackman. I forget exactly what he said, "Not only am I going to bust you for those two bags back there, but I'm going to run you in for picking your feet in Poughkeepsie."

He knew the line because Eddie Egan used it all the time. Hackman traveled with Eddie Egan. The Egan-Grosso interrogation technique is very simple. It's obvious, but it really works. They get a guy who is obviously into something. Because he was into something, we're all into something, so we all feel a certain guilt. There are questions that we all have the answer to, like what's your name and what's your address and what are you doing here, and there are some questions for which we don't have answers. So what interrogation technique there was, was one guy would come in with the question that one guy had to have the answer to and the other guy would hit him with some far-out thing that he didn't even understand the question.

Like, one guy would say, "What were you doing in that bar back there?" and the guy'd say, "Huh?" The other guy'd say, "Have you ever been in Poughkeepsie?" And the guy knows he's never been in Poughkeepsie, but he's saying, "How come this guy wants to know if I've ever been in Poughkeepsie?" The other guy wants to know something that he has the answer to. This guy's trying to hit him with Poughkeepsie. It's a double-talk kind of thing. It really gets down to a moment where one guy is saying, "Did you pass something to that fellow in the bar?" And he says, "Huh?" And the other guy says, "Did you ever sit down on the edge of a bed, take off your shoes and socks and run your fingers between your toes?" The guy was totally stunned.

8

Visuals and Camerawork

VISUALS — IDEAS AND IMAGES

KING VIDOR: In silent films, where we didn't have all the words to explain everything, we thought in terms of symbols, graphic arrangements, or possibilities. We were trained in these terms. When you had to explain something, you didn't think, "What's the exact word for this? The exact phrase or sentence?" You just thought, "What's the picture, the symbol?"

LOUIS MALLE: I feel very strongly that in making films now, for me, at least, the principle is not to take the audience, take their hand and tell them, "I'm going to show you that," or "I'm going to explain that to you." Just

201

ask them to participate, make their own selection, to sort of present them with something which is ambiguous and confusing and have the audience really bringing something. Part of the creation is theirs. This is a little difficult sometimes because I'm not sure audiences like it too much. Unfortunately, I think most of the time they prefer to be manipulated.

VINCENTE MINNELLI: I think the visual is very important. I think that the story and the actors are most important, of course, but their surroundings, their place and time in space, is very important.

ED EMSHWILLER: Images, it seems to me, have all kinds of reverberations. It's that whole varied, indefinable spectrum of reverberations that play against one another in an almost sensual or nonabsolutely specific way that appeals to me. The thing that I feel is that I am subject to pressures of all kinds — historical, personal, psychological, social, intellectual pressures that I can't weigh, but which press upon me and shape my seeing and my responses. So, when I am dealing with whatever thematic imagery or concepts that interest me at a given time, I respond out of all of these pressures that are multidimensional and I hope to capture the flavor of that multidimensional sense of what I'm dealing with. If I add these together, then I create a gestalt.

ALFRED HITCHCOCK: I think one of the biggest problems that we have in our business is the inability of people to visualize. What I am about to say is hearsay, but I remember David Selznick, the producer, when he was talking about Irving Thalberg, the great name in our business. Selznick used to say, "Thalberg is great with a finished picture." When you examine those words, they mean that the man lacked any visual sense. The film had to be made as quickly as possible, in eighteen days or twenty-one days. Then they looked at it on the screen and remade it. To me that seems to be an awful thing.

Imagine a composer sitting down with a blank music sheet in front of him, and a full orchestra. "Flute, give me a note, if you please. Yes, thank you very much," and he writes it down. It's the same thing, but a man can compose music directly on paper and what's the result? It comes out as gorgeous sounds or what have you. The visual, to me, is a vital element in this work. I don't think it is studied enough.

Go back to the early days. Go back to Chaplin. He once made a short film called *The Pilgrim*. The opening shot was the outside of a prison gate. A guard came out and posted a wanted notice. Next cut: a very tall, thin man coming out of a river, having had a swim. He finds that his clothes are missing and have been replaced with a convict's uniform. Next cut: a railroad station, and there coming towards the camera dressed as a parson with the pants too long is Chaplin.

Now, there are three pieces of film, and look at the amount of story they told. These are the things that I think are so essential, especially when you send your film into a foreign country, Japan, Italy, or wherever. If you send a film which, as I have mentioned elsewhere, is "photographs of people talking" all the way through, and that gets to a foreign country with subtitles underneath, the poor audience will spend the entire evening reading. They won't have time to look at the pictures.

GEORGE CUKOR: Maybe if I were aware of how to do it, I would be shooting all doorknobs turning instead of the actors' faces. But I think this. The placement of the camera, everything, is determined by the text. It is not the director that decides it. There is a truth in a scene and that's the only truth and the inevitable truth. If a waiter comes on with a cup of coffee, and that is very important, that must be featured. There's no point sticking to the star who is sitting there, doing nothing. Where the camera is placed depends very much on what the scene dictates, is about. It is not the director's choice, and to try to make it something else, to distort it, is to falsify it.

JACQUES DEMY: I like painting very, very much. Whatever you say, film is an image. It's a way by which one can be a painter. You can use the colors that a painter would use. It's all a matter of look. When I walk along a street, I am always attracted by color. Each person has to make his own choice. When I think of framing a picture, right away I think, "Where is something that is a good color?"

ALFRED HITCHCOCK: If it's a man wearing a top hat walking towards a manhole, the nicest shot you could do would be to put the camera on the ground, have the manhole in the foreground, and see the man approaching the hole wearing the top hat. Now, the next cut ought to be the head and shoulders of the man. You dolly with him and he drops out of the picture. You don't have to go back to the manhole anymore. He walks along and suddenly, whoomp, he goes. Now, to complete this, if you want satisfaction, you should now cut down to the manhole. He is lying there bleeding; the blood is pouring from his head. A policeman looks down, calls an ambulance. He's lifted up and taken to the hospital. The wife is brought to the bedside, and they say, "I'm afraid there is no hope." There is a fine line between comedy and tragedy.

WILLIAM FRIEDKIN: You are uncomfortable with that which you are least familiar. Fear, the essential principle of fear, has something to do with having something standing behind you. It's generally something behind you. So there are a lot of shots in *The Exorcist* of somebody turning around.

There is also a concept that we call the "expectancy set." The term was coined at the Maimonides Dream Laboratory in Brooklyn. What that really is is you're walking down the street, every twig that bends under your feet, every leaf, every footstep fulfills that expectation and makes you afraid. Expectancy set is what an audience brings with them to a Hitchcock film and what they bring with them to *The Exorcist*.

Now that it's in the papers that it's supposed to be a scary movie; people are scared when they're standing in line. The title comes on and guys say, "Oh, I can't look." And that's what you play on as a filmmaker. You play on the knowledge that fear is something behind you. It's the expectancy set. That's what you work on. That's what's at work on those characters within the film.

ALFRED HITCHCOCK: Let's say that you set up a suspense scene and you happen to have two characters who look the same. You're going to have the audience say, "Which man is that? Is that the other man?" You are going to distract them from the emotions. Keeping our mind on one thing involves many things, such as clarification, locale, who is what, making sure the characters are not wearing the same suit. There are many elements that you have to clarify, so that you leave room only for the emotions.

There are moments where you have to use a certain amount of footage to introduce the character. In that particular case you just didn't introduce them by small talk. You have a little boy playing and accidentally pull the veil off.

THE DIRECTOR-CAMERAMAN RELATIONSHIP

In a sense, camerawork is the most independent of all the traditional filmmaking functions. Outside of certain basic script requirements, any actor, any object, any setting may be lighted and filmed in a nearly infinite number of ways. As most directors do not possess the necessary technical information, they must rely upon a successful translation of their ideas to cameramen and their crews.

In preproduction consultations with the director, the cameraman should become aware of a certain overall style that will be necessary to convey best the intent of the film. A director, though he might not have specific ideas about the technique of a shot or its lighting, usually will sense when and where the camera should be. With this knowledge, the cameraman takes into consideration any technical or budgetary limitations and any particular dramatic requirements of actors. All these requirements in hand, they mutually set out to produce the most aesthetically satisfying shot possible, relative to the particular situation and to the film as a whole.

CURTIS HARRINGTON: I am very dependent upon the cameraman. I tell the cameraman many things. Sometimes I am very specific about what I want light on and what I want light off of. I will tell them where I want the most light to be. I always choose the camera angles. Sometimes the cameraman might suggest an angle, and if I like it or think that it is better than something that I thought about, then I have no ego about it. I would use it.

PETER BOGDANOVICH: In *Paper Moon,* in the café scene early on when she says, "I want my two hundred dollars," and all that, the last setup in that sequence is a face-off between the two of them and the waitress comes up and says, "Hi, there, precious," and Tatum says, "My name ain't precious." It was kind of a slightly low angle and that's exactly what I had in mind, that shot, but I didn't know enough to say to him, "Put the camera down low so we can see the girl coming." I just said, "Look, here's what I want. It's the last shot in the sequence and I want to get kind of like a Mexican standoff."

He said, "What's that?"

I said, "Well, look, give the impression of these two people opposing each other and you don't know which way it's going to go and they're sort of . . ."

And he said, "Well, maybe if we shoot low."

And I said, "That's good."

And he set it up and I looked through and I said, "Let's move in a little closer," because there was air on the side and I wanted to get as tight as I could get and still hold the head of the waitress.

That was a big contribution from him. He got the idea of what I wanted and he was able to give it to me.

Preminger once said to me that there were two kinds of good cameramen. He said, "There's the good cameraman who'll give you what you want but doesn't know why you want it. And there's the other kind who can give you what you want and knows why you want it." He said, "Of course, it's much more fun to work with the second cameraman."

ROBERT ALTMAN: Most of the collaboration with the cinematographer takes place before the film when we're really deciding what the film is going to look like. We start out with what we can control — well, we start out really with what we can't control. That starts our philosophy of how we're going to make it look. By the time we start shooting, he and I both know pretty much. Some pictures, I'll get very involved with the composition and camera movement and on others I won't get near the camera. It depends on the picture.

JAMES BRIDGES: I still don't know that much about the camera. I hire the best people, and I work with them and tell them what I want.

IRVIN KERSHNER: As *Loving* progressed, it became easier and easier, and there was a meshing of personalities and a meshing of vision. By the time we were halfway through, we never had to discuss anything about how we were going to do it. The cameraman and I would come into a situation and I would have an idea of how I wanted to do it, and we would start to stage it. Gordon Willis would be following along and would sometimes make suggestions. Most of the time, he would just be lighting it in his mind as I was doing the thing. It was just sort of automatic. He became sort of my right hand. We worked so well together that we didn't really have to discuss much. The discussions went on before the picture began, on a fairly conceptual nature. That, as you might guess, makes it kind of a pleasure.

ROMAN POLANSKI: A good cameraman can function only with a good director. It's very difficult to do good photography with a lousy director. It never happens, *almost* never, unless the cameraman takes it all over and makes a series of stills to which the theme, the rest of the film, is only an illustration.

JOHN CASSAVETES: I don't shoot many angles going back and forth. Almost everything is shot from the same place, from the same perspective, so that . . . it's very important to me that the cameraman has feeling, and can move with the figures as he feels it, rather than me saying, "Oh, we missed that."

MARTIN RITT: It really does depend upon who your cameraman is. You may ask for something and not get it, because it is not in the frame of what he does. You have to be shrewd to be able to understand your cameraman.

You have to understand what he does. If you made a mistake when you hired him, you may not get exactly what you want. He is not going to be able to change those lights, because the lights are psychological with him. He has been with them a long, long time. If he tries to do something which he is not about, then it's not going to work. It is very complicated.

I do have a very good working relationship with James Wong Howe. He is a very gifted and intuitive man. When he first reads a script, he might not see the picture. But after about a week of rehearsals and hanging around and seeing the behaviorism of the film, he catches it.

GEORGE CUKOR: I have had a great many good cameramen. I admire them very much. A director must give them courage to do their work. I will tell you some cases in point. I did a picture with Ronald Colman, *A Double Life*. Colman plays a star. There was a scene backstage. I thought, "I am not accustomed to being on the stage, and I want the audience to get the impression of what it was like. When I go backstage I am blinded by the lights." I wanted the audience to get that effect. I told that to the cameraman. He was very good. I told him to light a flare. He didn't do it. He didn't have the nerve. I had to go back and say, "No, no, no. I will take the responsibility." A cameraman has to understand what you are trying to get at. You have to understand his problem, and you have to give him courage. You have to say, "Do the goddamned thing."

JOHN CASSAVETES: I wouldn't tell Vic Kemper where to put the camera. Just get together with him and say, "Feel what you feel." All the long lens shots were Vic's, and there was one stationary shot in the whole scene.

He's the only cameraman I know who hand-holds with an Elemack dolly. He just walks around with it, pushes the cameraman, and has a terrific focus-puller that he has worked with for a long time. They talk to each other, back and forth. He sets up his moves. You could watch the camera moving, and you knew that it was going to be very good because he just has great feeling. So I would never worry about him.

MICHAEL WINNER: I always say to the cameraman when I start a picture — because I really don't believe that you should be befuddled by the fact that you don't know as much about the camera as they do — I always say, "I like to work quickly, and in order to do that you can't have many lights . . . because if you have a lot of lights, you'll play with them all day, and I won't be able to play my bit. I don't want to sit there while you put fifty-two lights in because I get terribly bored and so does everybody else. So, we'll give you two or three, and then you'll have to get on with it much quicker." Normally they compromise and end up giving you somewhat more than you bargained for and somewhat less than they're used to, and you still get along pretty quick. Richard Kline literally appeared with two or three lights, and he was holding two of them in his hand, and he'd say, "Ready." And I'd say, "Ready? I haven't got back to my chair yet." It was fantastic.

JACK NICHOLSON: If I wanted the cinematographer to just shoot this right here and I wanted to do it because I've got to be finished by two-thirty, I didn't want him to be worried what they'd see in dailies back at the studio, if it was underexposed or whatever. So I had a cameraman, Bill Butler. He pretty much made it clear to me if I wanted to shoot it, we'll shoot it. He gave me a sort of running lesson in photography. I would ask him what will this look like or where should I point it, or what light shall we use and what negative density will I have later on, and when I print it up is it going to go green?

I knew lenses and dollies and all that already from working around, and writing before. What I wanted to know was what you can get in a given situation. I learned by shooting something and then seeing it. I quickly caught up until I wouldn't have to use a light meter; I would know what I could actually shoot and what I couldn't.

STANLEY KRAMER: I have had a variety of cinematographers. I just finished with an elderly gentleman artist and I didn't know if he'd be right for this picture. I thought the vitality necessary for it might well be with a younger cameraman. But no. I worked with Robert Surtees and he was a dream, a joy. You look for somebody who doesn't come to work in the morning and says, "Where do you want the camera and what do we do? Do we do a close-up shot or a master shot or what?" You look for somebody who creatively makes a contribution beyond the texture and the lighting and your set which you can discuss in advance. You look for somebody who says, "Why don't we let him just go out of the shot and we'll hold on this and it will tell the whole thing." Somebody who is making contributions. I think that is very important, and again, that's unusual except for the most part in the younger men.

The younger men are coming up creatively because there are no shibboleths; they destroyed them all, which is good. I don't really look for anybody except somebody with whom I can work and if I have an idea or he has an idea, that we can entertain it. What more? You figure you don't take a man in the first place unless he's a craftsman.

ROBERT ALDRICH: This is a terribly sensitive area. I like to have the cameraman like the scene. I want to have him understand the way I would like it to look, so I often explain my ideas to him in terms of artistry or craft. I don't want him to tell me anything about what lens to use or where the camera should be. I like him to make as many setups a day that reasonably capture what we are trying to get. In addition, the relationship of the director and the cameraman should be one of understanding. The cameraman doesn't necessarily need to like you, and you don't have to like him. But, it is a must that you understand each other. That rapport is the most difficult thing to come by. Different cameramen have different temperaments.

OSCAR WILLIAMS: You should get a cameraman at least two weeks before you start to shoot, so that you can talk about things you want to do. You may want to do things like have angles, like to go past this microphone and around there to get everyone in focus. He may say, "We'll get a shot of the microphone and then cut to that over there." It's like that. You may want to do something by dissolving. But he will say, "You might just get the same effect through wide-angle." All of these things come from the relationship that he develops with the director. It's helpful one or two weeks before, because you're going to need him. You're going to need the cinematographer, because you decide on the concept with him.

PAUL MAZURSKY: The biggest mistake made in Hollywood is that they usually get the cameraman for a week. It's a terrible mistake. If possible, the cameraman and the director should be together for three or four weeks and go to every location and have time to sit and talk. . . . I try to as much as I can. It's very hard, because most cameramen are still on a job when you are getting ready to go. They may be finishing on Thursday and you start preparation with them on Monday. There are a lot of nighttime phone calls and "Great, great, we'll do this, we'll make tests," and there is very little time. I always take suggestions. The trick is to encourage them to give you suggestions.

JAMES BRIDGES: The first day we met, after the cameraman, Gordon Willis, had read the script, at the Plaza Hotel, he said, "What would you think of this?"

And I said, "That's terrific." So we laid out the shot.

Then there would be times when I would come in and say, "I want this and that and that," before we'd start shooting. I remember one day when

I didn't know how the hell to cover it, and I just took the actors and I said, "Go get some coffee and I'll call you." And then I blocked the scene, and made myself very happy. I said, "I want to be on this side of the room, but I don't feel like figuring out how I'm going to shoot it, so I'll see you later," and I went down and had coffee. And an hour later he came back and asked how I was going to do it. So we worked on it, and he made some suggestions. But basically it was just talking it out together.

HAL ASHBY: On *The Landlord* I tried to get all that — as to concept — out of the way before we started shooting. I mean, talking to my cameraman about what I'm feeling visually out of it before we ever start shooting. I took him to locations and said, "This place feels this way to me; does it feel the same way to you?" And so forth. I think there are times when you should get into paintings. I could see times in future films when it would help you with overall style and look to the film. But try and get all that out of the way first, so you don't run into every day saying, "I think maybe we should try this." Hopefully, when you start looking at your dailies after your first two or three days in the picture, you're going in basically the direction you want and you don't have to say, "Let's change that, let's make it a little darker mood or into something else." Fortunately, we didn't get into that. We got pretty much what we felt we both wanted.

RAOUL WALSH: You choose the angle and the setup, and you take the cameraman along and consult him about the light. If there's a mountain there and so on, "How long can we work on this side?"

He'd take the viewer and look through and say, "Well, the sun's liable to go at two o'clock." We'd work over there.

I'd pick the shots and then consult him about the light. "How long are we going to have light here?"

HOWARD HAWKS: I told Bill Clothier, "Look, I'm making a western, *Rio Lobo*. I utilize Remington's hard lighting on the street coming out of a saloon floor or a window. Now, I don't want yellow light to hit the faces of the people, but I want you to use a bunch of yellow light, use it on the back wall, on the street." He liked the looks of it and started experimenting. All you do is put a yellow gel on and you get a golden richness. It's getting what you want out of a scene. Sometimes I don't know how to get it, but the cameraman knows what I want. Some men, like Gregg Toland, who did *Citizen Kane*, are great. Lee Garmes was great. There was a scene in *Scarface* that I didn't like. He said, "I have an idea if you don't like the look." He turned out all the lights in the front and had back light coming through a window curtain and it made a silhouette. It became one of the really good scenes. A good man can help you.

MILOS FORMAN: Because I wanted to bring my cameraman over from Czechoslovakia, we made a very interesting compromise with the unions. They asked that we have an American director of photography. I didn't want to just pay somebody who would sit somewhere, so we asked if we can make a compromise so that all the people in the camera crew will be working. We had two directors of photography and a focus assistant, so the two can switch with each other and either operate the camera or take care of lighting, which was the ideal solution for me. I don't like a camera operator, because he's the man who's looking in the camera, but he isn't responsible when the actor moves a little unexpectedly. But when the director of photography is looking in the camera, he can make decisions.

Imagine you have two people talking to each other. The camera operator will never make a decision to follow this one or that one. He will just say: "Stop. Cut. I don't see them both." A director of photography, who is responsible, will make decisions and he will follow somebody and then he will tell me, "Listen, I followed him; is it all right?" And I'll say either yes or no and then we'll reshoot it or we'll print it.

There was a lot of almost improvisational movement in that strip-poker game in *Taking Off* when, for example, Lynn Carlin suddenly stands up. That was not rehearsed, so it's the director of photography's responsibility to go up. I like having the person who is looking in the camera being responsible.

JOHN CASSAVETES: I'm not a cameraman. But you generally light. Just take a lot of time to fill in. I mean, people see what's going to happen, really, basically. If this is the room, we're shooting this way, the camera's here. So you encompass all of it. I mean, you couldn't possibly work with the lights that are surrounding somebody and say, "Now, improvise, oh Jeez, you're in the shadow." You couldn't possibly do that, so the lighting would have to be much more general. But the soft lighting seems to work very well for improvisation, because it's a general light anyway.

FRANKLIN SCHAFFNER: There is a great tendency not to communicate with cameramen, and I have found that they want to know what you have in mind. I have found it's a reasonable question, and they take it reasonably well, when you have staged your master shot, to ask, "When do I get the set?" They will tell you, and now you know what you have to plan.

HASKELL WEXLER: When you work on a film, at least in my opinion, the director is the boss. And sometimes it can be horrible. Now there can be all kinds of problems for a cameraman, because a lot of times the directors don't know what they are talking about. If they say, "I want to have a little more contrast," or if they say, "I just want to barely be able to see this or that," or "I want that lamp very hot behind that girl's head." Well, what is very hot? Does he want a number four focal flood in there blasting down, or just hiss-hot? You have to put yourself in tune and try to understand what they want to do. I really believe that. It may sound less democratic, but I think it has to be that way.

JIRI WEISS: If that cameraman is a strong personality and you disagree, he possibly will say, "Well, choose another cameraman." And it depends on what you want to have, whom you want to have. In my opinion, the eye in the cinema is the most important author.

COSTA-GAVRAS: My cameraman on *Z* doesn't talk much, so *we* didn't talk too much. I showed him a few color pictures just to tell him exactly what kind of tones I wanted. I needed lots of very violent lighting and I wanted neutral insides, sort of flat lighting. He was worried because he thought then we wouldn't be able to see anything of the exterior. If there is no light in the inside, then the exterior will look completely white. "Does it bother you?" I ask him.

"I don't care; what about you?"

RAOUL WALSH: You sit down with the script and tell the cameraman, "Play this in shadow. This gal can't act very well. But this guy is a dog; don't light him at all." The cinematographer is used mostly for lighting and illuminating the sets. I did all my own blocking and staging.

GEORGE STEVENS: Don't be imposed upon by a cameraman with enormous seniority. So often the cameramen are terribly senior and want to do it the way they've always done it, or at least the way they did it the last picture — except in the rare cases of an inventive cameraman. So, to come in and take charge of that thing is something everyone is facing, and it happens in one form or another. It's very comforting to think you know the other fellow's work, and you don't have to ask him because sometimes you do have to tell him.

FRANKLIN SCHAFFNER: I've had my breath taken away by a cameraman who said, "Can we split this master in half, because I can't light the whole thing." Or suddenly one day after you have been after him day after day after day, and finally in the rushes it looks like what you really want, and you compliment him on this, and he says, "Well, I don't throw my Sunday punch every day."

Talk to a cameraman and tell him what you want, what conceptually you see this picture as. He will then come back technically and say, "I can get it this way; I will use a quarter fog filter all the way through, and we will depend upon the lab to wash, or we will desaturate or we will flash. We will time it so we can get what you want. But please don't inhibit me by putting filters on the camera, because we are liable to go foul." Now all this you can discuss with him. I find it difficult to discuss conceptually with an operator* what my sense of framing is. So that when I get on the machine and frame, I call them, and I say, "Here's the start." And as we take a move, I call them, and say, "And here's how it's going to end." And your breath is taken away very often when you're looking at dailies and that ain't the way you framed it. And it's only by the dailies that you can tell where you're going with this man who's got the sandpaper fingers on the wheels. The other thing is that you've got to have enormous confidence in this man, no matter how close you are to the camera. You can only visualize a certain frame. In a given moment, you may miss a given moment. And when you say to him, "Did you get it?" and he says, "Yes," and you say, "Next setup," you've got to believe him and trust him.

HASKELL WEXLER: When I worked as a cameraman, I directed every scene, but I had to keep my mouth shut as much as I could. But, then, when you are the cameraman, that's a nice position too, because if you are wrong you can just say to yourself, "Oh, that jerk doesn't know what he is doing." Or you say, "I would have done it better." You can say all sorts of marvelous things when you are second-guessing. But, when you are directing, you are totally responsible. I think that is the basic difference between director and cameraman.

HOW IMPORTANT? HOW DIFFICULT?

SERGEI BONDARCHUK: I found out all the secrets of cinematography in three months.

---

*The camera *operator* works the camera mechanism during the actual filming. He, in turn, may be assisted by focus-pullers, zoom lens operators, etc. They all function under the cameraman — variously known as "the first," "the director of cinematography," and, in England, "the lighting cameraman."

PAUL MORRISSEY: I've only had one assistant with sound. I light it. Anybody can go ahead and light it.

JOHN CASSAVETES: It's not really interesting, to me at least, to set up a camera angle. At some points in the filming you really want to take the camera and break it for no reason except that it's just an interference and you don't know what to do with it. It's like putting the top on a can that is bent. You can't really do anything with it.

The most difficult part of working on a film like *Husbands* is that the opinions of the crew really affect the people in front of the screen, and sometimes they don't see anything happening. They get despondent. You can feel them loosen up. You can feel you're losing the thing.

ROMAN POLANSKI: I never think of camera, not until the scene has been almost lit. I think camera is the last thing. You see, to think of the camera first is like tailoring a suit and then looking for a person who will fit it. I'd rather get the person and take the measurements and then make a suit for him.

JEAN RENOIR: The reason for my camerawork is not to cut in the middle of the acting of the actor, to have the camera hanging on the actor, following the actor, but to be just a recording instrument and not a God. Camerawork was especially dangerous in this city, in Hollywood. It became so important that in the mind of many people the camerawork was the only thing which was important. If everything else was wrong, the director wasn't satisfied, the actor wasn't satisfied. Well, the producer would arrive and say,"Please, you are fussy, both of you, looking for an impossible. The shot is sufficient like that and we must not waste time with such nonsensical tasks." But if the cameraman was looking to remove a little shadow at the tip of the nose of the star, he could take three days if he wanted.

CARL REINER: I do rely on a cameraman. I would like to have the best cameraman. I would have liked to have had Kubrick before he became a director. I want to get a cameraman before he is ready to become a director. I would like him to be with me on a picture just before he is ready to become a director. That would be the optimum for me. If I could have a guy like that, I would make some picture. But, a couple of times I invented a couple of ideas.

I think that mainly, in comedy, if you get very tricky with the camera, then you may lose some of the human relationship portrayal that you are trying to show. If you get tricky, then you relate face-to-face. You don't relate shooting through a guy's legs. Comedy is somebody reacting to something that somebody else does. Even a close-up may not be the best thing. You usually have to see both people or three people. The more tricky you are in comedy, I think the less effective you will be.

JAN KADAR: The work of the cameraman, as myself, is mostly behind the scenes. Telling you the truth, in the beginning when we started *The Shop on Main Street,* we didn't know exactly which style we were going to try to get. One thing that I did know in the beginning was something about the whole dramatic mood and structure of the picture. Do you remember the dinner sequence? They were getting drunk. I had to make a rehearsal before, because I didn't know how to shoot it. We agreed with the cameraman to do a rehearsal before the principal photography that was a full test. It was a part of the preparation period. I knew that I must not, may not, and would not interrupt the action.

LEO MCCAREY: I put the camera where I thought it was best. I didn't formulate any theories about it.

JAN KADAR: I am not a cameraman. I don't even take pictures, because I don't have any hand camera. What I do is with my eyes and what I have in my mind. I know very little about technique. It doesn't interest me very much. But, the moment when I get on the set, then I become a cameraman.

GENERAL APPROACHES AND TECHNIQUES —
SOME REPRESENTATIVE COMMENTS

BERNARDO BERTOLUCCI: I discuss with the cameraman and the art director the feeling and the movement. I'm very meticulous and boring about camera movement. . . . I tell the cameraman exactly the point, because I think the camera is a musical instrument. Paradoxically, you can make a musical without music but with camera movements. Audiences can imagine music in seeing the camera.

Composition and Camera Placement
ALFRED HITCHCOCK: I think mainly it is a matter of the interest in the composition. I have a horror of what I call the passport photograph: shooting straight in. It's dull, it's not interesting, and a slight variation on that is not so much the desire to get anything in the way of sharp angles,

low or high or what have you, but merely to avoid the standard level shots.

ALLAN DWAN: I think it's instinct. I think you have a sense of composition or you haven't. I think you might develop it as you can develop anything, but I think you have to have the basics. Again, that's mathematics, you know. There's nothing more beautiful than mathematical perfection. And that's really architecture.

When I use a cross-the-shoulder shot, I try as a rule to photograph the one who's listening rather than the one who's talking, because it's a better picture. Also, I get the feeling of the effect it's having. If I speak to you, the important thing is what effect am I having on you? And so I have to see whether it has by looking at you just as an actor peeking through the curtain at his audience can see what they're thinking and whether he's got them. He may not see them on account of the lighting but he knows he's got them or he hasn't. He's got that feeling. That's what I like to photograph; I like to photograph the listener.

GEORGE SEATON: Ford had the greatest trick in the world. He comes in in the morning with those dark glasses, you can't see his eyes, and he's got that dirty handkerchief. He says, "What do we shoot today?"

The assistant says, "Well, it's the scene where Duke, you know . . ."

"Yeah, well put the box there. Duke, you come in here, you meet the girl there . . ." and suddenly you realize this is the perfect place to put the camera. Now he's been studying all night, of course, you know, but he likes to give that performance because it doesn't come that easy. But everything flows toward the camera.

There's a wonderful story about when he was making a picture with Robert Montgomery, *They Were Expendable*. Bob Montgomery's first day on the back lot, PT boat in the pond, and Jack said, "Now, I'll put the camera here and the speedboat comes up here and you hop off, Bob, and she comes up here," and so forth.

So Montgomery, who had just directed his first picture, said, "Jack, you might not know it, but I just directed a picture at Universal and I've been thinking about this scene a great deal and wouldn't it be better if the speedboat came from here and I jumped here and she came in from this side, which would give an over-shoulder . . ."

You couldn't see his eyes, of course, and Jack said, "You think it's better that way, huh? All right, fine." He said, "All right, let's do it Bob's way. Put the camera here, so forth." And they do it and it takes two hours to light and shoot. He said, "How was that for you, Bob?"

Bob said, "Fine."

Jack goes over to the box, opens it, takes the film out and tears it up, and he says, "That's your version; all right, now let's put the camera here."

COSTA-GAVRAS: The actors are the first consideration. Because you can plan a scene and say the actors will be put this way, but maybe the actors won't feel at home that way. So first you rehearse it and discuss the angle. But very little and very quickly, really. I am a lot behind the camera. At least, once I have decided to place the scene and I have the actors doing it, then I am behind the camera. I see the framing and so on. And meanwhile, Coutard, the cameraman, is finishing the lighting.

ROMAN POLANSKI: The intimacy is not directly related to the angle but to the place where you put the camera. In *Rosemary's Baby*, if you had Rosemary walking into a bedroom and you put the camera on the other side of the bedroom and through the door opening see her walking into the room, it wouldn't be intimate. But if you put the camera behind her, behind it all, and the door opens and she comes in and you follow her, then it would be intimate.

Lighting

ALLAN DWAN: Lighting is a very important part of your intention when you're making drama. But comedy, when we were doing comedy, was more or less a flat light job. Shadows and artwork seem to annoy comedy and comedians. They didn't perform when it was artistic. They slowed down to admire it, I think. Who could do a pratfall if the scene's pretty? Most of them say, "If I do it here, you won't see me — there's a shadow." So we'd light it up. But in drama we'd play it for shadows and light, and that was our job.

ROBERT ALDRICH: Charlie Lang used to be Joan Crawford's cameraman. He would put up those shadows so that all you could see were her eyes. If she didn't hit the mark by an inch, she would be in total darkness. The cameraman really knows what he is doing. The actors are reasonably sober. The problem isn't that acute. But, it is acute if a guy wants to put one key light up there and wash the room out. There is no way that he can draw attention to that lady in the second row. This all doesn't become a problem if the cameraman knows how you feel before you start.

Lenses and Perspective

ROMAN POLANSKI: The wide-angle lens is used mainly for the depth of field, but I would have to talk a long time about it. I don't know whether it has any sense; maybe it does. Being hung up on visuals, it's very important for me to show on the screen what I see in life. I think the way the human being sees life around him, the world around him, would be closely comparable with a picture made by what you call the wide-angle range of lenses.

You mustn't forget that what you show on the screen is a picture. It's just a name that they have for it. It's a picture, it's not a reality, it's two-dimensional. So when you look at it from the side of the screen it changes totally the proportions. It gets shorter. The perspective applies to this picture. Once you have this in mind, you have to realize that what you show on the screen is not real life, but some kind of translation of real life.

There are certain things which don't apply in this picture like what's called, in psychology, constancy scaling. When you look at a perspective in real life, things don't appear smaller as they fall off in the distance; otherwise, if you look at your two hands, like this [Polanski demonstrates], they will both appear the same size, but the linear perspective shows that the right hand is half the size because the distance here is doubled. If you close one eye and align them, then they change suddenly; they will dramatically change in size, and you see that the right hand is much smaller. It's half the size. But if you glance at them without thinking, there's a mechanism in the brain called constancy scaling and the two hands appear to be the same size. Now, once you are aware of it, when you try to render the three-dimensional world on a picture, you have to compensate for this constancy scaling.

Painters do it by applying a false linear perspective. When you take the painting of a master, you see a street, and if you start to put rulers to the lines, you realize that the perspective is not correct. If you do it correct, like that Italian painter, Canaletto, who used the camera obscura, you see the perspective is always too sharp. It just looks wrong, although it is correct from the linear point of view. You have to compensate for it. Now when you have all this in mind, you realize the most important thing on the screen, for me, is to render the perspective the way I see it, not the way that it appears and not the way it is being deformed by long distance lenses.

Now, the ideal for me would be to use the one lens all the time, to come close with the same lens when I want a close-up and go far with the same lens where I want a long shot. It's very difficult, so you try to keep as close to it as you possibly can.

Now, I want to tell you one thing. It's not the same thing to have this shot of yours made with a long lens and then change the lens and cut on your close-up like that, because this is not true. I mean, it's true if I look at you from this distance.

The important thing in filming for me is my point of view, of course, because it's a question of taste, but the most important thing for me is to put the camera at the proper distance from the object at a distance from which I would find myself looking at that object; otherwise, when I turn to him and I look at him, I have to put my camera here, and then I have to find the lens that will give me the proper size. But it's not enough to put this camera here and have the same size, because he doesn't look like that.

He looks different from here than he looks from there. The linear perspective of his face is entirely different. The proportion of his nose to his ears is entirely different than it is from here. If you look at him through binoculars from the other end of this room, he will look entirely different because there's no more perspective, practically, in his face. So otherwise, when I look at you like this, I see more or less that much. My peripheral vision goes here, but I'm conscious of seeing more than this, so I would put my camera here and I will look for a lens which will show me that much, and I will come out with a wide-angle lens.

ALFRED HITCHCOCK: If you use a wide-angle lens, of course, you naturally change your perspective considerably. As a matter of fact, if you use a short-focus lens, say one-hundred-millimeter, you foreshorten; your standard view is about a fifty-millimeter. That would give you what the eye sees. When you don't use the normal fifty-millimeter, you make a room look too big and you send the back wall too far away. If you use a wide-angle lens, you make the set much bigger than it really is.

You see, sometimes you get involved with the whole question of the depth of focus. There is a whole group of people who think everything should be sharp in front and equally sharp at a distance, which in actual fact is almost impossible in real life.

I remember at Paramount, when they first introduced VistaVision. They did their first test out in the desert. They were making a film with Martin and Lewis, and when they saw the first results, they were overwhelmed and ecstatic that a hand in the foreground was sharp as a figure half a mile away. And what the hell that's got to do with picture-making I don't know, but they were delighted. They all thought this was a wonderful system. Of course, what the camera department failed to tell them was that if you shoot the desert then you have to stop down to a pinhole and it will make everything sharp, including five miles away. But the camera department was afraid to tell them. So they let them think it was VistaVision.

I was doing this picture *To Catch a Thief* at the time, and I remember the head of the studio, who shall be nameless, comes to me and says, "Look, in these close-ups of yours everything's blurred; that's not VistaVision."

I said, "So? The audience is not going to look round the head, they are going to look at the head we've got on the screen."

"Yes, but in VistaVision everything is sharp." So the camera department secretly went round to each cameraman and said to pile up the lights, so as to continue to deceive the front office. They went around to every cameraman on the lot and made him pile up the light so that everything was sharp.

MARTIN RITT: Some cameramen, if you want to use a zoom lens, they get kind of shaky about it. They say, "Well, it's not going to look good when you get into the fifty-millimeter part of it. We can't light it properly. We don't have enough light when we get in there." I don't like it. I have used it. My feeling about the zoom is: I'll use it if I can't get the shot any other way.

I remember I used it once in a shot that began on New York in a close shot. It was of the skyline. I pulled back across the Hudson River and went around and around. I came around almost three hundred degrees. There was a little figure seated on a chair in a marsh. Then I moved in. There was no other way to get the shot.

I am always bothered when a zoom is used, because it takes me right out of the picture. I won't use it unless I can't get the shot any other way.

Color versus Black and White

ROMAN POLANSKI: I think black and white is something totally artificial. There's no bearing to our perception of the world since we see in color. It's something which happened only because photography was invented first in black and white, and we got used to it. Also, it seems sometimes more real, because the photographs of real life which we saw in magazines and newspapers used to be black and white, also the newsreels. Everything that was connected with news, with newsreels, with real life, was always presented to us in black and white. This association is very strong.

Also, there is all the history of cinema, which was black and white, but to the new generation which is growing up with color television and color printing, this thing will become more and more artificial and arty, I would say. I think that it's a certain coquetry now, using black and white. However, it may render certain styles that you are after in certain situations and, obviously, certain directors use black and white to relate somehow to the black and white period in the cinema. If they make a film about the thirties, they use black and white. I don't.

On *Chinatown,* which is Los Angeles 1937, which happens in the heart of this town when this industry was created, I do it purposely in color, even in Panavision. I'm making a film which should look like a film made today, not a film made in 1937. A film made today, about that period.

Color gives us so many more possibilities. It's often misused; it's very difficult to do a good film in color, because it's very difficult to make it look good. But there's the same reason again with the pictures, not real life. In real life, you accept it the way it is, but when you put it flat, it looks entirely different.

ALLAN DWAN: Color photography has taken the whole art out of motion pictures because no lighting is required for colored pictures. Just put the light on; that's all you have to have. Light and get the colors. Once in a while, you can get an effect, but you lose the color if you do, so they insist on the color. And they look at it and say, "Too much purple. Too much blue. Too much this or that." But the art's gone.

In the black and white, you had to devise ideas, you had to get highlights, and you had to get shadows. You had to work on them and get them. That's what I mean by painting with the light. And that I liked. I liked that kind of work. You can't do that now. That's gone. With color, the color takes care of itself. You paint colors on the things, you put light on it, and the color'll be there. That's what color is. You take colored still pictures and they're great. But you take the same thing in black and white, and they say, "Well, it's mushy. There's no quality. There's nothing there. Why didn't they get a little highlight on the side, or something?"

So, I think that between color and the shape of the screen, the whole art's gone out of it. I think the thing now is a billboard on the side of the road that ought to be discarded. I hate the shape of it now. It's lost. It's awfully hard to compose. And you can't get any intimacy at all in a thing that shape. A big, long, narrow thing. And you want to work out intimacy. You've got so much left over on the sides of your intimate portions that you've got to fill it up with something, and it's distracting.

The Camera's Effect

JOHN HUSTON: The camera follows the mental processes. Film does. I think even more than that, more than many realize, it also follows physical processes. I'll give you an example. Look from this lamp to that lamp. Do that a couple of times. You blink. That's a cut. You don't do this because you know what the relationship is. You're used to this room now. You know what the spatial relationship is. So, when you look from there to there, you don't keep your eyes open. You rest your eyes and open them again.

I've seen recently scenes where they pan, one thing to the other, and it strikes me as tedious, and unaware of the way we think and our bodies do. I think this has come out of a novice's first experiences using the camera, and we could trace that. There is simply one example of how we're dictated to — as well we should be — by the behavior of our bodies and our minds.

I see on the screen very often the wrong relationship between people in a dialogue. Here they are talking where they should be eight feet apart. They're three feet apart or a foot and a half apart on some occasions. I think that the camera should discover what the right distance is. Most are now making rules which are of course to be broken. It would be very hard to make someone, even a comedian, amusing or funny by shooting up at them. I don't say this couldn't be done, but I think it probably comes from our memories as children — from those that are bigger, are wiser, stronger and nobler. We look up — same as you do with sculpture, monumental sculpture. Would you look down at your superior, or even God Almighty?

HAL ASHBY: I will try and get relationships set up from the front. It's that creative level, so everybody keeps turning on and gets it going and will talk about a scene and say, "Let's get it over here." And I'll work out the staging of a scene and then take a look through it. If the rapport's good and you're working well, you'll change the setup. You'll say, "That's fine, that's good"; or you'll move it over here a little bit and see it that way. But once you're into working, that rapport's usually clicking pretty good and you won't be very far off, and it gets them on too, you know, where they're going. You don't have to say, "Put it here; no, put it there," while they're standing around waiting for you to make up your mind.

And for George Cukor, it is basically true that the camera for the film actor has "the same energizing effect that the audience has in the theatre."

HOW THE MATERIAL NECESSITIES AND THE CAMERA INTERPLAY

ALLAN DWAN: Griffith didn't start to use the close-up until after I was in, I think. At least we didn't notice the close-up. Because like all the rest, he started being conventional. He used the full figures. Then suddenly he decided — I think he probably looked at some of Rembrandt's paintings or somebody's painting where there were just hands, and he said, "My goodness. Look at that magnificent face. I'm going to take the camera and go up and get a magnificent face and put it on the screen."

Now, he didn't make that move around much at that time because he would show the full figure or the three-quarter figure and *then* cut into the close-up of the face, banging it in, you know. And you'd jump up suddenly as you were talking to a person and he'd suddenly lunge forward and there was his head right in front of you. It was a funny effect. It did that to you when it first happened. It wasn't smooth. The camera didn't move in; it jumped in and gave you that shock that you get today with what I call hysterical cutting — that's back in, you know. It's bang-bang-bang-bang stuff. And sort of senseless cutting at times, and then close-ups that cut from there to there, hysterically. He just cut it in. They didn't object to that.

But when that head turned around or when that head moved across to another spot, then they roared. They said that the head is walking and it has no feet. The theatre owners made the complaints, but they said that they got complaints from their audiences. Just as I got complaints when I started to move the camera. And they said they got sick, seasick, at first, because it gave them a feeling of moving. They thought the seats were moving. The same thing you got when Cinerama came. And you had those awful feelings in the theatre, of your moving. And they were really effective. But we had that complaint.

When I went and made my picture, instead of jumping into the close-up, I dissolved into the close-up, or I moved into the close-up. I got the cameraman to learn how to change his focus while I moved his camera on wheels. I put the camera on wheels; they never had them on wheels. They had them on tripods, and they were anchored down and chained down so there'd be no vibration. I put them on dollies and moved them, shoved them up on people. And that, that alarmed the theatre, too. To see something come, they didn't know whether they had moved up or whether the screen was falling over on them or what. But things would come up on them. Movement bothered them at first. Then they got to like it.

JAN KADAR: You should not impose the camera on the dramatic content, but you should do just the opposite. So, we worked in the studio in the following way. I make it my homework. It's like a chess play. When you start one way, you have to do this and that so that you have five, six, seven solutions. But, I never told it to the cameraman in advance. I didn't tell it to my script girl either. I am talking now about shooting in the studio, the interior scenes, where the drama really occurred.

VINCENT SHERMAN: When working with Errol Flynn, I would have to stage everything so that I would photograph the left side of his face. He said to me that he didn't hear well on his right side. I once said to him that people were going to wonder what the other side of his face looked like. He said, "Oh, no, no, no." He thought that was his good side, and it was his good side. Every time he came into a room, that would be the side that would be revealed.

HOWARD HAWKS: The "New Wave" in Europe really ended up by doing the old stuff that had been tried before — the camera floating around, all that stuff we went through, camera on the floor, camera up above the people, and so forth. Finally, we realized we could tell a story better if we told it just as though we were looking at it. In *El Dorado*, the only way to do a scene was to put the camera on the floor and let a body fall out of a church steeple on it. One critic was terribly surprised. He said, "That's the first time I've ever seen Hawks get the camera off of eye level." I mean, I had to do it that way. We were just stuck. But there are plenty of things that you can do dramatically, characterwise.

VINCENT SHERMAN: The Epsteins, producers of *Mr. Skeffington,* had talked to the art director about getting the interior of a home with rich wood paneling. They wanted dark walls. Well, of course, in color it would have been very beautiful and simple to handle. But in black and white, these dark walls — when I went in and looked at them — I said, "My God, fellows, this is really going to be a problem to shoot."

I took in Ernie Haller, who was going to be the cameraman, and he said, "The only way I'm going to be able to bring light to these walls is to put banks of lights on the floor. Otherwise it will just be black." In many cases they are pretty dark, and it took just hours to light the damn thing. As a matter of fact, as a result of that particular picture, Warner issued an order that there were to be no more dark walls in the studio. It did take an inordinate amount of time to light. It was rich-looking and everything in the final product, but it cost me hours of time.

ALFRED HITCHCOCK: For the shot in *Frenzy* where we followed the murderer out of the house into Covent Garden, we used a hanging camera. You see you have a hanging camera and then you go by a fanlight, a glass panel in the doorway. Well, half of it, that's all done in the studio, you see, and that glass panel is slid away. Now you go up with the camera pointing down the stairs, so that you see the murderer, with a sort of stone face — he's not a cheerful chap, because he's going to get down to the business of raping the girl. Now you go up and you turn, and you look and they go in the room. The door closes. Now you go back a bit, because you're on overhead rails, and as you get near to the door with the fanlight over it, the door at the bottom of the stairs, you slide in the glass panel very quickly. Now you go down the corridor, in the studio, and then you get outside the door and a man goes by with a bundle.

Now you go to Covent Garden itself, and you repeat the going through the door and the same man going by carrying a bundle. That's where your cut is. Now you pull back, and now you show a façade. And what we're saying pictorially is: There is a murder going to take place, and nobody will ever know it, because at that moment I brought the sound up three times its volume, so that the audience subconsciously would say, "Well, if the girl screams, it's never going to be heard."

So the whole thing was something for the audience to imagine what is going on by the pictorial expression, which takes us right back to the visual again — telling as much as you can visually. Another example is that strange effect in *Vertigo*; it took thirty years to get. It really did.

When I was making *Rebecca*, I had a scene where Joan Fontaine is supposed to faint. I explained to Selznick I wanted to get the effect of her looking and everything seeming to go far away. Where I got the idea from was at the Royal Chelsea Arts Ball in London on New Year's Eve. I remembered at a certain time during the evening everything seemed to go far away. And I asked for this effect and they said they couldn't do it.

I tried again about five years later. For *Vertigo*, they tried different effects and finally it was arrived at by a combination of a dolly shot and a zoom lens crossing each other. Dollying in and zooming out. When the head of special effects came to me I said how much was it going to cost. He said fifty thousand dollars to put a camera high and take it up and zoom it, because of the enormous rig. I said, "But there is no one in the set." Why didn't they make a miniature and lay it on its side? "Oh, I hadn't thought of that." So they did it and it cost nineteen thousand dollars.

VINCENTE MINNELLI: Joseph Ruttenberg, the cameraman on *Gigi*, was very worried about the scene in Maxim's. He said, "Why don't we go for lunch one day and talk, because I have a few ideas."

I said, "Fine." So, we went there for lunch.

He said, "You know, this ceiling is marvelous, this Tiffany ceiling," and he says, "Of course the mirrors, we can block those out," and so and so.

And finally I said, "Joe, the whole quality of Maxim's is the low mirrors. They must be shown. They must reflect the entire room in them, and somehow hide your lights.

He said, "I was afraid of that." So, he hung those special bulbs where they were hidden. He had a terrible time of it, and he said afterwards that he couldn't make out in the studio where all the lights were available.

ROBERT ALDRICH: Unfortunately, if you have a long training, you are apt to be too cautious. You will say to yourself, "I know it can't be made." When that happens, your horizons and thresholds are going to be lower than they should be. They will not be higher. But, the cameraman doesn't want to make it sometimes. They will say that the light is going. You will tell them to open to $f 2.3$ and shoot it. If you don't like it. object and hold the slate upside down. There was that great sequence that Ford did, the raining sequence in *She Wore a Yellow Ribbon*, that won the award. It's the same old story. A guy says, "I object," and held the slate upside-down and got the Academy Award for best photography. It's absurd. What's the worst thing that can happen? The guy can shoot it the next day or two days later. Why go home?

A DISCUSSION — THE NATURE OF CAMERAWORK

We might propose that the best cameraman will be one who has a sense of the overall look of the film, who has the technical expertise to plan most completely for the realization of the film's visual requirements as determined by script, direction, etc., and who is sensible enough to create conditions that will urge any chance events toward a direction best suited to the entire film. Any number of photographic techniques and styles have evolved out of what is often a chance set of circumstances wherein directors and their cameramen have fused artistic sensibility and technical skill.

There are limitations placed upon camerawork as a result not only of its function in terms of the film as a whole and as a result of an individual cameraman's skill, but more as a function of what camerawork actually means. Should a camera be set up in a theatre to film a play or a dance, it would in no way capture what we consider to be the essence of those arts.

To be sure, a dance or a play can be filmed from, say, the position of a spectator. Indeed, we might let the camera zoom in and out, pan around, go blank periodically in order to simulate the role that our eyes play while observing these other arts. However, it must be recognized that what is being captured on film is not the dance in its danceness, or the play in its theatricality, but a transposed sense of the textures of space as they unfold through time. What this really means is that there is no one-to-one correlation between entities in and of themselves and what those entities come to mean within the framework of a film shot. For example, we might be sitting in the desert and have a tremendous feeling of the passage of time. The very stillness of the land, the sky, conveys to us a sense of the ultimate immutability of time. However, if we were to film exactly that scene, it would not be the inevitable flow of time that we would be capturing, but instead a certain fortitude in the very space of existence, a certain resistance to the very effects of time. As we have learned from films directed by Murnau, Lang, Ophuls, and many others, it is actually the moving or tracking shot and not the stationary one that often best represents the feeling of an indomitable temporal passage. That is to say, it is when the movie camera moves that we begin to experience the ravages of time, which are sensed during moments of stillness in the everyday world. What is called for, then, in the expert cameraman, is a certain basic intelligence and sensibility about the grammar of filmwork. The camera is not an extension of the human eye. It gives us an entirely new kind of eye whose defining properties are as different from our everyday vision as is the bowl of fruit painted as a still life different from the bowl on our dining room table, as are the rhythms and dynamics of music from the rhythms and dynamics of the common sense world. Camerawork allows us to become acquainted with what is a scene, not with what may be the emotional inwardness characteristic of the individual entities within that scene when considered in their everyday careers apart from the film.

While the human eye has a potentiality for peripheral vision, the film camera provides a sharp boundary for the area of its concern. The eyes inevitably roam, and therefore include more in their vision than that which is primarily focused upon. Peripheral elements for the film camera are, by definition, eliminated. With that elimination, the worldly environment of what we have focused upon is lost. Whereas anything we attend to in the everyday world we recognize as belonging in a larger environment, the film camera gives us a boundary leaving nothing on the outside except what is alien to it. The camerawork, then, is analogous to the frame imposed upon a painting. The camera, and the frame, shut out the world of everyday experience. In ordinary vision even when we are attending to a particular thing, we have, at least, a dim awareness of what is outside that thing. Also, in ordinary perception the very surface on which we focus is being pulled away from us by the object which lies beyond it and to which it belongs. We are always encountering appearances as being pulled away by realities which possess them. But even the highly mobile and flexible film camera can never know more than appearances. It cannot catch the recessiveness, the self-absenting quality of the actualities to which those appearances belong. The film camera functions like the brush of a painter. The French have often referred to it as a "caméra-stylo." The film camera is an instrument used in creating new appearances — the appearances of art — different from everyday appearances.

While the film camera is, and can only be, concerned with appearances, it nevertheless possesses the unique quality of having its created images able to point beyond those appearances toward a submerged common reality out of which they are constituted. The shots recorded by the film camera reveal dimensions of existence and its actualities which are not available through ordinary perception. If we establish the film shot as a primary unit of expression, we must make sure that we know just how much a shot can describe and indicate. There have been films which consisted entirely of one shot. In the case of short "experimental" films, this one shot usually is concerned with the enactment and embodiment of one particular process. For example, in *Welcome to Come* (1968, directed by Fred Camper), the single three-minute shot concerns itself with seeing, with the shifting of perceptual attention from one area to another. As in Japanese haiku, the actual content seems minimal whereas the scope of meaning may be great. The shot, in this case, not only presents the appearance of things in these two separate frames of reference, but is largely concerned with vitalizing the processes, the dynamics, of the act of seeing. In longer films that are composed of one shot (*Empire* by Andy Warhol, *Wavelength* by Michael Snow), the shot becomes more of a bounded window for our perceptual, sensual reactions. The concern in these cases is almost strictly causal-dynamic. Occasionally, even Hollywood has presented feature films consisting entirely of one shot or, at most, of several very long shots. In *Rope* (directed by Alfred Hitchcock, 1948) what is essentially a murder melodrama becomes a highly complex set of moral interrelationships. The incessantly moving camera scans, observes, and lays bare not only the appearances which it confronts, but those subterranean realities that have caused those appearances to arise.

The question then becomes, of what use is it to discuss the single film shot as a unit? Since the shot can be of virtually any length, since anywhere from one shot to thousands of them can constitute what we refer to as a whole film, since the shot may primarily enclose appearances or portray processes, or do both equally, it is necessary to regard the film shot not as a final unit of artistic expression, but rather as helping to constitute a whole context in which the film lives. That transcendent sense of the way things are that we encounter when viewing a film is not so much resident in the shots individually as caused by the shots being bound together in some ordered, shaped, and conditioned flow guided by an overriding artistic consciousness. When we seek to discover the artistic import of a film, it is not the shots in isolation to which we attend, but the overall consciousness that binds the film as an organic unity.

Another interesting aspect of the film shot is the way its scope of concern seems to vary from film to film. In the films directed by Douglas Sirk, for example, we sense that the frames tell their own story. That is, although we are aware that there is a unity to all the shots, we come to feel that this larger unity is constituted out of those specific appearances that the shot presents. This is not to retract the earlier statement that a film's artistic unity exists over and above the individual shots. It is to say, however, that that overall sense of appearances which the film provides issues forth from the actualities focused upon and interrelated within its frames. While in these Sirk films we sense that the appearances and processes of existence are resident in that which the frame is focused upon, there are other films, such as those directed by Roberto Rossellini, where we sense that the ultimate processes that seem to be the concern of the entire film are not bounded within the geographical confines of the individual shots. Particularly in Rossellini's recent "educational" work, there is an overwhelming lack of rigidity about the shots' structures. His well-known technical apparatus, which enables him to change the focal length of the lens during the filming of the shots (an automatic, remote control zoom device), is indicative of his shots' potential to inscribe a whole world of meaning from a number of different viewpoints. When he gives us a set piece of a group of men standing and talking, instead of cutting between close-ups of them speaking and reacting, he usually starts with a long shot and then comes in and zooms and pans between the men while they speak and listen. Our sense of the group as a whole is not lost when we zoom in — instead, the process of zooming in illuminates clearly that greater "boundedness" which contains them. The zooming in, the apparent shift of attention, does not isolate them from each other, but points to the larger context in which they exist. We may say, then, that the shots in a film sometimes are concerned strictly with that which they frame, and sometimes, by the very processes which act upon those shots, call attention to that which they do not frame.

Moreover, there are certain kinds of shots and a certain way of shooting that calls attention, rather than to the unity of the frame, to the tonality, the textures, described at any part of the frame. For example, the shots in films directed by Howard Hawks demonstrate a certain flatness, a lack of differentiation between background and foreground. As a result, in the frames and shots of Hawks's films, we may attend merely to a portion of the frame in this shot, another portion in the next shot, and so on, and still perceive as much meaning as we might were we to observe thoroughly the particularities of the whole frame.

Camerawork is best seen as a tool for the expression of artistic ideas and feelings. There would be no film without camerawork. However, beyond a certain level of competence in technical execution, beyond a certain resourcefulness of imagination, we have no guarantee that a film will be a unified work of art simply because it shows an excellence in camerawork. If, in examining film, we begin with the idea that camerawork is full-fledged artistic work and thus we must attend to the units of camerawork — the shots — in order to comprehend a film's artistic import, then we would lose a dimension, a depth of emotional richness which only the film viewed as a unity provides. Camerawork alone cannot be the master of space, time, and dynamic processes. Nor can camerawork alone reveal heretofore hidden depths of actualities in an interplay with the forces of existence.

Certainly, camerawork is part of the grammar of film, but grammar does not necessarily exhaust the potential form and meaning of its subject. A film's grammatical constructs help provide a context for that ultimate import which now and later will be infused into a film's being. A film shot is beautiful not if the reality which it illuminates is beautiful, but if, in itself, and in its relationship to the other shots in the film, it helps to exude a certain extended sense of the way things appear. We do not perceive a film's artistic merit by attending to the particulars of this shot or that, but by experiencing the total vision which the film presents to us. The appearances that a film forcefully presents are reliant upon camerawork for their portrayal, but not for their being. The eventful flow of the script, the gestures and presences of actors must also be counted as contributing to making those appearances be.

9

Film Editing

The most enjoyable part of directing or filmmaking for me is editing. It is literally the language of filmmaking. It is right there, and you learn constantly how dumb you are and how much you have to learn every time you take a picture into the cutting room.

— William Friedkin

I don't want to get into editing. I'm not interested in it. Editing is editing. It's all right. I have nothing against it. You get good effects from it. You want to cut to people in bathtubs, great. It works. Editing is a discipline that should be subservient to something else. It usually is.

— Paul Morrissey

THE ART OF FILM EDITING — AN ANALYSIS

After the film camera captures and works over the enactment by actors, objects, and settings of a script's eventful flow, we are left with a strange sort of substance, a substance that does not really have its counterpart in any of the traditional arts. This substance, a number of filmed images, has a sort of finality that we do not encounter in the substeps of any other art. While the developing process in the laboratory may affect some of the colors, shadings, and tonalities, the basic construction of the shots as registered by the camera is inalterable. The images, once having been

231

committed to film, represent a certain closed segment of action that occurs through some time span. No matter what occurs to the images in the remaining steps of the filmmaking process, they possess an absolute completeness as to what it is that they show. However, merely having a number of finalized images does not give us a film. The images must be connected, juxtaposed. They must be trimmed, manicured. They might become interwoven. They might appear side by side. Some of the images may be eliminated from the whole film altogether by the time the work is complete.

It is the job of film editing to take what is already a certain kind of finalized material and treat it as though it were raw material, as though it were open-ended. Because of this unique extra step in the course of making a whole film — this step that separates film from the theatre, from painting, from story, from music — much attention has been directed to the film editing process in attempting to determine if it is here that the art of film resides.

That we have film editing at all rests upon a number of assumptions. First, and most obviously, there must be a greater than one-to-one ratio between the amount of film that we shoot and the amount we care to end up with. This may occur for a number of reasons. If a shot involves some complicated technique, we will want to take it a number of times, hoping that the execution in one will be superior to another. If we are using actors, we may repeat a shot several times in order to insure that the performance will be as intended. If a shot calls for some natural occurrence (for example, sunset, clouds moving by, waves crashing against rocks), we may let the camera roll for a great deal longer than necessary in order to be sure we capture the exactly desired moment. Finally, in the case of scenes involving interplay between actors, between actors and objects, or between objects themselves, we may shoot them in a number of ways, from a number of different angles, so that we will be sure to have enough material to piece together a sequence with intercutting, reaction shots, inserts, and so on.

Another assumption underlying the necessity of film editing is that only after a scene, or even a single shot, is completed, is "played back," will we have enough distance, enough knowledge of the facility with which it was played, to know just when and where the cuts should occur. In the midst of choosing camera setups, rehearsing action or dialogue, and attending to technical execution, it may be difficult to anticipate the editing that will help to bring about the desired effect. With the distance of time, though, we will be in a better position to conceptualize the scene as a whole, to see how its parts might best be integrated.

Finally, in viewing the completed shots and scenes, we may notice various themes or even isolated points of interest that have occurred entirely by accident. No amount of planning can limit and bound the potentialities for nuance in performance, subtlety in technique, and out-and-out chance events and tonalities that will be present in the completed shots. Thus, film editing provides us with an opportunity to spot submerged elements and to bring them to the fore. Indeed, the whole idea for a scene may change upon our seeing the completed individual shots.

Eisenstein has posited that there are three basic editing techniques.* Parallel editing — where a number of stories may be seen to unfold concurrently (for example, Griffith's *Intolerance*, Keaton's *Three Ages*); editing by attraction — where images may be juxtaposed to reinforce one another, to underscore, to create metaphor; and accelerated editing — where temporal elements are altered to create new temporal modalities quite apart from the realities which constituted the substance of the shots. By confronting film shots in their durational and contextual aspects, film editing is concerned primarily with the juxtaposition and length of the individual shots.

In film editing, it is decided which shots are to be used where and when. It also is decided when shots should be broken up, when they should be preserved. Decisions are made regarding when cuts should occur from the subject of the activity to its object (reaction shots, inserts, flashbacks, and so on). Sometimes whole shots, even scenes, are deemed superfluous and are eliminated. Film editing, although confronted with rigidly produced shots, is able to plasticize them once again by exercising control over their temporal extension and their dynamic juxtaposition. Further, in editing, an all-important decision will be made as to when *not to cut*. Preserving the linear tension of a particular shot may be absolutely necessary if its power is to remain intact. There are traditional moments for cuts, especially in narrative films, which sometimes must be scrutinized with utmost care if only to avoid cliché, and thus the dissipation through familiarity of an emotional response from the viewer. Time shifts by means of flashbacks and flashforwards will be considered in light of the film's overall intention. In film editing, too, the need for special sorts of optical effects may be recognized. Dissolves, fades, superimpositions may be called for in order to underscore a particular theme. The juxtaposition of a film's shots and the determination of their duration are resolved only in the film editing process. A film is completed only after the work of the editing has helped to constitute a single integrated totality.

Film editing is concerned with selection. Elements are juxtaposed that otherwise might remain at a distance. Out of a plurality of opportunities, a

---

*Sergei Eisenstein, *Film Form: Essays in Film Theory, and the Film Sense*, Cleveland: World Publishing, 1965.

single integrated totality is made. Since it is the function of film to take all of nature, all space, all time, all causality as within its province, the task of film editing is a cosmic-minded one. Bits of these dimensions of existence are related to one another during the editing process. Moreover, these interrelationships are determined regardless of the ordinary laws of space, time, and causality. In a sense, later time may be placed before earlier time, future before past. Different locations in space are interwoven. Causal processes may be reversed. Film editing makes concrete a new spatial, temporal, and dynamic universe, which is revelatory of what is ultimately existent and what individuals in their route actually are.

The film editing process radically shifts about various portions of extension — the shots — and opens up for us the extraordinary pliability of these extensions. We gain a new insight into time when we see that a remote period can be juxtaposed with a present one without the intermediating times that occur in the ordinary course of nature, in the daily life. The future can be made to operate in the present and to work back and be involved with the past just as surely as the past can be brought into interplay with the future. Similarly, in juxtaposing the different parts of space, a new geometry is created, a geometry which is nowhere exemplified in the ordinary world. This new geometry is one of concrete occurrences with definite contours, hills and valleys, recesses and protuberances that are created right then and there. Finally, the freedom of film editing from ordinary causal processes allows it to make evident the relevance of anything whatsoever to anything else. This is a revelation of the richness and the endless flexibility and potentiality of every entity in the universe.

Film editing challenges the contours, the limits, of ordinary extension. In regulating the extensions by choosing the mechanical activity from shot to shot, from scene to scene, the parameters of movement, of transition (length of shot, ultimate linear position, cuts, fades, dissolves, special optical effects, and so on) should be chosen so as to enhance all elements. The transitions between shots must themselves occur so as to lend an import to both that they would not have had in isolation. Because film occurs dynamically through time, there is an additive, cumulative effect from one image to the next. Indeed, when one film is viewed many times, the transitions must be seen to be not only functional in terms of story line, but logically controlled in terms of the film's aesthetic design as a whole. It is especially when one is viewing one film repeatedly that the beauty of its transitional effects emerges. There is a true interplay not only between one shot and the following shot, but between that shot and its predecessor. We not only retain after-images while viewing a film, we remember what has been occurring. Of course, it is not so much that one piece of film influences another, but that our understanding, our grasp of the whole is enhanced.

Film editing begins with the extensional qualities of the objects, settings, and textures within the individual shots and infuses into them an overriding extensionality. The extensional qualities added to a film's whole during the editing take into consideration the extensions of the entities within individual shots, and the extensional qualities of the shots themselves as integral units, yet produce a more cosmically concerned dimension of extension. This cosmic extension is necessary to unify a film's many parts but is not derivative from any one localized entity, from any one shot or object within a shot. In a sense, the overall extensional quality of a film overcomes the limitations of the localized extensions; overcomes them, but is not foreign to them. A film's shots and entities within those shots present, during the editing process, a series of occasions to create an extension limited by the film's whole, but not by its parts. That which is inside each frame exerts a force, exists in a tensional relationship to all the other frames and shots, suggests an extension that is recognized and reworked in the editing to create the extended sense of the universe that is constituted out of a film's overall appearance.

If we say, then, that through the work of film editing — the determination of the duration of each of a film's shots, the modes of transition between them, and the linear placement of these shots in terms of the whole film — we can affect, indeed, determine, the extensional quality of the film as a whole, we also must recognize the final limitations placed upon the editing process by the other sorts of filmwork. André Bazin* has pointed out how the classical practice of film editing tends toward the baroque. Juxtapositions, while they may help to underscore and advance the interplay between certain thematic threads, may also snap the intensity building up within the individual shots by adding distracting and superfluous ornamentation. The compositional qualities, or framing, of a shot may themselves be lending an extensional dimension to the whole of a film that cannot be enhanced, but only interfered with or recognized and obeyed by the traditional work of editing.

In this sense, the deep-focus shot, or sequence shot (where all the action of a sequence occurs within one shot rather than a series of cuts), may be seen as a major editorial interpretation on the part of the director and/or cameraman and script writer. By composing in depth, by allowing sequences to be played out without cuts (although the camera may move

*André Bazin, *What Is Cinema?* Vol. I, Berkeley: University of California Press, 1967.

about), it might be argued that the traditional work of editing — the creation of an overall extensional depth — can successfully be integrated into the directorial or photographic style of a film. Bazin argues that by composing in depth or, better, by framing the elements — objects and actions — of a scene in such a way as to make cuts superfluous to its flow (in this case, cutting would be relegated to the role of a mechanical tool which helps us get from one scene to the next), we are doing exactly what normally is done by editing: setting up lines of action, planes of visual response.

We have incorporated those elements which we normally would look upon as transitional into the tensional, textural qualities of the frame. When we learn that, for example, many of the deep-focus shots in *Citizen Kane* are actually split-screen effects,* then it becomes apparent that the lack of cuts in such a scene does not indicate that there has been no editorial work. It means simply that the normal function of editing had been achieved in the actual staging of the shot. Bazin interestingly holds that the Kuleshov experiment† does not so much point up the potential art of film as it does attempt to analyze and dissipate the integrity and mystery, the ambiguity, of the film image.

Editing, for Bazin, is strictly a device out of the expressionist's arsenal with a potential, at best, for some kind of gross ordering and, at worst, for serving as a crutch for weakly conceived and composed images, thereby performing the analytical task which might have been better dealt with within the shot. For this reason, then, a film that contains no classical editing, no cuts between shots, no juxtaposition of elements need not be looked upon as possessing no editorial style, no evidence of editorial work. Looking at Hitchcock's *Rope* (1948), an entire film in seemingly one eighty-one-minute shot, we would not think to say that it suffers from a passivity in the editorial dimension. Indeed, since there are no instantaneous moments — cuts — where we detect the work of editing, the extensionality of the film is pervasive. We do not so much notice that there are no cuts as we do get caught up in the moving world of the film. To conclude that perhaps the film might be better if we had a few cuts here and there, a

*Peter Bogdanovich, article in *Esquire* magazine, October, 1972.

†There are many references throughout the film literature to the Kuleshov experiment. Here, a shot of a man is intercut with various objects to which he does not facially react; that is, he maintains an identical facial expression regardless of the object of his supposed attention. It is seen that, depending on the object, his facial configuration sometimes seems one of innocence, sometimes of voyeuristic leer, and so on. Alfred Hitchcock, in interviews, often refers to this as an example of the power of film editing to affect our perception of film images.

few bits of evidence that the cosmic extensionality usually seen as the work of editing was being imposed upon the images, would be not to accept the film on its own terms. As we would not criticize a painting that had no evidence of blue, or a play that did not follow the normal division into three acts, we cannot rule against a film if it shows no outward signs of classical editing. What we must look for is whether or not the traditional accomplishments of editing have been integrated into some other aspect of a film.

Films with little or no cutting, such as the early features of Andy Warhol, have been criticized for not utilizing the full potential of filmmaking techniques. Supporters of these films usually try to show how it is the very boredom in the universe which is being expressed, that the lack of cutting that leads us to a bored state somehow makes us aware of this dimension of existence. I think, though, that in a film with no traditional cutting we should not necessarily emphasize this lack of editing before we attend directly to the images in order to determine what the film is about. In Warhol films, for example, there seems to be not so much a concern with "boredom" as with the ways that entities present themselves through their surfaces. Objects, people, events in Warhol films are not derived from some "core of humanity" (as they might be in a traditional narrative film) but from the very surface of the universe, the universe's appearance. Thus, the occasional cuts in a Warhol film represent a way of moving from one surface to the next. This is not to say that Warhol eschews consideration of the temporal extension in his images, but that the temporal dimension is inextricably involved in the interplay of surface. In a Warhol film, a monologue, or a conversation between two people, might be interrupted by cutting to some brightly colored object, then cutting back to the discussion at a time later in its development. Or, there might be a cut from one conversation to an object, to some other event altogether. In these cases, the eventful flow of the film is described and conditioned by those very appearances that we perceive. The rapid jump cuts that often occur between the major sequences in Warhol films are to be seen not so much as the necessary mechanical occurrences because of a changeover in cameras, but seem to urge the events onward, to serve as the virtual source of time and change. Hence, in Warhol films, when there is an occasional cut that seems to be following classical lines (such as in *Sex*, when we are watching a scene in a room and there comes a knock at the door and we cut to the door), the function is not the analytical one described in the Kuleshov experiment, but is the stimulus to a whole sense of dynamics.

All of this is not to say that classical editing is unimportant to the art of film, but more that the breadth of application of editing principles may be wider than anticipated from a strict Eisensteinian description. When we define film editing as being concerned basically with the juxtaposition of shots, we lose the sense of the degree to which editing is dependent upon and often determined by those qualities of the images themselves. If instead we look upon editing as one of the ways that film can control the extensions of the universe, then we learn to rely more on the expressiveness of the images, and less on some external manipulation whose (by its very nature) intermittent control over a film's appearance will, it is hoped, help to bring out the images' underlying themes.

There are three sorts of relationships which the editing process may take in line with a film's images. First, editing may emphasize those extensional concerns indicated by the images. In this case the work of editing will be harmonious with and contributory to a film's overall unity. Second, the editing work might serve to inject a harmful tension between what the images seem to be about in themselves and the way that they are linearly placed in the unfolding of the film. Here, the editing will dissipate that unity strived for in the images — by camerawork, by acting, by setting, by event. Third, when confronted with a set of images that have no great artistic depth or unity, editing may help to construct a "patchwork" presentation of some sort of extensional interpretation. However, again, since the control of editing is explicit only at moments — the instants when cuts are manifest — the full reach of editing's power will not be exercised if it is not playing off some tendency inherent in the images. In this third role, the work of editing strives to construct out of materials that do not, in and of themselves, lend themselves to such a molding. We might say here that the work of editing is relegated to the function more desirably performed by script writing, directing, and so on.*

This is not to say that there cannot be a style evidenced in film editing. If we are presented with a selection of artistically made shots, there still are an enormous number of ways in which they can be interconnected. Exact temporal durations and the modes of transition may be decided upon in as many ways as there are film editors. There might be a particular editing style that best serves a certain combination of shots regardless of what film they appear in. Nicholas Ray has said that Sherman Todd, the editor of several of his early features, gave him a basic insight into the nature of screen action that was valid for all story, all acting, all camerawork.

However, there are many examples which indicate the ultimate independence of a directorial vision from the classical work of editing. In *Pickup on*

---

*See Jean-Luc Godard's discussion of the role of the film editor in *Godard on Godard*, New York: Viking, 1972, the essay, "Montage My Fine Care."

South Street, directed by Samuel Fuller, there often are times when the camera is on a tight close-up which normally would satisfy an editor. However, invariably, the camera tracks in to an extreme tight close-up. This added move, while being achieved by camerawork, and while offering a sort of editorial effect (as we normally might cut from, say, a medium shot to a normal close-up), can come only from a directorial vision. There is another sequence in the same picture where a girl is walking along in a subway station, trying to remember something that may have just occurred on the train. Today, the normal editorial style might have quick flashbacks to the event, demonstrating for the audience exactly what the girl is thinking. However, in the picture, there are no cuts at all in this sequence. Thus, Fuller seems more concerned with respecting the unity of the process than with explicating any particular individual perception or personality. Hence, he seems to be concerned with what Bazin might term "the integrity of the image."

If we were to film some action, say, a man walking to a lamp and turning it on, there would be virtually an infinite number of ways to shoot and cut this event. First, of course, the entire action may be shot in one piece, therefore not requiring any cuts. The placement of the camera in this case will determine the emphasis of the shot. With a stationary camera, we might emphasize the spatial coordinates of the lamp, the man, the man's hand, the environs of the room. With a moving camera, we might emphasize the process of the event with primary attention being focused upon the man's action, the lamp's resistance, or the room's essential change as a result of the light being switched on. Now, if the function of the event is to illuminate in the room some person or object that we did not know was there, then we might, after the lamp is switched, cut to the object of that shot. However, unlike in the Kuleshov example, we must be sure that the purpose of the cut is not *merely* explicative of the action, but serves to further the whole sense of space, of time, and of dynamics that we are working toward in the film as a whole. In the shooting of this scene, we must be sure that the frame compositions, too, have an import richer than the occasion of that moment. In this sense, script, acting gesture, camera placement, and movement must all unify to create the most complete statement possible of this particular occurrence. If, in a pedestrian manner, we were to cover the event from numerous points of view (that is, take stationary and moving shots of the room, the man, the lamp), then an editor could cut them together in such a way as to make perfectly clear the unfolding of the event. However, unless he also attends in terms of the film as a whole to those tones and textures called for by the event, then the editing will not have contributed to the film's unified sense of appearance. For Nicholas Ray, a certain technique of cutting *upon* action (that is, instead of staying on the man until the light is switched and then cutting to the room, the called-for cut occurs at the exact moment of switching) was developed, which made the action not only intelligible in terms of story line, but lent the whole process an artistic necessity. That is, the event became inextricably related to its effects, not merely serving as some functional predecessor in the sense of everyday causality. For Ray, this interrelationship between action and result could not have been achieved with a single image, only through the juxtaposition of the several elements deemed necessary to an understanding of the event in the framework of the entire film's sense of space, time, and dynamics.

Film editing may help to reveal a certain beauty inherent in a film's images. It also may serve to add to a film a cosmic sense that is not contained in any one image alone. But film editing is nothing at all if not primarily reliant upon the beauties of its raw material — the completed shots. The style and technique of editing within a particular film must serve to advance that film's larger purposes. The mere juxtaposition of a film's shots in some commonsensical causal line does not enhance the art of a film. The addition through editing of some unique sense of extensionality that is entirely foreign to a film's intention works against that film's overall unity as a work of art.

This is not to say that there is only a passive role for film editing. There is enough evidence on the part of outraged directors, cameramen, and writers that editing *can* enormously affect a film's overall appearance. When John Ford says that he never gets involved with the editing, indeed, never even goes to the editing room, it is because he has taken into consideration during shooting that editorial manner which will best serve the intentions of the film. A Ford film, according to most of the cameramen and editors who have worked with him, really can be cut in only one way. This is not to say that there cannot be certain modifications in the flow as a result of the editing. What this does mean is that that arena of filmic interpretation that normally is the domain of postproduction editing work is so ingrained in all the individual shots of a Ford film that there is minimal need for additional creative work at this point. This does not mean that a Ford film is a film with no editing. It shows instead how editing, rather than being a specific process that occurs at a specific time during a film's production, is related to a certain sense of the film's whole appearance. All films, even those with no cuts at all, evidence an editorial vision.

When Alfred Hitchcock says that upon completion of a script, his interest in the filmmaking process is ended, he means not so much that there is an equivalence between script and film, but that from the completion of the script on, the film's being in his mind is so firmly established that it then becomes strictly a matter of work to achieve his vision, that he has successfully anticipated the specific appearances that will, through camerawork, acting, and editing, come to constitute his film. The context for the film that he has created through an interplay with story (contributed by the screen writer) and his own filmic vision is so strong that normal variations and chance occurrences here and there in the shots, in acting performances, in editorial manner, cannot affect the basic thrust of the film, the overall sense of appearance that will come out.

When Eisenstein says that the art of his films is to be found in their editing, he does not just mean that his shots are bits of information to be made into art at some later date. More, he means that based upon his shooting style, his images require a certain kind of radical juxtaposition in order for their import to be revealed fully.

In *Spite Marriage* (1929), Buster Keaton is thrust into the impossible situation of emptying a flooded boiler room with one small bucket. Rather than soaking the scene for various slapstick comic effects while this hopeless predicament is grappled with (as would have most silent comedies of the day), the film shows us a rapid fade-out and fade-in to the fully drained boiler room with Keaton mopping up the last drop. Thus, rather than the staging of various visual routines mocking the very hopelessness, an editing effect was chosen that underlined the meaning of the scene (and the whole film): that film itself can work a certain magic not possible in the everyday world. However, if we were to concentrate on this resolution as being strictly the work of editing, we would lose sight of the fact that this editing effect would be meaningless apart from the context of the film as a whole. Now, it might be argued that the script could have said, "In this scene, we demonstrate how the magic of film is entirely responsible for Keaton's success in emptying the boiler room." Further, the cameraman might have said, "Let's not take the usual slapstick approach; in fact, we won't even shoot Keaton's struggle with the bucket — we'll let the editor work it out." I think it becomes clear that whether or not we decide that the entire artistic import of this scene is attributable to a specific editing effect, we still see that the editing effect is only serving a larger sense of the whole film rather than the ends of one isolated scene. To say that the beauty of that scene is due to its editing is to risk an appreciation of how that whole film, in all its parts, adds up to being an artistic unity. Certainly, if the editing of all the sequences is uniformly excellent, if we see that the main thrust toward artistic unity is beholden to the editing work in the film, we still should not conclude that the beauty of this film's editing work is responsible for the beauty of the film. When we react to the film's whole, we are not so much reacting to a series of cuts here and there, we are sensing an overall vision which, though it may be constituted out of editing processes in conjuction with camerawork, is nevertheless greater than any of its parts considered separately.

The work of editing is apparent at moments, at instants of transition. The beauty in a particular shot occurs linearly here rather than there because of editing, but the shot's beauty is still an independent quantity. Its edited position and function may be determined by values apart from it (script exigencies, qualities of acting performance . . .) but its spatial-temporal-dynamic dimensions are not entirely beholden to its juxtaposition amidst other shots.

In *Three Comrades* (1938, directed by Frank Borzage), we see a series of phone conversations that are played in a split-screen manner. (Robert Taylor speaks with Margaret Sullavan — they each occupy half the screen with a fuzzy line of interconnection between them.) One normal way to play the scene would have been to concentrate visually on one or the other of the actors while hearing the response as though it were coming from the tele-phone. The other traditional playing would intercut between the two speak-ers in order to see their facial reactions. Instead, in this film, we see both actors throughout the whole conversation. Now, this effect had been used in many films before this one. Usually it is seen as being a "tricky" or "clever" way of filming such a conversation. However, in this case, it seems to be furthering the theme of the film as a whole — the unity of space-time in a love relationship. Do we say that the beauty of the scene is due to a decision to eschew standard editing techniques in favor of the split-screen, or do we realize that, considering the overall intent of the film, there really was only this one way to present the scene in order to maximize its potential power?

There is another scene in *Three Comrades* where Robert Taylor phones a doctor. We see him enter a room with a wall phone on the left. On the right we see a bird cage. Taylor places the call and we cut to a medium shot of him on the phone. Because of the cut, Taylor's position and size in the frame has changed. We also lose sight of the bird cage on the right. The effect of this cut is to concentrate our attention on Taylor and his call. However, even though the bird cage is out of the frame, we are not particu-larly aware of its absence. That is, the cut, while visually eliminating elements of the frame, does not really alter our spatial sense in the scene. This happens not only because of the residual effects of the first image in our memory, but to a whole sense of space we perceive from this film that is not dependent on the specifics of the objects within the shots. That is, because of our whole sense of the visual field which is built up throughout this film, we come to respect not so much the integrity of objects in themselves, but the overall sense of texture, of light and dark, of shape which emerges during the viewing of the whole film. When this cut occurs from the whole room to Taylor on the phone, we do not think, "Well, we've lost the bird cage, so it must be unimportant." We do not even say to ourselves, "Now that the phone conversation has begun we must shift our attention from the room to the particulars of the call." Instead, what we feel is more of a continuous evolving of a certain sense of the unity of time and place — a sense that regardless of what we are specifically looking at, there is a whole "way of looking" that is unfolding.

In film, the thrust of our attention, then, is not so much on specific shots or cuts, on specific gestures of actors or lines of dialogue. When we watch a film, a whole sense of space, time, and processes of becoming unfolds. Along with this general sense, we are enlightened as to how the qualities of various entities become manifest and interact with one another to yield an overall way of looking at the world.

THE IMPORTANCE OF FILM EDITING

The importance or nonimportance of film editing seems relative to directors' intentions and approaches. Leo McCarey told Peter Bogdanovich that it was the pacing of his actors (for example, Cary Grant and Irene Dunne in *The Awful Truth*) rather than the editing that contributed most to the success of his comedies. For Alfred Hitchcock, the problem is a practical one. After the picture is shot, he leaves little work for the editor. . . .

ALFRED HITCHCOCK: Because this is the point: I mean it seems to me an extraordinary thing when you have, say, six million dollars' worth of film, that it might get into the hands of a very indifferent cutter. That's your problem.

Brian De Palma, a self-pronounced disciple of the Hitchcockian method, adds:

When I shoot a film, I know exactly what's going to end up on the screen. There are few surprises in the editing room.

On the other hand, there are proponents of the view that editing is an important and necessary step in the filmmaking process.

FRANKLIN SCHAFFNER: Some of the most stunning moments occur when you are in the editing room. You remember months that you spent with the writer. Your scene had to be directed to a certain comment on that scene in a line of dialogue. And it would take two or three days to come up with that particular exchange or line of dialogue, and now you have it. And two months later you are in the editing room, and you put the scene together, and the first thing you start doing once your visual pattern is set in the scene, is pulling out the dialogue. Because it's amazing how much the visual impact tells the story, how much there is that visually influences the story. And you can only think to yourself, "What was I doing months ago, wasting my time?"

FRANK CAPRA: Films are made both on the set and in the cutting room. The original instinct, or, let's say, intuition about a scene comes when you're making it. Then you prove it in the cutting room, and you *improve* it in the cutting room in many cases. It's a funny thing about film: you take a series of scenes, maybe five scenes, and perhaps there are twenty-five different ways you can put those five scenes together five at a time, and there's probably only one way that makes any sense, and you've got to find that one way. The others are meaningless. If you put scenes together in one way you get a certain power out of them, but if you put them together another way it's dull, it's flat. Now don't ask me why. I don't know why. I just know that that's it, that's part of the whole creative thing about making a film. You don't know why those things happen, because if you did you could get yourself a formula, and you could sell it to everybody.

The potential of editing is such that it can even "save" a film.

GEORGE STEVENS: I remember the first picture I directed, and I have never lost my interest in the cutting of film on account of it, because I saw, when it was put together, that I had to save my professional life. The film couldn't be shown; it was impossible. I went in the cutting room and worked with it enough so that it could just barely be accepted.

The non-Hitchcockian orientation also is common.

BARBARA LODEN: You really don't know what you've got for a long time. You see your rushes. You really don't know what you've got and you start editing. I think you have to keep adapting to it all the way along the line, the whole creative process keeps changing. I don't see how anybody could start out saying, "I'm going to make this, it's going to be exactly like this, and this frame's going to be like that and that frame's going to be like that," and they draw diagrams and everything. But I don't see how anybody can predetermine how their movie is going to turn out, or why anybody would want to, because it's a creative thing and it's changing every day and you're changing every day while you're working on it. You start to make a movie and when you finish it, you'll be a different person. I was.

Of course, whether or not the mechanics of editing are widely used in a film, the dimensions of editing — juxtaposition of images and determination of their extensionality — always are felt.

ED EMSHWILLER: Time is the big plus in filmmaking over painting to me. It's the very fact that you have sequence and you have control. I think we live in time, through experience; through musical flow or kinesthetic flow; or through just a meditative flow. A painting is there. It doesn't go through any progressions, permutations, and so forth. It may be as valid an art as any, of course, but to me the idea of the certain experience of the flow of concepts is very important. I like that flow.

THE DIRECTOR-EDITOR RELATIONSHIP

Once the effects, if not the practice, of editing are acknowledged, we turn to the next all-important director relationship. As with cameramen, editors possess a technical skill that requires directors to come to them. (It has been argued that that itself is a construct of the unions — the establishment of multiple jobs in multiple studio departments.)

ALLAN DWAN: We didn't have cutters. I did it myself. We did it by hand. We didn't have any instruments or machines. Everything was backwards actually. It's just the reverse. Whites were black and blacks were white. But I'd cut it with a pair of scissors. Where I wanted to end a scene, I just cut it and that'd be a scene. Then I'd get the next scene I wanted after that and we'd put it together.

Whether the relationship is one of mutual creativity between artists, or more the carrying out of an artist's vision by craftsmen — ranging from full-fledged editors to enthusiastic producers — is, again, open to question.

HOWARD HAWKS: You need a good film editor. He can supply ideas that might not occur to the director. But also you have a style of shooting yourself. For instance, I use a great deal of reaction stuff. I don't give a hoot about watching somebody read a line that has been read eighteen hundred times before, but I am more interested in somebody's reaction to it. All of that comes out in making it. One time I made a picture on location. I came back and looked at it and I couldn't believe I made it because the man had cut it together in such a fashion. He wasn't there for me to tell him how it was supposed to be cut. So I had to fire him and reprint one hundred thousand feet of film and do it all again. A good man can make or break a picture.

You find most of the directors — for instance, Hitchcock is an editor; Jack Ford is not — most of the directors who are any good have very definite ideas of how they made a scene. You can do amazing things by editing. You can take a scene away from somebody. You can cut out bad stuff. Sometimes you can mess it all up.

In *I Was a Male War Bride*, we did have an awful lot of trouble. Cary Grant got yellow jaundice; Ann Sheridan had pneumonia; I never thought it was going to be over. Zanuck looked at it and said, "Well, it isn't your fault, you had too many handicaps. We'll just take a few cuts out and maybe it will get by."

I said, "The trouble is, I have a contract that calls for three previews and I'm going to stand on that."

We had a preview that night and I've never seen a more enthusiastic audience. I said, "What do you want to cut out of it?"

He said, "Not a damn thing."

I said, "Well, I'm going to cut about three or four hundred feet and don't tell me about it because you don't know how to cut this one at all," and Zanuck was a damn good editor.

On the other hand,

VINCENT SHERMAN: Warner got into the final cutting of the picture. I must say that he was pretty skillful — a little brutal sometimes. His favorite phrase came when we would say, "Please, J.L., don't do that."

He would say, "Vince, it only hurts for a second. The audience will never know it."

ALLAN DWAN: I cut the first cut. I mean dailies. I didn't run dailies. I ran the film later. The editor would rough it up, put it together according to the numbers, then we'd go in together to see it. Under our agreements, we'd have to deliver a cut. Then we'd kiss them good-bye because the producer goes to work and what comes out after that is anybody's business. And Benedict Bogeaus could slash them up like nobody. He fancied himself quite an editor, and he wasn't. He'd injure a picture sometimes, but he had Jim Lester, who was a very good cutter. Bogeaus would tell him to do things and they'd run it again the next day. Jim would tell him, "Hey, I think that was a big improvement — that suggestion of yours," and it was exactly the same.

And Bogeaus'd say, "You see, I told you." And the thing would be just as we had it in the first place.

Lester was a good cutter, and he had a sense of cutting. He would help it. He'd do things that I'd look at and say, "That's an improvement. I like it." He'd put something in that he had that he thought would be better — a close-up or something, or leave one out or something. And some fellows have an instinct for that, and he had.

RICHARD LEACOCK: I always edit my own films. I don't believe that you can learn to shoot unless you edit your own material. I think that the only way to progress in shooting is to constantly edit your own material.

STANLEY KRAMER: The characteristics I would want in an editor, I think, are the characteristics that everyone who knows his craft very well would like in an editor. That is someone who is technically proficient and is able to carry out yesterday what he wants today. Now the reason I say that is because editorially speaking, I cannot imagine letting a film, with all the respect in the world for the editor, I can't imagine letting a film go out where with each frame I haven't said, *"There."*

There are many wonderful editors and creative editors, but the creative editors have got ideas. They want to be directors and they're right.

The editor today doesn't get enough of a chance to make the decisions unless he's working with people who don't know as much as he knows, in which case they are totally dependent upon him. So that if you ask that question you have to ask the question of somebody who actually needs somebody to technically get it together and show him the way it's going to go together and what can be done, how elastic the film really is. Also, somebody who's aware of all the techniques in sound, in dubbing, in everything that has to be done to a film. . . .

It's not too far from the writer's dilemma. There is this terrible burden of having a director translate what he wrote in the way he didn't think it should be. Everybody's got this beef in film because of this interdepartmental thing. But the editor has it particularly because he puts a thing in the first cut and sometimes he puts in a wonderful first cut. Sometimes not.

Now, my feeling is that you make a film. So much of it depends upon how it goes together and where the emphasis goes and how the coverage is used and what the impacts are. It seems to me that any director who doesn't stay with it frame for frame — because really a lot of direction is in the cutting room — isn't worth his salt. The damn film . . . you can move scenes out of order. You can cheat close-ups from other sequences; you can pull things up and tear them down; snip off part of a scene. Everything. Which is part of directing.

PERRY MILLER ADATO: On the Gertrude Stein film, I worked very closely with the editor. I had a wonderful editor. A lot of the things that are in any film, including this one, are contributions of the editor. The editor is very important. As a matter of fact, from the beginning I felt that the editor was so important that I offered him the associate producer credit. He never functioned as the associate producer, but his contribution was so important. And his assistant editor ended up doing several very good sequences himself.

PAUL MAZURSKY: I get very involved with the cutting a lot. I just cut myself out of this last picture. I work with the editor the whole thing through.

ARTHUR PENN: The relationship between director and editor is one of those phenomena where you really are just craftsmen, and then sometimes a little spark of magic happens, and it turns out to be art. It's probably independent of both persons. Something in the collaboration creates a point of view that is maybe a little larger than both individually.

VINCENT SHERMAN: I worked fairly closely with Rudi Fehr, who is now the head of Warners' editorial department. He would do like a first cut and then we would look together and make a few little changes. He knew the values that I was trying to get out of the film. It was self-evident in the film that was shot. Usually I would say that there wouldn't be many changes after the first cut.

HOWARD HAWKS: My pictures often are almost cut when we're finished shooting. It's assembled in shots. The editor comes down to the set and says, "What have you figured on doing to this?" He watches it being taken. He watches the film, and he goes out and he puts it together. By the next day he is ready to show it. If he is particularly pleased with it you see it right away, and if he is still working on it I can tell what's happening because he doesn't show it to me for two or three days. Some pictures you get two days after you're finished.

MARTIN RITT: I will not look at a first cut that the editor has put together. I am usually so upset by the end of the first reel that I can't see anything else. I say, "What in hell is the value to me? I haven't seen the picture that I made. How could they possibly know what I meant?"

There is something axiomatic in our world which says that you get a sense of the film. That harks back to the early days when a director came in and saw the first cut and went on to another picture. When he saw the cut, he would throw his ideas into the hopper. I find that to be totally destructive. I can't do it.

I go every morning. I get to the cutting room at nine and I sit there until eleven. I work on one reel at a time. Then I put it away. When I go through a film once like that, I know I am going to see the film that I intended. Then I can make a judgment about what is right and what is wrong. But I can't make a judgment based upon somebody else's idea of what I meant.

RALPH NELSON: I have a fair idea of how it's going to be cut but then I'll always let the editor have a chance first. He may come up with some fresh ideas that didn't occur to me and I'll buy them, anything that makes a contribution to the film.

VILGOT SJÖMAN: I work very closely with the editor, and that means, to a certain extent, I feel he needs his freedom. But as soon as there is something when we don't agree, then we have to work it through once again. But, if you have shot a scene with a lot of material, I think it's silly that I should sit there and do it if the editor's a guy whom I trust.

FEDERICO FELLINI: For my first picture, I was more pretentious. I wanted to cut, and I wanted to do everything. I didn't want to miss anything. But going on in years, I prefer to leave the cutter to his work. I don't want to see the rushes because, you know, the picture that you make is not entirely the picture that you have in mind. So if I'm going to see what I'm doing day by day, I start to see that the picture is becoming a little bit different. The day after, when I am going to shoot, I think of the things I have seen, not of what I am making; so I prefer to separate.

JAMES BRIDGES: I've been very fortunate. I work with one cutter all the time, by the name of Walter Thompson. . . . He cut Renoir's first film in America. He cut for John Ford *Wee Willie Winkie* and *Young Mr. Lincoln*. He's a terrific, wonderful cutter. I always work with him. I have it in my contract that on the sixth day or seventh day I have a projection room, and nobody is admitted except the cutter and myself, and we cut as we go along. He's always one week behind me, so by the end of the second week after the film is finished shooting, I see the first cut. And we even polish as we go, so that it moves very, very fast.

HAL ASHBY: On *Harold and Maude,* I had editors, but I cut it in the end — which is something I want to break away from, because I've been into editing and I don't like to do that. But I let the guys go through and get their first cut on it. What I'm always trying to do, because I've been an editor, is free them up and have them work as I did as an editor, and that was to please myself. I always went for that. I worked with a guy who was into that, so I got that, and that's the best feeling you can have. Because if you let the film turn you on, and you get pleased by that, then you're happy with it — unless you've really got somebody who's definitely got such and such. Somebody who's got that much money usually doesn't shoot that much film. You know, somebody says, "I really see it this way and this way and this way" — well, that's about all the film you're going to have to work with. I didn't run into that with those kind of people before, and I really wanted to free these guys up.

But it's very, very tough to find guys who give a damn. Most of them say, "Well, Jesus, you shot this, it should be in the picture." So you sit there for two-and-a-half hours the first time, and it looks like something in every scene is working, but it's either too long before it gets going, or it's over and it's staying on too long after what you've really got going with the scene is there.

SOME GENERAL WATCHWORDS

ROMAN POLANSKI: There are two reasons for cutting. One is that you can't carry it any further for technical reasons, and the other is that you need another shot. For example, I show a man sitting here and talking with these people. So I see these people, I see him and suddenly, somehow, he talks here and I turn and look at him, or he passes a glass of water to someone, so I have to cut. To pan would be nonsensical since it doesn't follow any physiologically known pattern, because when I look from here to you, I am not aware of what is happening. It is like a cut, you see. My eyes somehow disconnect for a moment when they swing over here. To render that, you have to cut.

But also, when you do a long shot you see you can do more. The acting is easier for actors because they have the run into an important part of the scene sometimes. It's also a question of — in general, a lot of ego on the part of the director. Every director wants to show that he can do it. I got over it; now what I do, I do sometimes a very long shot of a very complicated nature and then I do a very long shot which is the reverse, and then I cut them together. This is a second level. I know I can do it so I do it very long and then I don't have any regret about cutting it for convenience, for the benefit of the editing.

JAN KADAR: When you do a picture do it both ways. Then you can decide what is best on the Moviola. It's true. Who knows? It's the most beautiful thing about moviemaking. There is always a certain challenge. There is nothing so sure; there is always a certain surprise. You have to prepare the possibility of surprises for the later period of the work. I don't believe, for instance, in directors who are working so economically that they are not making any lines more than is necessary. I don't believe in it. Maybe some genius can do it. But I think that is quite mechanical. You have to leave a certain place for your game, which is the next period, the editing.

CARL REINER: There are stories that you cannot make a terrible actor great. You can make a good actor better, and you can make a great actor terrible. I mean you do have it in your power to help or hurt. You may steal a reaction moment that they did earlier in the scene. An actor may have done something quite different at the moment you are working with. But you may not want that. You may say, "My God, I don't want that. It doesn't work. It's too much." So you cut in a place that happened later where the actor may just be staring. You may help the actor that way. Also, it is your fault that you allowed him to do that originally. That is one thing that it took me a while to find out. The less you do the better. Less reaction is better. Let the audience fill in.

JAN KADAR: You will feel exactly that here you need something and here you don't. Sometimes you can sit at home at a table and think and think about it and it is never right. You have to use your imagination. And usually I have found that it is best in one piece. The dinner scene in *Shop on Main Street,* for instance: I would never put it together with nicely framed shots. I would put one camera here behind here, and another one here just so you could see the table, and the third camera over there on the other side. If I knew that everything would happen, then I wouldn't insert anything. Each cut or insert that I did in the scene because it needed something, never worked.

JIRI WEISS: It's the simplest thing in the world to take scissors and cut material and stick it together. If you have a very stupid film, kindly take the end and put it in the middle, take a part of the beginning and put it in the end, and make out of it something which no one understands. Put it on the screen and it's wonderful. I am deadly serious.

BRIAN DE PALMA: It's like the whole Hitchcock idea. You tell a story with little pieces of film, and each little piece of film is an important piece. It's not just tracking shots like Bertolucci choreographing a long tracking thing, because Bertolucci doesn't like to cut. Because once an editor gets in there he cuts and makes it look like everything else. He wants to have the whole thing in like one lyrical movement, but you can shoot that way. That's an approach to doing it, but I just try to have a visual conception.

Before I was a director, I was a very good editor. In fact, I probably edited better than I directed initially, and I have a very strong editorial idea for the way pieces of film should go together.

PERRY MILLER ADATO: The rhythm of the editing should never come from trying to compress your material. If you really don't have time to do it, then you have to take it out.

BERNARDO BERTOLUCCI: I don't assemble as we go along. I edit after we finish.

FEDERICO FELLINI: It's no more than two or three days to edit a feature film. It's a question of how you can organize your work. I mean, not your work, but your mind, you know? That's all. If you do a lot of shooting, then after, you have all that stuff, and you wait.

PAUL MAZURSKY: I don't change the story while shooting. Sometimes in the editing, I do. On every picture I've done, I've taken out thirty or forty minutes.

BARBARA LODEN: There are scenes that when we shot them we thought they were good and in the rushes they were good and as a scene they would be good. But in the context of the movie, it wouldn't work because it would stand out like a scene and you would get that telegraph, "O.K., folks, now we're going to have a good scene for you." And, you know, you just get that feeling a lot of times in the movies, when they say, "O.K., folks, get ready now because we're going to have a really good scene."

SOME METHODS AND EXAMPLES

PETER HYAMS: There is a thing about certain rhythms. It's a kind of tension you want to get, and sometimes you can do it better by moving than you can do it by cutting. There are instances where, just by a series of cuts, you can create that kind of nervousness, that kind of fidgety quality to what you want, and that could be very important to what you're doing. And so the worst thing in the world could be a very sustained master with people talking.

RICHARD ATTENBOROUGH: I believe in starting with the master and settling for the master and deciding when the master doesn't work, rather than the other way around.

VINCENT SHERMAN: Errol Flynn was tricky in one way. He never gave very much of what I call a "master scene." He would always keep his energy low and play the scene somewhat dull. Not very vivacious in the master scenes and the long shots. But when I got into the close-up, that was when he would be acting. That was unfortunate. Many times he would force me to cut to a close-up when I would have preferred not to. I don't think that it did us any great harm. But that was some of the typical stuff that happened.

WILLIAM FRIEDKIN: When I cut the chase in *The French Connection* . . . I used a track from Santana called "Black Magic Woman." I cut that whole chase scene to "Black Magic Woman." I didn't put any music in it in the picture. There's not a note of music in the chase. I just cut it to that tempo. There's like nice, sliding, long sort of guitar trills and licks and the thing sort of moved along nice to that and then there's some hard stuff and it slows down. But I had "Black Magic Woman" in mind when I shot that scene. The final cutting of it really happened out of a number of shots in that chase scene.

JACK NICHOLSON: For *Drive, He Said,* I planned on shooting a lot of angles. I planned the film to be an edited film; it's really the end of a cycle of thinking about editing that I got into while writing. The script that I wrote for myself before *The Trip,* and the two westerns with Monte Hellman of which I wrote one, were the first films, commercial, theatrical films, in America that I know of recently that had subliminal or flash cutting in them. Since then I'd gotten tired of seeing all movies solve their exposi- tional and motivational problems by simply showing either what they say is a vision of the mind, which it's not, or a remembrance of the past or whatever you have. Yet I know the appetite for speed in films is up in the audience and I wanted to force the cutting style without using the device of multiple time levels or inner-consciousness cutting.

It comes from the fact that I stayed with the structure of the novel, which is fairly ethical: a lot of characters and a lot of parallel stories going on, and that more or less forced a very driving cutting style.

ALFRED HITCHCOCK: For the shower murder in *Psycho,* there were seventy-eight setups and it took forty-five seconds on the screen. First of all, the leading lady was a bit squeamish about revealing herself, so I had to get a nude stand-in. It was made up of all those tiny pieces of film because the knife never touched the body at any time. Just an illusionary thing. We did the storyboarding beforehand, and in the editing we tight- ened it up and got the tempo going. There's no question that for any kind of violence that you want to portray on the screen, that's the way it can be done best.

Let me see if I can give you a comparison. If you stand in a field and you see a train going by half a mile away, you look at it and it speeds by. Now go within six feet of the train going by; think of the difference in its effect. So what you are doing is you are taking the audience right close up into the scene, and the montage of the various effects gets the audience involved. That's its purpose. It becomes much more powerful than if you sit back and look. Say you are at a boxing match and you are eight to ten rows back: well, you get a very different effect if you are in the first row, looking up under those ropes. When these two fellows are slugging each other, you get splashed almost.

In *Psycho*, once that figure comes in and starts to stab, you're in it. Oh, you're absolutely in it. The distance of the figures, you see. That's why I think barroom brawls in westerns are always a bore for me, because one man hits the other, the table collapses and he falls back over the bar. If they would only do a few big close-ups here and there, it would be much more exciting, instead of looking at it from a distance. But you see, they make a mistake, they think it creates a greater air of reality by seeing it at a distance and in fact they are doing the wrong thing.

GEORGE CUKOR: Hitchcock is a master. He is an absolute master. You can analyze it, but to do it you are going to have to turn yourself into Hitch. I think one should observe what he does. But unless you really know what you are doing, I would not do . . . tricks. I very often see things. I often see pictures and am influenced by certain scenes. We are all influenced that way. I see certain movements that Hitchcock has done and others have done. But I would urge the young director, "Don't do that. Invent your own movements."

To a certain extent, I preplan my editing before I shoot, but I am always surprised at what happens.

For example, in the picture that George Stevens did — he is somebody that you should watch. He is a wonderful cutter and a very good director. He knows what in hell he is doing. But in *A Place in the Sun*, there was something very fascinating in that. There was a scene and in the background there was a telephone on the wall. There was a doorway in the front. The boy went in there and went on the telephone. He spoke to one girl, came out, and just as he walked out, the telephone rang. He went back and talked to the other girl. That remained just on that one setup. I, as the audience, imagined some things.

It's most useful if you can get that audience's imagination going. That is fascinating. If they had broken the rhythm and cut to a close-up of him in that scene, then it would not have been nearly as effective. But, as for planning everything, one often gets surprises.

About my own experience, let's say in *My Fair Lady*, there was a scene when Rex Harrison was getting very frustrated. It was three o'clock in the morning, and Audrey Hepburn wasn't speaking it correctly. There was a beautifully written scene where he made this very inspiring talk about the English language. You weren't quite sure whether she understood it or not. She was sitting almost profile in the foreground, and everybody had a headache. Rex Harrison was in the back. He was sticking to it. He made this speech, and then he went back. She was still in profile in the foreground and he was in the back. He said, "Oh, well, all right, do it again."

Then she said, "The rain in Spain . . ." She said it correctly.

They rough-assembled this for me, and they cut to her saying it correctly. I said, "No, no, no." What they should have done there was just say it in the longer shot. You should have gotten him listening to it. She isn't aware of what she said, and then he says, "Again." She says it again correctly. Then she realizes that she said it correctly.

I did not play that, obviously. I thought that when she says it correctly, then you won't be on her. I found that it was much more effective not to be on her. It was much better just to have her in the foreground and play the reaction to that on Rex Harrison and Wilfrid Hyde-White. Those are the things that you cannot really plan. . . .

ABRAHAM POLONSKY: In *Willie Boy*, I had this flash-flood scene. We shot it. It was terrific. I want to tell you, there's nothing more impressive on the screen in the picture. We cut the scene into where it was supposed to be in the picture. We cut it properly, I thought. It interrupted the pattern of the escape, which was in the form of a fugue. The rhythm of it was interrupted. The flash flood stuck out like a thumb there, a very sore, aching thumb, which said, "Look at me, look at what a terrific flash flood I am." And I didn't want anything in that picture saying, "Look at me, look what a terrific thing I am." Because that's not what's terrific. So I eliminated it. Well, I want to tell you, they were terribly upset at the studio. This was "production value."

ROBERT ALTMAN: The way I edit film, really, is to start showing it, as I start getting to it, to small audiences, usually people that were involved in the thing. Eventually I start broadening that out a little bit as I get what I think is closer toward what I want. The only guide that I use is that if I'm with an audience that hates one of my films, the film doesn't look very good to me. I find that if I get to a point where I'm embarrassed by something on the screen, I just know that it should go. I have to see it a lot myself because initially I really like all this stuff. I think it's terrific, yet I know I'm wrong about a lot of it. I like it maybe for different reasons than somebody seeing it cold.

WILLIAM FRIEDKIN: On *The Exorcist* I got stuff in Iraq of the guys who stab themselves and do numbers and put daggers to their throat, which I got close-up, and all kinds of Iraqi life, and I got it all back in the cutting room and I said, "I can't do it. It'll really mess up this story if I do an essay on Iraq." But it was such a temptation. I mean, it's a once-in-a-lifetime thing. No Westerner has ever gone over there and filmed these places for any reason in a feature film. I might do a documentary on it, on the footage we got there, but even, there are three or four shots in there that shouldn't be in there now, but that I couldn't pull out because they're so beautiful. They're just so beautiful.

There's a shot of von Sydow walking through a bazaar where they're making shoes and it's done without any light. No lighting. It's all natural lighting. The sun pouring through these holes in this cave and it doesn't belong in the movie, but it's just so beautiful. You know, I had it out of there. I yanked it. We pulled it. And the scene played a lot better, moved a lot faster. I went to bed one night and Christ, I got up and I called the editor. I said, "Put those damn shots back in."

He said, "Why? They fuck up the scene."

I said, "They're so beautiful. They're gorgeous. I mean let's — Jesus Christ. You know, if they'll believe any of the rest of this stuff, they'll believe this shot." So we stuck it back in.

It means nothing. I assure you. It doesn't belong in the picture. It's just — I love it. The sound is so nice. All these guys making shoes, all the kind of rhythm thing. It's my favorite moment in the picture. It has nothing to do with the picture.

USING SOUND

SHIRLEY CLARKE: If you want two cuts that don't match to match, let the sound carry it over and it will fool the eye into thinking that it goes together. One of the best ways to get a unified sense of a lot of disparate images is to have the sound have a very strong line. That is one of the best ways to use music in film. In other words, not to use it merely to carry the emotion content.

JOHN SCHLESINGER: I have quite specific ideas of the kind of sound that I may want before I start, or during the movie. In the case of *Midnight Cowboy*, we used "Everybody's Talking," and I knew before we had even the vaguest assembly, I said to the editor, "Use it here, try it there, there, there, and there." We didn't always end up by using that precise place but we knew whereabouts we wanted it.

I remember the end, for instance, of *The Day of the Locust* was very much pinched musically from Penderecki and hearing that piece and shoving it into a rough cut very early on. It was mind-boggling, the use of it.

But it is just by one's own liking and knowledge of music that you try different things, because by the time you get to a composer they need some kind of quite firm direction. If they're a good professional, as the composers I've always worked with are, they quite like that, particularly if you know something about scoring.

When we get to the session, I'm very demanding because although I can't compose, I know when the score is too thick or when it wants putting into a different kind of sound or use of a woodwind, or we don't want strings or we want more strings or we want a solo violin or whatever. I think it's a question of layering, laminating film together, laminating the experience with different kinds of impressions during the making of it.

ROBERT ALDRICH: I think that the director ought to make the movie. I think that the musician is an extension of the director. I don't think that the music ought to be different than, or better than, or alien to, the movie. As a consequence of this, sometimes you make a bad movie and the music is pretty bad. Occasionally, in a good movie the music will be bad. But that is your fault. It is not the musician's fault. I know that there has to be music over the tag. I know there has to be music over the chase. You may know there will be a love theme, but where and how?

I don't preplan where the music is going to go. I spot the picture with the musician, and usually after the first cut. I happen to believe that in certain kinds of pictures, *Dr. Zhivago* kind of pictures, that thematic repetition is effective. I find that where it may bore you or me personally, it doesn't bore the widespread audience.

MICHAEL WINNER: The music is a big risk, because it's the only thing on the film that you cannot hear at all until it's finished. I mean with an actor you could have seen him act. With a composer, you may have heard a composition, but it isn't yours.

And you have this enormous cost of recording, and at the end of it you've really only got two choices, throw it out — in which case you're going to look a mug — or live with it. You're buying an unseen product, really. You can only go over the music in great detail with the composer and list exactly where you'd like it to come and what you'd like it to be and naturally you hope to have much guidance and ideas from him and hope it works out.

I don't mind a theme, but I don't think it's essential. I think it can be a big selling point. I think *Dr. Zhivago* without the theme — who knows?

I don't think you can expect to get a great theme. Everyone's got a great theme in theory. But the same composer who wrote *Dr. Zhivago* wrote six more films, and he didn't have a theme out of any of them. Again, you can't guarantee a performance. You know if you're going to get a brilliant performance. You don't know if you employ a well-known composer that you're going to get a brilliant theme.

ABRAHAM POLONSKY: I consider music a part of the film if it's a film that has music in it. And, therefore, although I don't tell the composer what to do, because I'm not a composer (although I'm familiar with music, obviously), I tell him where the music should go, and I tell him what it should be like. And then I treat him like an actor or a cameraman, even though music is an independent art. So is acting. So is writing. So is editing. So's photography. They're all independent arts subjected to the director or the script. So I treat the music the same way.

And I try and get the musician to respond to my sense of what the picture means, and then hope *his* talent, which I don't have, will invent something that will make my idea even better than it is. And more effective. In other words, I'm dependent on him at the same time that I'm telling him what to do. But I'm more dependent on him than what I'm telling him. And that's true of everybody you work with, including your actors.

RALPH NELSON: You work perhaps least with the composer, because you hire him and then he has six weeks to write the score, and the first time you see him again, I mean you spot this music in the film, say, "Here. I want it to come in here and out there, and this is the kind of sound I would like," but it's suddenly when he hears the sixty musicians there and lifts up his baton, you're hearing it for the first time.

HOWARD HAWKS: There is a whole lot of conversation with the composer. We go over a thing. We talk about it in general and he works on it. Then, finally, I believe that we have a running. "The music should begin here and it should finish here." We're not always right. Sometimes after we finish we say, "Let's chop off the music here." You know, fade it out, let's start it a little quicker, it just depends.

HAL ASHBY: I am not a musician, but I just feel it very strongly. I feel it with film very, very much. In fact, what I would like to do would be to get a composer who actually does, in essence, his score or does his songs and records them before I ever start shooting.

FEDERICO FELLINI: I caused my musician a lot of trouble, you know, when I said to him for a particular picture we couldn't have music, we could have just music as atmosphere. So I listened, maybe to five hundred records; it was very likely, because a friend of mine has a discotheque; he has folklore, oriental, African records. So I had a lot of records, and I chose from those records just this kind of barbaric and Eastern sound. And, for a lot of it I made just some melody in the beginning and the end.

Sometime, before we start, I like to have some tapes of music because I like music when I work. And so it helps because it is another little piece of the body of the picture that you put in your studio so you start to be more familiar. The music is a big help always because it puts you in a strange dimension in which your fantasy has stimulation. Sometimes, as soon as I finish a picture, I show the picture to Nino Rota, and we work very strictly and I tell him exactly what I wish, what I want, and we go with the piano and the Moviola and we can do the score.

WILLIAM FRIEDKIN: I can't read a note of music. I am, as Lalo Schifrin describes me, a musical dilettante. But I love music. All kinds — I listen to everything. I pick up on music and I'm very influenced by music. I'm as much influenced by musical references when I'm working as I am by anything else, like that Santana cut, that "Black Magic Woman." That whole chase in *The French Connection* came out of that. But I can't read a note of music.

JOHN CASSAVETES: On *Shadows*, the whole experience of getting people to do things was incredible. I didn't know what I was doing, really. None of us knew what we were doing. When lighting a scene, we didn't know what we were doing. We even did the music. I asked Charlie Mingus. I said, "Charlie, would you like to do this?"

"Yeah, what is it?"

"A film."

Charlie said he'd do it for nothing. He worked six months on the music and he wrote a minute and a half's worth of music. I don't know that that's wrong.

He said, "Listen, man, would you do me a favor? You have got to do something for me."

"Sure, sure," I say.

"Listen, I've got all these cats that are shitting all over the floor. Can you have a couple of your people come up and clean the cat shit? I can't work; they shit all over my music." So we went up with scrubbing brushes and cleaned up the thing.

Now he says, "I can't work in this place. It's so clean. I've got to wait for the cats to shit."

Finally we get it together to record. So, double session, three hours, double session with the projectionist sitting there and I'm watching. He's got fourteen seconds' worth of music. Everybody's saying, "Why don't you just tell Charlie to improvise?" All the advice then starts. So then he's got to improvise and he loves to sing and he started to sing and he played. He made everyone switch their instruments.

So I said to Charlie, "Charlie, Charlie, it was great; it really sounded great. Everything sounds great. The noise comes out; it really sounds great. It's perfect for the picture."

He says, "Man, I got to work six more months." He went away.

GEORGE CUKOR: They tend to bring the composer in later. I have always felt that the ideal picture would be if the composer worked along with the writers and the director. But, it has been my experience that the composer has come in later when the picture is more or less finished. When this happens he has to fit in. He has to fit his pattern in. Sometimes that works and sometimes it doesn't. I always find it very helpful if I know what the music is before.

Max Steiner caught the spirit of *Little Women*. He caught the charm of it and he didn't make it schmaltzy. At that time the tendency was to do a big Balaban and Katz overture and sentimentalize the thing. He didn't do that. I thought that we all did it rather tactfully.

JACQUES DEMY: Do you know what the big problem was in *Cherbourg?* Imagine that I am with Michel Legrand and we are working, and I tell him that the girl is going to her bedroom. She is in the dining room and she is going to the bedroom, and her mother is going to follow her. We would decide that two or three bars of music would have to go there.

We shot everything in *Cherbourg* on location. We were so poor that we couldn't make a set. I had to find a bedroom that was two bars away from the dining room. It was a very funny situation. We moved the dining room table, but it closed off the bedroom, and she would have had to run to get to the bedroom. Either the music was too short or it was too long so she would have to do something in between.

That was a great film to make. Everyone was singing. Often, when you speak about music, there are no words that you can find to adequately express what you are thinking. It is very difficult.

THE DIRECTOR'S CUT

RICHARD ATTENBOROUGH: It is possible to alter and vary — indeed, fundamentally change sometimes — the manner of performance with a Moviola. You do, if you play the scenes correctly and truthfully, have in that play and on the floor a veracity of reaction in terms of a scene, one actor to another, which you will judge to be true and correct. In other words, if I ask you a question and you have a reply, bearing in mind all the other elements that rush into your head before you make that reply, there is a certain pause or a certain manner in which you deliver that reply.

If we decide in the cutting room afterwards that we want to speed the scene or change the tempo of the scene, what do we do? We cut to you for your reply because you can't do it in the two-shot as that is played as we intended. We cut to you for your reply sooner than the thought process that you went through in order to give your reply and sooner, in truth, than would be possible.

You change the reaction of that man to the question, and, very often, grant it an implausibility, an unreality, by having jumped a thought process which would under normal circumstances have been there. And therefore, this whole question of editing and one's determination to edit and be part of the editing, I don't want to work for two years or two and a half years and say at the end of it, "Here you are, fellows. You take it over. You put it together how you please." I see no point.

That editing can affect the entire shape and outcome of a picture is evidenced by the fact that the Directors Guild of America has made important rulings about the director's right to "a cut."

VINCENT SHERMAN: I just feel that the director has the right to have the first cut.* I think it is a weakness in our Guild when the rule is not absolutely

---

*"First cut" refers to the first total assembly of a film, the first complete version. The Directors Guild long has insisted it be mandatory for a director to have the "first cut" — so that there is a record of his desired form for the finished product.

adhered to. I feel that the director should not only have the first cut, but he should have the opportunity to see his first cut in front of an audience. Then, if the audience doesn't approve, which is pretty discernible, the producer should take it over. But this business of saying that the director is too close to it, or the director has no perspective — well, maybe in some cases it is true. But I still feel that the director should have that first cut. He should also have the opportunity to see that first cut in front of an audience.

ARTHUR PENN: My right to a final cut was an outgrowth of my success. It also was something I fought for. It was something I gave up rather innocently on one occasion and lived to regret it. I'm referring there to *The Chase*. Since then, it's been really a basic rule that I would rather not do the film if I don't have that. This is no reflection on all the guys who don't have it. All I mean to say is, if the director doesn't have final cut, then one has to ask the question, "Who does?" If you ask that question, you have to answer it. And if you answer it, you have to say, "Well, the man who heads Fox has it, or the man who heads Warner Brothers has it, or the man who heads Columbia has it." Then you have to say, "Well, what are his credentials?" Would I, if I were the studio, assigning the right to make a film, say to the head of Fox, "You have the right to final cut," or "You don't have the right to final cut"? If I were to say, "You have final cut," I'd have to examine his credentials and I think they'd come up short of mine, by a long shot.

PREVIEWS

Sometimes it may be the preview audience which points to lulls that may go undetected through editing.

LEO MCCAREY: We finished *My Favorite Wife* and we found that after about five reels, the picture took a dip and for about two reels or more it wasn't funny. It wasn't as funny as what preceded it. It didn't come up to it. It was a lot of unraveling of a tricky plot. So, anyway, the cast was dismissed, the writers went home, the director went home to New York, and I sat there with the cutter trying to figure out what to do to save the picture. So we sneaked it out once more to be sure we were right that something had to be done and sure enough, right in the same place, it dipped, was very unfunny.

Then I got the wildest idea I ever had. There was a judge in the opening who was very funny and he dropped out of the picture. I decided to bring him back. What we actually did was to tell the judge our story problems in the picture and have him comment on them. And it was truly great. It became an outstanding thing in the picture.

GEORGE SEATON: Speaking of a big audience, the first preview of *A Night at the Opera* (which I consider a much better picture than *A Day at the Races*), we took it to Long Beach and, I give you my word of honor, there was not one laugh in the entire picture. Not one laugh — not even a chuckle. We came out into the lobby and Groucho wanted to kill himself. That was the first thing he wanted to do. And Chico was looking for excuses. He said, "Didn't you see the paper? The Mayor of Long Beach died today."

And Groucho said, "So did we."

And then Chico said, "They were supposed to have bank night and they had a preview instead and the audience was mad."

So Thalberg said, "I don't believe this. I just cannot believe that we can be this wrong." He said, "I don't want anybody to touch a foot of this film; we'll take it to San Diego tomorrow night." We took it to San Diego the next night and it played just like it plays and always played. I think we took out twenty feet and nobody, to this day, could figure out why that Long Beach audience sat on their hands.

WILLIAM FRIEDKIN: I'll never audience-test a film as long as I live. Never take a film out, like to the Preview House, where a guy pushes a button and a guy comes on the screen.

You know, they've got a joint on Sunset Boulevard. People sit there hooked into wires and boom. They run pilots — television pilots. A guy walks out. They tell you to push a button if you like this guy. Boom. A guy walks out, says, "Hello." Psst. Eighty-five people press a button that they don't like his face. He's out of the pilot. Really. They recast the part. I don't preview anything. If I had previewed *The French Connection*, they'd still be recutting it at Twentieth.

BUDD BOETTICHER: When you leave a picture, the director has a director's cut. And not enough directors, especially many of the young ones, take advantage of the cut. They can't do a damn thing to you until you say, "This is my picture. Now foul it up."

My favorite story — and I don't know who invented it, I like to think I did, but I am sure that it was before me — is about the big major preview of the young director's first hit. It is playing at Grauman's Chinese Theatre, like it used to be, and the place is packed. It's fabulous. They even know who he is. All the people converge on the young director for autographs, because he is in. He's got the best picture that has come out in years, and they didn't even know who he was until now. And he starts to sign the autographs, and two guys in dark suits disappear into the shadows. And you dolly in for a nice two-shot, and one is the cutter and one is the producer, and they are heard saying, "I think we can fix it." This is really true. Beware.

Herbert J. Yates didn't like the scene with Katy Jurado in *The Bullfighter and the Lady*, because he couldn't hear it. He was deaf. And he didn't want to wait to see what Bob Stack said. So he cut it out of the picture. And I found out about this the day of the preview, that the scene that was going to make her a star in her country wasn't in. So, I went into the cutting room and cut it back into the preview print. And Yates applauded with all of the rest of the people. He didn't even know that he had cut it out. I mean, you really do have to be careful with these things.

FRANK CAPRA: We made *Lost Horizon* and ran it in a small theatre at the studio for three hours, and I thought it was the greatest thing I'd ever made. So did everybody else. Two million dollars, half the yearly budget for the whole studio. Two million went on *Lost Horizon*, and with the other two million they made twenty pictures, so you know what was riding on this. We took it to a preview at Santa Barbara, and they began to laugh at it in the first five minutes, and kept tittering and tittering. It got louder and louder, but there was really nothing purposely they should laugh at.

Well, I went out of the theatre. I didn't know what the hell was happening. I went into the lobby to get a drink of water, and there was another man who wanted some water, and he leaned down first, looking up at me, and he said, "Did you ever see such a goddamned thing as they're running in there?" Well, I left the theatre altogether after that. I ran outside and walked up and down in the rain for three hours. It was an absolute disaster, an unreleasable film. Two million dollars!

So I went up to Arrowhead by myself, walked around the hills for a couple of days, went through every scene in that film, every word, and I couldn't understand why it should be funny, why they laughed at this, and why the whole thing was funny. The only thing I could think of, I don't know where it came from, but I thought that if I could just take the main titles and put them at the end of the third reel, well, it was worth trying. So I rushed back to the studio and said, "Listen, let's preview it again. I've made one change. I'm gonna stick the main title at the beginning of the third reel."

Cohn said, "For Christ's sake, it'll get out that we've got a bust."

And I said, "Well, we've got a bust." So we took it to San Pedro and they didn't laugh. Whatever it was, it was cured. Now don't ask me what it was in those two reels, because I don't know. I've forgotten. If anybody comes to me and says, "Well, gee, I had a preview that didn't go as well as I thought it would," I just say, "Burn the first two reels. It's a panacea for everything."

JOHN SCHLESINGER: When I'm telling a story, I imagine that it's to myself, seeing it for the first time. I think the greatest difficulty and the most essential thing to try and do is to remain objective through a very long period of time. It's difficult.

I don't believe in previews. I must say I get very paranoid, and when I show a film to a group of people I watch for waggling feet and for lighting a cigarette. Which can very often be totally misleading. People light cigarettes not because they're bored but because they need a cigarette and perhaps want to be more involved.

I hate the system of everybody going out to wherever with studio executives to preview a film. In fact, I have it written into my contract that I don't have to. I don't have to abide. I've never done it and I distrust it because I think panic very easily and quickly sets in and you finally have to be the arbiter, along with people that you trust.

I go through very destructive processes making a film. I will miscut it terribly, commit mayhem because you get so used to seeing a piece of material and you'll go, "Oh, we don't need this, we don't need that," and then look at it again and suddenly it's all gone and then you start putting things back. At least I do. It's a process that I seem to have to go through.

But you have to at all times try and remember the first time, if you did, you were excited — which is the only moment in cinema after all — the first time you see something you say, "It works," and that may be very early on. Then beware of destroying it.

DISTRIBUTION

Although the final cut, established after editing and previews, usually holds as the end product, there is one last interloper — the distributor.

JOHN CASSAVETES: You con people and you lie to them. You try to keep a little part of yourself when somebody says to you: "You figure it's the greatest picture ever made?" You try to keep a little part of yourself alive. It's the same thing if you are a cameraman behind a camera with a director who is uptight. They know the guy's uptight. What can they do about it? Can they say, "Look, you're uptight. Relax"? They are going to have to live with it afterwards. They will go out and have a drink, go home, argue with their wives and be unhappy.

There doesn't seem to be any solution within that traditional framework whereby people could say, "I am going into the movie distribution business for money," while we approach it behind the scenes as an art. We can't.

ROBERT ALDRICH: There are almost no pure distributors. The pure distributor is limited by the flow of the products and how good the products are. The distributors may be limited, but I have never met a broke distributor. On the other hand, I have met broke producers and many broke directors. First you make the movie and then you hire the movie theatres. That is, the distributor. Then you wait for the phone call. If the picture is no good, you'll blow it anyway. If the picture is good, they will take it for nothing and they may even give me back some of my money.

Nobody has ever won a suit against a major distributor. There have been some recoveries, but the cost of recovery is an admission by you that the thieving was done without their knowledge. In other words, they are not party to the act. Now, you know they robbed you and they know that they robbed you. But the only way that you are going to get part of the money back is to say that they didn't knowingly take it. On a picture, you can steal a half a million.

HAL ASHBY: I'm not crazy about too much stuff in advertising, but I did feel that on *Harold and Maude*, it was important to be provocative. Business was not good anywhere, except in Baltimore. In Baltimore, it was doing sensational business. So I said, "Why the hell is it doing good in Baltimore? Are they just all freaks in Baltimore, or what is it?" That seemed a little bit unreal to me. So they found out that the exhibitor or the theatre owner made up his own radio plugs and his own ads, and they were on the provocative aspect. "She's eighty and he's twenty and they're in love." And it's been holding up just fine in Baltimore.

ROBERT ALDRICH: There is no secret about how to distribute a picture. If you have a good picture, it requires two things: the ability and the money to go out and rent a theatre and have some clown do an ad. If that picture works, you are a distributor. But, if that picture doesn't work, then you can be Twentieth Century–Fox and you won't sell that picture.

HOWARD HAWKS: For television, they do some of the strangest cutting I've ever seen in my life. You worry about your main audience. You're going to get eight to ten times as much money before television. I don't see any reason to consider a later TV showing. If they want to do it, they'll find a way to bitch it up. Television is running now *Red River* twenty-eight times, and they didn't use the negative. They used an old work print and made dupes. It's filled with writing from a book on Texas. I tried that first and it was bad. Then I made narration with Walter Brennan and that was the way the picture went out. They didn't even bother to use the final print. I don't know what you can do about it. I'm too busy making pictures, not fighting old battles.

FOUR

"CINEMA"

10

Film as Art

What is cinema? It's projection of shadows — to use a word quoted from Hitch — on a rectangle. Of course, it's a convention. Because they are shadows, you can read so much into them. To me, the ideal film — which I've never succeeded in making — would be as though the reel were behind one's eyes and you were projecting it yourself and seeing what you wished to see.

There's a great deal in common with the thought processes. Singularly so. More so in film than in any other media. Usually the first few minutes of a picture — good pictures and bad — you're allowed to see what you want to see. But usually, after a couple of minutes, there is a sickening instant when we are brought back to reality and we know we are in a theatre looking at trash.

— John Huston

It sometimes is argued that film is too new an art form to analyze as rigorously as the traditional arts. It also is said that since film is at the mercy of technology to a greater degree than the other arts, then we cannot approach it as though it had reached its full potential. These arguments may be essentially irrelevant. After the first primitive man had painted his impressions of objects and events on the walls of his cave, the entire arena of painting was opened. Certainly, with the development of more sophisticated materials — canvases, brushes, paints — he was better able to recreate exactly what it was that he felt. However, the cavemen's images were no less of an abstraction than those of modern painters. They are as deeply moving and revelatory of the nature of existence as today's more obviously abstract art.

Similarly, when we attend to film history, we see that virtually the entire vocabulary of filmic expression was established within a few years of its beginnings. The early films of D. W. Griffith, Allan Dwan, Buster Keaton, and many others display the full range of cinematic possibilities. The French critic André Bazin has pointed out that it was not technology that guided the early filmmakers; it was the filmmakers that urged on those technological developments which were necessary to establish a full and fluid filmic vocabulary. Wide-screen, split-screen, rapid cutting, special effect superimpositions, and even color all were hinted at long before the technicians had solved their end of the problems. In fact, while many film historians point to the advent of sound in films as being that art's death knell, Bazin again observes that viewing a late von Stroheim or Renoir silent film is like watching a modern sound film. One senses that sound was a considered parameter for these artists, and that the technicians behind the scenes were ever being forced to hurry and catch up with their sophisticated cinematic sensibilities. "Sound came not to destroy but to fulfill the Old Testament of the cinema."* Sufficient time has passed and a sufficient number of obviously great artists and masterpieces in film have appeared such that to serve full justice to film, we must approach it on a footing with the traditional arts.

FILM AS CONSTITUTED OUT OF MANY KINDS OF WORK

Film is unique among the arts in the number of different activities that comprise it. Not only must there be an overall concept or feeling for the sense of actuality and existence that the film is to express; that concept

*André Bazin, *What Is Cinema?* Vol. I, Berkeley: University of California Press, 1967.

must be realized consistently through the camerawork, the editing, the acting (if people are to be used to animate certain dramatic themes), the screen writing (if there is to be anything beyond a completely improvised, virtually random selection of filmed scenes), and the sound (including such elements as music, dialogue, random "natural" sounds, and, of course, silence). As we would hold a foundry responsible for any of the qualities of a sculpting, then we also must attend to film laboratories, costume designers, set designers, make-up personnel, and so forth.

All of this has led many observers and practitioners to look upon film as some sort of compound, collaborative art. Logically, it makes some sense to assume that if there are a number of people involved in the making of a film, then there must be a number of potential artistic personalities who take part.

When we look at a large number of films, and when we attend to a particular film several times, we begin to sense two distinct functions that a film serves. First, what we usually perceive is a vague, diffuse set of themes — derivative from a conglomeration of harmonious or clashing styles. Sometimes, though, we detect a singular unified presentation of a particular vision of the space, time, and dynamics of the universe under observation and of the entities caught therein. In response to this dual role a film might take, various critical stances have emerged. Usually, each group champions one particular contributor to a film as being its true creator. It has been the fashion to attribute a film's artistic qualities either to its director, writers, actors, cameramen, or editors. Also, some hold that the ideal film will be one in which all the participants are artists in their own right, and are on a footing throughout a film's creation. In fact, such a film might be seen as virtually an anonymous work of art — one in which all phases meld into a singular view of the cosmos, but whose view is not attributable to any one of the participants alone.

To posit that there might be five potential artists in filmmaking (the director, writer, actor, cameraman, and editor) would be as arbitrary as to say that if film is an art, then there must be only one artist who is to be held responsible for it. Composers of film scores and sound editors might argue that, ultimately, their contribution is on a footing with the script writer's or with the film editor's. Make-up men, costume designers, and set designers might argue that without the environment they create for a film's action, then the cameraman's choice of aesthetic objects and an actor's potential range of expressiveness is highly limited. A film's working producer might say that without his overall control of the production — choice of script, production personnel, and actors — a film would be totally devoid of organization, and thus could not possibly be a work of art.

There are two difficulties with each of these positions. First, they tend to take the traditional structure of the film industry as being somehow endemic to the art of film itself. Actually, the division of labor that we so readily associate with film production is quite arbitrary. We have learned from the practice of many European filmmakers and from "independent" filmmakers around the world that one person, or just a small number of people may perform all the functions necessary to a film's production. Should we then conclude that these are merely specialized cases of our view of film as the receptacle of the artistic contributions of many — that is, do we first set out to analyze a person's artistry as a cameraman, then as an editor, and so on? Do we conclude that these cases represent some sort of ideal state of the art, where we know for sure exactly who is responsible for what? Or, finally, do we decide to take another stance altogether apart from the dissection of contributions in order to determine a film's artistic worth?

The second difficulty with most of the traditional critical views of film is that they do not seem to be derived from a personal submission to the actual overwhelming power of the film experience itself. This does not mean that one must make a film in order to understand the process. Rather, as with all encounters with art, one is struck first by the unity and totality of the particular view being presented. To perceive most fully the potential power in art, one first bares himself to the whole of the work; it is later that he goes back to examine all the variegated elements which have gone into constituting it.

We might envision an artist from another medium, say, a painter, attempting to make his first film. Assuming that he chooses some sort of narrative subject requiring actors, he would, nevertheless, probably attend first to the compositional qualities of each separate shot. He may first notice that his images are not static — that with the presence of people who are themselves living, energized beings, a sense of dynamics to be molded in the actual filming is present in a way unlike his painting. Thus, he may decide that the handling of actors is a most important dimension of the filmmaking process.

Then, he might notice that even when there are no actors present in a shot, the objects he is filming (even though he may regard them as primarily abstract shapes, sizes, and colors) serve a different function from the objects he is accustomed to painting. He realizes that in the filming, time itself becomes a force surging its way into his preconceived pictorial compositions. A filmed shot of a chair expresses a different sense of existence than he would have perceived having painted it, or simply photographed it. He also might find that by moving his camera from one position to another, yet another spatial sense of that chair is revealed. He comes closer to a complete understanding of that chair as its complete environment — both in its everyday role in the world, as well as in its specialized function in the film — is exposed. While it is true that he might have painted a series of pictures of that chair, all from different angles, he still would not have achieved the variegated experience of that chair which came largely from the spatial-temporal flow of the camera around it. Indeed, rather than moving the camera around the chair, he may decide to pan the camera away from it altogether. He now notices that even though the chair would not actually be seen by someone viewing that shot in the film, the chair has left some sort of perceptual residue both affecting and being affected by the elements in the image he has ended up with. Thus, he learns that the objects (whether considered as the entities that they are, or as some abstraction of textures suggestive of some dimension of space) in a film answer not only to themselves but to various dynamic processes which evolve in the course of that film. Hence, he may decide that it is in the realm of cinematography that the true art of film resides; that it is the positioning and lighting of a scene's elements, and the placement and movement of the camera that will determine just what spatial, temporal, and dynamic dimensions will be revealed.

Now, he views the resultant pieces of film for the first time. He learns that what he thought he was seeing through the camera has been altered. Perhaps the colors are not what they seemed to his naked eye. Perhaps the sense of rhythm established by the camera's movements seems modified when projected on a screen. If he had used actors, he may notice certain tensions during the filming between the performance and his intentions. These tensions may have worked to advance or to suppress his original filmic concept. Further, he may come to see that the dialogue spoken by the actors and the flow of events which unfolds seem to have a life of their own quite apart from the indications in the script. He feels that up to this point any number of the participants in the project may have played a dominant role in determining the tone of the film without his necessarily having realized it. But now, during the process of editing all the separately filmed pieces, he finds that he again can emphasize certain elements of his original ideas. Or, indeed, he decides that he will underscore the new thematic tendencies that have appeared. Through selection and juxtaposition of images, he is now exercising a new area of control over the film's ultimate appearance. He may decide that it is here in the editing that the true artistic direction of the final film is provided. Certainly a sense of the film's totality has been contributed by actors, cameramen, and writers, but to him it now seems to be the editing process that determines finally the sense of space, the rhythm, and the extent of the dynamic relationships which will characterize the finished film.

He may undergo, although perhaps to a lesser degree, similar experiences when trying to apply music or sound effects to coincide with the images. He detects that he can radically alter an image's appearance by the sound he prescribes to be associated with it. A sense of stillness in the image may be transformed into boisterousness by adding sound effects, and vice versa. And thus it is that in each stage of the filmmaking process, the filmmaker senses that he can radically alter the film's final appearance.

However, the great shock comes when he views the completed film for the first time as a whole. He is stunned to see that the film has a being and presence over and above any of the particular processes he has experienced. Critics and spectators may extract all sorts of threads and interconnections running throughout the entire picture that had never really occurred to him. The being of the final film overpowers any of the specific sensations he may have felt in its production.

FILM, THEATRE, AND THE OTHER ARTS

STANLEY KRAMER: Film is different from anything else, in terms of an art, because although film can represent the imprint most heavily of one man's thumb, still if you're a human being and an artist and you have feeling for people and you want to share many things with people, even if you are a writer, director, producer, you bring in with you the best cameraman, you get the best writer, you get the best director, you get the best musician. You bring all these people together and, since you brought them and you have paid them and you went after them to come to your baby and help nurture it, you want the maximum from them. In wanting the maximum from them in this medium, no matter how much you are in control, I can assure you that always the actor whom you dreamed of for the part cannot or will not read the line that's the most important to you the way you want it read. The cameraman says this will be diffused, but it isn't as diffused as you thought it should be. There are always four too many violins in the score, and you've heard the score on the piano and everything.

Every time I hear a young filmmaker say, "But I'll never make a compromise" . . . Baloney. All of life is a compromise. Don't compromise your principle. But it's one succession of compromises after another, an interchange. Now, the three months or the eight months or the eighteen months prior to the picture in preparation, you are readying yourself for this onslaught.

ED EMSHWILLER: My turf is different. Narrative film is of secondary interest to me. I'd like to put it this way: as I mentioned before, I come to filmmaking from graphics and visuals, and most filmmaking is really narrative. To my mind, most movies are illustrated stories. The real creative work is done by the writer. It's his concept. The director is simply an illustrator. Now, I've been an illustrator and I enjoyed visualizing stories that other people have written, but what I personally feel about filmmaking is that the emphasis has been on storytelling.

The novel has been the only form that's been recognized. Poetry has been left out. I'm using an analogy to film, in this case. I think there should be film poets. To me, the meanings that you get out of poetry are the types of meanings that don't lend themselves well to translation into prose. It's very difficult to translate painting into words. Even poetry is very difficult to translate from one language into another. It's that area of filmmaking that I am most concerned with, the kind that cannot be dealt with as easily, in terms of words, as literary forms. Now that may not be an answer to the problem, but it does give you a sense of my turf. It does identify the areas in which I am operating.

I've been invited to direct feature films, but I don't find it interesting to do plotted stories. If I'm going to spend the kind of time involved in directing someone else's story that's involved in making a feature film, I would much rather make a film in the manner in which I normally do, which is to say that I deal thematically in formal terms, almost musical terms, in choreographic terms. I face filmmaking as a form of choreographic exchange and I make film as a living experience, a growth exploration for myself.

STAN BRAKHAGE: I wanted to be a poet more than anything else; I just did not have the ability. Poetry and music are neck and neck in my life. Both of these arts mean much more to me than film. I spend my life with them. I try to get as many of the useful qualities from both of those arts as possible into my work. Artists are always stealing things and then transforming them through their own processes so they are totally new. Which is not too far removed from stealing a car and changing the license plates. I try like an old rook to steal anything useful in other arts. There are many films of mine that I can say were inspired by one kind of music or another. I get out of it as much as I can and then translate it into visual terms.

VILGOT SJÖMAN: At one time, I thought I would spend half a year making a film, the other half writing a novel. And we are two or three in the same situation in Sweden as I am. Bo Widerberg started out as a writer and he can't combine it. I never realized that until I had been working with film for some time. This is very strange because the theatre is still a writer's medium. You can combine theatre and writing. But film is definitely something else.

FRED ZINNEMANN: To me, film — if it has to be compared to anything — should be compared much more to a piece of music, because the basis of a film, to me, is to flow. And to arbitrarily chop it into curtains is to deny that very principle.

ROUBEN MAMOULIAN: The thing is integration. Let's take a symphony orchestra where the conductor is there for only one reason, to integrate the hundred men playing, to have each do his part without overdoing it or underdoing it, to tell them also how to do the different sections. If the orchestra is not integrated you have cacophony. That's why you can't listen to a good concert without a conductor. On the stage, you integrate a group of actors. You only have one movement on the stage. That's the movement of actors. That's all. That's not the case on the screen. On the screen you have three movements: one is the movement of actors on the screen, two is the movement of the camera, which means not only dolly shots but cutting — because cuts are movements, you jump around — three is the movement in cutting, or montage if you choose to call it. These three must be integrated into one harmonious whole so that none of them stick out. Then you get a perfect work with every emotional impact increased a hundredfold. Because, as you know, rhythm is the greatest force in nature.

FRED ZINNEMANN: If you wanted to study the parallel with music, you would say, "All right, let's say that a film could be like a symphony movement: The first movement written in sonata form. There is a main theme; then introduce the second theme; and then introduce the final third theme. Then you begin to play one against the other and elaborate on them and modulate and so forth. You finally bring it to conclusion, you know, the reprise and conclusion." That, to me, would hit the whole basic structure closely. . . .

Again, talking about music, you might say that you subconsciously decide what key it's going to be in. Why does it have to be in F major? Why couldn't it be E-flat? Or why not in B-flat? What is it that makes you do it? It's partly the feeling, and partly a deliberate thing, but there are many things that go into it; a lot of it is subconscious. You get a feel of what it is you want to be in, and in everything else you do, you try to approach that basic feeling.

NICHOLAS RAY: In the theatre, words are eighty to eighty-five percent of the importance of what is happening to you for your comprehension. In film, words are about twenty percent. It's a different figure, but it's almost an opposite ratio. For the words are only a little bit of embroidery, a little bit of lacework.

PAUL MAZURSKY: I think the biggest adjustment is that maybe some people are born with a natural understanding of this three hundred sixty degrees. That's the hardest thing, to know that what the camera sees and what has to be felt can be the cigarette ash, where in the theatre, it's really two-dimensional in that sense. It's flatter. To shake that off is interesting and tricky. If all of us shot this scene here now, I'm sure we would all do different things. But you start seeing visually and there's the trick. The detail is specific and the feeling of movement which in the theatre is different is a different set of problems. I think even acting is different in the theatre.

IRVIN KERSHNER: They say that on stage you have the proscenium arch. In film you have the frame line. Then you have a wall in back of the proscenium. That wall is finite. If you drew a perspective line from the actor in front of that finite wall back out into the audience, it would extend into infinity. In other words, you are sitting in the theatre and the real world is in back of you. It goes on infinitely and it comes to a stop at the finite wall. In film, the whole thing is reversed. You have a frame line which is the proscenium, and your eye is the beginning of all space, because it is a shifting line. Infinity is really the deep space in back of the people.

GEORGE CUKOR: I never wanted to go back to the theatre. I was in love with the film medium, Hollywood, I just took to it. Now, unless the theatre is absolutely first class, I'm bored to death and, when it's first class, I'm thrilled. There's a claustrophobia, you can't get up and walk out like you can out of a movie. I have done it on occasion when I say, "Christ, I cannot . . ." Tallulah Bankhead's judgment of a play was, she said, "When my ass gets tired, I know the play is a bore." Well, my ass doesn't get tired because it's well-padded, but suddenly my legs fall asleep and terrible things happen to me. In the theatre, I feel betrayed unless it's very good.

VINCENT SHERMAN: Being from the theatre, I had to realize that the camera can select only what it wants you to see. Little by little we would experiment with different things. Instead of doing the formula opening on a full shot, so you saw the full house or the full room and then went in closer as the scene progressed, we realized that sometimes it wasn't necessary to start off shooting the whole room. You could start with a person. You could start with something else, and then little by little you could reveal the room. Or it might not be important ever to see the full bedroom. A bedroom is a bedroom unless there is something distinctive about it from the story point of view.

ABRAHAM POLONSKY: Film has nothing to do with just those things like how it looks in color, and so on. Film is much more complex and deeper than that. It's a mode of spiritual communication. And it's different from music. One of the great disasters in film is the fact that some of its associates are powerful arts: music and writing. Of course, if the music and the writing lead too independent a life in that film, they can destroy the center of the film, which is the vision. The visual image is the center of the film. There's no doubt about it.

I've watched composers. I've watched pictures where I can't look at the picture because the music is driving me mad. I'm trying to listen to it. Now that is not the role of the music altogether, because how can I watch those images? At the same time, I don't want to subject them to each other, because that's wrong. And that balance is a balance in which, fundamentally, what counts is the image, even though I think words have an independent life if you use them like that. Nevertheless, I try not to let them destroy the images. And fundamentally, when I start to shoot the film, I will throw out anything.

PAUL MORRISSEY: I guess all directing consists of is following up. It's really like one foot following the other. One foot goes here, the other foot has to go there. To get a close-up, you have to go somewhere else. From somewhere else, you go into a close-up. I don't think about the technique of directing. I try to take the importance away from directing and just let it be very simple. Actually, I don't think about it. The things I like in a film are little nuances or line readings in an absurd situation. The lines take on different overtones to me.

MERIAN C. COOPER: While the picture's going on, if you say it's good photography, or a great piece of acting, or good direction, or great music, you've lost it. The picture's a dead duck. The whole idea is to keep mounting your emotions.

FRED ZINNEMANN: Flow is of the essence of cinema. I would say that my whole endeavor is to make it flow and make it build, rather than to present it in segments. A steadily mounting kind of thing, emotionally involving for the audience.

ED EMSHWILLER: There are a lot of ways of talking; some people speak one language, some people speak another. I am simply sharing with other people my vision. Some people will accept it and some people will reject it. That's what happens to all of us, and that's all there is to it.

VILGOT SJÖMAN: I think it's basically a very infantile need of showing yourself somehow. The basic motivation is not any kinds of nice and idealistic expression. I think you have a certain kind of nature and you want to express it. Many times I feel a lot of power in making films and I think these kinds of things play an important role.

REFLECTIONS ON THE ART OF FILM

STAN BRAKHAGE: My feeling would be that for this time of your life, it is ideal for you to work in a collaborative situation, to make a more social-minded film. I don't have any values in that sense. I don't think an artist is any more important than an advertiser, given that they are both equally good people. An artist is a specific thing, not a value judgment. It is unfortunate that people place dead artists on pedestals because they usually use those statues to beat living artists to death.

They are always giving artists honorariums, which means they are not going to pay you. They are always telling you that this is your big opportunity. A museum gives me a complete retrospective of my work. Then they come on that I'm the first independent filmmaker to get a complete retrospective and I'm only thirty-nine at that point. I'm getting this great honor, and I should be either sixty or dead. They tell me they aren't going to pay me any rentals for the films. So I said, "No."

I have had too much praise and not enough money. That you see is how the society started the situation, by putting dead artists on pedestals.

Anyone that presumes he is an artist is already considered an egomaniac just to say so. To me, "artist" means the same as electrician, plumber, garbage collector, doctor, what have you. It is a service which is needed. How many artists dare write in a motel registration, under occupation, "Artist"?

JIRI WEISS: The question is, to what extent should an artist express himself, and what is the responsibility he has to his public? As an artist, you have this tremendous urge, especially if you are a young artist, to speak out, to express yourself. And it is later that you begin to discover that there are other people, and they might or might not want to hear what you are doing. You can tell me that there are very great artists like Modigliani or van Gogh who get their fervor not thinking of their public. That they simply painted what they wanted to paint.

But the cinema is not that kind of a medium. The cinema is the kind of a medium where you communicate directly to people. René Clair said the cinema is a medium where today is seen by the eyes of today, even if you make an historical picture. This is why yesterday's picture is disagreeable. After twenty-five years, when it's a classic, you can look at it. Even the worst musicals, after thirty years, are somehow gentle and nice. Even the things you find which are frightful today, after thirty years somehow mellow with age. But you are working for today. And I wonder if I saw your film whether I would find any responsibility to the people you are working for. You are going to live in a very hard world. It's very hard. But still, the responsibility, you ought to keep it. Otherwise the advantage you had here would be completely wasted.

BERNARDO BERTOLUCCI: I am against every form of censorship, absolutely, because the power uses censorship always for political reasons.

ROUBEN MAMOULIAN: I am eclectic in my tastes. I've done everything — Gilbert and Sullivan, grand opera, drama, comedy, farce, gangster films, love films, musicals, and so on. I can't do the same thing because it bores me. I like variety. Therefore, I say, do anything that is good. I don't have a specific thing. . . . You see, by the time I was seventeen, I had subscribed to the slogan *ars gratia artis*. Art for art's sake. To hell with morality, with decency, with truth — art is something very exclusive and precious. I walked around like Childe Harold out of Lord Byron.

Well, by the time I got to be twenty, I outgrew this silly notion. And I firmly believe that art, like everything else, is for life's sake. It's not for art's sake. It should serve life. Everything should serve life. Everything should serve to add to the goodness and the beauty on this earth, to the dignity and the size of man. So he can walk proud again. Therefore, the only condition I have is that it has to have a seed of value. I'm not going to do a bedroom thing with people having intercourse through reel after reel. For one thing, it bores the hell out of me. It's a good thing to do and not a thing to watch, at least not to me.

What I feel strongly is that the artist — and I broaden this — the great majority of artists in every field are betraying mankind. To me, the hope of the future is in the arts. It's not in politics. It's not in economics. It's not in religion. It's in the arts. Because the arts are the only truly universal medium. The whole thing should serve to remind you that man still has a potential, that he's not just crawling on earth. He still has wings and he can fly. We need this reminder of faith, of optimism, to reestablish the dignity of a human being.

The greatness of Shakespeare — that's why he's viable, that's why he lives today, he'll live a thousand years from now — was that he knew man. But he told the truth about man. Not just the bad and not just the good. But the whole — all the facets. His villains were greater than life, but there was a potential in them. Even his worst villain, Richard the Third, tells you why he's a villain. He says, "If I can't be a good man with all my deformities, I can't be a lover, I can't be attractive, well, by God, I'm going to be a good villain." Hamlet says, "What a piece of work is a man! How noble in reason! How infinite in faculty, in form, in moving, how express and admirable! . . . The beauty of the world, the paragon of animals. . . . And yet, man delights me not. What is this quintessence of dust?"

Now, that's the whole truth. It's the potential and it's the quintessence of dust. If you've shown one without a touch of the other, you're a liar. It's not the truth. It's prejudiced. It's fragmented. If you show the heroic without the other, that is not the truth.

DOING WHAT'S "PERSONAL"

MARTIN RITT: The only way to function on any kind of a first-class creative level is to do what you are about. If you try to do something else, if you try to do something that you are not about, then you will go right on your ass. You may make money, but creatively you have got to go on your ass.

PAUL MAZURSKY: I think it depends on what you want to do. I want to be successful, but I don't want to be successful at the expense of making something that I don't care about. It takes a year and a half to make a picture, just about; two years for me because I write them. So if I were to do something I didn't have real passion in, I would lose my confidence early on. I'd hate myself and then start to get edged and pushed. I wouldn't do it.

MICHAEL WINNER: I do the best I can and try to bring personal qualities into my work, without necessarily fooling myself that every time I go to make a film I am dealing with perfection. I think that's the most dangerous thing, you know, when a filmmaker goes in every time to make a film which, somehow, because he's doing it, is all perfect. In the end, when people say it wasn't perfect, he says, "Well, that's your fault. It was really. You didn't see it." If you think like that, you're in terrible trouble, because you're kidding yourself. You must accept that we live in a somewhat imperfect world.

JEAN RENOIR: I do start with an idea, when I can. That's not so easy. I spent my life suggesting stories, and nobody wanted them. And it's still going on. I'm used to it, and I'm not complaining because the ideas which were forced on me were often better than my own ideas. A little mixture of what was brought to me and what I had in my imagination gave a happy medium which perhaps helped to make the picture a little more alive. Of course, you can always do a personal picture, a picture which would be the expression of your personality, even if you have to work on a story you don't like very much and within a frame which seems to be very severe.

Perhaps the first credit that you ask from a director is to know how to digest some types of food which were not at all done for him. You know the words: you must give up, give up, give up; but practically and in the final result it is your picture and not the picture of a neighbor. It's why I cannot give you any recipe about how to start a picture.

Myself, I was terribly helped in my career. I made about forty films and they were all proper refinements. Most of them had a normal career. Finally, the examination of my whole work is highly in favor of the way I did produce. But I owe the possibility to have done my films with this liberty to the most unexpected producers in the world.

WILLIAM FRIEDKIN: I'm not interested in the personal film. I'm interested in films for audiences, if it also happens to be personal. You see, it's too many people. If you've ever really been to the trough, you know that there are too many guys that contribute to the success of a picture. It's true that one intelligence can and does generally inform a project. It's usually one man's vision, but the fulfillment of that vision requires a great many talents.

RAOUL WALSH: We got into the training of "take everything." Just do it and get started and get out of here. Once in a while, you'd get a nice one, a gem, but the rank and file of them sometimes were not too hot. But, as I say, I was twenty-nine years with Warner Brothers, and in the early days, the picture was already sold.

I remember once, years ago, I made a picture in New York with Theda Bara — that was when Columbus came over, you know. It was a Spanish picture. The studio was in Fort Lee and we built a big Spanish set there, a big Spanish street. The day we started the thing, a blizzard hit New York, and it really was a blizzard. Well, Bill Fox was a nice old fellow and he said to me, "Raoul, what can we do?"

I said, "Well, Mr. Fox, I think that if we put a few domes on that set, we can change it to a Russian picture."

He called all the people and he said, "Get the Spanish costumes the hell out of here and bring the Russian costumes in." Now then, we made the thing in about three and a half weeks and the salesman came to New York for a preview of the product. Well, some fellows from Cincinnati were saying, "Gee, we advertised a Spanish picture. Where the hell is it?" Well, it was a Russian picture.

FEDERICO FELLINI: I think it is absolutely impossible not to be autobiographical. I think that *Satyricon* is maybe much more autobiographical than even *8½* because it is not an adapted biography. But maybe the anguish, the fear, the faith, the atmosphere that is in *Satyricon* — maybe that has to do with myself in a more immediate way. I think that the author of *Satyricon* is talking about his book in the same way.

PAUL MAZURSKY: The idea for *Harry and Tonto* didn't come from one person. My mother had a cat. It may have been that. It's a strange question. You do what you do. Everybody, in the end, does what comes from them or else they are really not dealing personally.

THE DIRECTOR AS AUTEUR

JOHN SCHLESINGER: At a certain moment the film must be the director's. It's not like the theatre, where you're seeing something from a fixed point of view. You know, we could all take a scene written by anybody and direct that scene totally different and give it our point of view and shoot it in such a way as to put the emphasis where we individually felt it should go.

GEORGE CUKOR: Alas, I am not an auteur, but damn few directors can write. They're very clever and they can go through the paces. As a director, you've got to think of your own limitations. There are certain things you're sympathetic with, and there are certain things you say to yourself. "Well, I can do it because I'm perfectly competent, but there're so many people who can do it much better than I can." I've been sent a script I think is charming and I said, "I think you ought to get an Italian director; it's madness to ask me to do it."

Now there are unexplored facets in a director. Offhand, I wouldn't want to say I'd be the boy to direct a western, but I thought I made a damn good try at it in *Heller in Pink Tights*. I'm very aware of that. You've got to think in your heart, "I can do that a little better than somebody else." That's an instinct; you read it and say, "Yes, I can do that." You're not always right, and naturally you can do a great many other things if you've been around. There are certain things that you are antipathetic to, you're allergic to. That shows on the screen.

GEORGE SEATON: Don't feel that you have to do everything yourself. I think it's a cooperative effort. I guess that I don't believe in the auteur theory. I think the cameraman, as Fellini says, should have some latitude. So should the editor, and I certainly believe in the writer. I became a director only to protect my own material as a writer because I think that's the only way you can do it. I think that writing and directing is a good combination. I am utterly opposed to somebody trying to do all three things because I think what happens is — as a director you love what the writer wrote, and as a producer, you just think that the director is great, and there's nobody there that's a friendly enemy to say, "You're talking too long, the scene is bad, do this." You've got to have somebody to fight against. Otherwise, as Frost once said about free verse, "It's like playing tennis without a net," and I think this is what happens.

JOHN HUSTON: Every picture is visually different so far as I'm concerned. I try and discover a new way of telling each story according to its own requirements, never to impose my own techniques — I'm not even aware of having any — on material.

MARTIN RITT: I am bowled over again with what I call "the arrogance of the auteur theory." I still think that the director is the most important person, but if he is not the writer, he can very easily change the meaning of the material.

RALPH NELSON: Film is a collaboration of many, many talents and skills. There has to be one man at the head of it, but he is not responsible for everything. Several years ago, there was a great altercation because the Writers Guild had negotiated with the producers, the MPPA, that nobody but writers could have a possessory credit. It would mean that people like Frank Capra, D. W. Griffith, Cecil B. DeMille, and all, could not have a possessory credit. They were trying to establish that the writer was the prime force behind the film. He's one of the contributors, but the director is the one who pulls all the elements together. But that would not in my opinion make him an auteur, unless he has conceived it, written it, directed it, did all the elements and basic redevelopments.

MICHAEL WINNER: I feel that in order to justify that sort of a credit, you should have contributed very substantially to the writing of the film, not necessarily by writing yourself but by having worked with the writer from very near the beginning, that you should have organized the film, even if not taking the producer credit. In fact, there was no producer on *Scorpio* although we gave the credit for technical reasons to somebody. He was not there at all by contractual and willing agreement.

And I think that you should then put your stamp on the film in the sense of editing it — which I do myself — and really be a part of it throughout. I must say that if somebody came to me with a completed and perfect script and said, "Would you like to do this?" I would still ask for the same credit, even though I would not be absolutely sure it was justified. Because we are in a slightly evil business where judgments are being made.

Well, it's rather like being in class each day, and the class is given marks, and if you have top marks you're put in a nice chair, and if you have bottom marks, you're made to stand in the corner. And on very foolish things, such as credits, those judgments are made. Anyway, on *Scorpio*, I certainly performed these functions I've described. I didn't have a heavy heart to take the credit, and I don't think I've had a film where I've had that credit where I've done less than I feel I should have done. I rather doubt that if I were doing less than I felt I should have done, I would say, "Take away the credit." Maybe I would be so noble that I would. I don't know.

THE DIRECTOR AS COLLABORATOR

ALLAN DWAN: I like all directors. I think every one of them has got something good. Some of them more than others. But what you've got to consider is this. You take it in steps. In the old days we worked completely alone. Alone. Completely alone at first and for a good many years. When we made a picture, we *made* the picture. Then there came a time when people like Thalberg began to come into the picture with good ideas backed up by enough money to follow them through with a good organization that surrounded you with excellent actors. And you got a lot of help. You were no longer the sole creator. You were the interpreter of their ideas. You began to use their very good ideas. And with all that help, you began to be better, whoever you were as a director, and everything connected with the whole enterprise became better because everyone in it was good. But you got a basis — you had a well-organized script from a good story, and if that basic person was good — call him the producer — if he was good, then your whole operation was good. Your whole picture was good. And you were good. That was a new school.

SAMUEL FULLER: The big argument today is: who makes the film? Who actually makes it? Naturally, the writer says, "I make it." The cameraman says, "Well, I don't make it, but I'm seventy to eighty percent responsible." The director says, "I make it." The producer, naturally, says, "I make it." And the editor . . . and all that. I think this is one thing that will be overcome. I'm no prophet, but I think that fifty, a hundred years from now, one man will make the film without any argument.

I know a lot of people don't like my argument — comparing it with a man who writes a book, the fellow who bound it should get credit, let alone the fellow who set it up, chose the type, the paper, the cover artist, the distributor. You can go on and on and on. That's all nonsense. It boils down to two people who are fighting as to who makes the film, who actually makes the film. One is the director and one is the writer. That's getting to a delicate battlefield now, very, very delicate.

NICHOLAS RAY: It's idiocy for a person to say, "Well, it was my idea, it was my idea, it was my idea." The film is the most dialectic of all the arts, the finest of all of the arts, but the most dialectic. Nobody makes a film alone, not even the madness.

ROBERT ALTMAN: I've got a kind of base, people who work with me most all of the time. Five or six people. Sometimes new people will come in, people will move out, but it's always collaboration. *Always.*

PETER HYAMS: I wrote a screenplay and I'm very fast. It was written in a very short period of time and I was done with it and I looked at the pages as if they were etched on tablets, and I was just thrilled with it. I was fully prepared to say, "That's the script." They turned around and said, "Well, that's not quite the script, love," and I then proceeded to get beaten to a bloody pulp and did more work on it and the script was better. Now, had I been all alone, had I been this wonderful auteur, walking around with my viewfinder, I have a feeling it wouldn't have been as good.

THE DIRECTOR AS STYLIST

ROUBEN MAMOULIAN: Style is really your point of view on the world, on life. How you see it. How you feel it. So it's not conscious. The style can vary according to the subject. But there are certain paramount things, though, which I don't know if I started from consciously. I don't know, I may have. Because sometimes I see some old films and I discover something I didn't realize consciously but unconsciously. This is purely personal because there can be as many attitudes as there are creative people.

But realism and naturalism is not for me. I'm not interested in it. I think it's too feeble an instrument. I think it's good for travelogues. It's good for documentaries or the newsreel. But not for fiction films. Of course, poetry lives forever. That's the most unrealistic foolish thing, right? In prose you have great realists like Tolstoy or Dostoevsky, great realists who really show you life. That certainly has a niche in the arts. So you can make a film thoroughly realistic and it belongs. But it is not the kind of thing I like to do because I think the realistic thing dies. All naturalistic painting is dead as a mackerel right now. Nobody wants it. They're all stylized. They're all imaginative. They're all poetical. I feel that any subject — it doesn't have to be a fantasy — any subject should be approached from a poetical point of view, and therefore stylized.

VINCENTE MINNELLI: It's hard to say how you assimilate a style for a certain film. It's going to be the right style for that film and not for any other. It comes from just living within those confines, you know, concentrating on them.

Well, once I told a story that illustrates what I think a director's function is. There was an old farmer who lost a cow. There were hills and fields and streams, and he searched for it for a long time and he couldn't find it. Finally, one day he had been gone about a week and he came back with the cow behind him. And everyone said, "Well, where did you find the cow?" And he said, "Well, I thought to myself, 'Where would I go if I were a cow?' And I went, and I did, and he was." So, you have to put yourself in a frame of mind where you say, "What would I do in these circumstances? How would I possibly make it reasonable, how can I make it live for me?" That's the way you do it.

ED EMSHWILLER: I like to use blocks of material to say, "Look at this," and then throw down a big heavy block that is shaped and formed in one way and then completely switch over and throw in another block right next to it. At first, they seem not to be about the same thing, but because they're next to one another, they are like a lot of our experiences in life which seem to be completely unrelated, but suddenly they make connections neither one alone would have conveyed. Suddenly you see and understand something that neither of these experiences would have told you by itself. And that's the kind of thing that I like to deal with. That means that I shift style, because style, very often, is a way of saying something and it's a stance — a way of seeing and viewing. So, by looking at something through several different styles or several different ways, I feel that I'm dealing more fully and, for me, more completely and more satisfyingly than if I did it all from one consistent standpoint.

JOHN HUSTON: If new ground is ever broken, it's purely accidental. I never set out to break new ground. It only occurs because the material requires it.

GEORGE CUKOR: The thing that determines what I do is the subject, the text. I would do *Little Women* differently than I would do *Travels with My Aunt*. It is quite a different style. It is farcical and comedic. I suppose you sniff what is in the air. I am not aware that I have changed. Obviously, I must be influenced by what is going on. I don't think, "Ah, yes, I think the audience will weep at this." I am not aware of that. I am only aware of what I am doing. I will say, "Yes, I think this will be effective or this will work." It depends very much upon the subject.

GEORGE SEATON: People always say, "I'm going to do it in this style." But someone else said, "Style is never the beginning, it's the result," and I think he's absolutely right. I think you have to start with an idea and then try to expand. It's geometric; you must start with a point and, if you take your pencil this way, it becomes a line. That's what I think Fellini was saying when he said his scripts were six hundred pages long. He starts with an idea and it develops as he's writing it.

PAUL MORRISSEY: I don't like to think I have a style. My style is in the casting and the peculiar mentality, the psychology of the people in the film. I don't care if they're photographed from the moon. I think if a picture is videotaped or shot with a fixed camera or the camera moves a thousand times and you have every angle to cover yourself from, unless the people find it more interesting, the way it looks doesn't interest me.

JEAN RENOIR: Everyone of us, we must build up our grammar, our method, like the recipe in a cookbook.

VINCENT SHERMAN: Unfortunately, the director doesn't always have control. Unfortunately, the head of the studio sometimes steps in and says, "I don't like the way this is cut. I don't like that music." Or he might say, "I don't like the way that it is photographed," or something like that. You would be surprised how the overall effect of a picture can be changed by certain things. The intent may change completely. It is a complicated subject, but in the final analysis, I think that what you are as a human being, what you feel about people and about life will come through in some ways in the films that you do. If you are cynical or skeptical and have no belief in people; if you have distrust, then I think that will come through. If you have faith in people and you have compassion for them, if you have understanding, then I think that too will come through. It can be demonstrated in different ways. Your attitude toward people and toward events will be manifested somehow or another in the work that you do.

ALLAN DWAN: Those are terms I've never quite understood — technique, style, and such. I was never aware of any technique. My job was to make the pictures in whatever way I thought they ought to be made, and I can't recall that I have any technique. I think it's instinctive. To me stories were mathematical problems, as most problems were. There's always a mathematical solution to anything. So I think that probably if I had a technique, I'd say it was a mathematical technique [manifesting itself] in logic, in naturalness, in the direction in which you went and the relationship of one thing to another. The inevitable laws of mathematics — they apply to drama and to life.

GEORGE CUKOR: Recognizing when something looks right, that I choose to say is style. That is what it is all about. How that is accomplished is a mysterious thing. Sometimes you make big decisions, but very often small decisions, decisions that you aren't aware of and, also, things on the set. You have a vision of them.

Yes, I suppose a director does influence, but maybe what sticks in my craw is the physical writing of the thing. I have too much respect for the writer, if he's good. Too much respect for what I can do. I want the best, I want the greatest help, I want the best cutters, the best designers, the best actors. That doesn't mean always the most celebrated ones.

ROUBEN MAMOULIAN: A lot of people are afraid of their own judgment and their own instinct. They're always underrating themselves. I think what makes a filmmaker is individuality. You don't want to be like me. You can learn nothing from me. What you can do, if there's some of these credos, something I believe in, if it hits a chord, let's say rhythm, you will use it your own way. That's not a detail. It's not a specific. The point is, when you get an insane idea, if you can theoretically justify it, do it. Don't back out. Do it, because it's going to be the best thing in the picture, believe me. It's always happened that way.

HOWARD HAWKS: One time, Louis B. Mayer had a brilliant idea. He was going to put Josef von Sternberg and me together and get a super-picture. Joe and I were quite good friends because I prepared his first picture that made him. We laughed about it and started to work on a story and developed a whole story. Then we started to talk about how to treat it. Well, Joe had always taken a little thing and built it up. I took a big situation and played it down. We both knew this. I said, "Joe, there is only one thing to do, let's go in and tell Mr. Mayer. You tell him your way, and I'll tell him mine. Let him choose, because we're no good to each other." So we did and, unfortunately, he chose my way. I told him big things that seemed fine to him and Joe told him little teeny things. But that happens all the time. I guarantee you that two directors that are any good can take the same story, change the name of the characters, change the name of the town, and make the picture, and it will be entirely different.

VINCENT SHERMAN: We all steal from each other. We are all stimulated by each other. I think this is true of any art form. I think it's true in the field of writing, of painting, of music. I think we're all influenced by our contemporaries and also our past masters. It's in the way you tell a story. It's in the way you do certain things. Eventually you hope that you evolve your own particular style.

GEORGE CUKOR: I have done a great many things. There are some where I would say, "Well, somebody else can do this one hell of a lot better than I can." But I think that one has to vary it. One has to surprise oneself. Otherwise, if you play it safe all of the time, it's not good. I try not to. Anybody who wants to be a director who advances and changes and keeps going has to be aware of that. Some people say, "I've done this scene over and over again." Some wise guy says, "I've never done it and I never will do it." One must realize that the cameraman and everybody there are the ones who have the experience. You must give yourself the illusion that you have never done it before. That makes it fresh.

JACK NICHOLSON: I'm not a very good stylist in anything that I do, but my approach is fairly methodical. I just don't go in and see what happens. I try and really define a structure. I have an overall viewpoint about what films are and what kinds of films can be made. I don't have a specific kind that I stick to, and I know how to make different kinds. My point of view is to get a whole experience out of the film. I don't think that by concentrating on any one thing you do that. Obviously, you have strengths based on what your experience has been.

I don't like to pander to audiences. I think there should be something of value given for somebody's time taken, spent for ninety minutes or a couple of hours in the dark. It can be just simple entertainment. I'm not given to philosophical statements because I find it's dangerous. It leads to time not being utilized. But I am very philosophical about myself. I always have my little scene where I consider it a good exercise to put a theme into verbal form rather than just let it ride. But mainly I don't like to be too boring.

BRIAN DE PALMA: You've got to look at your career and see what you're good at and what you're bad at. If you've seen any of my movies, you'll know what I'm good at and bad at, and you'll see why this movie, *Sisters*, is such a big step for me, because most of my movies before were sort of cold, intellectual, and satiric, and certain parts were good, but there was no structure. They sort of fell apart, and if you got through fast enough, you were okay. But this movie was a very conscious attempt to tell a story, to involve the audience with the characters, to work in a very cinematic style.

JACK NICHOLSON: There are certain sequences of *Drive, He Said,* which I think just suddenly drop into a whole different genre. There's a sort of suspense sequence in it which I shot differently than the rest of the picture. I like it myself when movies don't get hung up on staying in one style. I don't like turning to the camera too much, though I don't object to it, and saying this is a movie, movie, movie. In this film, I didn't do that, but also I don't like to delude myself that I've carried someone into another level of consciousness and they don't know sometime during the ninety minutes that they're in a movie theatre and I let them know I know through movie style.

RAOUL WALSH: The transition from silents to sound pictures didn't hit me in any way. I just kept the thing moving regardless of the sound. I took them out of the room and let them talk in the hall, if they didn't talk inside the room. I just kept going. Of course, it was pretty tough on a lot of actors and actresses who'd had no stage experience. I handled it the same way. Of course, there was a great upheaval amongst the directors when talking pictures came in. They called me a renegade because I was one of the first ones to do an outdoor talking picture. They said that they'd created such a medium with pantomime, you know, and now this talking stuff was going to destroy it all. I said it was going to destroy us if we didn't get along and get in with it. So they finally all came in.

RICHARD ATTENBOROUGH: I believe very much in content and I believe very much in content demanding the technique. Flash and style and pyrotechnics for their own sake I have no respect for at all.

INFLUENCES — PLUS AND MINUS

STAN BRAKHAGE: One has to remember that the first movie I ever saw was *Snow White and the Seven Dwarfs*. My childhood, like that of Gregory Markopoulos and Kenneth Anger, was saturated by Hollywood movies. Most of us still go to them quite gratefully and enjoy them in the same milieus that we did as children. So we are all the time borrowing possibilities from the Hollywood movie. They are also getting grammar from us. It looks at times that we are getting closer and closer together, but we're not, because the absolute division is the overall purpose of the work. The purpose of the Hollywood film is to help us share in the same cultish dream. It is the dance of the society, it is our tribal dance, whereas the artist is always really trying to create a new dream.

FRED ZINNEMANN: I think one can make marvelous films that have no beginning, middle, or end. In fact, I think the more we get away from that kind of setting up of general rules, the better off we'll be. I think we have suffered — as an art form — tremendously from the fact that a lot of arbitrary rules were enforced upon us by a lot of people who had no business doing it, and who only had authority invested in them by money — various executives who hired you for so much and told you how to make a picture. They did fill us full of all kinds of do's and don't's.

And if you go back, and if you examine the kind of rules that were put forth, you find two astonishing things. First of all, you find that they were totally arbitrary, such as L. B. Mayer's famous postulate, "There are only two kinds of women — mothers or whores." Or saying, "No matter what happens, the star's face must always be very well lighted — you've got to see the star's face," even if it's in the middle of the night in a railroad town. And so on. There was a whole slew of rules and regulations of that kind, and no matter how hard one fought against it, I suspect that insidiously some of it stuck. And it's very, very hard to get that out of one's system. But, even more surprising, in the thirties, the Hollywood films probably reached their all-time high as far as quality is concerned. That's the extraordinary thing.

From poetry to moving pictorialization, the influences on filmmakers are widespread. For the early practitioners, there was a master to emulate.

ALLAN DWAN: I very candidly watched Griffith and did what he did. It was a wonderful, successful thing to do. I'd see his pictures and go back and make them with my company.

For Leo McCarey, there was, in addition to John Ford, Frank Borzage, Charlie Chaplin, Frank Capra, and Ernst Lubitsch,

. . .Tod Browning. As much as one person is capable of imparting knowledge — personal knowledge — to another, he gave me a priceless legacy. He wrote all his own stories from scratch. They were all original. And I sat in on them and had a chance to suggest ideas. Then I went through the picture as script girl, taking notes on each shot, sitting next to him. Then I went in the cutting room and finally worked on the titles and saw the picture off.

BERNARDO BERTOLUCCI: I made one film as an assistant with Pasolini, the first Pasolini movie, *Accattone,* and it was really very exciting to see him because it was his first movie, so he was discovering what filming, shooting is. But it was my only experience before shooting my first movie. So nobody told me you have to know the connection between a sequence and the sequence after. You know, the problems exist from the moment when you start to think.

The influences on filmmakers need not be limited to other filmmakers. For Stan Brakhage, working from a more directly abstract formal approach, the techniques of composers have set significant examples.

STAN BRAKHAGE: Webern actually depends on repetition. He is in the mainstream of Western music. He depends on his subtleties by us expecting repetition which he does not give us. Webern is new and they regarded him as the great beast who tried to overturn music. We've come to realize that this is all very absurd. It depends very much on a tradition of development for any new development to exist. You cannot have El Greco until you have Michelangelo, because the figure would be totally incomprehensible. It was anyway to most people for several hundred years.

There is a chronology to learning. Each figure that is developed by a new artist is dependent on all the crucial figures of the past. This was very heavy on my mind during the making of *Anticipation of the Night,* because I wasn't taking anything for granted. Webern had that kind of importance that he permitted me to do structures that were not dependent on the baroque, any more than he was, where you do not have repetitions in any sense of the word.

Other modern directors do not hesitate to turn back to their venerated masters.

CURTIS HARRINGTON: The main conscious influence in my work is a director whose work I admire most. That is Josef von Sternberg. Even though I have never made a really Sternbergian film, I am still very influenced by him. I hope someday to do a film in his style.

I am very aware of film history. When I was younger, I lived in Paris for a couple of years, and I went to the Cinémathèque Française almost every night. They would show two or three films a day there, so I really had a marvelous education in the world history of film, both silents and sound. In that sense, I have all of that somewhere in my head. I may unconsciously borrow an effect or an idea that I remember because I am so oriented to film.

BRIAN DE PALMA: I think that Hitchcock probably has had the best story ideas and cinema ideas in the history of cinema, and I'm just trying to follow the master a little bit. I think the construction of *Psycho* is a brilliant idea — to involve yourself with a character and then kill him, you know. That's very consciously done here in *Sisters*, to involve you with a black man and then kill him. It's pure cinema. To me this movie is like a learning situation.

In my prior movies, they're fragmented. They sort of work in some parts and don't work in others. I have many sorts of styles to things I'm playing all the time. Now, this way I'm forced to work to a very strict form. I think for a director, it's a great growing process. Very few directors have a chance to grow in their careers.

STAN BRAKHAGE: Mark the cases of von Stroheim, von Sternberg, Orson Welles, D. W. Griffith. Most of these men, whom we recognize as artists, struggled with the studio situation. The pattern of hatred against them is almost always the same. Many of them were forced to become actors to make a living. It's the final punishment that Hollywood could put upon them, to make Erich von Stroheim, the man you most love to hate, become an actor in a film like *Sunset Boulevard* as a fallen director.

Some directors even may pay visual tribute to their mentors. Peter Bogdanovich, in his first film, *Targets*, made use of the "cinematic quote."

PETER BOGDANOVICH: I think most novelists begin by consciously imitating others to get a certain effect, not as parody or homage, but because the other writers "do it good," and you know it'll be good that way. There are people who criticize one for stealing. On the contrary, I think it's admirable, because I don't think that there is anything that's original anymore. It's all been done. They were doing it in the silent days, all this split-screen junk and fast cutting. I just interviewed Allan Dwan, and he said that he did it way back when he was making films in the 1920's. He said,

"That's the kind of stuff we threw away when we grew up." So, there isn't anything new.

One of my pleasures in making films is to sometimes reproduce shots that I've seen and loved. I love one of the corniest shots ever done. You see it in any chase, any Johnny Mack Brown western: the guy rides by, and you pan back to see the people who are chasing him. I just love that shot, so I used it in the chase in *Targets*. It's a good piece of grammar; it's a good sentence. It says, "Here he goes; now let's see how far back they are." It's a continuous movement, and the audience knows that nothing's been manipulated, that it's real. A lot of things like that give you pleasure.

PAUL MORRISSEY: There was a style of filmmaking once whereby each film did not have to make millions of dollars or be a great critical success. That was a technique of filmmaking where films were looked upon as inconsequential contrivances to keep the actors at the studio working. I think I'm consciously or unconsciously putting myself in a situation where I don't try to attach importance to a film. I just try to think about the casting and find interesting people and put them in front of a camera to play parts. It's an incredibly old-fashioned set-up, because I think the major films of the thirties, the mentality or the psychology involved in them, was a bit easygoing. Now filmmaking is such a small business that everything is critical. There's a lack of distance between the people who make the film and the film itself. I think that a lot of extra things find their way into a film made in an easygoing manner.

JAN KADAR: I told you about the philosophy of filmmaking. Why are you doing pictures? Maybe it is because you feel a certain attraction to this profession. You may have something to tell. Or you may be trying to learn a way to express yourself. There is not only one reason why we are in this field. I am doing pictures because I cannot do anything else. I am trying to do my best.

Naturally, you have to communicate something, so therefore you are doing pictures. Now, there is only one problem and that is how to fight all of the obstacles which force you to do something else to preserve your own integrity. But, the main reason why anybody is doing pictures is that one has to tell something or has to communicate something just as any other artist does. That's why we are doing it. If you want to do it for other reasons, maybe you can select a much more easy and more comfortable way of living.

Of course, becoming a complete filmmaker is not merely the result of "dues paid" in the Hollywood system. The impetus for artistic self-expression occurs in all areas of daily life.

STAN BRAKHAGE: One day someone — it might have been my mother — gave me a rose. It was very beautiful. I seem to have been very disturbed by things that seem to have no end into themselves, no purpose, no intrinsic value in my life, but were beautiful all the same. I could neither decide for or against them. It would be ridiculous to throw this rose out, I decided, but in time it really was annoying, so I began to photograph it. And then, almost immediately, all kinds of ideas sprang into my head, ideas that are very intrinsic with the rose. My whole life long, I have been involved with the flower and it certainly took on special meaning to me sometime when I was sixteen or seventeen. I read Gertrude Stein's poem, "A rose is a rose is a rose." There's a wonderful thing about the poem though it's been despised and made fun of by practically everybody. When this was pointed out to Gertrude Stein, she very wisely said, "This may be true, but do I have to point out to you that it is the most often quoted poem in the English language?"

DOCUMENTARY

Every second is a discovery if you really try to understand things, you know? So what I try to do is to recreate the process of knowledge.
— Roberto Rossellini

What is documentary film? Is it somehow more or less pure than "fictional" cinema? Has it any greater or lesser claim as being art? The question has not yet been answered adequately. Perhaps the problem is with the question itself. We usually assume that documentary film "documents" something. That is, documentary film *records* rather than *stages;* uses *non-actors* rather than *actors;* takes place in *actual locations* rather than *contrived sets; captures* and *reflects* events rather than *forcibly commenting* upon them; and, generally, is of a less glamorous bent than the standard fictional film.

Problems arise with these differentiations. Are Robert Flaherty's films (for example, *Nanook of the North, Man of Aran*) — utilizing "real people" but staging events — documentary or narrative/fictional? Are Roberto Rossellini's recent educational films for Italian television — using sets *and* locations, actors *and* non-actors, historical texts *and* dramatizations — documentary? Are Robert Bresson's films — using *all* non-actors, *all* locations, and *all* fictional story — narratives?

The answer might best be that these divisions are false and misleading. They provide a shorthand for gross categorization, but do not really inform as to a particular film's worth or position in the current art/entertainment/ educational modalities.

Jean-Luc Godard poses the question in his film, *Les Carabiniers*. Of the two founding fathers of French film, Georges Méliès and Louis Lumière, the former is usually considered the dramatist, the fiction-weaver, while the latter is taken as the realist, the documentarian. The former filmed rocket ships going to the moon, magical special effects, outlandish tales. The latter filmed trains arriving at stations. Godard argues that it was Méliès, presenting the world as he saw it, who was the documentarian. Lumière, rigidly representing objects and events as they seemed objectively to occur, was the fantasist, since we know that art, by its inherent inability to be truly representational, works only in the realm of appearances — appearances not equivalent to their submerged realities.

In this section, the views are presented of those who have worked in traditional documentary forms. Also, there are comments from some filmmakers who have created both traditional documentary and narrative works. Finally, the section is concluded with extensive comments by Roberto Rossellini. Rossellini has undertaken no less than a filmed history of the world. His recent "didactic" films — *Socrates, The Rise of Louis XIV, Augustine, Pascal, Descartes, The Struggle for Survival, The Age of Cosimo de Medici, The Messiah* — are extending the limits of traditional filmmaking.

WILLIAM FRIEDKIN: Documentary is a reordering of actuality. You have to select. I made a documentary called *The Thin Blue Line* about law enforcement in the United States. You go around and you order reality for the camera and in the cutting room. Directing is communicating with people, that's all. I mean, you'll never *learn* that. You have that or not. The best documentary filmmaker I know is unable to communicate with actors, makes great documentary films but gets in a fiction situation and he's tongue-tied. You must be able to communicate with people. That's acting.

ROBERT ALTMAN: I have a background in documentaries, but my feeling is that in films like *Nashville* and *California Split* particularly, what we do is set up the arena and create an event. Then we cover it as if it were actually happening. We just have a little more control. I can say, "Let's do it once again."

RICHARD LEACOCK: When we started, we set up a crazy set of rules: never ask anybody to do anything. If you missed anything, even if you missed them coming through the door, don't ask them to come through the door again. The reason for this we found through experience: it simply doesn't work. It sets up a whole psychological thing that is exactly what you're trying to get away from. Most people want to please you. They know you've come here with a camera and a tape recorder. Presumably, you want something. So they try and find out what it is you want and do it for you. So you get this funny thing — I just put down the camera and don't shoot until they finally say, "Well, this stupid ass obviously doesn't know what he's doing. To hell with him. I'm going to go ahead and do what I do anyway."

I went to Israel once with Lenny Bernstein — he happened to be a friend way back in college. Every time Bernstein produces a score, every time he blows his nose, you start shooting, you're really going to get him uptight. So I would go days, literally days, where I'd say to myself, "I don't care if he stands on his head and plays the piano with his back to us, I'm not going to shoot." This was in order to allow him to generate his own thing.

The only things that are rules for me are: don't interview, because that's, to me, a copout; and don't . . . well, I do break them sometimes. It happened on the stage. We did once, in that house, ask a direct question. "How do you feel about this?" But otherwise, you're just observing.

For instance, I spent three months looking at the leadership of the Ku Klux Klan and never had a single argument with them. When I did *Chiefs,* I didn't have any arguments with those cats. In fact, one of them gave me a pocket Mace gun to take home with me. Big Super-Chief, remember him? I'm just more interested in what makes people tick, than arguing with them, I guess.

BUDD BOETTICHER: I didn't feel that the definitive motion picture about bullfighting had been made. And I knew that you had to make that picture with one of two men who were then alive: either Luis Miguel Domínguin in Spain, or Carlos Arruza. Both were very close friends of mine. I chose Arruza because suddenly he fell on horseback and I realized that I had a combination of *National Velvet* and *Black Beauty* and *Blood and Sand*, rather than just showing the situation of the bullfighter throwing back the roses to the crowd, which had been done before. In fact, I had done it myself.

And I chose to make that picture, and I started it off as exactly the type of picture that you now see. Then I married a very lovely actress, Debra Paget, and I hadn't seen any of her pictures. I think that a director marries an actress in spite of the fact that she is an actress and not because of it. And I began to see her pictures and realized that she was a very talented girl who hadn't scratched the surface if she wanted to continue with her career.

So I rewrote this story that I love, the simplicity of it, because I didn't want to put words into Carlos's mouth. The minute I would start to tell him what to say, it was my picture instead of me showing his picture. That's why I kept it in this documentary style. I rewrote it and called it *Olé* and photographed a great deal of my wife as Mrs. Arruza. This was the only Hollywood element of the picture. Or London element — I hate to use Hollywood; it's a dirty word. What I mean is that she was the only actress in the movie. Then, when we were separated and ultimately divorced, I replaced her with a lovely actress, Elsa Cardenas, who redid everything that Debra did. Then, when Carlos was killed, I waited eight months and went to Mrs. Arruza, who was fortunately a very dear friend of mine — and kept Carlos and me from killing each other for about seven years — and told her that I felt that there was only one woman in the world who could play the part, because the part had to have the dignity that I insisted upon. She was shocked because she was satisfied with Elsa. She thought that I meant that I had decided on someone from Mexico for the part and she said, "Who?" And I said, "You."

SHIRLEY CLARKE: We spent six months casting *The Cool World*. Carl Lee spent four months getting into the actual street gangs and casting the kids from the major gangs that were around then. When we first began, we went to the schools and they would always bring forward the bright, young kid, and for a long time we kept thinking the script was an absolute fake; we'd get them to read it and it was just disastrous. Finally, when we got to the actual gang kids and whether they could read or not, we sort of would do improvisation things with them that were similar to things in the film. Suddenly, the script came back and it was at that point that we realized that we would stay with the kids and let them lead us, rather than feeling that the story had a plot that we had to follow.

There were certain things in each scene the kids had to accomplish. They had to learn lines, but basically it was always worked through setting it up so they were feeding it back to us before we started. Lines seemed to be coming from them. They had permission to say whatever they wanted and change anything they felt didn't sit right. Usually what they tended to do if we worked for a long enough time is get closer and closer to the original script, and they really wanted the security of the script. They needed to progress.

STAN BRAKHAGE: The eyes move quite fantastically over any given scene; they jump continually. Even when we think we are stony-eyed and staring at one spot, the brain flickers a variety of interpretations of this one spot. I have increasingly worked with this quality of seeing — this jumping. The problem is that most people are reading these films out of the trained experience of the normal film. To them, my film is making the statement that the subject or person is jumping and leaping about. But what I am really stating is that the eyes jump and move about.

I really think of my films as documentaries. All of them. They are my attempt to get as accurate a representation of seeing as I possibly can. I never fantasize. I have never invented something just for the sake of making an interesting image. I am always struggling very hard to get as close an equivalent on film as I can, as I actually see it.

I think that the difference between my function and cinéma vérité is that the event is much more consciously changed by the camera in my case. I am taking all of that on to myself. In cinéma vérité they interpret the effect of that on other people.

One thing that I think of as important in a work of art, in any medium, is a representation of the materials that make up that work of art. For instance, painters have always with very few exceptions, painted their names on the front of the canvas. Now when you find a painter who paints his name on the back, he tends to be a man who is involved with painting a window.

Andrew Wyeth tends to paint his name on the back of his paintings. He is of that school of art, very much in the minority, that comes out of Greece, where they say that "the painter painted so well these grapes that the birds tried to come and eat them." To most of the artists that I know, it would be a frightfully disturbing thing. In the first place, we don't want the birds pecking at our paintings.

The drive is honestly to make a film. That is one reason why I scratch titles. By scratching them, you start people off with an intrinsic sense of

what film is . . . that this is a film and not a window. Then I am using
flares, edge-flares. I am using many little effects. At times the camera
will be visible. I stick that in there when I feel that I have gone almost to
the point of creating a Hollywood film and people might start being
sucked up into the screen.

ROBERTO ROSSELLINI: I think that today we have to build a culture based on
knowledge. Not on emotion. You can have the emotion later. But you
must approach it through knowledge. You see, the truth is such a little
little thing that is very difficult to discover. Truth is more little than a cell
or a molecule or an atom, you know. So to approach the truth is really, is
really a tremendous effort. . . . True knowledge you can reach, perhaps,
one day too. That's a long proceeding.

I refuse to say, "That is the truth." What I am searching for is the
truth, but I don't know what is the truth. Through knowledge you can
approach the truth much more than through feelings.

We must admit that the sickness of our society and of our time is
specialization. So the action we must take is against the specialization,
and to see broad things, vast things. This is the point. You see, specialization is an invention very recent — of two hundred years ago, when
science quickly developed mainly technique. We need specialists to
build up the thing. And now we must admit that our culture is a culture of
specialists. Now we have collected enough knowledge. Now we must
pass to another kind of action: to put together all that knowledge, which
is very difficult because a true specialist is impossible at communication.

I am convinced that I am totally ignorant, and I know there are others
ignorant in the world like me. So I want to learn, and I want to have the
excitement of learning and discovering things. I want to convey what I
have discovered to the others ignorant like me. You see? And that's, in a
sense, the approach.

But I feel that today we are totally lost because we have not really a
real culture. You see, the things which are going on in the world, they
have a tremendous speed. The transformation, the new knowledge, the
new things are coming towards us at a tremendous speed. We have not
prepared to look at those kinds of things. We have not information,
because we must admit, I think, that the worst of the pollution today in
the world is the so-called information. There is such misinformation all
the time.

That is tied to another problem, tied also with the problem of education. I'm always repeating that the word *education* comes from the Latin
educere, meaning "castrate." And, you know, education is always cas-

trating, in a sense. Why is it castrating? Because there exists in the mind of the educators a type of man who they think is perfect, and they try to rebuild that man. And that is, I think, wrong.

Another kind of thing which is wrong in education is that we have tried always to remake the man of yesterday. The only thing which has value is the future, nothing else. So you must open your mind. You must know a lot of things.

Educational films are usually a failure because people have a very vague idea of what is educational. Education, in general, is taught like a message. I think that the mail takes care of messages. Why do we have to take care of the message, you know? The telegraph and the telephone take care of the message. People want to deal with education, or even outside of education, they want to convey a message, which I think is the wrong position.

Dealing with television, when I had started this sort of film, the lowest of the prices was paid for educational things. So, there is always very, very little money involved. And, when you have little money, so you have to find a way to do the things.

But the main thing is the confusion of the area of education. You see, for example, we must admit that education is conceived more or less like a training for the good taste. It is not the learning, which is another kind of thing. We use always the words *sensational, great*. The word *useful* we don't use at all.

You see, the approach is different between a fiction filmmaker and an historian. I don't think it's any real difference, you know. The differences are much more in the organization of the thing. A filmmaker of a feature film needs an organization, needs a distributor, needs some money to be invested. He needs to gain on that money, on that investment. As soon as you start that way, you are conditioned. You are conditioned by the things that are around. So it's impossible to be free.

I don't search for dramatization at all. I don't search to do something dramatic. I search for the most illustrative point, that's all. I am searching for the reality. Surely the reality appears to you what is more evident, what is more glamorous in a sense, you know? The paradox is a way to see reality, but I am not searching for paradox at all. . . .

I am really convinced that we are not talking enough in our center. The film has reduced us to some indication, to some *access* of the past instead of to the past. I think it's very amusing to go and to explore again the architecture of the past, so I use a great deal of dialogue because I think there is really the main thing of man. When I made *Open City*, we had passed through the war, we had passed through twenty years of fascism, twenty-two years of fascism. And the war ended and we were in the middle of the ruin. Just the ruin. So it was the first duty to try to get rid of the dust which was covering us and to understand a little bit what we had passed. That was it. So, again, there was a desire to understand and to be orientated in that kind of thing.

From then on, I have discovered in myself that to understand fully the particular thing, I must know everything. That's the reason why I made *Socrates* — just to look a little bit more carefully to the great civilizations. Now, Socrates — to me it seems, and I think that it is true — historically is right. He was very important and very original because he was against any sort of education, in a sense. You know, education in the sense that you take advantage of people. So at that time, the question was the development of eloquence. And *eloquence*, etymologically, means the capacity to convince. So his system was not a system of convincing, but was a system to push each man to be himself, and to be logical in his way towards everything.

I don't care if he really existed or not. I think he existed. But anyway, what is important is that Socrates is known all over the world. So who cares if he was a real person or not? It is that way of thinking which is important. You see, he thought he was the wisest person in the land because he discovered that he didn't know anything. That is a very wise attitude. And it is unique in the history of human beings.

I made just recently *Pascal*. Why Pascal? Pascal is a difficult character. He was at the beginning of science, and he was a scientist. And he was a theologian in the meantime. So that was a tremendous conflict in himself. And believe me, to make a film on Pascal, one needs to have a tremendous courage.

He was a virgin. Never had any love affair. He was always sick, suffering all the time. And thinking of God, just a boring person, you know? But he was a person, important to understand certain kinds of things. Now, if you see *Pascal*, and if you read only Pascal, if you are a mystic you can admire his own mysticism. If you are a mathematician, you can admire the work that he has done in geometry. But that's not enough. What is important is to see Pascal in the context of his own world.

For example, that was the period of the big trials against the witches. And he was there. He was participating in those trials. And he was believing; he was full of superstitions. I am full of superstitions too, but anyway, he had more superstitions than I. For example, one day he was sick. He was always sick, but one day he was a little bit more sick than usually. And what disturbed him was going on in his room. He got out all the water existing in the room. So, at least if he died, his soul didn't sink in the water. You see, it's incredible. And those things, they were absolutely accepted by everybody. By Pascal, by his father, by his sister. Because that was the rise of the moment.

So when you put a character like Pascal in that context, you understand a lot of things. It's possible to understand a lot of things. At least, so it seems to me. If you start to say, "Well, I want to do the real Louis XIV because Louis XIV has certain kinds of resemblance with certain kinds of political problems of today," you are completely in the wrong. But if you look only to him, and if by chance those kinds of things fit with certain realities of today, that's another kind of approach.

I didn't propose a model. If somebody has just the right eye, he can see how, for example, through the rise of the power of Louis XIV, how the power is a silly thing. And how the power gets advantage of the stupidity of man, or the innocence of man, eh? We know about that abstraction — conflict. We know everything, because we have a lot of filmmakers in the world. They tell us always about conflict. And they have reduced the conflict to very little. So they have conflict for sex, and things like that. There are few specialties more than that. But to understand is more vast a problem. What I am trying to do — but you know I am an old man so I can also be a fool, and I think I have the right to be a fool. Everybody has the right to be a fool. So I am forming that dream, and I can do something good and useful.

Everything which comes from man is dramatic. Everything is dramatic. Why not? You know, you can *emphasize* in dramaticism. But everything — to live, to breathe — is dramatic. I am not a philosopher; I refuse to be a philosopher, I refuse to deliver messages. I am just a worker, no more than that. That is my moral position in front of what I have to do. I am purely a worker.

11
Viewing Film

THE AUDIENCE

The Question

To what degree does the director allow his concern for the audience to affect the actual shape of his material?

FRANK CAPRA: I think of the medium as a people-to-people medium — not cameraman-to-people, not directors-to-people, not writers-to-people, but people-to-people. I didn't come from the stage or anything else. I had no training in any of the arts. I just stumbled into motion pictures and loved it, so this is just what I have formed from my own experience. You can

only involve an audience with people. You can't involve them with
gimmicks, with sunsets, with hand-held cameras, zoom shots, or anything else. They couldn't care less about those things. But you give them
something to worry about, some person they can worry about, and care
about, and you've got them, you've got them involved.

Everything is subject to the actors as far as I'm concerned. And as far
as the actor is concerned, I try to make that actor subject to that part, to
live that part and not act it, because my main objective is to involve the
audience, to get them when what they're seeing up there, when they
begin to believe it, and they become part of it and they become interested
in what's going on up there on the screen. And if I can involve that
audience that much, then that's remarkable. My pictures are made for
audiences, not on a one-to-one basis, but on a one-to-a-thousand basis.

FRED ZINNEMANN: It is an interesting subject for discussion: whether today's young picture-makers believe that they have an obligation to the
audience, or whether they are simply obligated to express themselves.
This is a very big question, because we were taught that we had the total
obligation of pleasing the audience and never mind how we felt about it.

I asked Peggy Ashcroft once — we were talking about the "Method,"
the acting method — "Do you have to cry in order to make the audience
cry? Do you have to feel the emotion at all to be able to get the audience
to share it?"

"Not at all," she said. "I feel it's my own private business; my job is to
make the audience feel an emotion — that's my work, that's what I do. I
don't have to cry to do it." And this is very interesting. Now, applying it
to picture-makers, some of us would feel that our vocation is to entertain
the audience, to bring something to them that's worthwhile — in terms of
an emotional experience, let's say. Others would say, "Well, to hell with
the audience — I want to put on film what I feel, and if they don't like it,
the hell with them." It's probably perfectly valid; and it would be very
interesting, because it's really the number one question of our time when
it comes to artists.

The Answer: Yes

SAMUEL FULLER: I'm positive that every director or artist, painter, whether
he says, "I don't care whether the people like it," instinctively does.
Otherwise, he wouldn't be doing it for public acceptance. Generally, he
would make a film, write a book, paint a portrait, and burn it. No one has
ever seen it. *That* is purely for himself. I don't believe the other. I don't

believe any director who says, "I don't think of the audience, I don't think of the front office." I don't believe a word of it. I think instinctively it has to be there in the back of his mind. And I can prove it.

You might feel it's very colorful to open up a movie with the Pope having an affair with a water hydrant. You know, even as you write it, or even as you shoot it, that it's not going to be shown. That's number one. Therefore, in your heart, you either were thinking of censorship, studio regulations, the Church, or the fact that the people would just band together and say, "This is too repulsive; we don't want to see it." That's all I'm trying to tell you. I mean instinctively. I'm using that as an exaggeration.

I believe that when a director shoots a scene and he has many, many people killed in a shot, he instinctively knows that when he goes over a certain number, it not only becomes horrendous or ridiculous, it's unacceptable. And so he cuts down on corpses. Why should a man cut down on corpses? Let's say he's shooting a scene based on the battle of Crécy and there are eight hundred fifteen men dead in that one afternoon. As a director, he knows not to show a dolly of eight hundred fifteen people dead. They won't sit still for it. You see, you do think of things like that.

In the mind of the motion picture director, when he's already reached three hundred dead, something within him has to say, "Forget about the accuracy, the authenticity; it's too much." Something within him says, "It's too much." It's because *he* thinks it's too much, since that's what excited him originally, was to show over eight hundred corpses. It's because you say instinctively, "I think they'll walk out here." So the director does think of the reaction of the audience, as well as his own interpretation of limitation. There's no doubt about it.

FRITZ LANG: In my opinion, I like audiences. I was always opposed to the American line, "An audience has the mentality of a sixteen-year-old chambermaid." If this would be true, I would be ashamed to work for such an audience. I like audiences, but I don't think you should give an audience something fifty steps ahead of them. I asked myself — why is the first work of a writer, of a screen writer, or of a playwright almost always a success? Because he still belongs to an audience. The more he goes away from the audience, the more he loses contact, and what I tried to do my whole life long was I tried not to lose contact with the audience.

ROBERT ALTMAN: Film can't go beyond the audience, so a perfect film could be made now that probably would be considered really good in fifty years, yet it would go totally unnoticed today, I think. Any success, anybody whom you hear of like me who is considered successful, we're really mediocre or we would pass everybody up. We're really just in that average middle cut of the thing.

I find that what interests me the most is what I want to do and that's to get to the point where I think an audience can see a film, finish it, have an emotional response to it, and say nothing about it, not be able to articulate.

I really get to the point where I don't like questions where people say, "Well, I don't think that guy would have done that under this set of circumstances." I don't want to deal with that. I think maybe part of the reason is the length of time I spent in television dealing with hundreds and hundreds of stories. Boy, you just knew why everybody did everything. I don't think we have to do that. You can take books and write all the psychology you want and nobody's going to answer the question, "Why did this guy really do it?" So I feel that to try to make an explanation in one instance — to create drama in a film — I don't say it's wrong but it doesn't interest me.

LASLO BENEDEK: Never underestimate an audience. Keep in mind that the audience is ahead of you. They don't have to be told. They discovered it, they know it.

JEAN RENOIR: Of course, you have to think of the public, and, very often, to think of the public from the beginning leads you to using mechanical devices. I have a nephew who is a cameraman, and a few years ago he made an extraordinary picture about Picasso. He had a transparency. Picasso was on the other side of the screen, painting. You see the beginning of a painting, of course a painting of not too great importance, but you see the progression. He was repeating, during his exercise, he was repeating something which to me is a big secret we should all share and use if we can: "Fill it." Those were his words. No empty space. You have a frame. The frame is a scene in a movie, or is the frame of a painting. You must fill this frame. You must give the feeling that the frame is too narrow. And I agree with Picasso. Very much.

WILLIAM FRIEDKIN: Usually, I want to make films for people to see in theatres. Now, there are any number of reasons to make a film; only one of them is so that people can gather in a theatre and see it and be moved emotionally. That's why I make films. So if that's why you're going to

make a film, then you've got to think up something that you think will be
of interest to somebody else. Then you need as much as you have of
talent and imagination, you need an equal part of ambition, and that's
something I cannot direct into you, or even tell you about. It's just got to
be there. It's like Louis Armstrong's definition of jazz. If you've got to ask
what it is, then you will never find out. I don't know how you raise the
money. You go on out and hustle up somebody. You tell him whatever
he's got to hear to get his bread to make your movie, unless you can
finance your own.

SAMUEL FULLER: I never met Woody Van Dyke, who directed *The Thin
Man*. I don't think that he was really bothered by anything, except that if
during the course of filming he decided it would be funny to show Nick
and Nora Charles do something, let's say take a bath together, and Asta
jumps into the tub with them, just to show a very happy family, that
would have been censored. This is an example. There might have been
twenty things that he thought of while he was making that picture, funny
things. There is censorship without censorship. He knew there was no
sense shooting it even.

ROBERT ALDRICH: Do I direct my films for a particular audience? If a
picture costs five million dollars, that question has been answered for
you. If a picture costs that amount of money, there is no way, if you have
any feelings of responsibility towards the people who put up the money,
not to make that picture for as broad an audience as possible. You had
better try to get the right, the left, and the center or you are not going to
recoup. So, on an expensive picture you are destined to get a wide
spectrum of individuals.

   The thing that I think was Lukas Heller's major contribution to *The
Dirty Dozen* was that he kept the humor enjoyable. I don't think that the
humor was ever directed in such a way that the picture became one for
kids. I think that the humor sustained itself across the entire range of the
audience. This is partially reflected in the success of the picture. It
wasn't just the "army joke" kind of humor.

   What I am saying is: If you are making a five-million-dollar picture,
then it has to be such that enough people are going to get out there and
see it to justify the expense.

The Answer: Maybe

JOHN HUSTON: I can't do any more than make a picture that I believe in and hope that there are enough like me to want to see the picture too. I certainly don't have an audience in mind. I am my own audience in a sense. The very idea of trying to manipulate — even to entertain — an audience when you get down to the specifics is quite beyond me — or trying to imagine what an audience would like. By God, I don't know what my best friend or wife or son or daughter would like. I only know what I like, and I hope that there are enough like me to feel the way I do about it.

CARL REINER: Being in the comedy business, you only go by the seat of your pants. This is true with anything. The only time you get in trouble is when you try to guess what the audience is going to do. If you say, "I think they will like it," then forget it. You don't know whether or not they will like it. You will keep being surprised. You have to look at it and say, "That tickles me." If it tickles you and it is too short, then you put something else in. You can only go by the seat of your pants. Somebody may come to you and say, "Hey, that's not that funny." You will say, "Well it may not be funny to him, but I won't know until I see it in front of an audience." You can only go by your own experience.

ABRAHAM POLONSKY: *Romance of a Horsethief* got mostly good reviews. It isn't a picture that everyone said was terrible. That's not true at all. It's just that no one went to see it. Now I think even if they had put a lot of advertising into it, people wouldn't have gone to see it. There must have been something about it that didn't fit into what people wanted to see, because they only go to see what they want to see. I know that. What attracts them is because it shocks them, and they want to be shocked in that kind of way, or because it pleases them, and they want to be pleased in that kind of a way. When I made it, I thought it would be very pleasing to people, and that they would go and enjoy it in the way I enjoyed making it. I was very surprised that they didn't.

I would really like to be very popular in what I do, and I will try. But I can only be popular about what I am — not popular about what they are. Especially when I think they're wrong about one thing or another. There's no way I know how I can satisfy that. In fact, I don't know what it is I'm supposed to satisfy.

ROBERTO ROSSELLINI: To me, it is the analysis of the known that's impor-tant. As to the people, they are free to do what they want.

ROUBEN MAMOULIAN: As a rule, the motion picture executives always contrast art and entertainment. So you see an old wise executive or producer saying, "This script is great box office, commercial stuff. This is no good. It's artistic. It won't get anywhere." And of course they're invariably wrong. If they knew what was box office they'd be doing nothing but hits, which they're not doing. They're all losing money. So, anybody who says this is commercial and this is not is an utter fool. Because no one can prophesy that. There's only one way to go about it: you like it. You're no different from an audience. If you like it, there's no reason a lot of other human beings aren't going to like it.

But the main thing is that you be in films, in the theatre, which is a very peculiar art, the most social of the arts. The artist cannot stand alone. The audience is part of it. In other words, you write a play and you say this is a great play and you put it on and nobody comes to see it. They don't like it. Well, somehow I feel it isn't a great play. There are rare exceptions, but very rarely, not as frequently as people who complain about all these marvelous masterpieces that never get produced because they're too good. I wish I'd seen one. Now and then something will happen that catches up later. A great play or a good play or a great film must find an audience. If it doesn't find an audience, there's something wrong with it.

If So, What?

GEORGE SEATON: You've got to put your ground rules down quite early. You've got to let an audience know what kind of a picture this is supposed to be, because otherwise, you know, if they sit there and their attention wanders and they start to say "What is this? I don't quite figure this out," I think you've lost them.

WILLIAM FRIEDKIN: You're working for the Warner Brothers or the Metro brothers or the Paramount brothers or whomever, all these guys who are putting up a lot of bread here and hope to get their investment back, and you're working for them and you're working for an audience, which has got to stand in line with three dollars, three-fifty on weekends, whatever. I don't know anybody who ever said, "Jesus, go see this picture because it's got a wonderful philosophy discourse in it." Or, "Go see this picture because it's really interesting." People want to see movies because they want to be moved viscerally. I do. If it doesn't get to me viscerally, I'm out. Now I sit there like audience, not like "Oh, I'm a scholar of film and boom, and I understand really what he —" Screw that. I mean, I'm not interested in an interesting movie. I am interested in gut-level reaction.

What I'm interested in is an entire audience in the palm of my hand. Boom. That's why they came there. There's a very famous story that Herbie Gardner told me about Alfred Hitchcock. Herb was flattered to have been invited by Hitchcock to come out to Hollywood and write a film for Hitchcock. And he says, "Wow, great opportunity." He gets out here and he finds that Hitchcock has drawn, has had the whole picture drawn out. It's all in cartoons. It's all drawn out. All he wants Gardner to do is write the dialogue or, in effect, the captions for what the people say, and Gardner says, "Jesus, I can't do this. I'm a writer. I'm not a cartoonist. Or a caption writer." He said he couldn't do that but he was so intrigued and honored to be invited by Hitchcock that he said, "I'm not going to do it, but I'd love to see these boards and see what they are."

He's looking at these boards and he sees in one frame, a shot of a guy being pushed off the Verrazano-Narrows Bridge. The guy's going over the Verrazano-Narrows Bridge. He's being choked and he goes over the bridge and two frames later, that same guy is sitting in a café, at an outdoor café, on Fifth Avenue, and Gardner couldn't make sense out of this and he had a meeting with Hitchcock and he said, "That's the same guy right in these two scenes?"

"Yes."

He said, "How do we get from the guy being pushed off the Verrazano-Narrows Bridge to he's sitting in a café on Fifth Avenue?"

And Hitchcock said, "The crew goes there."

He said, "Wait a minute. How do we get the audience there is what I mean."

Hitchcock said, "Mr. Gardner, the audience will go wherever I take them and they'll be very glad to be there, I assure you." That, I must say, if I have a philosophy in a nutshell about what you're trying to do as a filmmaker, that would be it.

COSTA-GAVRAS: The audience is manipulated anyway, by bad politicians, by bad popcorn-sellers, so if we can manipulate them in this way and teach them to be conscious of situations, then we must manipulate them. I don't think that when the audience comes out of the theatre they will have changed completely, but if, at least, they ask themselves one question then I think that's enough.

HOWARD HAWKS: I imagine you could put it this way. If you go to a picture and you hear people laugh, you know you've made a pretty good picture. There isn't much way of people appreciating the dramatics of a picture unless an awful lot of the people go in. And if they do, you are very pleased, and, incidentally, you make money, too. I have no desire to make a picture that's just for a small group. I want to make it for everybody. As a matter of fact, I don't worry about what critics say. I worry about whether or not people like a picture. I'll tell you one thing, you can't make a picture without help.

GEORGE PAL: The audience is not frustrating. They are a challenge, actually. They are just a challenge. We just have to be a little bit better and fool them a little bit more. It's like a magician. He is delighted when he can fool the audience. And I think that is the thing that is wonderful in motion pictures. That is, if you can do the impossible, you can fool them and scare them.

ALFRED HITCHCOCK: I want to give them pleasure. Same pleasure they have when they wake up from a nightmare. The first thing, you see, you have to remember the audience goes in anticipating something. They've read something about it in the ads, so it's a question of how much of the light-weight story you put up in the picture in the beginning. I believe it was Fellini who said, "Hitchcock made them wait for the birds to come on. I wouldn't have the nerve to do that." But I think it is a matter of figuring it out and then gradually, one bird just hitting the girl. And the gradual slow buildup.

Let's take a very, very simple childish example. Four people are sitting around a table, talking about baseball, five minutes of it, very dull. Suddenly a bomb goes off. Blows the people to smithereens. What does the audience have? Ten seconds of shock. Now take the same scene. Tell the audience there is a bomb under the table and it will go off in five minutes. Well, the emotion of the audience is different because you give them the information that in five minutes' time, that bomb will go off. Now the conversation about baseball becomes very vital, because the audience is saying: "Don't be ridiculous. Stop talking about baseball. There's a bomb under there." You've got the audience working.

Now, there is one difference. I've been guilty in *Sabotage* of making this error, but I've never made it since: the bomb must never go off. If you do, you've worked that audience into a state. Then they will get angry if you haven't provided them with any relief. That is almost a must. So a foot touches the bomb and somebody looks down and says, "My God, a bomb." Then he throws it out of the window and it goes off. That is an example of information given to an audience. You can't expect them to go into any kind of emotion without the information.

In *Vertigo*, it was the end of the book before it's revealed that it is one and the same woman. I decided halfway through to blow the whole thing, tell the audience the truth and not wait until the end. People were horrified. "What are you doing? Giving it all away?" I replied that if I didn't I'm starting another story. Jimmy Stewart has lost one woman. She's dead, she's gone, he was crazy about her, and she even drove him into a nursing home. Now he sees a girl on the street, he sees some resemblance, and he gets hold of her, gets into her room. From that point on in the book, he endeavored to change the girl back into the image of the dead woman he wanted to renew.

The reason I gave the whole thing away was to give additional values. First, we know who she is; added value, what will Stewart do when he finds out? We know something that he doesn't know. Now there is an element of suspense. Second, why does the girl resist him? If you haven't told the audience who she really is, you won't understand her behavior. Why she doesn't want to wear a gray suit, why she doesn't want her hair made blond.

There's a limit. If you stretch it out too long, they will start to giggle. They'll relieve the tension themselves. They'll do it for you if you don't do it for them.

ROBERT ALDRICH: There is a real luck factor. You think that in a big picture you have to have some insurance of knowing that the film is filled with enough momentum, adventure, and excitement to entertain. The story should have substance to interest enough people so they will want to come to see it. A great many very talented people have misevaluated these judgments time and time again. I have made the same mistake as often, if not more often, than other people. You hope for the happy mix, and you don't always get it.

ABRAHAM POLONSKY: I'm going to tell the audience everything I know. What I'm thinking about, what I'm feeling, what I hope things will be, what I think human relations are, what I think history's about, what I think philosophy is about. Anything that comes to mind. I think that's my business. I hope I have something worth communicating. I assume I have because I'm involved in it myself. So I don't question it.

ROBERTO ROSSELLINI: We are suffering of a sickness, the propaganda sickness. We are always trying to persecute people. I don't want to persecute people at all. I want to offer material through which they can draw their own conclusions.

GEORGE SEATON: Shaw once said, "Individually, an audience can be comprised of complete idiots, but collectively, they're very seldom wrong." I think this is quite true, and I've seen it happen over and over again.

JOHN HUSTON: I very seldom feel involved with my characters, but rather detached and fascinated instead of as though I were on the hero's side. I'd rather have an audience identify with the picture itself than with a character in the picture, feeling a fascination for the whole material rather than being emotionally involved with the hero or heroine or something of the sort. Some very fine directors do just the opposite.

GEORGE SEATON: On *The Awful Truth*, directed by Leo McCarey, with Cary Grant and Irene Dunne, this was the first comedy about divorce, which was pretty daring in those days. They took it to some theatre and nobody laughed at it, and they thought they had a disaster. I saw the preview because in those days, everybody at the studio went out to see the preview. Leo said, "Let me think about this, just think about it." So, about three days later he said, "I know why they didn't laugh. They didn't know that it was supposed to be funny." So he went back and reshot, or shot a scene which he added, and it changed the whole complexion of the film — where she accuses her husband of infidelity; she wants a divorce.

Now, what follows was not in the original picture. She picks up the phone and calls her lawyer. The lawyer gets on the phone and he gets away from the dinner table where his wife is. Irene says she wants a divorce, and the lawyer says, "Oh, now think about this. Marriage is a wonderful institution." Meanwhile, his wife is saying, "Eat your dinner or it'll get cold." And he says "Shut your damn mouth." To Dunne, he says, "Marriage is just so wonderful — you're married to a wonderful fellow," and his wife speaks again and he says, "The food stinks, and I'm not going to eat it. . . ." Now the audience laughs at this, and once that was started, the picture played and was a very successful, and critically successful, picture.

WILLIAM FRIEDKIN: I have set the sound level in each of the theatres where *The Exorcist* is playing, in the twenty-four opening engagements. I've set the sound level and the light level on the screen because it really turns out to be, I find, the most engrossing if not interesting part of filmmaking, and that's seeing what happens to the picture after you make it. Because no matter what you hear, the projectionist has final cut always. You've got to set the sound and light levels and take a hardline policy and make sure you get what you want.

Now at the National Theatre, we're setting the faders on twelve on the projectors. The manager at the National told me that he had gotten some complaints, that it was a little too loud, could we set it at eleven? So I said, because I like this manager — he's a terrific guy, he really knows his audience — I said, "Could we sit in the last row on opening night and listen to it at eleven?" And it was okay. I could hear everything, so I've taken it down a little. But periodically, I call him up and say, "Maybe you ought to put it on twelve tonight."

You know, if it's raining or something, I figure maybe there won't be too many people in the house, kick it up a little. So he kicks it up and he calls me and says, "We got some complaints."

So I say, "Put it back to eleven." But you'd be amazed. The standard generally for how much light you're supposed to have on the screen is fifteen and a half lamberts. Most of the theatres in the country run anywhere from three to twelve. So that it's almost impossible to have your picture seen in some of the best theatres in the country the way you shot it.

What we did on *The French Connection* and *The Exorcist* is, we had some people go around. On *The Exorcist*, I've got the best people possible doing it. On *The French Connection*, we sort of improvised it and all took turns showing up in all the theatres where the picture shows before the picture opens and setting the light level and the sound level in the theatre. In the case of some theatres, we replaced the screen. In the Gopher Theatre in Minnesota, the guy who we sent out said, "This damn thing is playing across the street from a whorehouse and a porno movie parlor, number one. Number two, there's potholes in the screen."

So I called up the head of distribution and he said, "How's it coming?"

I said, "Well, we'll have twenty-three prints ready, not twenty-four."

I said, "The Gopher Theatre in Minnesota is not getting a print."

He said, "Why not?"

I said, "Potholes in the screen."

He said, "They put up a hundred thousand dollars for the picture."

I said, "Fine. They can put up five thousand dollars and replace the screen." So we replaced the screen for them and billed them for it.

Cinema I in New York, which is a very good theatre, very good house, the guy who checked the theatre out for me called me back and said, "The stuff's running out of focus. The lenses are shot." So we replaced the lenses on the projectors at Cinema I. We replaced them at our expense. At the end of the run, they can either buy the lenses or go back to the crap that they're using for their next picture. I want them to see the picture in focus, you know?

I shot it in focus. I rejected about one-third of the prints that we made at the M.G.M. lab, which is an excellent lab. They do a great job; out of about three hundred thousand feet that they ran off for us initially, we rejected a hundred thousand feet; that is, myself and the people working with me to check prints, for the most part my editorial crew. We check every print that goes out. We're continuing to check prints right along, because that's something you'll find that you have very, very little control over, even at the top level and unless you really care, really care, and give it time and raise hell, you ain't going to get what you shot.

JEAN RENOIR: How important is the story? Well, it is the eternal quarrel between abstract art and figurative art. Now, to choose the point and the temperament of the author. If the author feels that he can express, that he can, himself, without the help of a subject, build a bridge between his own inside and the spectator, good. Myself, my preoccupation is slightly different. You know what is my preoccupation in pictures? When the picture is finished? It is that I would like the picture to give the feeling to the audience that it is unfinished. Because I believe that the work of art where the spectator, where the reviewer, does not collaborate, is not a work of art. I like the people who look at the picture perhaps to build a different story on the side.

You know, that was the marvelous thing in the silent days. You had to build your own dialogue. You were collaborating. But you can't do it today. But without any collaboration of the public, to me, we have nothing.

Figurative art and abstract art . . . If you are confronted with an abstract picture, everything depends on the talents of the author. Now, if you work with figurative art, that means if you show objects you can recognize on the screen, like faces, the situation is the same. But you know what is good? It is when the public says, "Oh, these couples didn't get along. The wife was disgusting." And the other one says, "No, no," says the man, "the wife is not disgusting. I like her. She must have reasons. I'm sure she was very unhappy when she was a little girl." You start to build stories around the story. That's a good picture.

You know, if art doesn't take us as collaborators, art is dull. We must be in communion, the artist and the public. And we must arrive at such and such a point where the public is the maker and the artist becomes the spectator. But, you notice I'm just dreaming aloud now. There is no rule.

You talk about the sympathy of the public. Of course we all want it. You know, you are in a preview, and your picture is a little dull. The public doesn't follow very well. All of a sudden on the screen some actor cracks a joke which you wrote unwillingly. But you had to do something, you had to fill a space. You hear a little laughter among the audience. You feel like a million. You are delighted. You would like to see who laughed — to kiss him.

Yes, we depend on the public. What is wrong is to believe the public is forcibly a crowd of ten millions of people. For some artists the public is ten people, or just one. That doesn't matter. The size of the crowd isn't important. What is important is that you are in communication with somebody, with a spirit which is not your spirit, but which can influence you for a short time.

The Answer: No

STANLEY KRAMER: No. It has nothing to do with the audience. The audience is the recipient of it and participates in it. But that chemistry is something that on some nights, after the picture is either cut or, sometimes, it has to wait until it's scored, I'm sitting there looking at it and I am saying to myself, "That's it." Now that may be it for me. I don't ask that it be it for anybody else but myself. I really don't. Because whatever the total patronization of the term, I really only have to, as you only have to if you deal in film, satisfy yourself. Which, if you ever do, finishes you. But you try to satisfy yourself and you are the only important person. Nobody else is important. You see, if the audience often enough doesn't agree with you when you've satisfied yourself or thought you've come close, then you just have to steal quietly away in the night and never be heard from again. Occasionally you've got to satisfy the audience with your tastes but you have to satisfy yourself first or you won't be worth anything as an artist in my opinion. And that's a luxury.

JACQUES DEMY: I just think about what I want to convey. But, I don't think about the audience. If you start in that way, you are ready for the worst. If you are successful and you have been yourself, then you have been understood. You have established a contact between you and the crowd. Think about what it means to want to please the crowd. The audience is made of so many people that don't think in the same way that you do. If you try to play to them, then you are lost. I think it is practically impossible.

COSTA-GAVRAS: While making *Z*, I really didn't think of the audience — to keep the attention of the audience. What was really interesting was to cover the path that the investigator followed to discover one thing after the other. Of course, I was terrified that all the part of the investigator — taking about twenty minutes in the investigator's office — would suddenly become terribly boring. But, actually, we had to keep it because I thought it was terribly important. We had to follow the way he did it.

FEDERICO FELLINI: I have never seen my pictures again so I am not in the condition to have a point of view about them, to judge them from a critical point of view. I can say I like the last one just because it is the last one and mostly because the people represent the result of many experiences.

ROBERTO ROSSELLINI: I have never seen again a thing of mine, and I refuse to, because I don't want to remain bound with things I have made. You see, for example, if I see a film of mine — an old film of mine — and I like that film, then I'm finished, you know. I will remain to copy that film for all my life.

MESSAGES

ROBERTO ROSSELLINI: I made a film on Socrates, and Socrates said something absolutely wonderful. He said the world is full of opinions and completely empty of knowledge. That's the truth. We have opinions but we don't know. I think, I hope, we are like that because I am like that, so I refuse to have an opinion where I don't have knowledge.

RICHARD ATTENBOROUGH: I wish to persuade those to whom power is important and authority is important that a display of tolerance and compassion is a display of even greater strength. I wish to make pleas of all sorts of causes. Now the cinema permits me to do this. And if I am granted the opportunity of being able to direct a picture of which I have total control, then my opportunity, in a medium which is probably the most poignant, certainly the most widespread communication medium that we've yet devised, is heaven-sent, is a godsend. I mean, to have that chance, to be able to make those statements, is the sort of thing anybody prays for. Therefore, I would wish to direct.

BERNARDO BERTOLUCCI: To have political effects, we have to change the relationship between audiences and the movie. I used to think — in sixty-eight — I thought the camera was like a gun and then I discovered that it was an illusion. I don't think you can do any political film, any picture with the good, right, correct effects, in this system of distribution. We must find in every place a different way. For example, in Italy, we tried to invent a new alternative system of distribution.

I think it's important to change really the attitude of the people looking at pictures. For example, if you tried to do a correct movie, a political movie, you will make a movie against the convention. If the movie's against convention, nobody goes to see the movie, so if nobody sees the movie, there are no political effects. That's basic.

ROBERT ALTMAN: I don't have anything that I'm trying to say. I have no philosophy that I'm trying to put across. I'm not saying, "This is what I think things should be." All I'm trying to show you is the way I see and think things are. I don't have any preconceptions about that really.

BOB TAYLOR: I don't like message pictures. You know, don't smoke dope. If I'm going to smoke dope, then I'm going to smoke dope. It'll kill you, whatever. So I don't like message things. But on the other hand, I think there should be a current always within a picture that sets an element of reality. That's what I'm trying to do with these animated features now, to get down to what, at least, through my eyes, I see to be reality. Conversely, when you have the freedom, you have to be careful. There are things that people will accept, and there are things that people won't accept.

FRED ZINNEMANN: If you accept the fact that films are not primarily an intellectual medium, then if you want to get any intellectual concepts across, it behooves you to put a very, very nice sugar-coating around it. And the more entertaining you can make it, the better — obviously. Otherwise, what right do you have to expect the audience to sit and listen to you? Of course, primarily you are there to put a picture in the theatre that people will pay five cents to go see. And they should come out and say, "Yes, we were entertained — it's an entertaining picture." If it isn't, then you have failed because then it is some kind of pompous

monologue. Nobody gives a damn, you know. We are not educators —
we're entertainers.

BOB TAYLOR: You know what's crazy, too, about pictures like *Traffic*, or any
picture that has a lot of meaning, everybody will pick out their own
theme. It's crazy. And if you want to be cool, you could take credit for the
guy who said, "Well, I thought it meant this," and you say, "Yeah, that's
exactly what I hoped to put across." There used to be a thing when I was
doing TV productions, where they thought the more characters you put
into a thing, the better chance you had of success, because somewhere
along the line, somebody would attach themselves to one of the characters. This is the same thing you had in silent pictures — the more meat
you throw into the thing, the more somebody's going to pick up on some
point, whip in, and say, "That's what they meant." Whatever meaning it
has for you, then it's right. It's impossible to sit down and really figure
out, especially where there are double meanings.

VILGOT SJÖMAN: I feel very stuck somehow. The problem is that I have
several ideas that deal with the left, but every time you are about to start
working on that, then you run into the following thing happening: as soon
as you touch a left theme, then you are bound to expose both the negative
and positive sides about it.

FEDERICO FELLINI: I don't make pictures just to propose problems. I think
that there is a connection between one picture and another one. Sometimes it is very difficult to explain why you made one picture instead of
another one. Just to make some newspaperman happy, I can invent a lot
of reasons why I made one picture instead of another one. But if I have to
be really truthful, I can't say that a director can really know why he
makes his pictures.

CRITICS

BUDD BOETTICHER: A newspaper reporter not very long ago said, "You
know, I don't want you to take this personally, but I saw one of your
pictures . . ."

And I said, "Wait a minute, cut. Before you go ahead with what you
are going to say, let me tell you something. It is about the most personal
thing that you can say. Now what were you going to say?"

And then he said, "Well, actually it wasn't really very important." So don't feel embarrassed about getting very emotional about what you do.

PETER BOGDANOVICH: There's a whole school of critics who think they like movies, but they don't. They think it's all very nice to like films, but within limits. You can't have a passion for them, because after all, it's still a bit juvenile to sit in a movie theatre for six hours. However, people who read books for hours are eggheads, geniuses. It's really a kind of Victorian antimovie theory.

PAUL MAZURSKY: I don't take most of the critics seriously, the above-ground critics. The newspaper people are writing for deadlines and you can't take them too seriously. I don't see how you can see ten pictures a week and do a legitimate job day after day. A couple of people have said things which, upon reflection, I found interesting. You have to say, "Well, if they all think this way, maybe there is something in there." But there is so much disagreement between them that you can start going crazy.

HOWARD HAWKS: I try to make the picture as funny as I can. Every time I go to France, I meet with twenty-five or thirty directors, and they know so much about the dialogue of the pictures. They analyze and ask me questions. France, England, Italy, on the posters over there my name is three times as big as Wayne's. I make sure those posters are where everybody can look at them. They don't even put the name of a lot of the actors up, they just put the name of the directors. They are very interested in how you make pictures. They go into it and analyze it and read things into it that I had no idea of when making the movie.

LEO MCCAREY: Somebody interviews you and says, "How did you come about getting such and such an idea? What happened to you in real life?" or something. And you start theorizing about why you came about getting the inspiration, and it probably had nothing to do with it.

ABRAHAM POLONSKY: You have to be able to analyze all those things out, as a good critic. And give everybody all the compliments they want, but criticize the film. That's the thing you're really paying attention to. Now, if you think that's a fiction, you say, "There're words and there're images, which is camera. Let's face it, without the camera, there're no images." You know what that's like saying? "Without the elements, there's no flesh." But nevertheless, there's a difference between carbon dioxide and organic tissue. And it's not just mere complexity, because something new has happened. Life. And if they can't tell that, what the hell are they talking about? I don't know what they're talking about. Anyhow, I love them all. Don't you? As long as they leave me alone.

ROBERT ALTMAN: The only thing that I learn from reviews, I think, is that people do look at the film from a different standpoint than I do.

THE CHANGING AUDIENCE

ABRAHAM POLONSKY: They've changed, all right. But they haven't changed as much as they think they've changed. What happens is that as cultural history changes — and it changes very rapidly in our society — the expectations for themselves change. So that things that would once seem viable no longer seem viable. That's to say that they have the conventions. The convention of resistance takes the place of the convention of acceptance. And the convention of work of one kind takes the place of the convention of pratfalls, depending on the kind of audience it is. They feel they're more sophisticated because everybody has music playing in their house all the time. Or they feel they're more sophisticated because they've gone to college. Right? And there've been a lot of things that they haven't paid any attention to, but they heard about it. So all this is different all the time. But what you do is destroy all that when you subject them to a work of art, a certain work of art. You destroy everything they've known. Now, if you destroy it too much, sometimes it's totally unacceptable to them because they have no convention with which to meet it, and they're very upset. But that's just too bad for them.

But sometimes you're lucky, and you accidentally do what they can accept, and then you're really lucky and the whole thing comes together. And you change, they change, and the work works. And some people, some artists, are very talented and gifted and they're always right, but most of them are wrong most of the time.

ED EMSHWILLER: The type of information that people accept visually today is very different from what they accepted ten years ago, simply through television ads. It's a different world, literally a different world. So now there are more people interested in my vision. I'm not unique. I'm part of the human community. There are others who have the same feelings that I have, the same tensions, interests. What I'm doing is saying, "For those of you who respond, look, this is what I feel and see."

ROBERT ALTMAN: I am literally trying to create an audience, to develop an audience and train an audience, educate an audience. The audience is growing out of the youth. The audience is growing and it grows faster than any of us can imagine. If I said, "I'm going to go back and try and get this other audience," I think I'd lose everything. I just don't know how to do it. And I think it's all going to be replaced.

FILM EDUCATION

You can't teach film, and I don't give a goddamn who says it, *you can't teach film*. You can experience it, but you can't teach it. I'm being paid to teach it, but I can't. I can provide an arena for people to have an experience.

— Nicholas Ray

JAN KADAR: I don't know what you will do with your education. When I see the opportunity arise where people can finally speak about movies and can exchange ideas, I think it is quite a step forward. I believe in the people who are trying to get into the industry. Sometimes you have to learn all of these things. I don't believe that everybody who leaves a film school will be a genius. But at least in this large field of moviemaking, television, documentaries, video tapes, and anything else, there are many things to do and especially so if you have a certain amount of education. I am a self-made man, but I don't believe in that anymore. That day is gone. I think if I started again, I would go into a school.

SERGEI BONDARCHUK: I feel that the role of any institution, any educational institution, is to somehow give a beginning for the persons acquiring an overall outlook on life, sort of a philosophy of life. No great teacher or professor, no matter what type of genius he has, can make a student acquire this interest for life, for learning, that he needs so much. And I think the sign of sort of an ideal pedagogue would be one that would help a person acquire and preserve a certain amount of individuality . . . this "born" individuality.

JAN KADAR: I think that the only thing that a school can teach — except the technique, which everybody can pick up very easily — is the way to think. That is the purpose of education.

ROMAN POLANSKI: My film school experience was very positive. I wasn't aware of it when I was in film school because I was bitching like everybody else about the waste of time. It was long — five years. But a few years later I realized how much I had gained through that experience. It was a very good school. A lot was happening, not only in the courses, which were of benefit to me, but in the discussions we had and in fights between the students.

They had big wooden stairs. It belonged to some king, a king of cotton or someone like that, or used to belong, I should say, and we used to sit on the stairs and drink beer and talk a lot and fight a lot and see a lot of films. The projection was continuous from probably eight in the morning until eight in the evening. The school was very closely associated with the National Film Archives, and at that time we could have anything we wanted. All we had to do was to fill out a little form to get a film and just say some reason for which we needed it, for our study, whatever it was, and we would have it.

Also, we saw a lot of new films at the school, and there were editing rooms in which we could work, and if we wanted to do something, we could do it. There they provided you with everything; we had a studio, we could make films, more than was actually required by the study. Strangely enough, some of the people wouldn't do films, although they were supposed to. That shows you that often people will say they want to make films but they are not actually ready for it.

We had some interesting courses in that school. We had a tremendous amount of photography during the first two years, still photography. Everyone was given a still camera for three years, and we would have to go through photography from the beginning. The first lesson was a piece of photographic paper and a leaf. We would put a leaf on it and shine a light on it and then we would develop it, and then we would go through all stages of photography, sometimes to very good results. I remember there were some great photographers, guys who had never had a camera in their hands before, and who developed this ability. It's important because it's pictures — maybe not moving pictures but nevertheless pictures.

TAMÁS RÉNYI: Let me tell you how a film director in Hungary gets started. We have a National Film School, the State Film School, which gives a diploma but not the possibility. The one who's just graduated writes a script and gives it in to either of the studios. He has already proven his abilities by making shorts before. But then who will make feature films among these graduates? Well, only God knows. On the other hand, we have a very good possibility and this is very important: the so-called Béla

Balázs Studio, which specifically gives opportunity for the graduates of the State Film School to make shorts.

SERGEI BONDARCHUK: In the Soviet Union, students are admitted that have completed ten years of education. This is comparable, in other words, to completing high school. There's a great deal of competition for entrance into the Institute. An example of this, well, it is approximately one hundred people who apply for one place, for one position. Therefore, the only way that one can be admitted is by way of a fairly strict entrance examination. And also, by certain contacts. But personally, I just don't understand how anyone can determine how a young man can have what it takes to become a director. I think I could determine whether a person has acting ability, but even then many people make mistakes.

There is something along the lines of an interview and certain courses work, but we did have definitely cases of students who on the fourth year were expelled from school because they did not have the abilities, professional abilities. What we have is something that is called an Art Room, a sort of laboratory. In this particular room both actors and future directors study.

I think the question is really, in effect, do you always have to go through the school to become a director? Or can you become a director without going through that school? Well, in theory, this could be, but it almost never occurs. Well, I know that right now there's a whole army of movie-lovers, and a few of them have become directors, but they have no specialized training. For example, I studied as an actor at the school in the branch of acting, and then I became a director. In our five-year Institute, those who are in the branch of directors usually start making a movie on the third year, or even the second year they start working out on it. And then as a final project, sort of like a dissertation, they do a final version.

ROBERTO ROSSELLINI: We [at the Italian film school, Centro Sperimentale] have to select the new students, and because we have a budget, we are quite fair but quite limited, too. We know that we are allowed only to get twenty-nine students to do good things, to give them a lot of film, to use a lot of film. Over three hundred people apply.

It's very hard. We must admit one thing. First of all, we don't need artists. Artists can do well by themselves. First choice is to put aside all the artists. So that was very easy. We remained with fifty-two and we made the choice of the twenty-nine, which was quite a cruel action to do.

I called the fifty-two and we discussed altogether, and we agreed in the choice of the twenty-nine with them, too.

The administration administers only the money, and the decisions are made together. At the school, the only thing is that we have to give them a chance to test themselves. There are five directors, so they will end it with five full-length films.

One thing is very clear, nobody in the school must read the scripts, nobody is allowed to read the scripts of the students, including the faculty. They want to make a film; that's the whole thing. They have cameras, they have film and have so much money, and it's up to them to do the thing. It's our goal to make people have experience. That's an experience. If a man realized that his thoughts until that day were stupid, it's a good achievement. You know, I don't want to teach, I don't want to educate. I want to offer possibilities for each one to be himself.

What is wrong with failures? There are millions of failures in the world. A failure is not a damage for anybody.

PETER BOGDANOVICH: A director now can "come up" without a background in any of the arts but film. I don't know that that's good. I didn't come from drama school, but from an artistic heritage. Up until now, no one has ever wanted to "be a director" while growing up. Now they do — from the age of eight.

That's good, and also dangerous. The thing that made the first generation of moviemakers so rich is the fact that they didn't want to make pictures when they started. Thus, there was a tension, always, between what they really wanted to do and what they found themselves doing. Griffith wanted to be a playwright. He wasn't a very good one, but he was a great director. There was a certain amount of disrespect for the medium which enabled him to do those things which no one else had ever done before. Ford would have been much happier as a naval hero. I don't think he took that much pride in movies. But he was a poet — so what can you do?

Dwan began as an electrical engineer, Walsh as a cowboy and sailor. McCarey began as a lawyer. Suddenly, they all were directing movies. There was an exuberance — what a crazy thing to be doing. After them, we had people directing movies who had been writers: Fuller, Wilder, and so on. They ended up directing because it was the only way to protect what they had written. Now who do you have? People from film schools who "want to be directors." I wrote about films because I couldn't get work as an actor or director.

MICHAEL WINNER: Cambridge University had no film course of any kind and still doesn't. Therefore, since there was nothing I could do that was like filming, I just chose by accident economics, because it was the only thing I hadn't done at school and I hadn't liked any subject I had studied at school. So I thought, "At least it's something new." I then found that a bit heavy going and switched to law because I thought it would be easier, and it was. I think that in a strange way those two combinations are very useful in film. Law teaches you a great clarity of thought. It teaches you a great practical knowledge. It teaches you a useful, clear thought process. And economics teaches you the use and distribution of money and resources. Film is enormously a matter of economics as well as art. So I think they both proved very helpful. I was, at the same time, the editor and critic of the University paper. So my dealing in film was as a voyeur and a bitchy critic.

PERRY MILLER ADATO: You learn a lot from seeing other people's films. I found that after seeing other people's films for twelve years, I learned how to make films.

FRITZ LANG: I learned only from bad films. When a young actor or a writer came to me and asked me, "What can I do to learn to make films?" I was always in a mess because I didn't know what to tell them. And I asked myself how I learned something. Now when I looked at the good films, I always was a very good audience. I was never interested in who the actor was, who the director was, or where the cameraman was. I lived with the film. I enjoyed it. It was an adventure. My interest was so full in the film that when I saw a lousy film which I didn't like, there was something which made me say, "Wait a moment, this is not good, this I would have done differently." In my opinion, this is the only way I personally learned. I don't know if another person could do the same thing.

ALFRED HITCHCOCK: I don't understand why we have to experiment with film. I think everything should be done on paper. A musician has to do it, a composer. He puts a lot of dots down and beautiful music comes out. And I think that students should be taught to visualize. That's the one thing missing in all this. The one thing that the student has got to do is to learn that there is a rectangle up there — a white rectangle in a theatre — and it has to be filled.

I personally never look through the camera. What for? To find out whether the cameraman is lying? I only consider that screen up there, and the whole film to me should be on paper from beginning to end — shot by shot, cut by cut — and each cut should mean something. It's not a matter of just letting the student do it one way or do it the other. There's only one thing. If you're composing music, you don't have alternatives, you have one way to do it. And that's what should be taught these young men. After all, you don't have a litterateur write three or four sentences and choose which one is the best later on. He writes the one sentence in his novel or whatever it may be; he assembles his words.

What is film? The assembly of pieces of film to create an idea, each cut joined one to the other goes by on the screen and has an emotional impact upon an audience. Now, I remember working at UFA in 1924. There was a writer called — actually I think he was one of the best film writers there was — Carl Mayer. And I worked at the same studio — I was a writer then, and an art director, I used to do both — and they were making *The Last Laugh* with Emil Jannings. And this film is to me the prime example of expressing a story idea even without titles. If you look at *The Last Laugh* today, you'll find the whole story is told visually from beginning to end. The only thing wrong with the silent film is that people open their mouths and no sound comes out. But, nevertheless, it's the visual that has to be taught — the fundamentals of the medium. It is the only new art of the twentieth century, but it is essentially a visual art. And that's the thing that has to be taught. Not by guessing and wondering how it will come out. They ought to be taught to know whatever they put down on paper will come out in a certain way.

They all want to start out being directors, and it has nothing to do with the proper training. It's a ridiculous concept. Now, going out with an eight-millimeter reminds me of when I studied art. I was sent to railroad stations and sketched people in various attitudes. But that was only a tiny fragment of the course — painting, composition, modeling, and all kinds of other courses to take, illustration, and so forth. So going with the eight-millimeter is only a tiny part. I mean what about them learning something about art direction, or sets? You'll find that these young men — these directors — not knowing their screen, will photograph a scene as they see it on the set, and they don't attempt to create for the camera. And that's one of the most vital things in the technique of motion picture — creating images. For example, we know that if you're in an office scene, they look at the desk, and the secretary is standing there, and so they set the camera up — the boss is seated in his chair. Well, they can't get it in until they've pulled the camera a long way back, and then they're too far away. What they don't learn is to lift that desk up eight inches, put the chair up, and bring the head of the boss in line with that of the secretary. Now this is creating for the camera. But they have to learn all those things, and it all comes back to that rectangle on the screen. How do you fill it? I mean look at the way close-ups are used, without any concept of orchestration. Now all cutting and all image size is orchestration. Don't go putting a close-up where you don't need it, because later on you will need it.

GEORGE STEVENS: A camera is a terrible defacement to people who want to express themselves, because they think it's automatic. And it's one of the most futile weapons the cinema has. I think of it as a fishnet. You know, you throw it out for great things and you come up with an anchovy, without putting this device to work and making it work, for what particular value it will have on that lonesome, solitary white sheet, with hopefully a large group of people waiting for something to happen. I'm terribly aware of this in the young people that are most interested in expressing themselves in film today. I'm quite interested in this and I'm tremendously hopeful.

But I see this Lorelei of the Arriflex, you know, destroying people's ability to focus in on the real nature of what they have to do. I'm terribly conscious of the Eyemo in an individual's hand. Somehow or other, he misdirects the current of effect that's coming this way onto the film. He feels the exuberance of his personal expression as he holds that and presses the button. He's expressing himself. It's his contact with something he wants to say — which is a total illusion. It has nothing to do with the sordid nature of a laborious business, of filming it and putting it together and then having some sort of magic of personality take place — of having seen, having put together elements of film in separate pieces, and then having it come off and say something that's subtle, hopefully, beyond the illustration that's apparent, that expresses the author, with the camera.

Biographies

These biographical sketches are in no way intended to offer a complete picture of any director's career. Rather, they serve merely to identify each person by suggesting the context from which he or she emerged. Unfortunately, in the film literature, such information as birth dates often varies from source to source. Therefore, even that statistic should not be assumed to be absolutely correct here.

In addition to the directors whose words appear in this book, several directors were referred to often in the course of discussion. For the sake of consistency, brief sketches are offered of these figures also.

Some of the reference sources used to compile this list were *Dictionary of Film Makers,* ed. Georges Sadoul (Berkeley, 1972), *International Motion Picture Al-*

manac, ed. Richard Gertner (New York, 1975), *The American Cinema,* by Andrew Sarris (New York, 1968), *The Filmgoer's Companion,* ed. Leslie Halliwell (New York, 1967), and *The Film Reader,* No. 1 (Evanston, 1975). Other excellent sources are the libraries at The American Film Institute and The Academy for Motion Picture Arts and Sciences.

Adato, Perry Miller. Spent ten years as a film consultant to CBS-TV. Produced and directed documentaries for NET on Georges Braque, Dylan Thomas, and Gertrude Stein. Emmy Award winner.

Aldrich, Robert. Born Cranston, Rhode Island, August 9, 1918. Directed his first feature in 1953 after several years as a production clerk and assistant director. Films include *Kiss Me Deadly, The Big Knife, Whatever Happened to Baby Jane?* and *Hustle.*

Altman, Robert. Born Kansas City, Missouri, February 20, 1925. Studied engineering at University of Missouri. Made industrial films in Kansas City. Co-produced and co-directed *The James Dean Story* (1957). Directed television for *The Alfred Hitchcock Hour, Bonanza,* and others. Films include *M*A*S*H, McCabe and Mrs. Miller, California Split, Nashville,* and *Buffalo Bill and the Indians.*

Ashby, Hal. Born Ogden, Utah, 1936. Attended Utah State University. Began as a film editor; worked with Norman Jewison on several pictures, including *In the Heat of the Night, The Thomas Crown Affair.* Films directed include *The Last Detail, Shampoo,* and *Bound for Glory.*

Attenborough, Richard. Born Cambridge, England, August 29, 1923. Studied at Royal Academy of Dramatic Art. Stage and film actor. Films directed include *Young Winston.*

Benedek, Laslo. Born Budapest, Hungary, March 5, 1907. Attended University of Vienna. Worked as writer, cinematographer, and editor. Films include *Death of a Salesman, The Wild One, The Night Visitor.*

Berman, Pandro S. Born Pittsburgh, Pennsylvania, March 28, 1905. Worked as assistant director and film editor. Pictures produced include *Of Human Bondage, Gunga Din, National Velvet, Madame Bovary, Butterfield 8.*

Bertolucci, Bernardo. Born Parma, Italy, March 16, 1940. Assistant to Pasolini. Directed *Before the Revolution, Partner, The Conformist, Last Tango in Paris, 1900.*

Boetticher, Budd. Born Chicago, Illinois, July 29, 1918. Attended Ohio State University. Films directed include *The Bullfighter and the Lady, Seven Men from*

Now, The Tall T, Ride Lonesome, The Rise and Fall of Legs Diamond, Comanche Station, Arruza.

Bogdanovich, Peter. Born Kingston, New York, July 30, 1939. Directed and acted on stage. Films directed include *Targets; The Last Picture Show; What's Up, Doc? Paper Moon;* and *Nickelodeon.* Also has written books and monographs on directors, including John Ford, Allan Dwan, Fritz Lang, Orson Welles, Howard Hawks, and Alfred Hitchcock.

Bondarchuk, Sergei. Born Ukraine, USSR, 1920. Actor in many Russian films, including *Othello.* Films directed include *War and Peace* and *Waterloo.*

Borzage, Frank. Born Salt Lake City, Utah, April 23, 1893. Died Hollywood, 1961. Worked as a coal miner. Became an actor and directed several westerns and silent films, including *Seventh Heaven* and *Street Angel.* Also directed numerous sound films, including *Three Comrades, A Man's Castle, I've Always Loved You,* and *Moonrise.*

Brakhage, Stan. Born Kansas City, Missouri, 1933. One of the most prolific and influential "experimental" filmmakers. Authored several books on film, including *The Brakhage Lectures, A Motion Picture Giving and Taking Book.* Films include *The Art of Vision; Scenes from Under Childhood; Lovemaking; The Horseman, the Woman, and the Moth; The Text of Light.*

Bridges, James. Born Paris, Arkansas. Actor and writer in theatre and television, including *The Alfred Hitchcock Hour.* Directed *The Baby Maker* and *The Paper Chase.*

Capra, Frank. Born Palermo, Italy, May 19, 1897. Attended California Institute of Technology. Films include *It Happened One Night, Mr. Deeds Goes to Town, Mr. Smith Goes to Washington, Lost Horizon, It's a Wonderful Life.* Autobiography: *Frank Capra — The Name above the Title.*

Cassavetes, John. Born New York, New York, 1929. Attended Colgate College. Stage, film, and television actor. Films directed include *Shadows, Faces, Husbands, Minnie and Moskowitz, A Woman under the Influence.*

Chaplin, Charles. Born London, England, April 16, 1889. Stage comedian with parents. Began film career acting in Keystone Comedies. Co-formed United Artists. Features written, directed, and starred in include *City Lights, Modern Times, The Great Dictator, Monsieur Verdoux.* Honorary Academy Award in 1971.

Clarke, Shirley. Born New York, 1925. "Experimental" and independent filmmaker. Features include *The Connection, The Cool World, Portrait of Jason.*

Cooper, Merian C. Born Jacksonville, Florida, October 24, 1893. Died April 21, 1973. Worked as co-director and producer on *King Kong* and numerous documentaries. Produced several of John Ford's films. Special Academy Award in 1952.

Corman, Roger. Born Detroit, Michigan, April 5, 1926. Attended Stanford and Oxford University. Worked as a story analyst and literary agent. Has produced over 200 films and directed over 60 of them, including *The Pit and the Pendulum*, *Tomb of Ligeia*, *The Wild Angels*, *The Trip*, *Bloody Mama*.

Costra-Gavras, [Constantin]. Born Athens, Greece, 1933. Attended the University of the Sorbonne. Worked as assistant director in France. Directed and wrote *The Sleeping Car Murders*, *Z*, *State of Siege*, *Special Section*.

Cukor, George. Born New York, New York, July 7, 1899. Actor and producer on Broadway. Films directed include *Dinner at Eight*, *Little Women*, *David Copperfield*, *Holiday*, *Pat and Mike*, *A Star Is Born*, *My Fair Lady*, *Travels with My Aunt*, *Bluebird*.

Demy, Jacques. Born France, June 5, 1931. Worked as an assistant and made short films before directing features such as *Bay of Angels*, *Lola*, *Umbrellas of Cherbourg*, *Model Shop*, *Donkey Skin*.

De Palma, Brian. Born Philadelphia, 1940. Attended Columbia University. Made short films and documentaries before directing features such as *Greetings!* *Hi, Mom!* *Sisters*, *Phantom of the Paradise*, *Obsession*.

Dwan, Allan. Born Toronto, Canada, April 3, 1885. Trained as an engineer at Notre Dame University. First worked in the business end of film, but became the most productive of all filmmakers. Films directed include *The Iron Mask*, *The Three Musketeers*, *The Sands of Iwo Jima*, *Silver Lode*, *Slightly Scarlet*, and hundreds of others.

Emshwiller, Ed. Born Lansing, Michigan, 1925. Attended University of Michigan. Studied painting and worked as an illustrator. Became a leading independent filmmaker, whose works often included abstract dream and dance sequences. Films include *Thanatopsis*, *Totem*, *Relativity*.

Fellini, Federico. Born Rimini, Italy, January 20, 1920. Worked as a cartoonist. Co-wrote several films with Rossellini and others. Films directed include *La Strada*, *La Dolce Vita*, *8½*, *Juliet of the Spirits*, *Fellini Satyricon*, *Clowns*, *Rome*, *Amarcord*, *Casanova*.

Ford, John. Born Cape Elizabeth, Maine, February 1, 1895. Died August 31,

1973. Directed over 125 films, including *How Green Was My Valley, The Quiet Man, The Man Who Shot Liberty Valance, The Searchers, Seven Women*. Won four Academy Awards and the first American Film Institute Life Achievement Award.

Forman, Milos. Born Czechoslovakia, February 18, 1932. Studied drama in Prague. Worked as script writer and assistant. Films directed include *Loves of a Blonde, Fireman's Ball, Taking Off, One Flew over the Cuckoo's Nest*.

Friedkin, William. Born Chicago, Illinois, 1939. Worked in television assisting and directing documentaries and daytime shows. Came to Hollywood for David Wolper. Features include *The Boys in the Band, The French Connection, The Exorcist*.

Fuller, Samuel. Born Worcester, Massachusetts, August 12, 1912. Worked as a newspaper reporter. Started writing and directing films after World War II service in the 1st Infantry Division. Features include *The Steel Helmet, Pickup on South Street, House of Bamboo, Underworld U.S.A., Shock Corridor, Dead Pigeon on Beethoven Street*.

Griffith, D. W. Born La Grange, Kentucky, January 23, 1875. Died July 23, 1948. Worked first as an actor and playwright. Made hundreds of short films before directing features such as *The Birth of a Nation, Intolerance, Broken Blossoms, Orphans of the Storm, Way Down East, Abraham Lincoln,* and *The Struggle*.

Harrington, Curtis. Born Los Angeles, California, September 17, 1928. Attended University of Southern California. Made shorts, documentaries, and "experimental" films. Associate producer and writer for several features before directing such films as *Games,* and *What's the Matter with Helen?*

Hawks, Howard. Born Goshen, Indiana, May 30, 1896. Attended Cornell University. Prop boy, editor, and writer after being a car racing driver and fighter pilot. Directed classic films in all genres, including *Bringing Up Baby, Air Force, Scarface, The Big Sleep, Red River, Gentlemen Prefer Blondes*.

Hitchcock, Alfred. Born London, England, August 13, 1899. First was a technician, art director, and writer. Started directing in England, then came to America where his films included *Rebecca, Notorious, Shadow of a Doubt, Strangers on a Train, Vertigo, Under Capricorn, Frenzy, Family Plot*.

Huston, John. Born Nevada, Missouri, August 5, 1906. Son of actor Walter Huston, he was an actor and writer before directing *The Maltese Falcon*. Other films include *The Treasure of the Sierra Madre, The African Queen, Moulin Rouge, The Misfits, Night of the Iguana, The Man Who Would Be King*.

Hyams, Peter. Born New York, New York, July 26, 1943. Attended Hunter College, Syracuse University. Worked for CBS News and made documentaries before directing television and the features *Busting* and *Peeper*.

Kadar, Jan. Born Budapest, Hungary, April 1, 1918. Studied at the Bratislava Film School. Imprisoned in a Nazi war camp; finally was able to make documentaries for Czechoslovakia. Films include *Shop on Main Street* and *Lies My Father Told Me*.

Keaton, Buster. Born Pickway, Kansas, October 4, 1895. Died February 1, 1966. Trained in vaudeville. Acted in two-reelers with Fatty Arbuckle. Later wrote, directed, and starred in his own films, including *Sherlock Junior, The Navigator, The General,* and *Steamboat Bill, Junior*. Special Academy Award in 1959.

Kershner, Irvin. Born Philadelphia, Pennsylvania, April 29, 1923. Attended Temple University, University of Southern California. Cameraman and writer. Made documentary films before directing such pictures as *The Hoodlum Priest, Loving, A Fine Madness, Return of a Man Called Horse*.

Kramer, Stanley. Born New York, New York, September 29, 1913. Attended New York University. Worked as an editor, writer, and producer; directed such films as *The Defiant Ones, Judgment at Nuremberg, Inherit the Wind, Ship of Fools, Guess Who's Coming to Dinner?*

Krantz, Steve. Born New York, New York, May 20, 1923. Attended Columbia University. Directed television before working on such animated features as *Fritz the Cat* and *Heavy Traffic*.

Kubrick, Stanley. Born New York, New York, July 26, 1928. Photographer and magazine writer. Made documentary films before directing features such as *The Killing, Paths of Glory, Lolita, Dr. Strangelove,* and *Barry Lyndon*.

Kulik, Buzz. Born New York, New York, 1923. Directed television episodes and features such as *Brian's Song* as well as feature films such as *Sergeant Ryker* and *Shamus*.

Lang, Fritz. Born Vienna, Austro-Hungary, December 5, 1890. Studied architecture and painting. Wrote several films before directing the silent *Die Nibelungen, Metropolis,* and others. Then made *M* and *Das Testament des Dr. Mabuse* before fleeing Germany. Directed over twenty films in Hollywood, including *You Only Live Once, Rancho Notorious,* and *The Big Heat*. Appeared as an actor, playing himself, in Jean-Luc Godard's *Contempt*.

Leacock, Richard. Born London, England, 1921. Worked as a documentary cameraman (including on Robert Flaherty's *Louisiana Story*) and directed as well as photographed such "documentary" features as *Primary, Football, The New Frontier*, and *Chiefs*.

Loden, Barbara. Born Marion, North Carolina. Actress and writer. Appeared on stage in *After the Fall*. Directed and starred in the film *Wanda*.

Malle, Louis. Born Thuméries, France, October 30, 1932. French filmmaker somewhat identified with the *nouvelle vague*. Directed *Les Amants, Zazie dans le Métro, India, Le Souffle au Coeur*, and *Lacombe, Lucien*.

Mamoulian, Rouben. Born Tiflis, Russia, October 8, 1897. Attended Lycée Montaigne, Paris, and Moscow University. Directed opera and stage plays before such films as *Applause, City Streets, Dr. Jekyll and Mr. Hyde, Queen Christina, Golden Boy, Blood and Sand*.

Mazursky, Paul. Born Brooklyn, New York, April 25, 1930. Nightclub comic and actor before writing and directing such movies as *Bob and Carol and Ted and Alice, Harry and Tonto*, and *Next Stop, Greenwich Village*.

McCarey, Leo. Born Los Angeles, California, October 3, 1898. Died July, 1969. Assistant director, writer, and director for many Laurel and Hardy shorts before directing such features as *Duck Soup, The Awful Truth, Ruggles of Red Gap, Going My Way, The Bells of St. Mary*.

Minnelli, Vincente. Born Chicago, Illinois, February 28, 1913. Theatre set and costume designer before directing such films as *Meet Me in St. Louis, An American in Paris, The Bad and the Beautiful, Some Came Running, Gigi*, and *A Matter of Time*.

Morrissey, Paul. Born New York, New York, 1938. Attended Fordham University. Worked in independent film production prior to joining Andy Warhol's group, where he directed *Flesh, Trash, Heat, Andy Warhol's Frankenstein*, and *Andy Warhol's Dracula*.

Neame, Ronald. Born London, England, 1911. Worked as cameraman and producer before directing such films as *The Horse's Mouth, Tunes of Glory, The Prime of Miss Jean Brodie, The Poseidon Adventure*.

Nelson, Ralph. Born New York, New York, August 12, 1916. Actor and writer for televison before directing such films as *Requiem for a Heavyweight, Lilies of the Field, Charly*, and *The Wilby Conspiracy*.

Nicholson, Jack. Born Neptune, New Jersey, 1937. Writer (*Ride the Whirlwind*) and actor (*Easy Rider, Five Easy Pieces, The Last Detail, Chinatown, One Flew over the Cuckoo's Nest*), as well as director (*Drive, He Said*).

Pal, George. Born Cegléd, Hungary, February 1, 1900. Puppeteer and animator. Won six Academy Awards for special effects. Directed such films as *Tom Thumb, The Time Machine*, and *The Wonderful World of the Brothers Grimm*.

Penn, Arthur. Born Philadelphia, Pennsylvania, September 27, 1922. Attended Black Mountain College. Television and stage director before making such films as *The Left-Handed Gun, The Chase, Bonnie and Clyde, Little Big Man, Night Moves*, and *The Missouri Breaks*.

Polanski, Roman. Born Paris, France, September 18, 1933. Studied at Lodz Film School (Poland). Wrote and directed several shorts before directing such features as *Knife in the Water, Repulsion, Cul-de-Sac, Rosemary's Baby, Chinatown*, and *The Tenant*.

Polonsky, Abraham. Born New York, New York, December 5, 1910. Attended City College of New York, Columbia Law School. Teacher and writer (novels, stories, reviews) before writing scripts (*Body and Soul*). Wrote and directed *Force of Evil, Tell Them Willie Boy Is Here*, and directed *Romance of a Horsethief*.

Ray, Nicholas. Born LaCrosse, Wisconsin, August 7, 1911. Studied architecture at University of Chicago. Wrote before directing such films as *They Live by Night, In a Lonely Place, Johnny Guitar, Rebel without a Cause*.

Reiner, Carl. Born New York, New York, March 20, 1923. Actor and writer (*Your Show of Shows, The Dick Van Dyke Show*) before directing such films as *The Comic* and *Where's Poppa?*

Renoir, Jean. Born Paris, France, September 15, 1894. Son of painter Auguste Renoir, made ceramics before writing. Directed nearly 40 films, including *La Grande Illusion, La Règle du Jeu, The River, The Golden Coach, Le Déjeuner sur l'Herbe, The Elusive Corporal*.

Rényi, Tamás. Born Hungary, 1929. Attended University of Budapest. Worked at textile mill and made films for Hungarian army. Assistant to Fábri before directing such films as *Tales of a Long Journey, Deadlock*, and *The Valley*.

Ritt, Martin. Born New York, New York, March 2, 1920. Attended Elon College. Stage actor and director before making such films as *The Long Hot Summer, Hud, The Great White Hope, Sounder*.

Rossellini, Roberto. Born Rome, Italy, May 3, 1906. Attended Classical School. Wrote for films before directing *Rome — Open City; Paisan; Germany, Year Zero;*

Flowers of St. Francis; Stromboli; Europa 51; Voyage to Italy; Fear; India; Socrates; Pascal; Augustine; The Age of Cosimo de Medici.

Schaffner, Franklin. Born Tokyo, Japan, May 30, 1920. Attended Franklin and Marshall College. Served in U.S. Navy. Wrote and directed for television before making such films as *Planet of the Apes, Patton, Papillon, Islands in the Stream.*

Schlesinger, John. Born London, England, 1926. Wrote and directed for television and documentaries before making such films as *Darling, Midnight Cowboy, The Day of the Locust,* and *The Marathon Man.*

Seaton, George. Born South Bend, Indiana, April 17, 1911. Wrote and produced stage plays before joining M.G.M., where he wrote, among others, *A Day at the Races.* Directed and wrote such films as *Miracle on 34th Street, Country Girl,* and *Airport.*

Sherman, Vincent. Born Vienna, Georgia, July 16, 1906. Attended Oglethorpe University. Stage and film actor and writer before directing such films as *The Return of Dr. X, Underground, Mr. Skeffington, The Adventures of Don Juan, The Hasty Heart, The Damned Don't Cry, The Young Philadelphians.*

Sirk, Douglas. Born Skagen, Denmark, April 26, 1900. Attended University of Hamburg. Stage actor and producer and film director in Germany before coming to United States. American films include *The First Legion, Magnificent Obsession, Written on the Wind, Tarnished Angels, Imitation of Life.*

Sjöman, Vilgot. Born Sweden, 1921. Novelist and a student of Ingmar Bergman. First film, in 1962, *The Mistress.* Later work includes *My Sister, My Love; I Am Curious — Yellow; I Am Curious — Blue.*

Spielberg, Steven. Born Cincinnati, Ohio, 1947. Attended California State College. Made films as a teenager. Worked in television (*Duel*) before directing *The Sugarland Express, Jaws,* and *Watch the Skies.*

Sternberg, Josef von. Born Vienna, Austria, May 29, 1894. Died December 22, 1969. Made *The Blue Angel* in Germany before coming to America to make his Marlene Dietrich series (including *Morocco, Dishonored, Shanghai Express, The Devil Is a Woman*) and others (including *An American Tragedy, The Shanghai Gesture,* and *The Saga of Anatahan*).

Stevens, George. Born Oakland, California, December 18, 1904. Died March 8, 1975. Child actor, cameraman, and script writer before directing such films as *Alice Adams, Swing Time, Woman of the Year, Gunga Din, A Place in the Sun, Shane,* and *Giant.* Winner of D. W. Griffith Award and Irving Thalberg Award.

Stroheim, Erich von. Born Vienna, Austria, September 22, 1885. Died May 12, 1957. Emigrated to United States in 1906 and became an extra, an actor, and an assistant. Finally directed several films, including *Blind Husbands, Foolish Wives*, and *Greed*, while continuing to act.

Taylor, Bob. Associated with Steve Krantz on *Fritz the Cat*.

Vidor, King. Born Galveston, Texas, February 8, 1895. Attended Tome College. Cameraman, prop boy, and assistant on a number of shorts before making such films as *The Crowd, The Big Parade, Hallelujah! Our Daily Bread, Duel in the Sun, Ruby Gentry*.

Walsh, Raoul. Born New York, New York, March 11, 1892. Attended Seton Hall University. Worked as an actor before directing over 100 films, including *Thief of Bagdad, High Sierra, Gentleman Jim, Pursued, White Heat, Band of Angels, The Naked and the Dead*.

Warhol, Andy. Born Philadelphia, Pennsylvania, 1930. Attended Carnegie Institute of Technology. Painter, sculptor, mixed-media artist while making such films as *Sleep; The Chelsea Girls; I, A Man; Bike Boy; Lonesome Cowboys*.

Weiss, Jiri. Born Prague, Czechoslovakia, March 29, 1913. Made documentaries before directing such films as *Wolf Trap, The Coward, Ninety in the Shade, Murder — Czech Style*.

Welles, Orson. Born Kenosha, Wisconsin, May 6, 1915. Welles directed, wrote, and acted on stage, in radio, and films. Directed such works as *Citizen Kane, The Magnificent Ambersons, Lady from Shanghai, Chimes at Midnight*. Won The American Film Institute Life Achievement Award, 1975.

Wexler, Haskell. Born 1926. Cinematographer for educational, industrial, and documentary films before becoming a leading cinematographer for features (*Who's Afraid of Virginia Woolf, In the Heat of the Night*). Directed *Medium Cool*.

Wilbur, Crane. Born Athens, New York, c. 1888. Died October, 1973. Lead actor in *Perils of Pauline* series. Wrote over 40 films and directed over 30, including *Canyon City*.

Williams, Oscar. Born Virgin Islands, 1941. Attended San Francisco State College and City College of New York. Fellow of The American Film Institute. Made short films and wrote scripts before directing *Five on the Black Hand Side*.

Williams, Paul. Born Massapequa, New York, 1943. Attended Harvard University, Trinity College. Made shorts and documentaries before directing *Out of It, The Revolutionary*, and *Dealing*. Currently producing as well.

Winner, Michael. Born London, England, 1935. Attended Cambridge University. Film critic and screen writer before directing such films as *The Jokers*, *The Games*, *Chato's Land*, *Scorpio*, *Death Wish*, *Won Ton Ton — The Dog That Saved Hollywood*.

Zinnemann, Fred. Born Vienna, Austria, April 29, 1907. Attended University of Vienna. Studied law. Worked as a cameraman and extra. Directed shorts and then features, including *The Men*, *High Noon*, *From Here to Eternity*, *A Man for All Seasons*.

Index of Names and Titles